GENDERING THE NATION:
CANADIAN WOMEN'S CINEMA

Since Nell Shipman wrote and starred in *Back to God's Country* (1919), Canadian women have been making films. The accolades given to film-makers such as Patricia Rozema (*I've Heard the Mermaids Singing*), Alanis Obomsawin (*Kanehsatake: 270 Years of Resistance*), and Micheline Lanctôt (*Deux actrices*) at festivals throughout the world in recent years attest to the growing international recognition given to films made by Canadian women. *Gendering the Nation* is a definitive collection of essays, both original and previously published, that addresses the impact and influence of almost a century of women's filmmaking in Canada. Embracing new paradigms for understanding the relationship of cinema to nation and gender, *Gendering the Nation* seeks to situate women's cinema through the complex optic of national culture. This collection of critical essays employs a variety of frameworks to analyse cinematic practices that range from narrative to documentary to avant-garde.

KAY ARMATAGE is the chair of the graduate program in Women's Studies at the University of Toronto.
KASS BANNING teaches cinema studies at the University of Toronto.
BRENDA LONGFELLOW is a filmmaker and an associate professor at Atkinson College, York University.
JANINE MARCHESSAULT is an assistant professor in the Department of Film and Video, York University.

Edited by Kay Armatage, Kass Banning,
Brenda Longfellow, Janine Marchessault

Gendering the Nation:
Canadian Women's Cinema

UNIVERSITY OF TORONTO PRESS
Toronto Buffalo London

© University of Toronto Press Incorporated 1999
Toronto Buffalo London
Printed in Canada

ISBN 0-8020-4120-5 (cloth)
ISBN 0-8020-7964-4 (paper)

Printed on acid-free paper

Canadian Cataloguing in Publication Data

Main entry under title:

Gendering the nation : Canadian women's cinema

Includes bibliographical references and index.
ISBN 0-8020-4120-5 (bound)   ISBN 0-8020-7964-4 (pbk.)

1. Women motion pictures producers and directors – Canada.   2. Feminist
motion pictures – Canada – History and criticism.   I. Armatage, Kay.

PN1995.9.W6G46 1999   791.43'082'0971   C98-933053-2

University of Toronto Press acknowledges the financial assistance to its
publishing program of the Canada Council for the Arts and the Ontario Arts
Council.

This publication was made possible with the support of the
Toronto International Film Festival Group and the
Ontario Film Development Corporation.

ONTARIO
FILM DEVELOPMENT
CORPORATION

SOCIÉTÉ DE DÉVELOPPEMENT
DE L'INDUSTRIE
CINÉMATOGRAPHIQUE ONTARIENNE

In memory of
Joyce Wieland (1931–1998)
and
Kathleen Shannon (1935–1998)

and to our daughters
Camille, Klara, Jessie, and Alex

Contents

ACKNOWLEDGMENTS xiii

Gendering the Nation
KAY ARMATAGE, KASS BANNING, BRENDA LONGFELLOW,
JANINE MARCHESSAULT 3

Pioneer

Nell Shipman: A Case of Heroic Femininity
KAY ARMATAGE 17

Documentary

Studio D's Imagined Community: From Development (1974) to
Realignment (1986–1990)
ELIZABETH ANDERSON 41

Anti-Porn: Soft Issue, Hard World
B. RUBY RICH 62

Storytelling and Resistance: The Documentary Practice of Alanis
Obomsawin
ZUZANA PICK 76

A Cinema of Duty: The Films of Jennifer Hodge de Silva
CAMERON BAILEY   94

Keepers of the Power: Story as Covenant in the Films of Loretta Todd,
Shelley Niro, and Christine Welsh
CAROL KALAFATIC   109

To Document – to Imagine – to Simulate
RON BURNETT   120

Avant-Garde

Feminist Avant-Garde Cinema: From Introspection to Retrospection
JANINE MARCHESSAULT   135

The Scene of the Crime: Genealogies of Absence in the Films of
Patricia Gruben
SUSAN LORD   148

Narrative Fiction

Gender, Landscape, and Colonial Allegories in *The Far Shore, Loyalties*,
and *Mouvements du désir*
BRENDA LONGFELLOW   165

A Minority on Someone Else's Continent: Identity, Difference, and the
Media in the Films of Patricia Rozema
ROBERT L. CAGLE   183

Barbaras en Québec: Variations on Identity
CHANTAL NADEAU   197

Mourning the Woman's Film: The Dislocated Spectator of *The Company of
Strangers*
CATHERINE RUSSELL   212

Fragmenting the Feminine: Aesthetic Memory in Anne Claire Poirier's
Cinema
JOAN NICKS   225

Two plus Two: Contesting the Boundaries of Identity in Two Films by
Micheline Lanctôt
PETER HARCOURT   244

Cowards, Bullies, and Cadavers: Feminist Re-Mappings of the Passive
Male Body in English-Canadian and Québécois Cinema
LEE PARPART   253

Querying/Queering the Nation
JEAN BRUCE   274

Playing in the Light: Canadianizing Race and Nation
KASS BANNING   291

SELECTED BIBLIOGRAPHY   311
CONTRIBUTORS   317
INDEX   321

Acknowledgments

First, we thank the funders of this volume. Many thanks to Piers Handling of the Toronto International Film Festival Group and James Weyman of the Ontario Film Development Corporation for their ongoing commitment to the anthology. Thanks to Will Straw and the Centre for Research on Canadian Cultural Industries and Institutions for supplying funds for the bibliography and index. We also thank Cinema Studies, University of Toronto, for administrative support.

Individuals we wish to thank for their encouragement and help include: Marc Glassman for assistance in finding the project a home; Karen Boersma, formerly of the University of Toronto Press, for her initial support; Emily Andrew for her unfailing passion, patience, and guidance through the editing process; Jill McConkey for her continued efforts; Frances Mundy for her gentle persistence; Barbara Tessman for her painstaking attention to the manuscript; Robin MacDonald and Rosemary Ullyot of the Film Reference Library for their assistance; Shemina Keshvani and Tracey Izatt for their contribution to the volume's coordination; Catherine Munroe and Jill Shillabeer for compiling the index; Nicole Santilli for helping with translation; Pat Banning for her sharp eye.

We would also like to acknowledge Joyce Mason's efforts (with Anna Gronau's assistance) in initiating the project and to salute Cinematheque Ontario 1995 board of directors, especially Dot Tuer, for its recommendation that the project continue.

Our appreciation goes to the anthology's contributors for their hard work and sustained enthusiasm. We are especially grateful to those who wrote original pieces. And, of course, there would be no *Gendering the Nation* without the imaginative and hard-won achievements of the women filmmakers themselves.

GENDERING THE NATION:
CANADIAN WOMEN'S CINEMA

Gendering the Nation

Kay Armatage, Kass Banning, Brenda Longfellow,
Janine Marchessault

As editors of this anthology, we came together from a conviction that Canadian women's cinema represents a richly diverse and evolving body of work that has contributed both to Canadian cinema and to an international feminist film culture. We felt that the films produced by Canadian women deserved a focused and dense exploration that would draw upon the critical discourses of Canadian cinema and women's cinema. Assembling the book allowed us to look back at the films that mobilized our ideas and desires; films that educated, provoked, and inspired us; films we carried around inside us; and films that too often escape memory. Despite all the challenges that women's cinema continues to face in this country (the precariousness of funding structures at all levels, the diminishing spaces for the distribution or exhibition of non-theatrical films, and the conservative discourses of post-feminism and global capitalism, to name but a few), there is still much to celebrate.

In 1973 in Toronto a handful of young women organized Canada's first women's film festival, Women and Film 1896–1973 International Festival. Fuelled by the women's movement, it offered a form of representational consciousness raising. The goal was to reclaim the lost history of women filmmakers and to celebrate the contribution made by women outside the purview of a masculinist orthodoxy. Although we can no longer share the heady assumptions of the era and consider gender as self-evident or women as undifferentiated, it is satisfying to note that the dreams of the festival organizers have been partially realized. Their hope that the festival would contribute to the evolution of constructive theories and criticism of films by women[1] is resolutely answered in the pages of this anthology twenty-six years later.

Canadian women have been making films since Nell Shipman, writer and star of *Back to God's Country* (1919), mushed across the snow-blinding Canadian landscape, instituting Canada's first woman's entry into filmmaking; since Jane Marsh's *Women Are Warriors* (1942) called the housebound Canadian woman to industrial arms by dissolving images of domestic appliances into images of factory pistons; since Beryl Fox took her television crews into the dark psychic sites of the sixties in *Summer in Mississippi* (1964) and *Mills of the Gods: Vietnam* (1965); since Joyce Wieland constructed *Water Sark* (1964) and *Rat Life and Diet in North America* (1968) on her kitchen table. By the end of the sixties the women's movement had spawned the first generation of 'out' feminist filmmakers documenting women's lived experience with breathless immediacy. In the seventies a fearless few broke through feature filmmaking's glass ceiling, and in the eighties and nineties communities previously unheard from smashed the barriers of race and sexuality. Films like Léa Pool's *La Femme de l'hôtel* (1984), Patricia Rozema's *I've Heard the Mermaids Singing* (1987), Deepa Mehta's *Sam and Me* (1991), Mina Shum's *Double Happiness* (1994), and Lynne Stopkewich's *Kissed* (1996) charged onto the international film scene, garnering major awards and critical acclaim. Led by Studio D at the National Film Board, Canada equally established itself as a pioneer in the field of feminist documentary.

Canadian women's cinema is not necessarily an equitably shared tradition. Its tremendous range and diversity owe much to circumstance; birth, economics, geography, language, funding institutions and, most importantly, the prevailing attitude toward women in each particular decade inform what films get made and what cinematic conventions will shape them. At the same time, the production of films by women has been affected by the same formative influences experienced by their Canadian male counterparts. Yet the *gaps* in women's production over the decades repeat a familiar pattern. After Nell Shipman's pioneering presence in the silent era, explored in this volume by Kay Armatage in relation to heroic femininity, a hiatus ensued that was not broken until the state formed the National Film Board of Canada (NFB) in 1939.

Enter Evelyn Spice Cherry (*By Their Own Strength*, 1940), Jane Marsh, Gudrun Bjerring-Parker, and Margaret Perry, who were hired by John Grierson to join the NFB filmmaking team. In spite of its obvious self-interest (Grierson needed extra hands for the war effort), the NFB launched contemporary English-Canadian women's film production, establishing Canadian women's strong ties to the documentary. These women joined the chorus of 'interpreting Canada to Canadians' by making films about regional life and the war effort.[2]

Gudrun Bjerring-Parker's poetic documentary *Listen to the Prairies* (1945) reconfigures the Canadian landscape tradition by juxtaposing singers at a Winnipeg music festival with the topology of Western Canada. On the East Coast, Margaret Perry captured localities in numerous documentaries. *Grand Manan* (1943) explores the life of fishing folk on the Bay of Fundy, while *Glooscap Country* (1961) explains, through poetic rhythmic form, the origins of Nova Scotia through a local Mi'kmaq legend. Independent Judith Crawley's *The Loon's Necklace* (1950) remains in the national collective unconscious of generations of Canadians.

Canadian television produced some of the most powerful documentaries in the sixties. Beryl Fox wrote and directed two exemplary CBC films, *Summer in Mississippi* (1964) and the award-winning *Mills of the Gods: Vietnam* (1965). Some thirty years later, these films remain compelling. *Summer in Mississippi* interrogates the now infamous disappearance and murder of three young civil rights workers. *Mills of the Gods* is both a unique document and an exemplar of the sixties' penchant for irony, offering an impressionistic view of the war in Vietnam and its effect on the populace.

Quebec's Office national du film (ONF), the French side of the NFB, inaugurated its pioneering series En tant que femmes in 1972. Six films were produced: *Souris, tu m'inquiètes* (Aimée Danis, 1973), *J'me marie, j'me marie pas* (Mireille Dansereau, 1973), *A qui appartient ce gage?* (Jeanne Morazain, Susan Gibbard, Marthe Blackburn, Francine Saia, Corinda Varny, 1973), *Les Filles du Roi* (Anne Claire Poirier, 1974), *Les Filles c'est pas pareil* (Hélène Girard, 1974), *Le Temps de l'avant* (Anne Claire Poirier, 1975). Similar to the NFB's Working Mothers series in the Challenge for Change program, these films offered private portraits of the condition of women. They focused on issues such as love, day-care, marital relations, social institutions, abortion, and return to work after childbearing. A mélange of testimony and fiction, these '*films-témoignages*' were unique to Quebec women's films of this period.[3] Widely distributed within Quebec, they provoked much debate.

With the formation of Studio D in 1975, women could turn to subjects that directly related to them. Under the directorship of founding executive producer Kathleen Shannon (director of *Would I Ever Like to Work*, 1974), the women's production unit at the NFB became the first publicly funded women's studio in the world. In her essay on Studio D, Elizabeth Anderson provides a crucial account of its founding. The realization that women's films needed to be supported by a unit run by women making films for women grew out of a distinctly Canadian articulation of culture, one that relates cultural production to institutional structure out of the necessity of giving indigenous filmmakers access to funding, distribution, and – most importantly – audiences. The films produced at Studio D were touchstones for the women's movement and continue to benefit and educate.

Although many of Studio D's films achieved widespread recognition (*Not a Love Story,* 1980, and *If You Love This Planet,* 1982), the unit's initiative was not without its contradictions. As Elizabeth Anderson argues in this volume, the studio's interpretation of feminism often relied on an increasingly standard meta-narrative of women's oppression, which tended to be shaped ideologically by a particular stream of thought within the American feminist movement. Studio D's particular version of feminism in *Not a Love Story,* as B. Ruby Rich's essay underlines, embodied a pro-censorship feminist morality play that came to be enormously influential in establishing a certain hegemonic mode of thinking about pornography not only in Canada, but throughout North America. Such a narrow perspective was certainly at variance with the work of independent documentarians who were influenced by different political goals – filmmakers such as Janis Cole and Holly Dale, for example, who in the 1970s and 1980s explored alternative approaches to eroticism, female sexuality, and the sex trade; or Quebec independents Sophie Bissonette and Joyce Rock (*A Wife's Tale,* 1980), who shared a specific class consciousness, maintaining a persistent focus on working-class women.

Yet many of the Studio D films of the seventies nurtured the independent filmmakers who would follow. In the mid-1980s, when Rina Fraticelli succeeded Kathleen Shannon as executive producer, Studio D produced films that challenged the universalist themes of the Canadian feminist documentary. The permanent stable of contract filmmakers was disbanded and there were concerted efforts to construct bridges to independent women directors through augmented assistance programs (NIFT and PAFPS) and through the initiation of training programs for indigenous and diasporic women. Various filmmaking communities were affected, and two feature films grew out of this realignment of priorities: *The Company of Strangers* (1990) by long-time Studio D director Cynthia Scott and *Forbidden Love* (1992) by Toronto independents Lynne Fernie and Aerlyn Weissman. Playing at the juncture of documentary and fiction, *The Company of Strangers,* as Catherine Russell argues in her essay in this volume, breaks down the oppositions between the Hollywood woman's film of the 1940s and conventional feminist documentary approaches. The terrain of women's desire and experience was also reconfigured in *Forbidden Love*, a history of lesbian life in Canada during the 1950s. In her article, Jean Bruce situates the innovation of the film in its explicit queer aesthetic, intertextuality, and postmodern lesbian flair. Both of these films speak not only to the evolution of new hybrid forms of filmmaking within the National Film Board but to developments that had been brewing since the 1980s within the larger context of feminist politics. It was precisely during this period that the binary of sexual difference as a political form of identification and a central theoretical category began to break down. The focus shifted to the examination of differences within, as gender was challenged as the sole defining characteristic of identity, and issues of race, ethnicity, and sexual orientation became prominent sites of production. Several black-authored documentaries on the lives of African-Canadian women, for example, were produced by Studio D during this period, including *Black Mother, Black Daughter* (Sylvia Hamilton and Claire Prieto, 1989), *Older Stronger Wiser* (Claire Prieto, 1989), and *Sisters in the Struggle* (Dionne Brand, 1991). In the history of women making films in Canada, a complex identity politic has always informed film practices.

Women's presence within the National Film Board, however, had never been limited to Studio D. Singer, songwriter, and filmmaker Alanis Obomsawin has been producing films on Native issues since 1967. *Kahnesetake: 270 Years of Resistance* (1993) documented the historic standoff between Mohawk warriors and the combined military power of the Quebec Provincial Police and the Canadian army. As Zuzana Pick contends in this volume, Obomsawin's films stand outside the conventional documentary traditions of the NFB through their provocative, confrontational approach to authority and the unique relations they forge with their subjects. In her essay, Carol Kalafatic discusses the central continuity between Native storytelling traditions and the work of Indigenous filmmakers Shelley Niro, Loretta Todd, and Christine Welsh. As Loretta Todd says, storytelling 'carries the culture'; it provides a way of building community and surviving the continuing effects of colonialism. The specific contradictions and discursive frames faced by black filmmakers working within state institutions are explored by Cameron Bailey in his essay on Jennifer Hodge de Silva's *Home Feeling: Struggle for a Community* (1983), a Toronto production of the NFB that documented the effects of policing on Toronto's Jane–Finch 'Corridor,' a community with a large black population. Filmmakers such as Obomsawin and Hodge de Silva are part of the racial group they deal with; in their films, the need to tell their *own* stories is paramount.

While in English Canada the distinction between documentary, narrative, and experimental forms has been maintained both institutionally (through festivals and funding agencies) and in theoretical and critical discourses, in Quebec the generic distinctions between fiction and documentary have led to a tradition of narrative experimentation and cross-fertilization of poetic forms in literature, theatre, and film. Indeed, Anne Claire Poirier, the only woman director at the ONF during the 1960s and 1970s, pioneered in developing a hybrid form that mixed documentary elements with poetic narration, fantasy, and dreamscapes in films such as *De mère en fille* (1967) and *Les Filles du Roi* (1974). Unlike many English-Canadian films, which often focused on an individual woman struggling to affirm herself against inherited layers of social obstacles, the feminist subject in Poirier's films was always articulated as a collective subject, a subject, furthermore, aligned with the history of Quebec national narratives. As Joan Nicks, Peter Harcourt, and Chantal Nadeau elaborate in their respective essays, francophone Quebec women – Anne Claire Poirier, Paule Baillargeon, Mireille Dansereau, Micheline Lanctôt, and Léa Pool – created poetic and narrative forms to represent the contradictory impulses of desire, subjectivity, and the quotidian experiences of oppression that women live.

Quebec women filmmakers outside the ONF were less influenced by a liberal feminist politic and by cinéma vérité than by French feminists such as Simone de Beauvoir, Luce Irigaray, and Julia Kristeva, for whom experience is complicated by language. Taking their cues from the Quebec nationalist cultural struggle, Québécoise filmmakers of the seventies emphasized difference and the fracturing of conventionalized realist representations to articulate new social subjectivities. Mireille Dansereau's *La Vie rêvée* (1972) used a multiform structure – part fantasy, part consciousness raising – to fashion a girls'-own sexual adventure. *La Cuisine rouge* (Paule Baillargeon, 1977) employed Brechtian tableau and broad farcical acting to confront the difference in gender experience. Anne Claire Poirier's *Mourir à tue-tête* (1979), which shocked spectators with its dramatic inscription of a violent rape, became a cause célèbre, provoking broad social discussion of the issue. Through a formal engagement with multivocality, Poirier produced an analysis of sexual assault as both social transgression and visual and narrative representation. Léa Pool's feature debut, *La Femme de l'hôtel* (1984), inaugurated a continuous stream of introspective dramatic features.

While Québécoise filmmakers were evolving new forms in documentary and feature filmmaking, Anglo-Canadian directors attracted to formal experimentation tended toward, as Janine Marchessault's essay suggests, a feminist avant-garde tradition that grew up alongside and to some degree in opposition to Studio D. As the luminous origin of this tradition, Joyce Wieland carved out an original feminist aesthetic in experimental films like *Water Sark* (1964) and *Hand-Tinting* (1967), using the arts and artefacts of the domestic environment and her own body to challenge perception and erode the visual distinctions between subject and object. Unlike the more austere modernist preoccupations of other structural filmmakers of the era, Wieland took a wickedly playful approach in *Rat Life and Diet in North America* (1968) and in her Canadian epic *Reason Over Passion* (1967), in which she methodically deconstructed the myths and icons of official state nationalism as embodied in the dispassionate rationality of Pierre Elliott Trudeau.

Another major influence on the feminist avant-garde in English Canada was the development of Anglo-American film theory that interrogated issues of representation and desire, the relation of the spectator to the text, and the question of the female gaze. Filmmakers began to employ strategies that foregrounded women's relation to language; issues of naming and women's attempt to speak within a patriarchal language that was constructed and maintained along lines of sexual difference were of seminal importance. Patricia Gruben uses language against itself in her neo-narrative films, as Susan Lord points out in this volume. The challenges to documentary truth claims, to the illusionism of fiction, and to the identity-constituting functions of representational systems are realized by decontextualizing the quotidian.

The ongoing negotiation with institutional sites, an inevitable part of women's filmmaking practice, is further complicated at the feature filmmaking level, where the demands for high capital investment and market considerations subtly shape possibility. Interestingly enough, however, the two hottest Canadian feature films of the last two decades, *I've Heard the Mermaids Singing* (1987) and *Kissed* (1996), were produced almost entirely outside conventional funding formulas (*Kissed*) or at the low budget end of state support (*Mermaids*). It is in such arenas that the site of production can be one of great creative freedom and risk taking. Indeed, while English-Canadian feminist cinema up to the mid-eighties had been polarized between a documentary and an avant-garde tradition, emerging filmmakers such as Rozema began to incorporate avant-garde techniques into narrative feature films. As Robert Cagle observes in his essay, the role of fantasy as a central psychic preoccupation runs through all of Rozema's films – a tendency that certainly echoes the early works of the

Québécoise feminist filmmakers. The effects of different institutional and historical climates on women's feature filmmaking is explored in Brenda Longfellow's essay, which examines the connections between Joyce Wieland's *The Far Shore* (1975), Anne Wheeler's *Loyalties* (1985), and Léa Pool's *Mouvements du désir* (1994) in terms of their representation of landscape and gendered national identity.

During the last decade women's film production has witnessed a profound shift in focus, style, and authorship. While the struggle for national identity has been an enduring framework for critical examination of Canadian cinema, recent films by women demand new critical perspectives to situate effectively these radical shifts in material production. It is a challenge to find coherence in an activity so eclectic and wide ranging. This anthology was conceived as predominantly thematic and auteurist, in critical dialogue with the central theoretical traditions within Canadian film studies. The aim is to provide a crucial conceptual intervention into this monolithic framework, with its assumptions of a unitary Canadian identity and its roots in seventies cultural nationalism. Such generic meta-narrative concepts of identity have severe limitations in their applicability today. As Linda Hutcheon, among many others, has maintained, the modernist drive toward constructing the nation along the lines of a centring discourse of homogeneity and universal interest has always failed in Canada, given that there is no singularity of religion, language, or ethnicity that could ground a 'long' history or 'deep' national myth of origins. In Canada, which has historically been dominated by colonial powers and internally colonized by centre–periphery inequalities of wealth and resources, the centre is, as Hutcheon maintains, always de-centred, 'always elsewhere.'[4] National identity in Canada is articulated against an imaginary centre and mediated through regional, ethnic, and, as we insist, sexual and gendered identificatory priorities.

To raise gender as a category, however, is also to encounter a proliferation of difference. Whereas once it was commonplace to assume that films made by women, on whatever subject, would be inflected by 'the woman's perspective,' the comfortable assurance of a unitary gendered identity has been profoundly questioned over the last decades. Lee Parpart's essay identifies various types of 'female gazes' in films by Joyce Wieland, Karethe Linaae, and Lynne Stopkewich. In her essay, Kass Banning foregrounds racial resonances in Deepa Mehta's *Sam and Me* and Mina Shum's *Double Happiness*. Films by women range from those based on broad social issues, such as the effects of poverty, war, and race relations, to the specifics of women's lives. In addition, the different film genres represented – the dramatic feature, the documentary (theorized in Ron Burnett's 'To Document – to Imagine – to Simulate'), the various avant-garde practices, and the hybrid cultivar – make a homogeneous assessment difficult.

Spanning some eighty years of filmmaking, the genealogy of films by Canadian women is rich, though intermittent. The sporadic nature of women's filmmaking owes much to the underlying political, economic, and institutional factors that have historically influenced Canadian film production. At the same time, the larger cultural constraints and social movements that have shaped this century have additionally determined who was afforded the opportunity to produce films, and when.[5] Women's cinema in Canada cannot be separated from the larger history of Canadian cinema, a history determined by the political economy of Canada's cultural industries and institutions. Canadian women's cinema has been nurtured by separate though interconnected histories: the political economy of film production in Canada; the establishment of federal and provincial funding agencies such as Telefilm Canada (and its predecessor the Canadian Film Development Corporation);[6] the founding of federal and provincial arts councils such as the Canada Council, the Ontario Arts Council,[7] and, in Quebec, the Société générale du cinéma (SOGIC); and the public institutional histories of the National Film Board of Canada. Over the last three decades, these institutions have increased funding and access to the means of production to women. While women filmmakers' responses have varied, one thing remains clear: no matter what the institutional site, from the artisanal mode of experimental film to the corporate pressures of feature filmmaking, the history of women's films in Canada remains inextricably tied to the vicissitudes of state cultural policy. Until the 1970s, cultural policy was at least implicitly based on the premise of national self-definition or a vague definition of 'the social good,' but the current agendas of policymakers have meant a renewed prioritization of viability in the marketplace. Today, in an era of the Multilateral Agreement on Investment, the North American Free Trade Agreement, and the new technologies of dissemination, wherein film production is increasingly oriented toward competing in a global marketplace, the cultural project of creating a distinctive indigenous cinema is even more challenging.

Contemporary developments in film practice and cultural critique also have signalled the need to rethink traditional paradigms. Eschewing conventional, all-too-familiar themes of Canadian film criticism – those that uncritically support realist practices, historical nostalgia, 'invisibility,' landscape imagery, or 'loser' or victim scenarios – this anthology was conceived to foster the development of new paradigms of relations between cinema, the nation, and gender.

Three sets of questions have grown out of the preparation of this anthology. The first concerns the theoretical implications of gendering the nation. That is, what is the relationship between the discourses of women's cinema, with all the tensions between particular and universal concepts of gender that attend such a category, and Canadian cinema, with all the tensions between particular and universal concepts of nation? Are gender and nation equal categories of identity and forms of culture, mutually determining and relational? Or is gender subsumed by nation?

The second set of questions came to the fore after the anthology was completed, the point at which we could examine its content with a little distance and reflect on the shape it had taken. Why has the project of gendering Canadian cinema resulted in a book conceived at least in part in terms of authorship and textual analysis? Does an examination of national cinema necessarily entail an auteurist approach, an emphasis on films and filmmakers?

A third set of questions emerged, encompassing the previous two. In the contemporary era of globalization, signalled in Canada by increasing numbers of co-productions and by the erosion of those institutions that supported a national culture, is the epistemological category of a national cinema or women's cinema outmoded? In the cultural diaspora of blurred borders and hybrid identities, does the project of gendering the nation bear the marks of an archaic modernist nationalism, or a problematic liberal feminism?

Linking nation and gender together to think about cinema leads to a redefinition of place. Our sense of cultural identity is not formed as a static response to the perennial refrain 'where is here?' but arises out of what cultural geographer Doreen Massey has called 'a global sense of place.' Massey describes this sense of place as encompassing 'a mixture of wider and more local social relations whose imbrication produces unique effects and identity formations. These relations are further defined in their specificity by an accumulated history of place, with that history itself imagined as the product of a palimpsest of different sets of linkages, both local and to the wider world.'[8] Nation, as both imagined community and socio-political boundary, is thus understood as mediated by those differentiated experiences. Within this framework of a localized conceptualization of difference, gender disrupts the imagined community of nation at the same time as particular experiences of national belonging call into question the often essentialized and romanticized community of women. Neither of these terms is static; both are subject to historic evolution and change.

Canadian women's cinema must be seen as a relational practice, in dialogue with broader institutional and historical contexts of feminism and feminist film, both national and international. Recent developments in cultural critique offer appropriate frameworks for situating Canadian women's cinema beyond single-issue gender determinants. Contributions to this anthology provide competing, sometimes conflicting, approaches to individual films. Articles ask tough questions regarding the diversification of feminism and its impact on the possibility of actually naming Canadian women's cinema within a specifically national context.

A wealth of written material has appeared in academic journals (mostly Canadian, some international) and film magazines over the last few years. These valuable articles offer analyses that critically situate women's cinema within a specific Canadian context. The best of these pieces are collected here, augmenting the scope of the chapters written specifically for this anthology.

NOTES

1 Kay Armatage and Linda Beath, 'Women and Film,' catalogue essay in *Women and Film 1896–1973 International Festival* (1973), 4–5.

2 There were casualties: John Grierson could match the tyranny of any Hollywood mogul. Jane Marsh's final cut of *Women Are Warriors*, for example, hardly resembles the ambition of her original treatment on women's contemporary situation. Notwithstanding Lorne Green's relentless voice of authority and the film's propagandistic goals, *Women Are Warriors* remains a charming document. The delightfully crude correspondences between women in Russia, England, and Canada, coupled with the equations between domestic and industrial labour, foster nostalgia for what appears to be a less complex existence. After a final disagreement with Grierson, who refused to let a woman head his 'Canada Carries On' series, Marsh resigned from the NFB in 1944.

3 See Louise Carrière's 'Les Thématiques des femmes cinéastes depuis 1960,' in *Femmes et cinéma québécois* (Montreal: Boréal, 1983).

4 Linda Hutcheon, *The Canadian Postmodern: A Study of Contemporary English Canadian Fiction* (Toronto: Oxford University Press, 1988), 4.

5 Canadian cinema survives alongside several American media empires. This history, so well documented in numerous books, profoundly impeded the development of an indigenous film industry and ensured the invisibility of

Canadian films on Canadian screens. See Peter Harcourt, 'Introduction: The Invisible Cinema,' *Cine-Tracts* (Spring–Summer 1978), 48–9; Peter Morris, *Embattled Shadows: A History of Canadian Cinema, 1895–1939* (Montreal: McGill-Queen's University Press, 1978); Joyce Nelson, *The Colonized Eye: Rethinking the Grierson Legend* (Toronto: Between the Lines, 1988); Manjunath Pendakur, *Canadian Dreams and American Control: The Political Economy of the Canadian Film Industry* (Toronto: Garamond Press, 1990); Ted Magder, *Canada's Hollywood: The Canadian State and Feature Films* (Toronto: University of Toronto Press, 1993); Michael Dorland, *So Close to the State/s: The Emergence of Canadian Feature Film Policy* (Toronto: University of Toronto Press, 1998).

6 While women in the mid-1980s still received less than 15 percent of funding from these agencies, and thus continue to illustrate marginalized histories within marginalized histories and the perpetual dialectic of inclusion/exclusion, women have benefited intermittently from these institutional histories. In 1984, the Ontario Film Development Corporation (OFDC), a new institution with a mandate of encouraging innovative work, invested in Patricia Rozema's first feature, *I've Heard the Mermaids Singing*. It became a smash hit, winning the Prix de la jeunesse at Cannes and the City of Toronto Award for best Canadian feature at the Toronto Film Festival. But these institutional infrastructures are constantly shifting: in 1995 when the Conservative junta took over in Ontario, they cut off practically all funding to OFDC.

7 At the federal and provincial arts councils, women have been more successful in terms of support. This is one of the effects of decentralized decision making, where grants are adjudicated by a council of peers, with a mandate to support innovative work. The Canada Council and Ontario Arts Council have nurtured work by experimental filmmakers such as Barbara Sternberg, Patricia Gruben, Midi Onodera, and Ellie Epp.

8 Doreen Massey, 'Power-Geometry and a Progressive Sense of Place,' *Mapping the Futures: Local Cultures, Global Change*, ed. John Bird et al. (London: Routledge, 1993), 61.

PIONEER

Nell Shipman: A Case of Heroic Femininity

KAY ARMATAGE

Historiography

New historiographical approaches are emerging in discussions integrating cinema history with film theory. As Tom Gunning writes, 'anyone can see that the apathy toward history evident in film theory in the early and middle seventies has been replaced by a mode of interpenetration ... Now ... film historians have appeared for whom film theory played a vital role and who are as interested in exploring what a fact *is* as in discovering one. Likewise theorists have realized increasingly the importance not only of the historian's facts, but of historical research and speculation in approaching issues of spectatorship, narrative structure, and the role of gender.'[1] Gunning goes on to say that 'It is no accident that much of the exciting new work being done in film history is being done by women. Recognizing their marginalized place in traditional discourses, these scholars have undertaken a rediscovery of women's experience of cinema which has led to a fundamental questioning of the established concerns of history and its dominant methods.'[2]

Feminist Historiography

For many years feminist historians in all the arts have questioned dominant historiographical conventions. Within their ranks, a repeated topic of debate has been the efficacy of simply interpellating women historical figures into mainstream history without questioning its historiographical assumptions. Feminist historians have also argued that the conventional emphasis on the role of heroic figures and the master narratives of the past have been significant factors in obscuring the role of women in history. In *Old*

Mistresses (1983), Griselda Pollock discussed the theoretical problems of such simplistic historical interpellation of women artists into fine art history, and called for new critical methodologies as well as new historical categories.

In an update of this position, Irit Rogoff writes:

Constructing a speaking position and a narrative voice from which to engage with the identity of women culturally constituted on the margins of modernism entails several acute paradigm shifts. Not only do the parameters of historical periodicity and historical value need to be shed, but the very interplay of voices and 'telling' needs to be reworked. The reconstitution of erased voices and their recuperations into existing narratives, structured as 'probing models,' achieve little more than a similar history gendered female. Perhaps it is not the materials and attempts of their alternative marshalling which we need to address but the modes of telling and retelling, the full consciousness that the narrative is endlessly and circularly retold, that the missing voices and erased identities cannot, should not, be robustly reconstituted.[3]

For feminist film scholars there are pressing reasons to make 'trouble in the archives.'[4] Feminist film theory has remained to a large extent situated within the established canon of classic narrative cinema. With a few rigorously restricted exceptions such as Sandy Flitterman-Lewis' *To Desire Differently* (1990), we have not stirred up significant trouble in the archives. In the other humanities disciplines such as literature and art history, feminist scholars began 'contest[ing] the canon'[5] fairly early on, producing a seismic shift in the definition of feminist criticism. As Jane Gallop outlines in *Around 1981* (1992), in literary studies feminist criticism moved in its first half-decade from a concentration on the examination of representations of women in the canonical (male-produced) literature to the recovery of texts by women writers and a taxonomy of women's literary traditions. By 1981, feminist literary criticism *was* the study of women writers. If such 'reconstitution of erased voices and their recuperations into existing narratives "has achieved" little more than a similar history gendered female,'[6] nevertheless we are undeniably richer for it. By now, we have not only a treasure-trove of women writers from the past with which to pleasure ourselves as women readers, but we have produced a more welcoming publishing climate for contemporary women writers from many geographical and cultural heritages, as well as new theoretical rubrics with which to consider them. When I read Rogoff's disclaimer, 'that the missing voices and erased identities cannot, should not, be robustly reconstituted,'[7] I am reminded of B. Ruby Rich's ancient complaint about feminist film theory, that we are asserting the absence of women subjects and spectators even in the face of our presence.[8] Indeed, we seem to be bent on prohibiting our presence in favour of 'uncertainty, ambiguity, and disorientation.'[9]

In cinema, a number of factors combine to suggest an historical configuration with rather differently modulated significance for women historical figures and for feminist film historians. The novelty of the medium in its pioneering period, combined with its status as a popular entertainment growing alongside vaudeville and the 'legitimate' theatre – terrains already occupied by women – resulted in a period marked (albeit briefly) by the presence of women in proportionately greater numbers than in subsequent years until the late 1970s. It would be foolish to argue that cinema was anything like a 'free zone' for women, escaping utterly the discrimination against women endemic to the other arts and the culture as a whole. But in its earliest days at least, cinema had not yet begun to effect the deliberate exclusion of women found in the other more established arts such as poetry, music, and painting, in which women were systematically denied access to the educational and professional institutions which shaped the arts. We had to wait about seventy years, until film schools were established all over the world, to feel those effects.

In time, the number of women in cinema would decrease dramatically with the monopoly practices that accompanied the coming of sound, the rise of the large Hollywood studios, and the founding of the immediately powerful technicians' unions which were dominated by organized crime and admitted only men to their membership. All three of these factors came together just at the end of the silent period. For the first thirty years, however, women pioneers in cinema were numerous, including Olga Preobrajenskaya, Esther Shub, and Elizaveta Svilova in Russia, Lotte Reineger and Leni Riefenstahl in Germany, Alice Guy Blaché, Germaine Dulac, and Marie-Louise Iribe in France, Adrienne Solser in Holland, Lottie Lyell in Australia, Elvira Notari in Italy, and Alla Nazimova, Mabel Normand, Lois Weber, Margery Wilson, Mrs Wallace Reid, Dorothy Gish, Nell Shipman, and numerous others in the U.S. This period is a site from which we can make 'trouble in the archives,' as Griselda Pollock writes, by 'contest[ing] the canon – the received and authorized version of the stories of modern art and its way of defining the visual image as the expressive site of an authoring self.'[10]

Nell Shipman is an exemplary figure, for her story parallels the entry, participation, and finally exclusion from cinema that was experienced by women filmmakers as a group in the first stage of film history.

Biography

Nell Shipman was born Helen Barham in Victoria B.C. in 1892, to a poor family of somewhat genteel British roots. With her mother's permission, Nell left home at thirteen to become a player in a small touring vaudeville company. Eventually, instead of bringing money to the family, Nell required help. In a show of support for women's career ambitions at a time when independent single women formed a very new social group, Nell's mother joined her on the road, making her costumes, feeding her, and generally looking after her. By sixteen Nell had played every sort of vaudeville role and circuit. In 1910, at age eighteen, a leading lady, she became Canadian impresario Ernest Shipman's fourth wife and gave birth to a son two years later. She had already written and starred in her first film, *The Ball of Yarn*, which was so bad, she admits, that even Ernie couldn't book it.[11] She directed her first film in 1914, 'an outdoor yarn' starring a handsome young leading man, Jack Kerrigan, in a buckskin suit.[12] She acted in films for Famous-Players-Lasky and Vitagraph, and turned down a seven-year contract that would have made her a star with Goldwyn. Her stated reasons: 'I did not like the way they dressed their contract players. This was in the period of curly blondes with Cupid's-bow mouths; and Wardrobe's main idea was to bind down a bosom with a swatch of shiny material which met yards of floaty gauze at the waistline and looked like a flowery pen-wiper. This long-legged, lanky, outdoors gal, who usually loped across the Silver Screen in fur parkas and mukluks, simply gagged at such costuming. And had the nerve to refuse it.'[13]

In 1915 she starred in *God's Country and the Woman*, a James Oliver Curwood–Vitagraph feature that was to become Nell's big break. The film's handsome budget of $90,000 reflects the stature of James Oliver Curwood (1878–1927), a well-known short story writer specializing in western, wilderness, and animal tales, and Shipman's ascending trajectory as a star. From the moment of her first association with Curwood, Nell was known as 'the girl from God's country,' driving a team of sled-dogs, snowshoeing, canoeing, and 'undergoing pages of Curwoodian drama.'[14] *Baree, Son of Kazan* (1918) was another Curwood feature, followed by *Back to God's Country* (1919). This magnificent adventure set in the Canadian north features Nell as the heroine, saving her invalid husband's life and bringing the villains to justice through her bravery, fortitude, and wilderness acumen, as well as her rapport with animals. Although Shipman did not direct the film, she wrote the screenplay as well as starring as the protagonist of the narrative, and it is evident from historical accounts that she played a central creative role. The film is in every frame a vehicle for Nell Shipman. *Back to God's Country* was an enormous critical and box-office success, reaping profits of 300% and cementing Nell's reputation as a star.

During the course of the *Back to God's Country* shoot, Nell began an affair with Bert Van Tuyle, who was working on the film as Production Manager. When the production was completed, her partnerships with both her producer/husband Ernest Shipman and writer James Oliver Curwood ended. Nell was so infatuated with Van Tuyle, a handsome former racing car driver, that she made him co-director of her movies and partner in her company, Nell Shipman Productions, formed in 1921. Between 1922 and 1924, they located in Upper Priest Lake, Idaho, living in a log cabin twenty-one miles from the nearest road and fifty miles from a railway line. To get out in winter, it was dogsled and snow-shoe across the frozen lake, a two-day walk in the best of weather, and nightmarish in the blizzards. In her autobiography, Shipman describes a heroic real-life adventure, chasing Bert when he left the cabin raving in delirium from frost-bite, herself barefoot for part of the journey because her socks had gotten wet and she knew better than to allow them to freeze on her feet.

Nell and Bert, cast and crew, lived up there in Priest Lake, making movies independently. Shipman was already known for her zoo of wild animals, including the famous Brownie the bear as well as numerous 'untameable' animals such as elks, coyotes, wolves, a cougar, wildcats, skunks, eagles, and owls, and more easily domesticated animals such as raccoons, deer, porcupines, beavers, marmots, muskrats, rabbits, dogs, and cats. A map of Lionhead Lodge, the Shipman establishment at the tip of Priest Lake, indicates the prominence of the ten animal buildings, not counting eight malamute houses and a beaver dam. Nearly all of Shipman's films featured animals in prominent roles, functioning as romantic agent, comic relief, victim, or hero. As I shall argue below, they also figure as central elements in the definition of feminine subjectivity in her narratives.

Shipman wrote, directed, and starred in at least two more feature films, *Something New* (1921) and *The Grub Stake* (1923), using a skeleton crew, doing all her own stunts, wrangling the animals, and supervising the editing. When the films were finished she would trudge across the lake to the nearest town and put on a vaudeville-type show at the local hall to raise money for her train fare to New York, where she would try to sell the films for distribution.

History: Just the Facts

An independent entrepreneurship in cinema was possible at the time. By 1908, 14th St. in New York City was well established as 'film exchange row.'[15] By 1912, there were 138 movie theatres in New York City alone[16] and the following year saw the formation of many distribution companies with large syndicates. The Protective Amusement Co. offered two features per week to one hundred syndicate-affiliated theatres.[17] These companies made use of national distribution circuits developed for theatre and vaudeville in the late nineteenth century, circuits already supported by the communications-transportation infrastructure of telegraphy and rail-roads.[18] What rapidly became a vast North American circuit was propped on the low costs and almost limitless duplication of prints, and the virtually daily conversions of legitimate theatres to movie palaces. By 1923, even towns with populations under 10,000 would commonly have more than one movie theatre operating seven days a week.[19] 'The process of selling your product in this climate was simple: you just put your film under your arm and kept going down 14th St. until one of the film exchanges offered to buy your picture. Until well into the silent period, even the price was standard: ten cents a foot.'[20]

By mid-way through the 1920s, however, independent production of this sort had become virtually impossible. Even earlier in the period, competition had been fierce; spying, sabotage, and straightforward theft were commonplace. With the financial and technological gearing up for sound, the film industry was interpenetrated by big business and organized crime. This new formation of the industry saw the rise of the big studios and the monopoly practice of vertical integration of production, distribution, and exhibition. The exhibition and distribution circuits which remained unaffiliated with studios were rapidly closed down. All of the stalwarts of the silent cinema collapsed along with Shipman – Selig, Biograph, Vitagraph, and Essanay, as well as Solax (Alice Guy Blaché's company) and other tiny independents such as Kalem.[21] Shipman's cottage industry mode of production, as Peter Morris points out in his afterword to Shipman's autobiography, was out of step with the new industrialization of Hollywood.[22]

Biography – The End of the Story

Bert Van Tuyle's delusions of grandeur were the initial cause of the demise of Nell Shipman Productions. *The Girl from God's Country*, which Van Tuyle produced, went disastrously over budget, and Nell Shipman Productions was never able to recoup the loss. Van Tuyle was also a drunkard. Nell stuck with him through the bankruptcy of the company, but finally let him go. After her production company collapsed and Bert Van Tuyle left, Nell Shipman married artist Charles Ayers, and supported herself and her family for the duration of her career as a writer – a place in the industry that remained open to women through Hollywood's classic period. Nell Shipman's career trajectory thus parallels not only the history of the silent cinema itself, but also represents in microcosm the history of women's participation in the industry.

At the personal level, she remained plagued by her disastrous selections of male partners. As Nell pursued her obsessive attempts to revive her career in the film industry, third husband Ayers became afflicted with permanent artist's block due to the humiliations of being supported by his wife and began a series of extra-marital affairs. She let him go. She married a fourth time to a man who had as many aliases as he had creditors, and bounced around America with him until he passed away. She died alone, 'broke to the wide,' with the manuscript of her autobiography waiting for publication.

History and Theory

Even in a period of transition and transformation, doxas rise up fast and sharp. It is already apparent that there are limited reasons for approaching an historical text. Tom Gunning allows that 'analysis of the individual film provides a sort of laboratory for testing the relation between history and theory. It is at the level of the specific film that theory and history converge, setting up the terms of analysis. We could even say that the individual text stands as a challenge to both theoretical and historical discourse, revealing the stress points in each as they attempt to deal with the scandal of the actuality of a single work as opposed to the rationality of a system.'[23] He suggests further that we should be looking for specific nodal issues: e.g. 'the way individual works can *transform* aesthetic norms, not simply actualize them' or in order to 'reveal the individual texts as contradictory and dynamic.'[24] He cites Lea Jacobs's work on censorship and *Blonde Venus* as exemplary for its analysis of the conflicting impulses of producers and directors in response to the Production Code:

An historical textual reading uncovers the conflict still alive and wriggling throughout the film itself, as modes of discourse continue to struggle for dominance in our reception of the film. [Thus] an historical analysis of a text does not simply dissolve it into its positivistically discernible elements ... but into its processes of production and reception ... What [historical readings] undertake is more than a placing of a text into an historical context. The context itself is seen as a field of conflicting discourses and the dynamic of the text derives from this complex genesis. Therefore historical textual analysis demands more than micro-analyses. The analyst must establish the clash of discourses that surround the text.[25]

Feminist Theory and History

Sandy Flitterman-Lewis is equally firm in her notions of what feminist film historiography and a history of feminist film practice would entail. 'A feminist cinema must necessarily conceive its challenge textually,' she declares. A feminist filmmaker, she goes on, must understand the entire cinematic apparatus, including the fact that the apparatus is designed to produce and maintain its hold on the spectator by mobilizing pleasure through the interlocking systems of narrative, continuity, point of view, and identification.[26] A history of feminist cinema, therefore, will construct that history in terms of textual resistance to the dominant mode.[27] Flitterman-Lewis has chosen her exemplary filmmakers wisely: Germaine Dulac, for example, who worked in France during the same period as Shipman was working in North America, operated within an intellectual, political, and aesthetic milieu in which she was able to work consciously as a feminist. A writer as well, Dulac theorized in her own terms the necessity to deconstruct the dominant model, emphasizing the materiality of the cinematic signifier vs. the conventions of narrative causality and visual continuity of the traditional cinema. In short, Dulac precisely suits Flitterman-Lewis' historiographical prescription.[28] No 'negotiated' reading required here, for we have 'the clash of discourses' in full battle mode in these consciously 'oppositional' texts.

Old and New Configurations of Femininity

The case of Nell Shipman is not so amenable to such readings. Far from oppositional to the dominant mode, Shipman was scratching her career out of the wilderness, trying her best to compete in that dominant commercial cinema. At fifty miles from the nearest railroad, she was well out of earshot of the clash of discourses. Shipman's is not a cinema that poses the *difference* of women's filmmaking,[29] but one which plunks its ample derriere firmly on its generic base. As controller of the discourse, her 'attempts to originate the representation of her own desire'[30] map almost exactly onto patriarchal configurations of femininity – complete with pipe-smoking hubby, burbling baby, and Great Dane on the hearth rug. Finally, Freud's 'normal' woman, and loving it.

In Shipman's films we find, *a fortiori*, a patriarchal, non-oppositional construction of femininity. Shipman's character includes an intuitive rapport with animals and nature which functions as constitutive of feminine subjectivity. It also emphasizes an unproblematized heterosexuality, which features a closeness to and unclaustrophobic comfort in her own body that is displayed with at least moderately exhibitionist gusto. The heterosexual feminine body on display is accompanied perforce with an acknowledgement of her potential victimization due to the spontaneous lust that in such melodramas is constitutive of villainous subjectivity. We even find something approaching hysteria, madness, even stupidity, in the almost pathological femininity of the Shipman character. For my contemporary students, Shipman/Dolores *in Back to God's Country* represents everything that as feminists they deplore in a woman. Furthermore, she makes absolutely no attempt to 'restore the marks of cinematic enunciation so carefully elided by patriarchal cinema.'[31] It's a bit embarrassing, really. Here I find myself identifying with Irit Rogoff's 'scholastic mortification' upon finding that her subject, 'a woman whom [she] had constructed in [her] mind as an autonomous female artist, a feminized version of the masculine participant in the heroic avant-garde project of the pre-war years' was in fact replete with 'thoroughly conventional bourgeois anguish.'[32]

What I intend to argue in this chapter is that it is within the terms not only of conventional narrative cinema but also of conventional patriarchal definitions of gender that Nell Shipman's work defines heroic femininity. I contend also that within such a patriarchal construction of femininity we can find definitions of sexual difference which speak from an historical moment in the past directly to feminist concerns of the present.

Femininity and Genre

Shipman's work with animals and the natural settings of her films were amongst their chief commercial features. As genre, wilderness and adventure stories had topped the literary bestseller lists since the early teens, with Zane Grey and Jack London the leading exponents of the form. T.E. Harre's *The Eternal Maiden* (1913), a tale of feminine virtue in an 'Esquimaux' setting, was an early example of the trend towards settings in the Canadian north.[33] Novels of the Canadian woods took off in popularity around 1914, with authors such as Ralph Connor, Harold Bindloss, H. Footner, Virgie Roe, B.W. Sinclair, and Alice Jones among the top sellers,[34] although their fame did not rival the lasting prominence of Zane Grey and Jack London. By 1917, 'the novel of adventure or mystery, ... [and the] story of the great outdoors still made up a considerable part of the year's fiction,' but the genre was beginning to be nudged off the top of the best-seller lists by novels of contemporary everyday life or of exotic romance.[35] Well into the twenties, however, the wilds of the Canadian Northwest were a 'commonplace' setting for popular fiction,[36] and in cinema, the genre of wilderness films remained a minor staple of the film industry, continuing to be made well into the fifties.

Shipman's earliest successes as a star had been in films based on James Oliver Curwood novels or short stories. Curwood had had modest success with the wilderness and local colour adventure novels which dominated popular fiction in the first decade of the 20th century, but with the publication of *Kazan* (1914), a story of an escaped sledge-dog who returns to his own wild wolf kind in the Canadian Far North, his fame had begun to equal that of Jack London's *White Fang* and *Call of the Wild. Kazan* was followed in 1915 by *God's Country and the Woman*, a 'lively melodrama of the Canadian Northwest.'[37] *God's Country and the Woman*, a story of a 'love so deep and confident in the breast of the hero that it pierced the curtain of apparent unworthiness in which the heroine had felt it necessary to cloak her own actions,' enjoyed great sales and was made into a film which began the partnership between Shipman and Curwood, and which would label Nell Shipman forever as 'the girl from God's country.' In 1917 Curwood returned to the animal kingdom with *The Grizzly King* and *Baree, Son of Kazan* (1918), the latter of which again starred Nell Shipman in the film version. By the end of the war, James Oliver Curwood had achieved a short-lived position alongside Zane Grey and Jack London as the best-selling authors of wilderness adventure.

Many of Curwood's novels were made into films, including *God's Country and the Woman* (1915), *Baree, Son of Kazan* (1918), *Back to God's Country* (1919), *The Golden Snare* (1921), *Code of the Mounted* (1932), *Red Blood of Courage* (1935), *Call of the Yukon* (1938), *Call of the Klondike* (1950), *North-*

west Territory (1952), *Northern Patrol* (1953), *Yukon Vengeance* (1954), and a remake of *Back to God's Country* starring Rock Hudson (1953). Although amongst film genres westerns were always reliable as the most popular genre, nevertheless both dog stories dating from *Rescued by Rover* (1903) and adventure films had been staples of the distribution syndicates. With Curwood, Nell Shipman had come to a productive partnership.

As not only the star of the films but the screenwriter/adaptor of the Curwood stories, Shipman routinely shifted the protagonist's position from the dog to the woman, and effected concomitant shifts in the working of the narrative as well. Thus into this circuit of commercial cinema, popular genre, animals, and nature, Shipman inserts the new variable, heroic femininity.

Femininity and Nature

In her autobiography, Shipman offers her down-to-earth, pragmatic analysis of her first encounter with Brownie the Bear:

Big Brownie was my first wild animal encounter on camera unattended by Keepers, guns, wire, whips or cages. At Vitagraph I'd handled sled-dogs but now I was acting with a free, large bear who might bite, hug or merely swat. She reared, put an arm about my waist, drew me close, gave me a tentative sniff, then licked my cheek, pushed me gently aside and dropped to the ground at my feet. While I relaxed in her embrace I knew my theory was okay, and that it was a fifty-fifty deal between human and animals. Had there been a seedling of fear in me I would have felt it sprout, recognized alarm or a least a faint quiver of concern. It could lie in the deepest, darkest thought-cell but would communicate. It simply was not there. All about us and within us was serene, untroubled, unquestioned. No personal bravery in this, just a fact of communication.[38]

Shipman's femininity is in part defined by and through such intuitive natural connections. This was a feature of the Shipman character not only in the Curwood adaptations, but in her own independent productions as well. In *Trail of the North Wind* (1923), for example, the construction of feminine subjectivity hinges around communication with animals of all kinds. Dreena the heroine (Shipman) is identified as the 'story-girl' because she listens to the tales told by the creatures of the wild and translates them into human language, and the film opens with a montage of alternating comic and lyric wilderness scenes with dogs, ducks, donkeys, and baby skunks. Such montages and tableaux exhibiting the tame animals and Shipman's communication with them are trademarks of her films. William K. Everson complains of *The Grub Stake* (1923) that 'Midway through the film, its narrative comes to a virtual halt when Shipman's character discovers a Disneyesque hidden valley, shares a cave with a bear, and communes with nature and wild animals for a reel or two.'[39]

Back to God's Country (1919), for many years the only feature film of Shipman's that was known, includes the most excessive of all the displays of human/animal communication. In an early scene, Dolores (played by Shipman) lolls about in erotic play with Brownie the bear, nuzzling his snout and tweaking his ears, as skunks, squirrels, raccoons, and baby foxes cavort about her. Such moments of intransitive display are central to the Shipman oeuvre; they become generic elements equivalent to the star turns in Fred Astaire or Gene Kelly musicals, functioning pivotally in the construction of the central persona as ego ideal. And just as in Astaire or Kelly films, the casual and effortless grace which marks the exhibition of the star's extraordinary capabilities indicates that such achievements are not the result of practice, effort, training, or the like, but rather innate, natural, endemic. Indeed it is such superhuman qualities – displayed with such 'natural' insouciance – which justify stardom. In Shipman's case her extraordinary communication with the world of nature is an essential element in the constitution of heroic hyper-femininity. Rather than the narrative coming to a virtual halt, as Everson complains, I would argue on the contrary that the plots of Shipman's films are very often devices constructed precisely to afford such moments of intransitive heroic display.

The Naked Feminine Body

In *Back to God's Country*, the construction of feminine subjectivity operates not only upon Shipman's intuitive communication with animals and nature, but this natural connection is relayed to a level of heroic defiance of social convention. As a character and as a star, Shipman doffs the fetters of ladylike decorum, to cavort not only in nature, but *au naturel*. The famous nude scene, for example, which was fully capitalized upon in advertisements for *Back to God's Country*, cannot be explained away by the usual relations of economic and sexual exploitation that are rebuked by contemporary 'no nudity' clauses in the more powerful female stars' contracts. Diegetically and extra-textually, this is one of the scenes which again defines Dolores/Shipman's femininity through a closeness to her body, and through essentialist connections to nature. Those elements are also inextricably linked to a fearless rejection of social hypocrisy that brooks no moral outrage and to Shipman's own control of the cinematic discourse as enunciator.

The scene originally functioned, in Shipman's script, to convey a simple definition of the elements of femininity, situating Dolores firmly within nature as the essentialist landscape of feminine subjectivity. The scene was first shot with Shipman wearing a modest flesh-coloured wool bathing costume. After the first take, however, when she saw the wet thick wool bunch and wrinkle about her body, Shipman firmly stepped in, shedding the costume and directing the cinematographer so that the mise-en-scène would invite no prurience while still making her unadorned flesh amply evident.[40] For the period, the gesture indicated a sense of easeful corporeal display at a time when melodramatic heroines were marked by Gish-like modesty and nudity appeared in films only in scenes of epic debauchery. Indeed, such a forthright 'naturalness' in relation to the naked female body didn't surface again amongst women until the 1960s.

The historical spectator's readings of the scene, like our own, would be guided by diegetic inscriptions of Dolores' virtue, her 'naturalness,' and her femininity, sustained diegetically and semiotically from the early scenes of the film. In addition, the movie was advertised with posters which featured a drawing of Shipman pulling a shawl across her evidently naked body as she stood knee-deep in water. In the trade papers, the promotion was even more explicit, featuring a sketch of a naked female body arching lyrically on tip-toe, with this advice to exhibitors: 'Don't Book 'Back to God's Country' *unless* You want to prove that the Nude is NOT Rude.'[41] Thus the historical spectator's readings would also be marked by the interpenetration of the textual by the extra-textual (the promotion and advertising strategies), inviting a reading which invoked not only a provocative challenge to the constraints of contemporary mores about the display of women's bodies, but which also ascribed a forthrightness, fearlessness, and control of the discourse to Shipman herself as enunciator and star.

Feminine/Canine Relations

It is in Dolores/Shipman's relation with the dog, however, where the connection between conventional definitions of femininity, here heavily inflected with an intuitive rapport with the animal/natural world, are aligned most transparently with courage and heroism.

Back to God's Country is at core a dog story, based on James Oliver Curwood's *Good Housekeeping* short story 'Wapi the Walrus' (collected in *The Golden Book of Dog Stories*, ed. Era Zistel – no longer in print). In contrast to the relatively domestic achievements of the dogs in other Shipman films such as *The Bear, The Boy and The Dog*, and *Trail of the North Wind*, *Back to God's Country* presents the dog Wapi (played by matching mastiffs Tresore and brother Rex) in a much more heroic mode. A variation on the bad dog story, *Back to God's Country* features Wapi as a fierce mastiff who responds to the gentle touch of a woman's hand. When the time comes for the inevitable chase and rescue, Wapi is at the woman's side, her salvation and – almost – her heroic lover. Paradoxically, such scenes define Shipman/Dolores' helpless femininity, her fearless heroism, and her control of the discourse. And they define them as intertwined.

Femininity and Extra-Sensory Inter-Species Communication

An uncanny extra-sensory communication materialises between Wapi and Dolores. Before they ever meet, there is a cut from Dolores on ship to Wapi at the trading post, followed by the title, 'Like a great winged-bird the Flying Moon [the ship] brings to Wapi a strange and thrilling message from the white man's world of his forefathers.' Wapi senses Dolores' presence, although they have not met, and that knowledge is linked (through the intertitle) to an atavistic memory of his forefather the Great Dane Tao, whose Chinese master was murdered by the 'white man' in the film's prologue. This intertitle is followed by a close-up of Wapi in vicious killer mode. Again in the scene in which the villain is trying to get his way with Dolores on ship, her plight is intercut equally with shots of Wapi far away across the ice, straining at his leash at the trading post, and shots of Nell's helpless husband lying injured in his bed in the next cabin. Wapi, like her husband, senses Dolores' plight. This also occurs before Wapi and Dolores meet for the first time.

In one of the most affecting scenes in the film, the scene in which the woman and the dog finally meet, Dolores' fearlessness and her femininity are marked by her actions and underscored by the intertitles. Dolores/ Nell has decided to take matters into her own hands, and strikes out across the ice and snow to seek help at the Trading Post, never suspecting that the Post is run by a man in cahoots with the villainous ship captain who is plotting Nell's seduction and her husband's death. Cut to Wapi snarling viciously in close-up, fighting with the other dogs. Blake, his owner, takes a whip to Wapi just as Dolores/Nell approaches. Without hesitation, she flings herself between the whip and the dog. Dolores' fear-lessness and her courageous attempt to rescue the abused dog are under-lined by Blake's warning of the threat from the dog himself: 'Look out! That dog is a devil ...' (intertitle). But as he speaks, the killer dog miracu-lously becomes quiet, as the intertitle – by this point in the film virtually synonymous with Shipman's discourse as enunciator – comments 'A new miracle of understanding, roused by the touch of a woman's hand.'

Whereas the display of inter-species communication in the other films demonstrated that remarkable understanding as idiosyncratically symp-tomatic of Shipman as persona and star, in *Back to God's Country* the con-nection between inter-species understanding, femininity and courageous heroism is made explicit and shown to be essential to the nature of femi-ninity. It is '*a* woman's hand' – not necessarily *this* woman's hand – which promotes the animal's peace; the 'miracle of understanding' is explicitly connected to gender. Moreover, in this film, as in most of Shipman's work, she stands for Everywoman, for she is virtually the only female char-acter in an all-male world.

The mutuality of the connection between the dog and the woman is underlined by a scene depicting the dog remembering or desiring: a shot of Wapi chained to a stake dissolves to a matching shot of Dolores at the dog's side, embracing him. That memory or wish triggers the dog's action, for he breaks his chains and follows Dolores' scent to the ship. The scene closes with an iris in on the woman embracing the dog and kissing him on the face. This kiss signals the transformation of the dog into heroic lover, displacing the husband until the closing scenes of the film.

Racial Difference and the Power of Sisterhood

The Prologue of *Back to God's Country* gives the dog Wapi an heroic gene-alogy. Brought by a Chinese man to the north, both dog and immigrant become victims of the white man's racism. The Chinese dog owner is first insulted and then murdered in an episode of callously racist violence, and the noble and gentle dog is subjected to 'forty dog-generations' of the White Man's abuse, until Wapi the Killer emerges as the result. The rhetorical flourishes of the Prologue establish the intertitles as central to the enunciative apparatus of the film, which will soon come to stand for Shipman's authorial voice. These titles do not shirk either moral attitude or affective sympathy as they tell Wapi's tale. At the outset of the film, then, Shipman as enunciator distances herself firmly from those White

Men, and the marks of that difference are found not only in gender but in attitudes of racism or anti-racism.

I will not argue a non-racist purity for Shipman by any means. The quotidian racism of Shipman's era is evident in the use of phrases such as 'yellow man' and 'half-breed' and in the comic representation of the soap-eating Inuit women, as well as in the romantic feminizing of the oriental Other, who is immediately assumed to be gentler, more civilized, and more sensitive than the white brutes into whose den he stumbles.

Later in the film, however, Shipman once again underlines her anti-racist impulses, in the only scene in the film in which Dolores connects with another woman. The sailors on the Flying Moon have brought some 'eskimo guests' on board, and the quotation marks of the intertitle ironically underscore the white men's racist and sexist designs. When one of the aboriginal women resists a would-be seducer, Shipman/Dolores steps in to assist her. This moment is clearly both anti-racist and proto-feminist. As in the Prologue, it is Shipman/Dolores' femininity, marked here as a doubled difference of gender and ideology, with which we can finally identify. But sisterhood is not powerful enough, and both women are overcome. Shipman/Dolores will live to save her own virtue and her husband's life, but she cannot change the Inuit woman's destiny.

In these moments Shipman's patriarchally defined femininity slips from the bonds of mere historical curiosity, and bespeaks an anti-racist and proto-feminist heroism that reaches out of the past directly into current feminist debates.

Hysteria at the Climax

The climax of the film depends upon a two-step relay of negative and positive elements, hysterical and heroic forms of femininity. Dolores/Shipman is mushing across the arctic landscape, her injured husband laid out in the sledge, while the villain is in hot pursuit with his dog team. At one moment, for no earthly reason, Dolores drops the revolver and leaves it behind. The text jeers with an insert: (medium close-up) gun up to its handle in snow. Here we have a moment of the type we used to find with such glee in the classic realist text, that instance of overdetermination when the ideological imperative overcomes narrative plausibility, the text is fissured, and a moment of spectator alienation breaks the hold of narrative continuity. It's the moment when everyone groans. That groan signals a recognition of the discursive pressures upon the woman protagonist to be scatterbrained, incompetent, and stupid, to conform to a patriarchal stereotype of hysterical femininity. And they groan again only a few seconds later when, as if to underline the patriarchal operations of the text, the invalid husband briefly rouses himself to say 'Dolores, give me the gun' (intertitle). In close-up, Dolores responds by hanging her head in shame. Here we have the quintessentially feminine moment, the moment beyond language, when words have left her, and her only language is the purely affective language of emotion. It is, as Catherine Clement writes, a 'losing song; it is femininity's song.'[42] In Rogoff's terms, Dolores is here 'the site of uncertainty, ambiguity, and disorientation.'[43]

In Shipman's text, however, that moment beyond language is simultaneously the woman's moment of shame and the instance of the spectator's recognition of the overdetermining operations of the narrative in the construction of femininity. 'Here we can perceive the need for negotiations between contradictory forces, between middle-class bourgeois conventions regarding an appropriate emotional and moral climate for women and the eroding questions being formulated regarding identity and fulfillment for women.'[44] For Gunning, we find that de rigueur clash of discourses, alive and wriggling across the text!

Feminine Heroism

It is at this moment, and out of the very depths of the damages that such an overdetermined femininity has produced, not only upon the character of Dolores but also upon narrative plausibility, that the climax of the film is constructed.

From this point in the tale, Wapi occupies the position of an heroic lover, taking up the traditional melodramatic function of the human male protagonist, who must rescue the imperilled heroine. As the chase begins, a title indicates that Wapi's 'hour of destiny is at hand.' Close-ups of Wapi are intercut with shots of Dolores worrying and the villain approaching in this high-speed chase by dog-sled – a scene rivalled in its quintessential Canadianness only by the canoe chase in Joyce Wieland's *The Far Shore* (1975) – and a title pierces the dog's consciousness: 'Sensing the swift approaching menace of the men he hates.' Cut to close-up of Wapi. A few minutes after Dolores' moment of shame, a still photo of Wapi in close-up forms the uncharacteristic background to the generic title 'Her Last Hope,' dramatically marrying signifier and signified in one image underlining the relation of feminine desire to the animal subject.

This rather complex relay of inter-species desire, it must be recalled, is the creation of the woman screenwriter and star. The dog, then, in the expression of its desire, must be seen as the representation of the excessive desire of femininity, a transgressive desire which exceeds the capacity for satisfaction through relations with the woman's human lover/husband.

As Wapi runs off to attack the dogs pulling the villain's sled, an intertitle intones: 'Fighting at last the greatest of all his fights – for a Woman.' Once again, the enunciative apparatus draws the connection between the feminine and the heroic action; the dog at its most heroic functions merely as the agent of the woman's desire. And once again – thank goodness – we have that welcome clash of discourses: on the one hand, the narrative and specifically generic demands for an action climax overdetermining the woman's helplessness in the scenario, and on the other, the discursive connections that previously have been established between the woman, the animal, and essential femininity, producing her as the controlling agent in the action. It is due to her intrinsic qualities as a woman that she can command the obedience of this heretofore untameable beast. Her hysteria and her helplessness, then, become the masquerade, but such excessive femininity masks not masculinity or its lack (as in Riviere and Doane[45] respectively) but the even more profound (though retrograde) well-springs of essential femininity.

The rewards of such normative essentialist femininity are made explicit in the denouement. With hubby safely tucked into bed at Fort Confidence, Dolores kisses Wapi in close-up, and the scene ends with a sweet iris in and fade to black. Dog and Woman – together at last. But the iris out positions Dolores as replete in the achievement of the totality of excessive feminine desire: she is centered in the frame, with pipe-smoking hubby by her side and former heroic lover Wapi now transformed into devoted nurse-maid to the burbling baby on the hearthrug.

Conclusion

In most of her films, Nell Shipman played the leading role, always of the heroic stamp. Husbands or lovers were either absent or incapacitated: they fell ill, were injured, or were simply 'artistic.' Nell inevitably had to save the day, for what with the travails of the wilderness and the villainy of the antagonists, there was always a day and a life that needed saving. Her amazonian beauty, the easeful presence of her body (cross-hatched with equal parts of hysteria, display, strength, and bravery), her great sense of moral justice, and the instinctive connection with animals and nature: these are the signs of her essential femininity, and simultaneously the source of the heroism which allows her to resist conventional narrative inscriptions of the woman protagonist as victimized and rescued. These are not simply Meaghan Morris' 'imaginary acts of piracy,'[46] but precisely Rogoff's 'endless negotiations ... the circularity of advance and retreat, of point/counterpoint negotiations' which allow historical 'parameters to expand while changing [women's] position in relation to [them].'[47]

Out of the uncertainties and failures, out of the negotiations between an essentialist construction of feminine subjectivity and heroism, between generic convention and control of the discourse, between ideological complicity and radical anti-racism, finally emerge dramatically different models of femininity played out in a gendered narrative of heroic achievement. The negotiations between contradictory forces are not only endless but immense: between the requirements of genre and transgressions of social mores, between the heroic character which Nell Shipman created as her exemplary persona and her humiliating failure as a producer in the film industry, between her staunch commitment to her work and her own career and her repeated infatuations with male partners who alternatively exploited her and failed her. As Rogoff writes, 'Nothing better exemplifies the contradictory nature of modernism – its weaving together of a valorized and radical concept of production with a traditional and unrevised legacy of the symbolic order – than the work of women within it and of their historiographic position in relation to it.'[48]

For Shipman, then, we must recast the old critical model dramatically, from the female spectator to the female adventurer, from the desiring body to the bear, the dog, and the raccoon, from the masquerade to the mukluk. But if we follow in Nell Shipman's snowshoed footsteps, we may make some gains in the recognition of female subjectivities of the heroic stamp, and with them the beginnings of women's cultural traditions in cinema.

Known Nell Shipman Filmography

The Ball of Yarn (scen./star, 1910); *Outwitted by Billy* (Scen., Selig Polyscope Co., 1913); *Under the Crescent* (scen. & star, 6 two-reel episodes, Universal, 1915); *Under the Crescent* (novel, publ. Grosset & Dunlap, 1915); *God's Country and the Woman* (from James Oliver Curwood short story, co-dir./co-scen., star, 1915); *Baree, Son of Kazan* (from Curwood story, co-dir./co-scen., star, 1917); *Back to God's Country* (dir. David M. Hartford, scen. Nell Shipman, prod. Ernest Shipman, starring Nell Shipman, Canadian Photoplays Production, 1919); *Something New* (scen./co-dir., star, 1920); *The Girl from God's Country* (prod./scen./co-dir., star, Nell Shipman Productions, 1921); *The Boy, The Bear and the Dog* (prod./dir./scen., Nell Shipman Productions, 1921); *The Grub Stake* (prod./co-dir./scen., star, Nell Shipman Productions, 1923); *Trail of the North Wind* (prod./dir./scen./star, Nell Shipman Productions, 1923); *Light on Lookout* (prod./dir./scen./star, Nell Shipman Productions, 1923); *The Golden Yukon* (co-dir./scen., star, Sierra Pictures, 1927); *Wings in the Dark* (scen. Nell Shipman, dir. James Flood, stars Myrna Loy & Cary Grant, Paramount, 1935); *The Clam-Digger's Daughter* (fragment, 1947).

NOTES

This article was originally published in *Feminisms in the Cinema*, ed. Ada Testaferri and Laura Pietropaolo (Bloomington: Indiana University Press, 1995).

1 Tom Gunning, 'Film History and Film Analysis: The Individual Film in the Course of Time,' *Wide Angle*, vol. 12, no. 3, July 1990, 5.
2 Gunning, 1990, 14.
3 Irit Rogoff, 'Tiny Anguishes: Reflections on Nagging, Scholastic Embarrassment, and Feminist Art History,' *Differences*, ed. Griselda Pollock, vol. 4, no. 5, 1992, 39–40.
4 Griselda Pollock, 'Introduction,' *Differences*, vol. 4, no. 5, 1992, x.
5 Pollock, 1992, x.
6 Jane Gallop, *Around 1981* (Bloomington: Indiana University Press, 1992).
7 Rogoff, 1992, 39–40.
8 B. Ruby Rich, 'In the Name of Feminist Film Criticism,' in *Issues in Feminist Film Criticism*, ed. Patricia Erens (Bloomington: Indiana University Press, 1990).
9 Rogoff, 1992, 61.
10 Pollock, 1992, x.
11 Nell Shipman, *The Silent Screen & My Talking Heart* (Boise: Boise University Press, 1987), 40.
12 Shipman, 1987, 43.

13 Shipman, 1987, 46.

14 Shipman, 1987, 50.

15 Fred Balshofer, 'Going Into the Film Business,' in Richard Dyer MacCann (ed.), *The First Film Makers* (Metuchen: Scarecrow Press Inc., 1989), 37.

16 Jeanne Thomas Allen, 'Copyright and Early Theater, Vaudeville, and Film Competition,' in John L. Fell (ed.), *Film Before Griffith* (Berkeley: University of California Press, 1983), 170.

17 Allen, 1983, 177.

18 Allen, 1983, 178.

19 Garth S. Jowett, 'The First Motion Picture Audiences,' in *Film Before Griffith*, 1983, 201.

20 Balshofer, 1989, 38.

21 Paul C. Spehr, *The Movies Begin: Making Movies in New Jersey 1887–1920* (Newark: Newark Museum, 1977), passim.

22 Peter Morris, 'Afterword,' in Shipman, 1987, 216.

23 Gunning, 1990, 6.

24 Gunning, 1990, 11.

25 Gunning, 1990, 11–14.

26 Sandy Flitterman-Lewis, *To Desire Differently: Feminism and the French Cinema* (Urbana: University of Illinois Press, 1990), 3.

27 Flitterman-Lewis, 1990, 22.

28 Flitterman-Lewis, 1990, 26.

29 Flitterman-Lewis, 1990, 21.

30 Flitterman-Lewis, 1990, 22.

31 Flitterman-Lewis, 1990, 22.

32 Rogoff, 1992, 38–39.

33 Edward Everett Hale, *The American Year Book: Literature and Language Bibliographies from the American Year Book, 1910–1919*, 71.

34 Hale, 1919, 91.

35 Hale, 1919, 135.

36 Hale, 1919, 197.

37 Hale, 1919, 111.

38 Shipman, 1987, 80.

39 William K. Everson, 'Rediscovery,' *Films in Review* (April 1989), 231.

40 Shipman, 1987, 79.

41 *The Moving Picture World*, July 24, 1920, 42.

42 Catherine Clement, *Opera, or the Undoing of Women*. Trans. Betsy Wing. Foreword Susan McClary (Minneapolis: University of Minnesota Press, 1988), passim.

43 Rogoff, 1992, 61.

44 Rogoff, 1992, 62.
45 Mary Ann Doane, 'Masquerade Reconsidered: Further Thoughts on the Female Spectator,' *Discourse* 11.1 (Fall–Winter 1988–89).
46 Meaghan Morris, *The Pirate's Fiancee: Feminism, Reading, Postmodernism* (London: Verso, 1988), 16.
47 Rogoff, 1992, 62–63.
48 Rogoff, 1992, 61.

DOCUMENTARY

Studio D's Imagined Community: From Development (1974) to Realignment (1986–1990)

ELIZABETH ANDERSON

This essay emerged from a much larger case study of Studio D and the National Film Board of Canada (NFB) in which I explore the problem of defining and redefining the culturally plural nation in the late twentieth century. In that larger project, my doctoral thesis, I study the connection between Canadian national identity and cultural production, as well as the interactions between gender identity and national identity, by showing how Studio D negotiates a position for itself within a nation-building institution. Using gender as an interpretive framework and highlighting film as central to the production of national identity, as well as other collective identities, I argue that the unlikely alliance between a feminist film collective and a federal cultural institution produces tensions that complicate the production of a unifying Canadian identity. Through an historical and cultural analysis of the discursive formation of Studio D's feminist community, I show how Studio D filmmakers have been both complicit in and potentially disruptive of dominant discourses of nationhood, national identity, and national unity.

Although this essay is by necessity less detailed and less ambitious in its scope than the larger project, I have attempted to maintain the integrity of the original by telling an informative and compelling story. In the first section I focus briefly on the early years of Studio D, situating its formation within the context of the North American feminist film movement. I describe some of the studio's first productions in order to illustrate how the social realist aesthetic of these documentaries was not only representative of a popular feminist film genre, but also referenced an NFB tradition active since Grierson's day. I have chosen not to focus on the most well-known and, in some cases, notorious Studio D productions of the early 1980s, namely *Not a Love Story* (1981) and *If You Love This Planet*

(1982), because these films, and in particular *Not a Love Story*, are already covered in detail elsewhere in this volume (see the essay by B. Ruby Rich on *Not a Love Story*).

Rather, I have chosen to devote more analysis to certain events and struggles that took place during Studio D's second decade because they highlight the contradictions of doing feminist work within a nation-building institution. These events – including the internal struggle over resources at the NFB, the restructuring of the studio in order to provide more access to independent women filmmakers, and the instalment of various initiatives to open up the studio's resources to women of colour and Native women – forced Studio D filmmakers to reimagine their feminist community to make it more inclusive and more representative of the differences among women. With this redefinition of their community, Studio D filmmakers, most of whom up to this point were white and middle class, had to come to terms with their race and class bias and learn to broaden their focus on gender identity to include other forms of identity. Not surprisingly, the struggle to redefine Studio D's community took place alongside attempts, both inside and outside the NFB, to redefine and reimagine the (culturally plural) Canadian nation. My interest is in how, when challenged with the realities of multiculturalism, Studio D's liberal feminism and the NFB's nationalist discourse end up looking and sounding remarkably similar.

Studio D (1974): Founding a Feminist Film Unit at the NFB

It has occurred to some of us that the NFB has not had a very good record in the past of fulfilling its mandate of 'interpreting Canada to Canadians and the rest of the world, etc.,' when we consider that 53% [*sic*] of the population is female, and that point of view has hardly been expressed. Women have a different approach to society, and we must be our own spokeswomen.
Kathleen Shannon, April 1974[1]

Questions of naming and identity have always been at the forefront of the dialogue on Canadian film. This concern with specificity shares a common motivation with feminism – naming our difference. Both 'isms' – nationalism and feminism – privilege the desire to name, to classify and to distinguish themselves from the Other. (Not coincidentally, feminism's Other, patriarchy, often behaves indistinguishably from Canada's Other, the United States.) So naming the Canadian feminist filmmaker can constitute a double articulation of specificity. It can

also mean confronting some of the pitfalls of a nationalistic posture, among them narrow definitions and exclusionary categories.
Kass Banning, 1987[2]

In August 1974, after years of intense lobbying by women at the National Film Board of Canada and months of discussion between various women employees and management, English production announced the creation of Studio D, the first publicly funded women's film production unit in the world. Soon after, three women, Margaret Pettigrew, Yuki Yoshida, and Kathleen Shannon, set up operations in the basement at NFB headquarters in Montreal.[3]

Nearly twenty-five years after the official NFB mandate was enshrined in the 1950 Film Act, Shannon, a sound editor at the NFB since 1956, challenged the rhetorical 'inclusiveness' and 'unity' of the mandate, and argued that women's 'different approach to society' needed expression at the NFB. Perceiving a gap between the rhetoric and the practice, Shannon took English production management to task for their failure to 'interpret Canada to [all] Canadians,' and attempted to destabilize and disrupt the NFB's national narrative by exposing its gendered bias. In effect, she asked: How are women to be configured in the imagined community of the nation? In whose interest is the NFB acting if women are largely excluded from the image-making process at the NFB? She offered a solution: as more than half the population of Canada, women must produce images about and for women if 'in the national interest' is to have any real meaning. This essay examines the various internal and external forces that combined to make this solution possible.

Feminist Film Movement: Theory and Practice

One should not underestimate the way an active and visible North American women's movement and a burgeoning international women's film movement contributed to a climate more receptive to the importance of women's cultural production at the NFB. In the late 1960s, American independent feminist filmmakers got their start in film collectives that were associated with the New Left movement.[4] The most important of these groups was Newsreel, a production and distribution collective that was located in New York and San Francisco and that specialized in political documentaries. In 1971, New York Newsreel produced *Janie's Janie*, a film portrait of a woman named Janie who lived in the white ghetto in

Newark. The film, funded by the New Jersey Board of Education, was made by a crew of women and men.[5] In response to pressures for a film about women, San Francisco Newsreel produced *The Woman's Film* in 1971. *The Woman's Film* focused on social structural definitions of women's issues and intercut footage of interviews from several different women's lives.[6] This format, a blending of the individual and collective, the personal and political, was replicated in Shannon's Working Mothers series (1974–5), which was made under the aegis of the Challenge for Change program at the NFB.[7] Both the individual and collective approaches, in their attempt to balance the stories of individual women's lives with an analysis of how all women were defined and delimited by socio-political structures, served as prototypes for other feminist documentarians.[8]

According to Julia LeSage, the feminist/social realist documentary emerged as a specific genre in the late sixties. The feminist documentary 'used a single format to present to (primarily female) audiences the ordinary details of women's lives – told directly by the protagonists to the camera – and to follow their frustrated but sometimes successful attempts to enter and deal with the public world of work and power.'[9] In valorizing the experiential, feminist documentarians, who were often feminist activists, hoped to persuade female audiences, through identification with the protagonists in their films, of the necessity for collective political action. In effect, these documentaries were a cultural embodiment of the marriage between the personal and political. As LeSage states, 'these realist documentary films both depict and encourage a politicized "conversation" among women, and in these films, the self-conscious act of telling one's story as a woman in a politicized yet personal way gives the older tool of women's subcultural resistance, conversation, a new social force as a tool for liberation.'[10] Indeed, the early social realist documentaries can be viewed as visual representations of the popular and largely undocumented consciousness-raising groups of second-wave feminism.

The First International Festival of Women's Films, held 5–12 June 1972 in New York City at the Fifth Avenue Cinema, provided a forum for the exhibition and discussion of the rapidly growing corpus of feminist films.[11] This festival inaugurated the British–North American feminist film movement in a very public way. In 1972–3 women's film festivals were held in four countries: following the success of the first festival in New York, the Women's Event, a five-day festival that included screenings and discussions, took place in Edinburgh, Scotland, in August 1972; over two months in the spring of 1973, the National Film Theatre in London screened women's films; and in June 1973 the Women and Film International Festival opened in Toronto and then made an eighteen-city tour of Canada.[12] In a newsletter describing these events, Canadian independent feminist filmmaker Barbara Halpern Martineau assesses the impact of the festivals, and particularly the impact of the feminist film movement on Canadian film practices and Canadian women filmmakers. Showing great prescience, she argues that 'We need a women's film centre, run by women, with an archive, a film theatre with regular showings of retrospectives and new work, a library, resources for making films and learning to make them, and resources for generating publications. Wouldn't Canada be a good place for this?'[13]

During the early to mid-seventies, several groups emerged in Canada that hoped to 'reclaim and promote women's work in film.'[14] In essence, these feminist media groups and production collectives, many of which had a special interest in media education, hoped to shift the focus from women as consumers of films to women as producers and directors. They emphasized educating the public about mainstream media stereotypes, creating an audience for women's films, and putting women filmmakers in contact with one another. To generate further interest in women's films, these groups used particular strategies such as touring the provinces with films for screenings and post-screening discussions, setting up video libraries, and publishing catalogues of available films and videos by and for women.

In 1974, in several cities across Canada, women created mobile film libraries that served as media workshops. For example, the Women and Film Touring Media Bus out of Toronto travelled Ontario and showed films in public settings, conducted workshops on media-related topics, and rented videos and films to groups and individuals for private screenings. Out of this experience, a group called innervisions/ARC (Access Resource Catalogue) produced a catalogue of films and video tapes by, for, and about women, available in Toronto. According to a letter announcing their services, the group claimed that 'the purpose of this catalogue is to stimulate the use of film or video as a grass roots communication tool.'[15] In addition to the catalogue, innervisions/ARC organized film screenings that they hoped 'would become a forum for discussion of media and for exchange of experimental ideas.'[16]

Women in Focus, a feminist film collective formed in Vancouver in 1974 under the direction of Marion Barling, wanted to 'provide alternative images of women' and to train women in filmmaking.[17] In an interview many years after Women in Focus was founded, Barling spoke of her

expectations for the collective: 'I wanted to see a women's aesthetic established: see a women's sensibility represented, understand what it is and
what comes out of it when you view the world through it. My general
vision was to literally put women in focus.'[18] Women in Focus operated
for nearly twenty years as a film and video production, distribution, and
exhibition space for women on the West Coast. Other feminist media collectives founded during this time are Reel Feelings in Vancouver (1973),
Reel Life in Halifax, the Vancouver Women and Film Group or ISIS
(1973), and innervisions/ARC in Toronto.[19]

Like the artist-run centres founded throughout the 1960s and into the
1970s, these groups relied on grant money from provincial and federal
arts councils to stay afloat. Women in Focus, for example, received grants
from two different sources: the Secretary of State Women's Program, and
the Canada Council. Without the institutional support or operating budget of a large federal cultural institution, its existence was often threatened.[20] Despite the fact that Women in Focus and Studio D shared a
cultural context, a socio-political ideology, and certain strategies, these
feminist film collectives had very different futures in store for them.

Although Studio D's place within the NFB was often precarious during
its first years, and even after, the women who started the studio had the
advantage of job security and, eventually, a fairly consistent amount of
institutional funding. Thus, from the start, Studio D's institutional setting
granted it a legitimacy not conveyed on more independent organizations.
It could be argued that this institutional legitimation worked against
Studio D by eroding its connections to feminist film culture. As women's
film production increased and funding decreased, competition for government funding grew stiffer. In a competition for federal resources,
independent women filmmakers working outside Studio D usually lost
out. Ironically, the feminist film movement, one of the most important
impetuses for Studio D's creation, and independent women filmmakers,
some of whom got their start as Studio D freelancers, were often considered outsiders to the women's film culture forming at the NFB. I will
return to this point shortly. I turn now to the early documentaries produced at Studio D.

Early Film Projects: Developing a Feminist Documentary Aesthetic

On the cover of a 1976 pamphlet describing the work of Studio D, the traditional NFB logo – the male form 'eye' – is transformed into the symbol
for woman, and the much smaller NFB 'eye' is placed in the position of

the heart on the larger logo's 'body.' Inside the pamphlet, under the heading 'What Is Studio D?' the studio's mandate is laid out: 'Studio D is a filmmaking unit within English production at the National Film Board of Canada. It provides a forum for women filmmakers. Studio D brings the perspective of women to all social issues through the medium of film, promoting personal, social and political awareness. Studio D addresses the specific information needs of women audiences. Studio D provides an opportunity for women to develop and express their creativity in film, and to move into filmmaking occupations that have been dominated by men. Studio D provides an environment where women can work together in a collective atmosphere of mutual support.'[21]

In Studio D's second official year of existence (1976–7), its budget jumped from $100,000 to $600,000. This increase made it possible for Studio D staff producers, and freelancers hired to direct films, to start producing films reflecting the studio's mandate. Additionally, in the spring of 1975 the studio sponsored a series of camera, editing, and sound workshops, and that summer, six female apprentices were hired for three months to support NFB filmmakers on specific projects.[22] The freelance and apprentice-training programs became important components of Studio D's mandate. All the films made before 1979, in fact, were made by freelancers. During its first four years as a full-fledged production unit (1975–8), Studio D produced the twenty-three short films in the Just a Minute series; seven of the ten films in the Children of Canada series; two films in co-production with regional NFB studios using freelance directors; a full-length documentary on American feminists; a short film about a full-time housewife and mother in transition; three 'film portraits' of individual women; and an archival package on the representation of women in NFB films of the 1940s and 1950s.

Like Shannon's Working Mothers films, made before the inception of Studio D, many of the early studio films focused on individual women's lives, placing them in a larger socio-historical Canadian context. For example, *Great Grand Mother* (1975), a co-production with Filmwest Associates and freelance filmmakers Anne Wheeler and Lorna Rasmussen, attempts to recover the histories of Prairie women through diaries, letters, and manuscripts. The film integrates archival photographs, interviews with five contemporary Prairie women reminiscing about their lives in an oral-history mode, historical re-enactments, and shots of prairie landscapes. Bonnie Klein's *Patricia's Moving Picture* (1978) is an autobiographical portrait of Patricia Garner, a wife and mother who lives in British Columbia and who, through discussions with other women at a local women's centre, decides to make changes in her life that lead to greater independence. Straying somewhat from the focus on individual women, *Some American Feminists* (1977, by Luce Guilbeault, Nicole Brossard, and Margaret Wescott) provides an historical perspective on the American feminist movement. The film profiles several well-known American feminists including Kate Millett, Betty Friedan, and Rita Mae Brown. In monologue and dialogue talking-heads style, these women discuss sexuality, art, politics, and economics. The film serves as an intellectual history of a specific time and place.

Teresa de Lauretis's description of 'one type of film work' popular in the early 1970s corresponds to the developing Studio D aesthetic. This type, the social realist documentary, 'called for immediate documentation for purposes of political activism, consciousness-raising, self-expression, or the search for "positive images" of women.'[23] B. Ruby Rich labels this film type 'validative' because it 'function[s] as a validation and legitimation of women's culture and individual lives.'[24] This type also comes under the banner of 'issue film.' The more explicitly political films, associated with left activists and liberal feminists, employ 'didactic' and 'propagandistic' strategies.[25] These films privilege content over form, and their main representational strategies include voice-over narration, talking heads in dialogue or monologue, direct address to the camera, and scenes depicting subjects and protagonists in 'real life' situations. While the content of early Studio D films varied widely, the aesthetic form was fairly consistently didactic.

During the late 1970s, the realism of many (mainly North American) feminist documentaries came under attack from feminist critics.[26] Studio D was no exception. During its second decade, critics of the studio, namely independent women filmmakers who wanted more access to government resources, argued that the overuse of the didactic form (particularly in the case of *Not a Love Story*, Klein, 1981), at the expense of more experimental or, indeed, more contemporary forms, was one more example of how out of touch the studio was with the feminist film community.

The Realignment of Studio D's Imagined Community

In June 1986, after thirty years at the NFB and twelve years as executive producer of Studio D, Kathleen Shannon announced that she would be taking a sabbatical leave. As executive producer, Shannon had overseen the growth of Studio D from an operation run by three women in the basement of the NFB's labyrinth-like building on the outskirts of Montreal to an internationally recognized production studio employing twelve permanent staff members (nine women and three men) and numerous freelancers. Over the years, Shannon had worked tirelessly to provide women with film training and to increase women's professional opportunities at the board, and by 1986 the Studio D repertoire included over seventy films. In her letter of resignation as Studio D's executive producer, Shannon cited exhaustion with the NFB bureaucracy as one of her prime reasons for leaving.

Shannon's leave signalled an important shift in Studio D's environment. Although members insisted that the studio's structure was non-hierarchical and run as a feminist collective, Shannon's authority had been firmly in place and generally uncontested.[27] And, because her name and influence had become synonymous with Studio D, her absence inevitably created an empty space, an authorial vacuum, or, in Shannon's terms, a 'strategic moment.'

In February 1987, following a nationwide search for a new executive producer, NFB management announced the appointment of thirty-seven-year-old Rina Fraticelli, a Montreal (anglophone) native, a former social worker and teacher, a feminist activist, publisher, and theatre arts administrator with no background in film. In one of her first public speeches as executive producer of Studio D, Fraticelli outlined the challenges facing the studio in its second decade. Calling this new decade Studio D's 'second wave,' Fraticelli stated that 'the challenge of the next decade is to make more and better films; to grow more and more accomplished in the grammar and the art of filmmaking in order to create ever more disturbing, more acute, resonant, compelling, precise, conscious and truthful views of ourselves and each other, and of the events and dynamics we are all caught up in.'[28] The key to understanding how Fraticelli's ideas represented a radical break from Studio D practices and aesthetics is the word 'more.' To Fraticelli, more not only applied to the measurement of political relevance and social consciousness of Studio D films, but also to the recruitment of more filmmakers from outside the majority white middle-class culture of Studio D. Fraticelli would take on this challenge in 1990.

By the end of the 1980s the Studio D social realist documentary form was familiar to most Canadians. Indeed, many people recognized the studio's documentaries as identical in form to typical NFB products: featuring talking heads and voice-over narration, they were didactic in tone, and, though marked by high production values, were aesthetically limited. In terms of content, Studio D films produced during the 1980s tackle large social and political issues related to women. *Not a Love Story* uncovers the world of pornography. *Behind the Veil: Nuns* (Margaret Wescott, 1984) records the history of women in religion from 'pre-Christian Celtic communities to the radical sisters of the 1980s.' Donna Read's *Goddess Remembered* (1989) deals with the contemporary interest in women and spirituality and features interviews with women who study 'goddess-centered societies.' Several films, including *If You Love This Planet* (Terri Nash, 1982),[29] *Speaking Our Peace* (Bonnie Klein, Terri Nash, 1985), and *Nuclear Addiction: Dr. Rosalie Burtell on the Cost of Deterrence* (Terri Nash, 1986), focus on the women's peace movement in Canada and the dangers of nuclear war. *To a Safer Place* (Beverly Shaffer, 1987) documents one woman's attempt to survive child sexual abuse. *Abortion Stories from North and South* (Gail Singer, 1984) is a cross-cultural survey of attitudes on abortion and abortion practices; it includes very little Canadian content.

A spate of films from this period examines the world outside Canada. *Dream of a Free Country: A Message from Nicaraguan Women* (Shannon/Stikeman, 1983) looks at the role of women in the Nicaraguan revolution. *No Longer Silent* (co-produced, Laurette Deschamps, 1986) focuses on the lives of women in India and the struggle of Indian feminists against injustice. Ironically, the very ambitiousness of these projects, including their tendency toward sweeping historical survey and broad generalization, weakened their political message.[30] With the exception of *To a Safer Place* and *Speaking our Peace*, these films are also noteworthy for their minimal Canadian content and context. Arguably, when in 1985 NFB upper management proclaimed that Studio D had a national mandate to fulfil and had achieved 'international brand name' recognition, the studio shifted its production priorities. In an attempt to internationalize its product and message and to keep up with the production demand from both national and international audiences, Studio D turned away from the local and specific evident in earlier films like *Patricia's Moving Picture*, the Working Mothers series, and *I'll Find a Way* (Shaffer, 1977). Attempting to appeal to the imaginary middle of the women's community in Canada and in other countries, Studio D simultaneously narrowed (through its allegiance to social realist documentary techniques and formats) and widened (with historical survey films taking on large institutions and espousing 'universal' themes) its production repertoire.

In the late 1980s, Studio D launched several production initiatives designed to create a more diverse set of representations, to give access to a greater number of women filmmakers, and to encourage more formal experimentation (combining fiction and documentary methods, for example). When Fraticelli joined the studio in 1987, she sought to reinvigorate its programming by, for one, exposing studio filmmakers to the work of independent women filmmakers who had begun to reject the didacticism of earlier feminist film forms.[31] Additionally, in 1987 she revived the Federal Women's Film Program (FWFP, a partnership between Studio D and government departments, started in 1980), and charged it with producing shorter, basic informational films dealing with issues of immediate concern to Canadian women, including domestic violence, reproductive choice, career choice, health care, and aging. With FWFP focusing on the more pedagogical films, Studio D was freer to produce more creative, aesthetically challenging films.

To celebrate the fifteenth anniversary of Studio D in 1989, Fraticelli conceived of a production project titled Five Feminist Minutes. The studio invited women from across Canada to submit film proposals for five-minute 'snapshots of the world from a feminist perspective.' With this project, Fraticelli hoped to open up the studio to a more diverse group of 'voices' from the independent filmmaking community. One of her inspirations for this project was the Five-Minute Feminist Cabarets, or Fem-Fests, that she had started with other feminist artist-activists in Toronto in the late 1970s. These feminist cabarets, which took place on a Monday night every year before International Women's Day, showcased the work of new and established feminist artists and performers.[32] Another inspiration for the project was Shannon's Working Mothers series, because Fraticelli admired both the representational specificity and range of this project; she believed it was an excellent model for how to accentuate the particular, the local, and individual, while simultaneously showing the interconnectedness of women's experiences, the various structural problems they face, and the need for systemic social change. Above all, Fraticelli wanted to return to the mandate at the beginning of Studio D, but update it by asking, What are the current feminist issues? and What is feminism in 1989?[33]

In a 1989 article detailing the restructuring of Studio D, Fraticelli is quoted as saying, 'On the eve of the year 2000, we look forward to continuing to celebrate the richness and diversity of women's culture, vision and experience; and to enjoying the increased involvement in Studio D of native women, women of colour and other minorities.'[34] Fraticelli's structural framework for instituting these goals was New Initiatives in Film (NIF), a program that ran from 1991 to 1996 and that was 'designed to address the under-representation of Women of Colour and Native Women in Canadian film.'[35] To help with the conceptualization of this program, Fraticelli hired Sylvia Hamilton, a black filmmaker and civil servant from Nova Scotia who had worked for the Secretary of State in race relations.[36] Over the course of a year, Fraticelli and Hamilton worked together to draft a plan that they hoped would be 'bureaucracy proof' and 'good for the long haul.'[37] Their methods for gathering information included discussions and meetings within Studio D, and across the NFB, and with members from the women's community and from the filmmaking community across Canada.[38] In April 1990 they presented their sixteen-page proposal to Studio D and to managers in English production.[39]

To argue the case for NIF to Studio D staff, Fraticelli made the analogy 'as Studio D to the NFB, so NIF to Studio D.' She made it clear to them that NIF would not be a 'challenge' to the original project but instead a 'further differentiation' within the project. Additionally, she argued that NIF would lead to a 'greater consciousness of different perceptions.'[40] In their proposal, Hamilton and Fraticelli place their argument in a broader institutional context: 'For Studio D, NIF concretizes a newly articulated goal of substantially increasing the participation of Native Women and Women of Colour within the studio. This program may be viewed as the beginning of a broader institutional response to issues of equity, and the corrective measures necessary to bring a stronger correlation between the NFB's mandate and the current reality of its implementation.'[41]

In the NIF proposal – as had been done with earlier initiatives like Challenge for Change and Studio D – Fraticelli and Hamilton directly link film to social change and the empowerment of particular communities. Again though, as with Challenge for Change and Studio D, it is the institution that provides the organizational base for this empowerment. There is an important distinction between NIF and the earlier programs, however: the organizers of this program start with the assumption that women of colour and Native women *recognize* that if their stories are to be heard and known they must 'gain control' of the processes of representation. In other words, these women – members of different communities – because they are aware of the power of dominant representations, must use film not only to challenge dominant representations, but also to diversify representations of 'the women's community' and the other communities to which they belong.

In the sections of the proposal describing the practical implementation of the program, Fraticelli and Hamilton attempted to respond to the need to balance institutional support with more grassroots methods. There were three main components to the program: the Resource Bank, the Summer Film Institute, and the Internship Component. The Resource Bank and the Summer Film Institute were financed through

Studio D's programming funds, while the Internship Component was jointly financed by the NFB and Telefilm Canada, a public broadcasting agency set up in 1983 to help finance film and television productions.[42] Fraticelli and Hamilton emphasized the 'national nature' of all three components of the program: the Resource Bank, first available in June of 1990, was distributed throughout Canada; the Internship Component offered production experience at Studio D in Montreal as well as at regional studios; and the Summer Film Institute, located at Montreal headquarters, would be available to women across Canada. Importantly, in the context of NIF, 'national' specified the commitment to include women from all regions of Canada and from rural as well as urban areas.[43]

In the fall of 1991, Studio D released *Sisters in the Struggle*, a film co-directed by Dionne Brand and Ginny Stikeman, which documents the contemporary struggles of black Canadian women against racism and sexism. Just two years earlier, while NIF was in its initial planning stages, Stikeman and Brand had teamed up to realize *Older Stronger Wiser* (1989), the first film in the Women at the Well series. To a certain extent, this series, which focuses on the lives of black Canadian women, paved the way for future productions that developed out of NIF. The collaboration between Trinidadian-born, Toronto-based filmmaker, poet, and activist Dionne Brand and Studio D producer (later executive producer) Ginny Stikeman provided a model for the Internship Component of NIF. Additionally, *Older Stronger Wiser*, which features five black women talking about their lives in urban and rural Canada between the 1920s and 1950s, and *Sisters in the Struggle* represented a distinct break from the more universal survey films of the mid-1980s. Instead of going overseas to explore various issues that affect women, Studio D stayed at home and began to look at how different groups of women in Canada, during different historical periods, lived, worked, organized, and loved.

With the 1992 release of *Forbidden Love: The Unashamed Stories of Lesbian Lives*, Studio D again proved its commitment to broadening its audience constituency and expanding its aesthetic range. Fraticelli brought co-directors Lynne Fernie, a feminist activist and multimedia artist from Toronto, and Aerlyn Weissman, a filmmaker from Vancouver, to Studio D in 1989 to start developing their project.[44] This co-production was the result of the meetings Fraticelli had arranged early in her tenure between independent feminist filmmakers and Studio D staff. Originally, Studio D had planned for Fernie and Weissman to do a film that surveyed lesbian history internationally. While researching their film, however, they came

across archival materials that suggested that Canada would be a particularly rich site for excavating lesbian histories. Not feeling the imperative
to survey Canadian lesbianism, Fernie and Weissman decided to focus on
a specific aspect and time of the history of lesbians in Canada.[45] Additionally, because Fernie and Weissman believed that Studio D films often
ignored the Canadian context, with *Forbidden Love* they wanted to take on
the 'politics of specificity.'

Interested in using formal strategies to make accessible, pleasurable
films, Fernie and Weissman bent Studio D aesthetic rules in *Forbidden
Love*. In fact, Fernie characterized the film as 'an attack on the didactic
aesthetics' of Studio D. Their first line of attack was the decision not to
have voice-over narration. As Fernie explained, 'We constructed it so
someone didn't have to come in with an explanatory text.'[46] At the centre
of the feature-length film are contemporary interviews with nine lesbians
of diverse race, class, age, and regional backgrounds who talk about their
experiences with lesbian bar culture in Toronto, Vancouver, and Montreal during the 1950s and 1960s.[47] These women's stories are illustrated at
times with archival footage from the period. The interviews and footage
are intercut with a fictional love story based on a lesbian pulp novel and
shot in the style of that genre. In their appropriation of the lesbian pulp
genre, Fernie and Weissman counter the stereotypes of lesbians that
often pervaded these books. Their version of events has the couple
together in the end, well-adjusted, and leading openly lesbian lives.
Importantly, this version also contradicts some of the stories of the interviewees. Most of the interviewees talk about the difficulties they faced in
encountering multiple forms of discrimination once they chose to fully
embrace their lesbianism.

Conclusions: Politicizing Aesthetics

Although Studio D did respond to calls for greater inclusion in its hiring
and production practices, it can also be argued that Studio D's attempts
to give greater voice to marginalized groups and to produce more varied
images of women were largely token efforts – token because they did not
often lead to substantive structural change or to power sharing. NIF, for
example, was not its own production entity: even though Claire Prieto
was named program producer in 1994, Studio D's executive producer
continued to play a large role in overseeing the program and making program decisions. And, because NIF shared resources with Studio D, it
often had to compete for these ever-shrinking resources. Efforts, then, to

make Studio D films more inclusive and reflective of the Canadian multicultural reality were not necessarily matched by efforts to recruit women of colour as staff members or to share power with women of colour. For the most part, the Studio D community itself – that is, permanent staff members and former staff members who were reassigned to other units at the NFB – remained white and middle class. Thus, it appears that while Studio D filmmakers were willing to be more inclusive in their films, this inclusivity did not always carry over to the workplace.

Of course, Studio D's failure to enact more substantive structural changes within its own community can be attributed in part to cuts in both Studio D and NFB budgets. However, there is another way to examine this failure. I would like to suggest that Studio D's tendency toward tokenism and its failure to be more inclusive both point to a veritable crisis in its project, in large part related to the studio's adherence to Grierson's idea that documentary film has the potential to define and *unify* a community. This crisis, in turn, is directly tied to the crisis in multiculturalism in Canada and North America, which revolves around the problem of defining and redefining the multicultural nation in and through cultural products.

What, then, did Studio D filmmakers hope to gain in producing more films – and more innovative films – for larger audiences about marginalized groups? Are we to interpret Studio D's attempts to be more representative in its films, and to grant opportunities to filmmakers who are members of underrepresented groups, as attempts to bring marginal voices to the centre? And, if these voices and groups are brought to the centre, do they run the risk of being neutralized, of becoming voices that add to rather than intervene in the national story? Is the point to enlarge the imagined community of Canada? And, in enlarging this community, do these voices that tell of plural histories lose their particularity and eventually come under the umbrella of Canadian history, singular?

Are Studio D images, then, just that – *images* that add to an *image* of diversity? Are these films, in effect, a form of collective cultural therapy – a comfortable, distant way for audiences to sample the lives of people who exist at the margins of the national community without having to fully engage on an everyday basis, in face-to-face encounters, with what it would take to create a more equitable, culturally plural democracy? Do images of diversity – what may be termed an aestheticized multiculturalism – substitute for the difficulties of actually working through and debating differences? If so, is this enough? I pose these questions, not to devalue Studio D's project, but to shed light on the contradictions and irresolvable tensions in doing cultural work – particularly work within a state-run institution – that is committed to some form of social change.

It is possible to interpret Studio D's project as both interventionist and additive. Early on in the studio's history, its filmmakers pushed for important institutional changes at the NFB, and, in the process, created a space for the production of films for, by, and about women. Once they achieved some measure of institutional credibility and authority, however, and were asked to share their resources and power with more diverse groups of women, they had to confront their own exclusionary practices. When first revising definitions of their imagined community, they relied on an additive framework; while they granted representational authority to some women of colour and Native women, they circumscribed this authority by delaying the process of making substantive structural changes. These structural changes largely reproduced the race- and class-based hierarchies present in the larger society.

Although Studio D filmmakers brought innovations to the documentary form in terms of changing its content, featuring women as subjects, and placing greater emphasis on the audiences for their films and the context in which they were viewed, for the most part they shared Grierson's belief that documentary film was, above all, a nation-building vehicle. It was their reliance on this belief that restricted their project in the end. For, in taking seriously the belief that documentary film could potentially unify the Canadian nation, one must also subscribe to the idea that nations are by definition exclusive and exclusionary.

At several points in NFB history, Studio D's liberal feminist discourse overlapped with the NFB's liberal humanist discourse and conspired to produce a discourse of Canadian national identity that reflected a 'unity in diversity.' Films such as *Forbidden Love* and *Sisters in the Struggle* break from this allegiance to liberal pluralist discourse because they embrace differences within communities of women, recognize the fluidity of identities, and refuse to reaffirm the imaginary centre. These films suggest a more diverse Canada, at least in image. And, in an image-based culture, aesthetic versions of multiculturalism and sexual pluralism play an important role in educating people about difference. Dionne Brand, poet, feminist, and anti-racist activist, and co-director of *Sisters in the Struggle*, however, warns against the dangers and limitations of state-sponsored, aestheticized multiculturalism: 'Multiculturalism is more than watching folk dances and eating spicy foods. People have to have equal access to equal justice, equal jobs, equal education. Those are the bones and blood of multiculturalism.'[48] A more substantive multiculturalism would mean that old hierarchies would have to break down, power sharing would have to be the rule, differences would be debated fully, and true democratic equality would have to be realized. And, perhaps most importantly, a more substantive multiculturalism would mean that we would have to begin to imagine the nation quite differently – that, for instance, we would have to reimagine the nation as a community, or even collection of communities, that is built on difference and a commitment to transformative change and challenges.[49] Our larger cultural project then is to begin to imagine and represent – perhaps through films that fundamentally interrogate the ways in which we place boundaries around our social identities – how we live at the intersection of multiple identities, multiple communities, and multiple worlds.

In March 1996, two years after Studio D celebrated its twentieth anniversary and, perhaps more importantly, five years after it made its resources more accessible to women of colour and Native women filmmakers by providing professional development opportunities through the New Initiatives in Film program, the NFB announced that it would be closing Studio D. This decision was made in the context of federal cutbacks to the arts and as part of a larger NFB plan to lay off nearly a third of its employees. Under the plan proposed by the NFB film commissioner, Sandra MacDonald, the system of lifetime employment for NFB filmmakers would cease, regional theatres and video libraries would close, and the annual budget of $80 million would decrease by $20 million. This structural change of course marks the end of an era of generous government support for the arts in Canada and greatly reduces the NFB's role as a producer of films 'in the national interest.' Most importantly, it signals the end of Studio D as a production studio. Though it is unclear how women filmmakers will fare under the new system, to some extent this move also signals an end to federal support for feminist filmmaking. No matter what independent women filmmakers in Canada think of Studio D filmmakers and their products, the studio has helped develop and expand feminist film production by providing a resource and training base for numerous women filmmakers in the last two decades. It remains to be seen what ramifications Studio D's closing will have for the larger feminist filmmaking community in Canada.

NOTES

1 Kathleen Shannon, 'Proposal for Women's Program (English) 1975–80,'
  1 April 1974, NFB Archives, Montreal.

2 Kass Banning, 'From Didactics to Desire: Building Women's Film Culture,' in
   Work in Progress: Building Feminist Culture, ed. Rhea Tregebov (Toronto:
   Women's Press, 1987), 149.

3 Studio D was one of ten films units in the English production branch at the
   NFB. In addition to Shannon, Margaret Pettigrew and Yuki Yoshida became
   Studio D staff members. Yoshida started working at the NFB as a wardrobe
   mistress in 1956, and was then trained as a unit business manager. Margaret
   Pettigrew, who later became a producer and stayed at the NFB until 1995,
   worked with Shannon on the Working Mothers series.

4 Jan Rosenberg, *Women's Reflections: The Feminist Film Movement* (Ann Arbor, MI:
   UMI Research Press, 1983), 6–7.

5 Ibid., 20.

6 Ibid.

7 In 1967, several filmmakers from the documentary studio (Studio B) at the
   NFB developed the Challenge for Change program. This program, which was
   active until 1981, focused on the use of film and, later, video technology to foster community participation in social change. Kathleen Shannon honed her
   filmmaking skills in this program.

8 Rosenberg, *Women's Reflections*, 48.

9 Julia LeSage, 'Feminist Documentary: Aesthetics and Politics,' in *Show Us Life:
   Toward a History and Aesthetics of the Committed Documentary*, ed. Thomas Waugh
   (Metuchen, NJ: Scarecrow Press, 1984), 224. LeSage was a proponent of the
   realist documentary form because she believed that the didacticism of many
   feminist documentaries was necessary to politicize women. Like the consciousness-raising techniques of the 1970s, many didactic feminist documentaries
   were used as tools to validate women's experiences and teach that gender
   (and gender oppression) was the most determining force in women's lives.
   The realism of these documentaries was often unproblematically viewed as a
   direct translation of women's everyday lives. In the early 1970s and into the
   1980s, feminist film critics debated the value of didactic feminist documentaries. For example, B. Ruby Rich's influential essay on *Not a Love Story*, which
   appears in this volume, attacks the didacticism of the realist form and argues
   that the moral authority claimed by Bonnie Klein and her anti-porn stance
   assumes a natural, fixed female identity that serves only to re-enforce dominant views of women and female sexuality.

10 Ibid., 237.

11 According to Jan Rosenberg, in 1971 'nine explicitly feminist films were completed and screened, and by the end of 1976 over 250 films had been produced.' *Women's Reflections*, 19.

12 Barbara Halpern Martineau, *Women's Film Daily*, August 1973, 36.

13 Ibid., 44.

14 Philinda Masters, 'Women, Culture and Communications,' in Ruth Roach Pierson, Marjorie Griffin Cohen, Paula Bourne, and Philinda Masters, *Canadian Women's Issues*, vol. 1, *Strong Voice: Twenty-Five Years of Women's Activism in English Canada* (Toronto: Lorimer, 1993), 405.

15 Innervisions/ARC open letter, September 1975, in Pierson et al., *Canadian Women's Issues*, 436.

16 Ibid.

17 Masters, 'Women, Culture and Communications,' 399.

18 Ibid.

19 *Interlock*, March 1975, 20–1.

20 Lack of funding and internal conflict led to the group's dissolution in the early 1990s.

21 Studio D literature, 1976.

22 Chris Scherbarth, 'Studio D of the National Film Board of Canada: Seeing Ourselves through Women's Eyes' (Honours BA thesis, Carleton University, 1986), 34.

23 Teresa de Lauretis, 'Rethinking Women's Cinema: Aesthetics and Feminist Theory,' in *Issues in Feminist Film Criticism*, ed. Patricia Erens (Bloomington: Indiana University Press, 1988), 288–9.

24 B. Ruby Rich, 'In the Name of Feminist Film Criticism,' in *Multiple Voices in Feminist Film Criticism*, ed. Diane Carson, Linda Dittmar, and Janice R. Welsh (Minneapolis: University of Minnesota Press, 1994), 37.

25 E. Ann Kaplan, 'Theories of the Feminist Documentary,' in *New Challenges for Documentary*, ed. Alan Rosenthal (Berkeley: University of California Press, 1988), 95.

26 Kaplan, along with Rich and de Lauretis, argues that the realist form is limited because it tends to gloss over contradictions in women's lives and rarely depicts differences among and between women. The attack on realist feminist documentaries also came out of a general unease with realism and the dominant belief that realism is a transparent, true record of the past or of experience. Elaine McGarry, in particular, argued that the use of realism in feminist documentaries plays into dominant ideologies and representations of women and life because realist codes seek to deny the ways in which all representations (and particularly those produced by the cinematic apparatus) are socially constructed.

27 Anita Taylor, 'Implementing Feminist Principles in a Bureaucracy: Studio D, The National Film Board of Canada,' in *Women Communicating: Studies of Women's Talk*, ed. Barbara Bate and Anita Taylor (n.p., 1987), 285.

28 Rina Fraticelli, 'The Story so Far,' *Perforations* 2, no. 1 (August 1987).

29 Controversy surrounded the distribution of the film in the United States. The State Department declared the film a 'national security risk,' in part, because it used footage from an old Hollywood movie in which a character played by Ronald Reagan spoke anti-Japanese sentiments. The film was banned from distribution in the United States for many months. Ironically, Terri Nash won an Oscar for her film in 1983.

30 *To a Safer Place* (1987) by Beverly Shaffer is an exception. It tells the story of a Canadian woman in her thirties learning to live as a survivor of incest. In contrast to the 'survey films' of this period, *To a Safer Place* found its power (and its audience) by focusing on a specific issue, a specific woman, and the Canadian context. The film very successfully tapped into feminist-therapeutic responses to the problem of family violence and child sexual abuse. Significantly, its Canadian content and context crossed cultural and national borders. While in Montreal, I met a Japanese woman who had seen *To a Safer Place* in Japan. She was very affected by the film, particularly since the issues presented in the film are not discussed openly in Japan. As a result of seeing the film, she had come to McGill for graduate studies to research Studio D and Beverly Shaffer.

31 From the late 1970s and throughout the 1980s, Canadian independent women filmmakers such as Patricia Gruben (*The Central Character*, 1977), Kay Armatage (*Speak Body*, 1979; *Striptease*, 1980), Midi Onodera (*Ten Cents a Dance (Parallax)*, 1985; *The Displaced View*, 1988) and Brenda Longfellow (*Breaking Out*, 1984; *Our Marilyn*, 1987) began to experiment with form and to question processes of representation in their work by, for one, playing with the arbitrary division between fiction and social realist documentary film techniques. Sexuality, interpretations of history, and the fluidity of racial, ethnic, and gender identity took centre stage in their films.

32 Masters, 'Women, Culture and Communications,' 405.

33 Interview with Rina Fraticelli, 1 June 1994.

34 'Studio D Moves Ahead,' *Playback*, 17 April 1989.

35 'New Initiatives in Film, Working Document,' prepared for Studio D by Sylvia Hamilton and Rina Fraticelli, April 1990, 1.

36 Hamilton co-directed *Black Mother, Black Daughter* with Claire Prieto in 1989. *Black Mother, Black Daughter* tells the story of black women in Nova Scotia, past and present.

37 Interview with Fraticelli.

38 'New Initiatives in Film, Wrking Document,' 2.

39 Fraticelli completed her stint as executive producer soon after the proposal was accepted; she continued to work on NIF as a freelancer for the first six months of its operation.

40 Interview with Fraticelli.

41 'New Initiatives in Film, Working Document,' 4.

42 The joint financing of the Internship Component of NIF is important because it meant that NIF trainees were not fully accountable to the NFB bureaucracy. Additionally, Telefilm sponsored many independent film projects, and its involvement in the NIF internship program kept the organization aware of new talent. From the perspective of NIF trainees, financing from Telefilm at an early stage in their careers helped increase their chances for further funding. In our interview in June 1994, Fraticelli characterized the joint financing as a 'safeguard.'

43 'New Initiatives in Film, Working Document,' 6–11.

44 Although Fraticelli brought the project to Studio D, Margaret Pettigrew and Ginny Stikeman are credited as producers because the film was completed after Fraticelli left in 1990 and under Stikeman's tenure as executive producer. The film took four years to make and had a budget of one million Canadian dollars. Interview with Fraticelli.

45 Interview with Lynne Fernie and Rina Fraticelli, 1 June 1994.

46 Will Aitken, 'A History Film with Good Sex,' *Globe and Mail*, 19 Nov. 1992.

47 In an interview, Weissman explains why she and Fernie took care to respect and preserve the stories and contexts of the women they interviewed. 'Lynne and I felt quite strongly that it was important not to overlay the experiences of these women with a vocabulary of nineties feminist discourse. We really tried to structure the film in a way that would allow the women to speak for themselves, to give their experiences as they lived them, but to provide their contexts as well.' Quoted in 'Adult Entertainment: An Interview with Aerlyn Weissman,' *The Womanist*, Spring 1993.

48 Quoted in Marc Horton, 'Double Discrimination: Film Board Project Probes the Class Struggle of Black Women,' *Edmonton Journal*, 9 Oct. 1991.

49 Perhaps Kathleen Shannon, one of the main protagonists in this story, best exemplifies this commitment to transformative challenges and finding new ways to enact social change. After leaving Studio D and the NFB for good in 1992, she returned to British Columbia and ran a guest house and retreat house for women who needed a place to rest, a safe haven from domestic abuse, or a place to recover from drug addiction. Shannon died in 1998.

Anti-Porn: Soft Issue, Hard World

B. RUBY RICH

Why has the anti-porn movement been so popular with the dominant media? My suspicions are not benign. For one thing, in a society that has failed to distinguish between sexuality and pornography, the anti-porn movement is a perfect vehicle for lumping all feminists together into one posse, a bunch of sex cops out to handcuff the body politic's cock. The ensuing ridicule can always offset any serious statements. Second, the subject offers the chance to talk about sex, something the mainstream media are never loath to take up. Third, the anti-porn movement is probably seen, and rightly so, as profoundly ineffectual, unlikely ever to make a dent in the massive commercial sex industry it would seek to topple. The porn companies don't have to worry about any consumer boycott by women; we're not their customers. It is even possible that the anti-porn forces get press because they represent no threat. *Not a Love Story* – portentously subtitled 'A Motion Picture About Pornography' – can open at the 57th Street Playhouse in a gala premiere, emblazon the *Village Voice* and the *Times* as well with ads, boast a prestige distributor and a first-class PR firm, and even make it onto the evening news. Just in case there's any lingering doubt about its moral fiber, keep in mind that it's showing at the same theatre where *Genocide* just ran.

The Appeal

Documentary films, like fiction, have a script. The script may not be written before the shooting, as with fiction, but in that case it gets written in the editing room. *Not a Love Story* is no exception. Director Bonnie Klein, producer Dorothy Todd Henaut, and associate director and editor Anne Henderson seem to have scripted a religious parable.

The pivotal figure in the parable is Linda Lee Tracey, a stripper with a comedic 'Little Red Riding Hood' act. She performs the role of the reformed sinner, without whom no religious faith could be complete. Her redemption seals the film's theme, binds the audience to it, and provides the necessary narrative closure. *Not a Love Story* opens with a series of valentines, ranging from soft-core Forties style to an up-to-date hard-core *Hustler* version, but clearly it is the Sacred Heart that takes over by the end.

Linda Lee is the real star of the film. A Montreal media personality famous for her annual 'Tits for Tots' charity-strips, she was a find for the film-makers. It is she who accompanied director Klein on all the interview sessions, frequently asking the questions herself, challenging the hucksters, haranguing customers from a soapbox on the street. If Klein empathizes on-screen, emoting outrage and concern, it is Tracey who acts, reacts, and takes the risks. Just how much of a risk is made clear toward the end of the film. The audience has already been buffeted by pornographic images and film clips, appalled by the attitudes of the porn kings, overwhelmed by the statistics, and alternately inspired and outraged by what has been shown and said. As the culmination of its guided tour, the audience gets to be present at a photo session set up between porn photographer Suze Randall and our by-now heroine, Linda Lee, who has decided 'to find out what it feels like to be an object.' In her willingness to embrace this risk, Linda Lee becomes the film's dramatis persona, the one character who is transformed, within the film, by the very experience of making the film. As if Christ had come back as a latter-day Mary Magdalene, she literally offers up her body for our, and her, salvation.

Halfway through the film, Linda Lee comments that 'it's starting to get to me at an emotional level.' She meant: the pornography. But I mean: the movie. *Not a Love Story* is, for me, more depressing than inspiring, more irritating than enlightening. The film hits its emotional stride early on and stays there, never straying into detours of social analysis, historical perspective, or questions of representation. Klein sets the tone with her pose of womanly empathy, polite outrage, and respectability. She recounts her decision to make the film after her eight-year-old daughter's exposure to porn magazines at the local bus counter. I suspect many viewers' responses to the movie will rise or fall on the issue of identification with Klein. Mine fell. An aura of religiosity began to permeate the proceedings. Method and message began to blur as the film gained in momentum, upping the emotional ante into a cathartic finale.

Not a Love Story is no call to arms, but rather an exercise in show-and-tell. Gaze at the forbidden, react with your choice of anger or outrage or grief (or the male option: guilt), and leave a changed person. When Linda Lee undergoes her debasement at the lens of Suze Randall and subsequently emerges transformed and cleansed – running on the beach in the film's last frames – she is enacting a ceremony that the audience communally shares. A change in consciousness, a change of heart. Look here and weep. Post-screening goings-on, both at the New York premieres and in Canada, fortify the scenario. After-film discussions have turned the theatre into a secular confessional, eliciting testimonials, women's resolutions to confront their mates' porn collections, teenage boys swearing to forgo the porn culture that awaits them, male viewers alternately abashed or exploding in anger, etc. According to polls of the film's audiences, people are moved from seeing pornography as harmless to viewing it as harmful by the end of the film. Conversion cinema in action.

In this moral tale, each character has a clearly prescribed role. Klein, who appears on-screen to supply an identificatory figure for the audience, plays the missionary in a heathen land. Seeking out the purveyors of porn, she is seen unearthing the sins of the world in order to combat them and save our souls. Blue Sky, Raven, and other peep-show workers and strippers all play the collective role of victim. Porn photographer Suze Randall, who photographs hard-core spreads in her studio, plays the classic madame: she who sells her own kind but probably, deep inside, is a true believer. The porn moguls interviewed are surely the forces of evil, whether represented by the sleazy panache of publisher David Wells or by the endearing just-like-your-Uncle-Henry spirit of one sex emporium manager. The male customers constitute the legions of rank sinners. A San Francisco–based group of men against male violence assumes the guise of penitentes; matching a Sixties wire-rim style to an Eighties sensitivity, they take the sins of their kind upon their shoulders and expiate them. There is, of course, a roster of saints: Susan Griffin, Kate Millett, Margaret Atwood, Kathleen Barry, and topping them all, Robin Morgan, who, with husband Kenneth Pitchford and young son, presents her own version of the Holy Family. Addressing the camera with a philosophical fervor (except for the more casual Millett), the saints embody the forces of righteousness arrayed against the sinful.

Is the appeal of the film, then, a religious one? A desire to pass through the flames, be washed in the blood of the lamb, and come out a new person? I think not. Instead, the anti-porn film is an acceptable replacement for porn itself, a kind of snuff movie for an anti-snuff crowd. In this ver-

sion, outrage-against replaces pleasure-in, but the object of the preposi-
tion remains the same. Cries of outrage and averted eyes replace the
former clientele's silent pleasure and inverted hats; the gaze of horror
substitutes for the glaze of satiation. The question, though, is whether this
outcry becomes itself a handmaiden to titillation, whether this alleged
look of horror is not perhaps a most sophisticated form of voyeurism.
The ad campaign reinforces the suspicion, with its prominent surgeon-
general-style warning about the 'graphic subject matter' that viewers
might want to avoid ... if avoidance is indeed the desired goal.

The film's own methods compound the problem. While it would be
unrealistic to ask *Not a Love Story* to solve problems the political movement it addresses has so far ignored, it's reasonable to expect the film to
take up those problems relevant to its own medium. A host of issues
raised by pornography are applicable to cinema, ranging from voyeurism
or objectification to simple questions of point of view. Instead of facing
these challenges, though, the filmmakers seem unquestioningly to accept
and deploy traditional cinematic practices. Given their subject matter,
this decision creates a subtext of contradiction throughout the film.

For example, the early scenes of strippers performing their act are shot
from the audience, a traditional enough technique for a rock concert
movie, but problematic here. Doesn't such a shot turn the viewer into the
male customer normally occupying that vantage point? Doesn't the camera's privileged gaze, able to zoom in and out at will, further objectify the
woman on stage? Worse yet is the scene shot in a club equipped with
isolation-masturbation booths, wherein the women on display communicate with the male customers via a glass window and telephone, with the
duration determined by a descending black-out shutter timed to the
deposit of money. The cinematographer lines the camera up with this
same shutter, positioning us behind the shoulder of a male customer in
the booth, protected by shadows even as the woman called Blue Sky is
exposed to our view. The cinematographer takes this alignment with the
male customer one step further by zooming in for a close-up on Blue Sky
– thereby presenting us with an intimate view not even available to the
real-life customer. (At such moments, Klein's use of a male cameraman
becomes an issue.) Why visually exploit this woman to a greater degree
than her job already does? Why make the male customer our stand-in and
then let him off the hook, without either visual exposure or verbal confrontation? Why not let us see what Blue Sky sees? Instead, the filmmaker
proceeds to interview two of the women from within this same booth and
from the customer's seat. Now the man has departed and we remain

sophisticated consumers, out for the show and the facts, coyly paying money when the inevitable shutter descends.

The filmmakers efface their own presence whenever the movie enters the sex emporiums. While Klein is prominent in the other interview sessions, she does not appear at all in the clubs. Furthermore, no second camera ever shows us the steady gaze of this one filming the scene for us, the performer's 'other' audience. True, we see the male audience – but only from the vantage point of another member of that audience. The camera is protected in its invisibility by the filmmaker, just as the male customers are in turn protected in their anonymity by the camera.

This is a serious mistake, but it's a clue to the film's attitude. At no point does the camera offer a shot from the point of view of the women up on the stage. We're never permitted to share their experience while they're working – to inhabit their perspective when they're supposedly being most exploited and objectified. The result is a backfire: we remain voyeurs, and they remain objects – whether of our pity, lust, respect, or shock makes little difference.

Not all the problems arise out of shooting; others occur in the editing room, particularly in the choices of sound–image combination. The key scene is Linda Lee's porn photo session with Suze Randall, whose presence overwhelms us with frequent calls for such props as 'the pussy light,' and 'the pussy juice.' Although the scene has Linda Lee speaking as she starts to pose, her voice gives way to a voice-over of Susan Griffin explaining Eros. Only later do we get to hear Linda Lee's comments. Why use Griffin's words when the film could have reinforced Tracey's image with her own explanation? Instead, the considerable power she wields elsewhere in the film simply evaporates.

The power of the pornography included as exhibits throughout the movie does no such evaporation act. Why does the film present us with the porn materials intact? Any number of methods could have been used either to intensify their impact or to diminish it. Some kind of manipulation of the image is standard practice in films incorporating pre-existing footage. The filmmakers chose not to, with two possible results: either we're made to undergo the degradation of porn or we're offered its traditional turn-on. Klein wants the audience to eat its cake and have it, too.

In sum, *Not a Love Story* is very much a National Film Board of Canada product: concerned, engaged, up to the minute on social questions, but slick, manipulative, avoiding all the hard questions to capture the ready success of answering the easy ones. It may have a different subject from other NFB films, but its methods are inherited. These methods have been developed for decades, and they work. If *Not a Love Story* is successful, that will be because of its emphasis on emotion, the presence of Linda Lee Tracey as a genuinely appealing star, the shock of the porn characters, and the sympathy of Bonnie Klein as our Alice in Pornoland. Not incidentally, the film offers some of the porn its audience wants to see but wouldn't be caught dead seeking out in Times Square. Most fundamentally, though, the film's fate will signal the prospects of the anti-pornography campaign itself. The basic questions are not, finally, about *Not a Love Story* at all. They concern the past and future of anti-porn politics, the reasons for its appeal, and the questions of priority it raises.

Displacement, Confusion, and What's Left Out

There are many unanswered questions in *Not a Love Story*, the title itself not the least of them. Assuming that pornography is not about love, what is it? The film privileges the words of Susan Griffin, who defines one of the central tenets of the anti-porn movement: pornography is different from eroticism. Kate Millett says the same thing, as have countless others. But, what is pornography and what is eroticism? One is bad, the other is good (guess which). Fixing the dividing line is rather like red-lining a neighborhood: the 'bad' neighborhood is always the place where someone else lives. Porn is the same. If I like it, it's erotic; if you like it, it's pornographic. The rules don't seem much clearer than that, so the game gets murkier by the minute. Ready?

Two stories. Back in 1969, when I first started thinking about this distinction, my best friend worked as an artist's model; so, eventually, did I. She would model for painters but never for photographers, since with them you'd have no control over who saw your body. Once she broke the rule and modeled for a mutual friend, a photographer who did a series of nude photographs of her that we all loved. He had a show in a local gallery. One photograph of my friend was stolen out of the show. She went into a terrible depression. She was tormented by the image of an unknown man jerking off to her picture. Test: was that photograph erotic or pornographic?

Back in 1980, a woman I know went to spend the day with a friend's family. Looking around the house, what should she discover but the father's personal copy of the Tee Corrine cunt coloring book. Made for the women's community, the book usually was found only in feminist bookstores. Test: is the book erotic or pornographic?

I have other friends and other stories. Surely it is not merely an image which is one thing or the other, but equally (if not foremost) the imagination that employs the image in the service of its fantasy. It is time that anti-porn activists stop kidding themselves about the fine distinctions between eroticism and pornography. If any extra test is needed, the film offers us one in its final freeze-frame shot of a bikini-clad Linda Lee, snapped in mid-air, seaweed in hand. It is meant as an image of 'wholeness, sanity, life-lovingness' according to the filmmakers, but it comes out looking more like a soft-core Tampax ad. Is this image, perchance, pornographic as well?

There is no end of definitions as to what pornography is or isn't. For me, that's no longer the point. I have read the statistics, thank you, on whether porn causes violence or violence causes porn, taken part in the chicken-or-the-egg fights, steered clear of the currently chic analyses of porn in academic circles. I'm as fed up with pornography being identified as sexuality (in some circles) as with anti-pornography being identified as feminism (in other circles). The books, the articles, and now the films have been rolling out.[1] Such widespread acceptance is always a clue that the problem has moved elsewhere. Why is pornography so important, finally? Is it important enough to be consuming all our political energy as feminists? Certainly it is seductive. It offers no end of discourse, arguments, connotations, and denotations in which we can immerse ourselves, no end of soul searching and pavement pounding which we can enact if so moved. But whence comes its assumed political priority, and does the issue deserve it?

The film, like much Women Against Pornography campaign rhetoric, tends to identify porn both by what it is *not* (a love story) and by what it *is* at its most extreme (sadism, torture dramas). The film, like the anti-porn movement lately, emphasizes the extent to which sex-and-violence is the contemporary face of porn. But such a focus dodges the dilemma. If violence were the only problem, then why would the film include extensive footage of the strip shows and peep booths? If only violent sex were the object of wrath, then why would any Women Against Pornography group picket a non-violent live sex show, or girlie line-up? In fact, the reliance on violence-condemnation in the rhetoric is a clue to the appeal of the anti-porn movement. Women today are terrified at the levels of violence being directed at us in society – and, to take it further, at powerless people everywhere. As one porn actress in the movie eloquently put it, we're 'the fucked.' Women are terrified at the crazy spiral of rape, assaults on abortion rights, sterilization expansion, domestic battering, and anonymous bashing.

Terror is not an effective emotion, though. It paralyses. The fear of escalating violence, accompanied by the larger social backlash, has resulted not in massive political action by feminists but rather in a reaction of denial, a will not to see the dangers ... a desperate desire to see, instead, their disguises. Turning away from a phalanx of assaults too overwhelming to confront, the Women Against Pornography groups turn instead to its entertainment division, pornography. But whether symptom or cause, pornography presents an incomplete target for feminist attack. The campaign against pornography is a massive displacement of outrage that ought to be directed at a far wider sphere of oppression. Just as the film narrows the hunt down to sinners, villains, and victims so too does the anti-pornography movement leave out too much in its quasi-religious attack on the Antichrist.

The hunt for archetypes, darkly submerged drives, and other assorted ghouls of the pornography industry and the pornographic imagination has left livelier culprits out in the cold. So long as the conversion experience is the primary method, then the social, economic, historical, and political determinants get short shrift. As long as they continue, of course, it is unlikely that Dorothy Henaut will get her dream – announced opening night – of seeing the porn industry dry up and 'wither away.'

The emphasis on violence has masked the central issue of male–female power relations which we see reflected and accentuated in pornography. Any woman is still fair game for any man in our society. Without an understanding of these power relations, no analysis of porn will get very far. It certainly won't be able to account for the prevalence of fake lesbianism as a staple of pornographic imagery (without violence). It certainly won't be able to account for the difference between straight porn and gay male porn, which lacks any debasement of women and must raise complex issues regarding sexual objectification. If an analysis of porn were to confront its basic origin in the power relations between men and women, then it would have to drop the whole eroticism-versus-pornography debate and take on a far more complex and threatening target: the institution of heterosexuality. Here, again, is a clue to the anti-porn movement's appeal for some battle-scarred feminists. Is it, perhaps, more tolerable for the woman who might attend *Not a Love Story* to come to terms with how her male lover's pornographic fantasy is oppressing her in bed than to confront, yet again, how his actual behavior is oppressing her in the living room ... or out in the world?

Also left out of the picture are all questions of class and race, subsumed under the religious halo of good versus evil. Does it do any good, however, to view the women employed in the porn empire as victims? Linda Lee herself, in the movie, describes having gone to a Women Against Pornography demonstration in New York and feeling the other women's condescension. Or, as 'Jane Jones' told Laura Lederer in the *Take Back the Night* anthology, 'I've never had anybody from a poor or working-class background give me the "How could you have done anything like that?" question, but middle-class feminists have no consciousness about what it is like out there.'[2] As long as the economic forces and social choices that move these women into the commercial-sex world remain invisible, they themselves will continue to be objectified, mystified, and misunderstood by the very feminist theorists who, wine glass in hand or flowers nearby, claim to have all the answers. The film equally ignores questions of race, even though the porn industry, in its immense codification, has always divided the female population up into racial segments keyed to specific fetishes.

Issues of race and class, here, are particularly troubling in that they divide so clearly the filmmakers from their subjects. One friend of mine, herself a Puerto Rican activist, pinpointed the cause of her outrage at the film: 'All these years, she [Klein] was never bothered by my exploitation. Now, suddenly, *she* feels exploited by my exploitation, and it's *this* feeling that really upsets her.' The film never acknowledges that there might be a difference between the physical debasement of the women who earn their living in the sex industry and the ideological debasement of all women caused by the very existence of that industry. On the contrary, the anti-pornography movement has never taken up the issue of class. If it had addressed questions of class with attention or seriousness, then it might have avoided the seeming complicity with the State (like its notorious participation in the Times Square clean-up campaign, evidenced by its acceptance of office space by the forces advancing the street-sweep) that has made so many feminists wary of the anti-porn movement's real politics. Instead, the total and very apparent isolation of the filmmakers from the women who populate the various sex establishments in their film cannot help but make the viewer uneasy. Empathy? Forget it. To put it bluntly, the anti-porn campaigners seem to view the women working in the commercial sex industry much the same way that the Moral Majority seems to view pregnant teenagers. The powerful sense of identification that has been such a keystone of feminist politics is absent; in its place is a self-righteous sense of otherness that condemns the sex workers eternally to the position of Bad Object (pending, of course, any Linda-Lee-like transubstantiation).

Also overlooked is the above-ground face of porn, its front-parlor guise as legitimate advertising. This was the first target of WAVAW (Women Against Violence Against Women) in such actions as the attack on the Rolling Stones' infamous Black and Blue billboard. The *Hustler* cover image that made the movie audience gasp (a woman churned into a meat grinder) made its feminist debut in the early WAVAW slide shows. Such actions have faded in recent years, as debate, theory, and red-light-district pressure tactics took over. *Not a Love Story* alludes to the intersection of pornography and advertising, even illustrates it at points, but never explicates the connections. The anti-porn literature does the same, condemning the continuum without analyzing the linkage. Hasn't anyone heard of capitalism lately? In order to use women to sell products, in order to use pornography to sell genital arousal, there has to be an economic system that makes the use profitable. Porn is just one product in the big social supermarket. Without an analysis of consumer culture, our understanding of pornography is pathetically limited, bogged down in the undifferentiated swamp of morality and womanly purity.

Significantly in these Cold War times, the differing attitudes of Nazi and Communist societies are not cited equally. The historical usage of pornography by the Nazis (who flooded Poland with porn at the time of the invasion to render the population ... impotent?) is mentioned by Robin Morgan in the film and has been cited by others in articles and talks. No one ever mentions (with whatever reservations) the contemporary abolition of pornography in Cuba or in Nicaragua. There, it is one part of an overall social program; here, it must be the same if it is ever to succeed in transforming our systems of sexual exchange.

The single-issue nature of the anti-porn movement is one of its most disturbing aspects. Once the 'final solution' has been identified, there is no need to flail away at other social inequities. I'd guess that its avoidance of social context is another of anti-porn's attractions. Racism, reproductive rights, homophobia, all pale beside the ultimate enemy, the pornographer. How politically convenient for a Right-leaning decade. It is precisely this avoidance of context, this fetishising of one sector or one crime, that is the distinguishing feature of life under capitalism. It is also, of course, the same fetishism and fragmentation that characterize the pornographic imagination.

Retro Politics

How can it be that I, as a feminist, even one who objects to pornography and subscribes to many of the arguments against it, can at the same time object just as strenuously to the anti-pornography movement and to the method, style, perhaps even the goals, of *Not a Love Story*? Or that many other feminists share my objections? The answer, predictably enough, is political. It has to do with the conviction that, in the fight against pornography, what gets lost is as serious as what gets won.

Behind the banner of pornography is the displaced discourse on sexuality itself. Indeed, if the anti-porn campaign offers a safety zone within which the larger anti-feminist forces abroad in Eighties America need not be viewed, it also offers a corresponding zone that excludes personal sexuality. This depersonalizing of sexuality is the common effect both of pornography and of the anti-pornography forces. It is a depersonalization that is all too apparent in the film.

Only Kate Millett speaks with ease, in her own voice, and from her own experience, lounging on the floor with one of her 'erotic drawings.' It is impossible to connect the other spokeswomen personally to the texts that they talk at us. Both Susan Griffin (with unfortunately, nature blowing in the wind behind her head) and Kathleen Barry (framed by drapes and flowers) speak abstractly, rely on the third person, and bask in an aura of solemnity that punches all of the film's religioso buttons. When Robin Morgan hits the screen, an even greater problem appears.

It is here that we realize just how much space the film has preserved for men. Not only has its debate been framed entirely in terms of heterosexuality; not only have we been forced to watch always from the seat of a male buyer; but now we are made to accept feminist wisdom from a woman in tears, reduced to crying by the contemplation of the great pain awaiting us all, and capable of consolation only by the constant massaging of a sensitive husband (in a supporting penitente role) and a prematurely supportive son, who flank her on the sofa as she tells of women's suffering, boyhood's innocence, and men's innate desire to do right. Isn't this going too far? Middle-class respectability, appeals to motherhood, and now, elaborate detours aimed at making men feel comfortable within the cozy sphere of the enlightened. Any minute, and the film will go all 'humanistic' before our very eyes. Men didn't used to play such a central role in the feminist movement. Nor did women used to put quite such a premium on respectability and sexual politesse.

What has happened here? It has been an unsettling evolution, this switch from a movement of self-determination, that trashed billboards and attacked the legitimacy of soft-core advertising, to a movement of social determination, that urges legal restrictions and social hygiene.

When the anti-pornography movement traded in its guerrilla actions for the more recent route of petitioning a higher authority to enact moral codes, the political trajectory went haywire. I do not agree with those who go no further than a pious citing of the First Amendment in their pornography discussions; while the vision of free speech is a benevolent one, even at times a practicable ideal, I am cynically aware of its purchase power in this society, especially in a backlash era. While I do not, therefore, agree that WAP can simply be conflated with the Moral Majority, and that's that, I do think the notion that a feminist agenda can be legislated in our society is a naive, and ultimately dangerous, one.

Judith Walkowitz, in her essay on 'The Politics of Prostitution,' traced the political ramifications of the British 19th century anti-prostitution campaigns, cautioning that the feminists lacked the cultural and political power to reshape the world according to their own image.[3] Although they tried to set the standards for sexual conduct, they did not control the instruments of state that would ultimately enforce these 'norms.' Nor do we today. Nor are feminists likely to countenance any such movement to set, let alone enforce, some notion of sexual 'norms.' This proscriptive tendency in the anti-porn movement is not offset by any counterbalancing emphasis on an alternative sexual tradition (except for the elusive eroticism). Is it a coincidence that one of the film's anti-porn demonstrators could be a stand-in for Mercedes McCambridge in *Johnny Guitar*? The anti-porn movement has a tendency to promote a premature codification of sexuality, and *Not a Love Story* may suffer for that emphasis.

Perhaps the film actually arrived just one season too late in New York. The questions of sexual norms and sexual codification exploded at the 1982 Barnard conference on 'the politics of sexuality' with a coalition of WAP and others pitted against women espousing 'politically incorrect sexualities.' The conference has trailed in its wake a series of attacks and counter-attacks, a sensationalizing of the proceedings, and one of the worst movement splits of recent times. Again, my perennial question surfaces: Why pornography? Why this debate? It seems that after a long hiatus, following Ti-Grace Atkinson's polemical assertion that 'the women's movement is not a movement for sexual liberation,' feminists have come back to sexuality as an issue to discuss, argue, and analyze. It is not, however, clear why this debate should focus either on pornography or on sadomasochism (the two extremes at the conference), why it should short-circuit its own momentum by immediate codification.

It's time that the women's movement got back on track. While Robin Morgan weeps on the sofa, there are worse things happening in the world. It's time to acknowledge the importance of analyzing pornography, assign it a priority in the overall picture, and get on with the fight. Pornography is an issue of importance. It is becoming much too fashionable to 'study' pornography in academic circles to dubious effect. Unlike many of the theorists doing that work, I would agree instead with Monique Wittig in 'The Straight Mind' when she stresses that, while pornography is indeed a 'discourse' it is also for women a real source of oppression.[4] That said, however, I would suggest that women desist from putting ourselves through the study of it. Finally, here's a proper subject for the legions of feminist men: let them undertake the analysis that can tell us why men like porn (not, piously, why this or that exceptional man does not), why stroke books work, how oedipal formations feed the drive, and how any of it can be changed. Would that the film had included any information from average customers, instead of stressing always the exceptional figure (Linda Lee herself, Suze Randall, etc.). And the anti-porn campaigners might begin to formulate what routes could be more effective than marching outside a porn emporium.

As for the rest of us, it is time to desist, stop indulging in false and harmful polarities, and look around. Outraged at the abuse of women in our society, there are any number of struggles that can be joined on a broad social front. Outraged at pornography's being the only available discourse on sexuality, there is a great amount of visionary and groundbreaking work to do in the creation of a multitude of alternative sexual discourses, a veritable alternative culture of sexuality, that people can turn to for sexual excitement instead of porn. It's about time we redefine our terms and move on, with the spirit of justice and visionary energy that always used to characterize feminism.

As the first mass-audience film to take up the subject of pornography, *Not a Love Story* is an important work. It opens up the issues even if it closes them down again too soon. For the people whom the film makes think seriously, for the first time, about pornography, it is a landmark. It is fascinating to hear that the audience at a recent midweek daytime screening was all single men; is it encouraging that none of them walked out? Or discouraging that they could stay? Perhaps the film sins, for all its righteousness, in being simply too little, too late, even though it's the first of its kind.

Because it can help move the political debate on to the next stage, *Not a Love Story* deserves attention. Because it shows all too clearly the stage the debate is now in, it deserves criticism.

NOTES

This article was originally published in the *Village Voice* 27, no. 29, 20 July 1982, and was reprinted with revisions in *Feminist Review* 13 (Feb. 1983). It owes its existence in part to the encouragement and fantastic editing of Karen Durbin, my *Village Voice* editor. In addition, the article benefited from extended conversations with Fina Bathrick, Lillian Jimenez, and Sande Zeig.

1 See, for example, Irene Diamond, 'Pornography and Repression: A Reconsideration,' *Women: Sex and Sexuality* (Chicago: University of Chicago Press, 1980) 129–44; Bertha Harris, 'Sade Cases,' *Village Voice* (18 May 1982) 46; Gina Marchetti, 'Readings on Women and Pornography,' *Jump Cut 26*: 56–60; Lisa Steele, 'Pornography and Eroticism' (an interview with Varda Burstyn), *Fuse* magazine (May/June 1982) 19–24; Ellen Willis, 'Feminism, Moralism, and Pornography,' *Beginning to See the Light* (New York: Knopf, 1981) 219–27.

2 Laura Lederer, 'An Interview with a Former Pornography Model,' *Take Back the Night* (New York: Bantam, 1982) 45–59.

3 Judith Walkowitz, 'The Politics of Prostitution,' *Women: Sex and Sexuality*, 145–47, or see the updated version, 'Male Vice and Feminist Virtue: Feminism and the Politics of Prostitution in Nineteenth-Century Britain,' *History Workshop Journal 13*: 77–93, with an introduction by Jane Caplan.

4 Monique Wittig, 'The Straight Mind,' *Feminist Issues 1* (Summer 1980) 103–12.

Storytelling and Resistance: The Documentary Practice of Alanis Obomsawin

ZUZANA PICK

Alanis Obomsawin is the best-known of the Native documentary filmmakers in Canada.[1] Born in New Hampshire in 1932, she spent part of her childhood near Sorel, Quebec, on the Odanak reserve of the Abenaki nation. She lived there with the family of Jesse Benedict, her maternal aunt, until she moved at the age of nine with her parents to Trois Rivières. Of the period in her life at Trois Rivières, Obomsawin recalls her cultural estrangement and, as the only Native child at school, her first encounter with prejudice and racism.[2] After moving to Montreal in the late 1950s, having learned English during a two-year stay in Florida, she performed as a singer and a storyteller, making appearances on reservations, in prisons and schools, and at music festivals.[3]

In 1965, she was invited by Wolf Koenig and Bob Verrall, both veteran producers at the National Film Board of Canada, to act as a consultant on various projects dealing with Native people.[4] Obomsawin directed her first film, *Christmas at Moose Factory*, in 1971 and, after joining the permanent staff at the NFB, produced and directed two films in 1977: *Amisk* and *Mother of Many Children*. Since then, her accomplishments on film, stage, and television, as well as her work with young Native people and her activism on behalf of Native rights, have earned her a Governor General's Award (1983), a Native Arts Achievement Award (1994), and honorary degrees at Concordia University (1993) and Carleton University (1994).[5]

Although the release of *Kanehsatake: 270 Years of Resistance* (1993), a documentary on the explosive events of the summer of 1990 that drove the Native 'problem' into the spotlight, brought national and international recognition to Obomsawin, her previous documentary work remains relatively unknown. Characteristic of Obomsawin's work is the emphasis on the affirmative resolve of First Peoples to revitalize their cultures, reclaim their right to self-determination, and envision a new and better future. As she has said, 'Native filmmaking is important because there are so many communities, cultures, and traditions. Many traditions have been lost, some are coming back, and some have remained underground for a long time. There was survival of the people through everything. It's so important to document how the people feel and what they have experienced. Each family and tribe has its own history. So there will never be enough people making documents.'[6]

Obomsawin is a filmmaker who is committed to redress the invisibility of First Peoples. Her documentaries reveal a deep commitment to and solidarity with Native causes, documenting how political struggle has changed the lives of Inuit, Métis, Cree, Mohawk, Ojibway, and Mi'kmaq communities.[7] Obomsawin's own engagement in First Nations' politics is revealed by films that are grounded within ongoing struggles and in 'full awareness of the contradictions at play,' to use Thomas Waugh's description of committed documentary practices.[8]

Like the work of other Native filmmakers, her films have been produced by the NFB and sponsored by the federal Department of Indian Affairs. Although her films appear to fit into the style institutionalized by the NFB, which emphasizes information and education, Obomsawin's practice sidesteps the prescriptive imperatives of the NFB didactic documentary. Her films rework documentary conventions and place representation at the service of a Native political and aesthetic agenda.

Her work demystifies notions of disinterested observation in cinéma direct by inscribing her presence in the film, as narrator and subject. In her hands documentary practice becomes a rhetorical intervention that places the enabling subject at the centre of discourse. The interview, used to shape point of view, becomes a valuable instrument to validate individual biography, make intelligible the ongoing struggles for Native self-definition, and contest Eurocentric narratives of First Nations history. In addition, Obomsawin's documentaries challenge what Brian Winston calls the 'Griersonian obsession with the victim' organized around the 'image of [a] heroically suffering humanity.'[9] Her work subverts the objectifying tendencies of the social documentary by revealing a heartfelt respect for the past and present of the people she has filmed. Obomsawin's approach to human emotion is premised on creating a place for empathy that promotes the circulation of affect between protagonist and viewer.

As a result, Obomsawin has been able to negotiate the difficult path between the human solidarity that permeates her films and the partisan, often controversial perspective that motivates her work as a Native documentary filmmaker. Thus, her films have fundamentally altered the way in which the cause of First Peoples has been communicated to non-Native Canadians. She has been successful in altering common perceptions, both about the ability of Native communities to take charge of their destinies and about the urgency of institutional change. In the process, as Peter Steven suggests, Obomsawin's films 'live beyond their original context ... largely because of the strong emotions she generates on the screen.'[10]

Self-representation and the Testimonial Narrative

Obomsawin's documentary work makes consistent use of the on-camera interview because, as she has stated, 'the basic purpose [of my films] is for our people to have a voice. To be heard is the important thing, no matter what we're talking about – whether it has to do with having our existence recognized, or whether it has to do with speaking about our values, our survival, our beliefs, that we belong to something beautiful, that it's O.K. to be an Indian, to be a native person in this country.'[11]

Yet Obomsawin takes the interview one step further. In its different modes (conversant, off-screen as pseudo-monologue or narration), the interview provides a space from which people can speak and subverts the 'culture of voicelessness' that has, in the words of Emma LaRoque, 'literally and politically negated' the 'vast storehouse of our oral traditions.'[12] Obomsawin's use of the interview, a staple of direct cinema, has a political and aesthetic function that draws on the tradition of Native storytelling (and other modes of oral history). It becomes a vehicle whereby Native history can be validated, pre-contact and colonial experiences can be retold.

What distinguishes Obomsawin's work from standard historical compilation documentaries is that the interview challenges pre-established categorizations of discourse and representation. In this way, the interview also evokes the testimonial narratives that, as Chon Noriega points out in regard to Latin American radical practices, are a preferred vehicle, 'to give "voice" to communities or a national identity, not in a passive sense, but rather through "constant, ongoing discussion" between filmmakers and film subjects.'[13]

Most importantly, in Obomsawin's films the interview – as a testimonial narrative – ceases being simply a statement, an interpretation or an account. It shapes point of view and becomes an explanatory template for self-representation. The interview is characterized by a tension between first- and third-person address, between individual agency and group identity, to enable the circulation of subjectivity across a range of narrative registers.[14] While third-person address is mostly reserved for historical and collectively shared knowledge, first-person address inscribes the complex negotiation between what is experienced simultaneously at the personal and the communal level.

Moreover, the interview in its testimonial form affectively anchors the relationship between Obomsawin and her social protagonists, between social protagonists and audiences. As such, the interview implicitly acknowledges the collaboration between the social subject and the filmmaker who records and edits the narrator's testimony. As Obomsawin has explained, the process of filmmaking depends as much on personal involvement as on collaboration. Through private conversations and individual (and sometimes collective) consultation and advice, the filmmaker builds a level of trust between herself and her subjects. As a result, her work speaks from what Steven calls an 'insider voice' – a voice that speaks individually and collectively from within Native culture.[15] Furthermore, this relationship between Obomsawin and her subjects is visually and aurally inscribed into the film either by her contiguous presence in the frame or the role she assumes as a narrator. In this way, the spectator becomes, in the words of Noreiga, '"complicit" not through a one-to-one identification with the narrator, but through an identification with the narrator's project.'[16]

Kanehsatake: 270 Years of Resistance, for instance, disrupts the standard protocol of the interactive documentary by structuring complementary functions of agency. The opening segments illustrate how this rhetorical strategy operates, and how the filmmaker and her interviewees assume concurrent roles as narrators, interlocutors, participants, and witnesses. The confrontation that occurred in Oka, Quebec, during the summer of 1990 between the Mohawk and the provincial police and federal military is introduced in the pre-credit by Obomsawin's opening statement ('The story you will see takes place ...') and is accompanied by a drawing that locates the Kanehsatake, Akwesasne, and Kahnawake territories, and by shots of the golf course and the Mohawk cemetery in the Pines. Positioned inside the Pines, the camera establishes the centrality of a Native point of view, which is maintained throughout the whole film (as in the sequences recorded from behind the Mohawk barricades and the Treatment Centre) to represent the social dynamics and political dimensions of the Oka conflict.[17]

The title sequence deals with events that led to the shoot-out between Mohawk warriors and the Sûreté du Québec (SQ). This sequence marks a shift in location (the Pines and the Mohawk cemetery) and address (on-camera interviews with Kahentiiosta, Ellen Gabriel, and Robert 'Mad Jap' Skidders). Narrated by Kahentiiosta, Gabriel, and Skidders, the confrontation in the Pines is visually rendered through the juxtaposition of images originating from broadcast television and home video and Obomsawin's film crew. Because Obomsawin's film crew arrived after the shootout, the raid itself is conveyed through a series of swishpans of the forest, accompanied by the noises of gunshots, implying chaos. It ends with a pastoral shot of the Pines and the golf course, suggesting the uneasy calm that followed.

The representational contrast in the confrontation and its aftermath is reinforced by a contrast in rhetorical forms. These forms range from chronicle to autobiography, interpretation, and reminiscence, and they integrate affective, experiential, and interpretative modes of speech. By bridging distinct forms of discourse, these rhetorical forms reveal the multilayered character of testimonial narratives. Obomsawin's voice-over narration ('the people in the Pines are very sad about the shooting of Corporal Lemay'), spoken in her characteristically soothing voice, and in present tense, evokes what the shot of the Pines cannot represent. Gabriel's on-camera response to the SQ tactical team, whose faces were concealed behind shielded helmets ('we were fighting something without a spirit'), voices the anxiety in the face of colonial aggression, bringing the conflict to a symbolic level. At another level, Kahentiiosta's description of Mohawk resolve ('but we weren't leaving') suggests self-assertion. Both Skidders's interpretation of Lemay's shooting (with Obomsawin appearing, this time on camera) and his account of the behaviour of police during the raid ('they started screaming and taking off') evoke bewilderment and uncertainty.

These opening sequences of the film disrupt the unified position of the narrating subject. Not only is the narrative multivocal, but the non-homogeneous sources of the visual records destabilize point of view and reinforce the impossibility of submitting a single 'interpretative frame' from which the events surrounding Lemay's death can be coherently re-arranged.[18] These segments illustrate what Obomsawin herself has said about her film: 'There are many stories to Kanehsatake, or Oka, or Kahnawake during the crisis – thousands of stories.'[19]

Ethnographic Imagery and Subjectivity

Obomsawin's films place the protocol of documentary at the service of alternative modes of historical and ethnographic representation. *Mother of Many Children* (1977) is such a film. While documenting how First Nations women experience life from birth to old age, the film situates the multiple ways in which First Nations women's identities and experiences have been historically shaped and articulated.

Mother of Many Children suggests, through its aesthetic and discursive strategies, the unpredictable ways in which colonization affects Native efforts to retrieve the scattered pieces of First Peoples histories. It translates into a documentary structure the Native dilemma of self-representation, and renders visible the predicament faced by Native filmmakers when they have to rely on images inherited from traditional, European-centred anthropology.

The two sequences that make up the birth segment of *Mother of Many Children* are a good example of a reflexive strategy that exposes the tension between one regime of knowledge, which is embodied and localized, and the other, which is imaginary and deferred (the discursive and representational archive of colonialism). On the one hand, the stylistic contrast between these sequences brings out differences between contemporary and traditional representations of childbirth. The sequence that shows the birth of a baby girl in a Fort George hospital to Alassi Anakayak, a Cree woman from the Eastern Arctic, is recorded in the style of observational documentary. The interview with Césare Newashish, a Manowan Elder from Atikameok Iriniokaa, is given mostly off-screen. On the other hand, these two sequences establish a tension between lived experience and historical memory, between the affectivity of mother–child bonding and the third-person plural account of how in the past Cree women managed pregnancy and delivered babies.

In addition, Newashish's narrative reveals the tension between Native storytelling and the silent subject of colonial imagery. Although the affiliation of Newashish's narrative to oral history is obvious, oral history is not idealized. While Obomsawin's off-camera translation of Newashish's on-camera account de-fetishizes the speaking subject, the elder's account is laid over archival footage. This juxtaposition suggests that what is remembered by oral history – what constitutes the historical consciousness of the Manowan Cree – cannot be reconciled with ethnographical knowledge, as represented by the archival footage. The normative bond between speech and representation is suspended, exposing a multiple self shaped by sedimented layers of historical consciousness.

Newashish's narrative begins with 'they always lived in the bush and canvas tents there were none,' and ends with the remark 'she was more

powerful than man.' It is accompanied, respectively, by traditional ethnographic images of a traditional tepee and then of an older woman. These
photographs, like all the archival stills used in the film, assert the local
and the specific. Images showing Native family groups and individuals in
a variety of domestic and occupational situations appear to have been
selected for their affective, rather than their descriptive, value. Thus, the
alternation between testimonial narratives and ethnographic imagery in
Mother of Many Children functions as a 'recuperative strategy in the face of
the erasure of difference characteristic of colonialist representation,' as
Gareth Griffiths points out in relation to Aboriginal representation in
Australia.[20]

This strategy also has a corrective function that fits well into the agenda
of the political and aesthetic enfranchisement that guides Obomsawin's
documentary practice. In *Mother of Many Children* this agenda is illustrated
in the 'walking out' ceremony. Performed for the camera in a northern Cree settlement (and described by Obomsawin's voice-over), this
sequence concentrates on ritual and affective gestures. What is significant
in this segment is the appropriation of the traditional ethnographic protocol. The parade of women and children, and the welcoming embracing
and somewhat timid kissing of the babies by the men in the tent, inverts
the anonymity and lifelessness of the archival stills seen previously in the
birthing segment. Moreover, this sequence foregrounds – through the
subjects' direct look at the camera – the 'impulse to "pose," to control
one's photographic representation.'[21]

Mother of Many Children is a powerful, cross-cultural statement that is
'made with full, sometimes painful awareness of what has come before
and of the representational residue available for adaptation, rejection,
and redress,' as Bill Nichols has noted of new forms of ethnography.[22]
This imaginative deployment of documentary devices also defies the rigid
taxonomy of ethnography, itself a colonial construct, and creates a tension between stable categorizations of self (and group) and social relations. *Mother of Many Children* offers a poignant portrayal of matriarchal
cultures that have, over the centuries, been pressured to change and to
adopt new habits and customs.

Visual Materials, Knowledge, and Representation

In Obomsawin's films, archival materials and found footage signify the
historical conflict between the knowledge that First Nations people
hold about themselves and the knowledge that others have constructed

about Natives. This strategy is the cinematographic equivalent of what Georges E. Sioui Wendayte has termed 'Amerindian autohistory.' Amerindian autohistory strives 'to demonstrate, by showing convergence with non-Native documents, the "scientific" validity of Native historical sources (written, oral, pictographic, mnemonic, esthetic, etc.) as testimonies of Native perceptions of themselves and their world.'[23] While this approach validates Native sources as legitimate historical accounts, it also recognizes that 'accredited colonial documentary sources ... continue to exist as the ultimate fortress of Euro-American discourse on Amerindians.'[24]

Yet, these Eurocentric images also become a site from which master narratives can be challenged and counter-narratives can be told through a process of reframing and repositioning. This strategy is present in most of Obomsawin's films; it manifests itself concretely in discrete segments that set up the films' historical and thematic frameworks and are made up of illustrations, paintings, photographs, and film clips. Some of these images are archival; others are contemporary or have been specifically commissioned for the film. Initiated by the filmmaker's own voice-over narration, these expositional sequences complement the historical, cultural, or testimonial narratives of the film and, at the same time, unsettle the epistemological stability of didactic documentaries. By alternating archival and contemporary images, Obomsawin's films forge powerful and visually engaging links between metaphoric and metonymic narratives to represent the ritualistic and contingent aspects of social and cultural Native experience.

Among these representational forms, drawings, illustrations, and etchings perform a greater variety of functions than do archival footage and still photographs. In *Incident at Restigouche* (1984), for example, Native representation is constructed as a process that acknowledges change and that situates how Mi'kmaq traditions continue under different forms in the contemporary world. The film contests the traditional antinomies – pre-contact/colonial, old/new, Native/Euro-American – by parallelism and repetition. A pastel drawing of a river landscape is alternated with night-time shots of Mi'kmaq fishermen. The drawing's implicit romanticization of America as a 'land of abundance' is superseded by Chief Metallic's account about how the Mi'kmaq adopted European fishing techniques. In addition, the waterfall in the drawing is used again to articulate a Native-specific view of representing history. It introduces a musical segment where found footage on the life cycle of the salmon is accompanied by 'Salmon Song,' performed by Willy Dunn. With the closing images of a crying baby, and of two young smiling children, the lyrics of the song link Native cosmology and cultural survival.

First used in *Incident at Restigouche*, and again in *My Name is Kahentiiosta* (1995), courtroom sketches illustrate individual narratives – the trials of Donald Germain and Kahentiiosta, respectively – and render representable those aspects of Native experience that have been made invisible. In *Incident at Restigouche*, sketches challenge the neutrality of images of court proceedings and expose the systemic racism of the Canadian justice system. The voice-over commentary (spoken by Obomsawin and a male actor) names the judge and reads the charges brought against the Mi'kmaq fishermen in May 1982, while the interviews (with Germain and witnesses Richard Barnaby, Fay Metallic, and Sally Caplin) expose the way in which the court testimony of Natives was delegitimized. Similarly, sketches in *My Name is Kahentiiosta* are used to show what happened after the Mohawk left the Treatment Centre on 26 September 1990. Accompanied by Kahentiiosta's testimonial narrative, the sketches visualize situations that could neither be documented by the camera nor by a sympathetic photographer, like the bus trip to the Farnham military base and the trial at the St Jerôme courthouse. While this strategy explicitly acknowledges the limitations imposed on documentary filmmakers, it constructs a new visual space for Native self-representation.

In *Mother of Many Children*, female initiation is presented through Marie Leo's story of her own initiation. This narrative takes an epistolary form and is accompanied by black and white drawings that emphasize the ceremonial aspects of the transition to womanhood. Complemented by archival stills (an Indian settlement in winter, a tent made of fir branches, women preparing food for winter storage) and family photographs, these drawings validate the place of ritual and tradition in the construction of identity.

The sketches made by Bob Verrall – and animated through an optical printer – for *Kanehsatake: 270 Years of Resistance* mimic, through viewpoint and camera movement, the forced migration of Mohawk begun with the arrival of Sulpician missionaries in 1566 and ending in 1721. The recurring drawing of the Sulpician church in Oka – shown frontally, as if seen from the river – surrounded by the forest, signifies colonial intrusion and the estrangement of Mohawk from their traditional land. These commissioned drawings make up for the scarcity of Native historical visual sources. This production of Native representations (like the rearticulation of history and discourse through testimonial narratives) implies an awareness of how First Nations peoples have been represented and how their history has been told.

In Obomsawin's films, the combination of images from diverse sources creates a space to visualize cultural knowledge and social experience, retrieve traditional and contemporary stories, and question colonial representations. Most importantly, Native history and knowledge are presented from multiple perspectives that enable both individual agency and collective identity. This approach reflects what Gerald McMaster and Lee-Ann Martin have termed a 'meeting of cultures' that foregrounds 'historicity, cultural conquest, Aboriginal title, identity and sovereignty.'[25]

The Aesthetics of Affectivity

In *Poundmaker's Lodge: A Place of Healing* (1987) and *No Address* (1988) – as in *Mother of Many Children* – multiple voices speak for, and within, the experience of being a First Nations youth. These two films establish a discourse through which self-abuse and healing is effectively represented as a process of self-recognition.

Poundmaker's Lodge: A Place of Healing is centred around the accounts of the young men and women who have come to St Albert (north of Edmonton) to break out from the vicious cycle of alcohol and drug abuse. Through their interactions with the social workers, medicine men, and elders at the Poundmaker's Lodge, the film reveals the struggle – in the words of Chief Poundmaker (spoken by Brian Eyahpaise) that open the film – 'to find a place in the world for our people.' *No Address* deals with homeless Natives who live in the streets of Montreal. The film's main protagonist is Tonatsee, a Great Whale Cree. Through him, the film generates an affective context for the plight of inner-city Natives whose only support to find a way out of drug abuse and prostitution comes from a handful of agencies (the Montreal Native Friendship Centre, La Mission Colombe, and Dernier Secours.)

What distinguishes these two films from Obomsawin's earlier work is the dramatization of individual stories and the personalized segments that reveal, with extreme sensitivity, the long road toward recovery. Affectivity in these films is the result of empathy, but also of respect for the young people. By maintaining a discrete distance, the camera establishes a private space for emotional release. In *Poundmaker's Lodge*, for instance, when Leslie Brunon, a twenty-five-year-old man, breaks down, unable to submit himself to the healing powers of the fire in the sweat lodge, the filmmaker lets him walk away from the camera.

Amid the bleakness of the young Native men and women's stories, there is always a precarious sense of hope. The relentless presentation of pain is counterbalanced by lyrical images of hope. The recurring image of a tepee set against a Prairie sunset in *Poundmaker's Lodge*, for instance, becomes a representational motif for centuries-old traditions of Native empowerment through spirituality. The promise of restoration is furthered in the lodge sequences where the young people gather in a circle to burn sweet grass and vocalize their anger. In *No Address*, Obomsawin uses the bleak winter landscape as a backdrop for the stories of those she calls 'the orphans of the city' and establishes how the Montreal Native Friendship Centre has become a physical and emotional refuge for young Native alcohol and drug abusers. The film follows the journey of each character from derelict neighbourhoods and abandoned buildings to the centre, from a self-destructive recklessness to a still precarious, but genuine, awareness of the need to take control of their despairing existences.

While both films denounce the systemic racism that has disenfranchised Natives, they also construct a social and psychological framework for hope through solidarity and empathy. As Robert Houle suggests, 'this social realism is what makes Obomsawin's narratives potent and cathartic, they are like the axiom which says one has to deal with the poison before a process of healing can begin.'[26]

Nowhere is affect more prominent than in *Richard Cardinal: Cry from a Diary of a Métis Child* (1986). This film chronicles the story of a boy who, between the ages of four and seventeen, was placed in sixteen foster homes and twelve shelters, group homes, and lock-up facilities and who, after three attempts, killed himself in June 1984. The film relies on the alternation of quotations from Richard Cardinal's diary (read by David Mitchell) with dramatized images of Richard as a young boy (played by Cory Swan), interviews with his brother, Charlie Cardinal, and some of the foster families with whom Richard was placed, and Obomsawin's voice-over commentary to narrate the tragic outcome of the child's story.

The opening sequences of *Richard Cardinal* set up distinct ways to reconstruct Richard's life by moving from the shots of a young boy in a field of wild flowers to photographs of Richard. A line from the diary ('Dear Chuck, if I die, try to understand') and a black-and-white photograph of Richard's body hanging from a white birch tree act as catalysts for the film. At the same time, the account given by foster parents Terry and Leo Crother of Richard's final days serves as a motivating drive for the film. The purpose of the film is validated by Leo's efforts to bring

Richard's death to the attention of government officials and by his reasons for taking pictures of the body ('somebody else should see'). This affective investment in disclosing the tragic circumstances that led to the boy's suicide is confirmed by Obomsawin's on-camera presence in the early sequences of the film.

With its retrospective narrative structure, compelling imagery, and persistent questioning of the treatment that Richard received, the film reveals the systemic inadequacy and racism of child welfare policies. The excerpts from Richard's diary set up a space from where a withdrawn and abused Métis child can speak, evoking the anguish that leads so many young Natives to suicide. Accompanied by images of Swan in a variety of settings, these excerpts have an affective impact on the representation of agency; they foreground the liberating potential of self-expression.

The film's re-enactment sequences have a double function. First, they reveal a dark world of abuse, fear, violence, and neglect. Richard's account of his arrival at the Jones home is illustrated in a sequence that shows him locking himself into a car and then being led into a building by a man. Shots of Richard sitting alone in the car, with a small suitcase on his knees, and of his crying face while being reassured by the social worker that 'everything will be fine,' portray his well-founded apprehension of what awaits behind the tiny basement window of the room assigned to him. The re-enactment sequences also provide an insight into a private world, one where a child can do those things that children should be able to do. Shots of the boy playing a flute, chasing after frogs in a pond, collecting flowers, and skipping along a railway track set up an alternative perspective. As Obomsawin has said, 'I want people, who look at the film, to have a different attitude next time they meet what is called a problem child, and develop some love and some relationship to the child – instead of alienating him.'[27]

Richard's tragic search for an identity is condensed into the final images of the film: Richard as a young boy running along a railway track, his arms filled with wild flowers, and, in voice-over, a diary excerpt speaking of sadness and depression. These melancholy saturated images represent, at an affective level, what the film has so successfully attempted to articulate: the need to rescue children who have lived similar situations, and to allow them to speak about those experiences. As such, *Richard Cardinal* reiterates the premise behind Obomsawin's documentary practice: 'Obomsawin calls film a "place" where Native people can talk to each other about their losses, their memories of injustice, their desire to share what is good about their way of life, and with that sharing viewers of her documentaries perhaps arrive at a better appreciation of how the dispossessed, dislocated, and disoriented try to come out of an abyss.'[28]

Storytelling through Documentary

Obomsawin's films constitute a compelling and politically important contribution to a family album where the stories of First Nations people in Canada are told, where their setbacks and victories are recorded with anger, compassion, and respect. Native people are no longer the silent 'other' and 'exotic' object of colonial representation; rather, Native subjectivity and agency are localized. Knowledge and history are embodied through narratives that express the struggle to reclaim the right of First Nations communities to imagine a better future. Each film explores the bewildering journeys of individuals and communities who have fought for self-determination. Obomsawin's work resituates Native history and tradition, social experience and mythology.

The bonds established between First Nations peoples and place serve to reconstruct Native identities in ways that reflect the twin sense of alienation from and belonging to the Canadian landscape. As a documentary filmmaker and Native activist, Obomsawin recognizes herself as a storyteller within a tradition where, in the words of Loretta Todd, 'storytellers were part of the governing of their nations, as they were holders of cultural history ... Through story, dance, song, ceremony ... the holders of the culture kept the histories and the visions alive, told by image and voice, by word and by action.'[29]

Obomsawin's skill as a storyteller is eloquently and effectively rendered in the historical segment of *Kanehsatake: 270 Years of Resistance*. This segment contextualizes the events of 1990 within the historical conflict between the Mohawk and successive colonial powers. It follows a shot of a military helicopter landing behind the Sulpician church in Oka, which Obomsawin's voice-over introduces as being the place 'where the trouble all began 270 years ago.' Illustrated with historical prints, paintings, Diorama reconstructions, archival stills, Mohawk family photographs, and contemporary drawings, this historical exposé centres around four historical moments.[30] The expositional form taken by this narrative is complemented by exegesis, as in the description of the Two Mountain wampum. Spoken by a male voice, this description reproduces the traditional oral recital of the Great Law of Peace by the wampum keepers of the Iroquois Confederacy Longhouse. The last episode in this historical segment tells the story of Chief Sose Onasakenrat (also known as Joseph Swan), who fought to claim the land back from the Sulpicians in 1869, and includes a dramatized exchange between Chief Onasakenrat and a Sulpician priest.[31] In this way, the film negotiates the complex history that has forced Native people to take up arms because, as Obomsawin has stated, 'for hundreds of years, our people tried everything. Nobody listened until now.'[32]

Kanehsatake exposes moments of intense emotion. The mounting tension at the barricades, for instance, is conveyed through reactions of anxiety, anger, and frustration by individual Mohawk warriors. Thus, what the film offers is more than a Native account of the events that were broadcast live into Canadian homes.[33] It provides an uncompromising and partisan perspective of what happened around the Oka golf course to open up a space from which Mohawk historical narratives can be re-articulated and Native struggles for self-determination can be legitimized.

The aspects of Obomsawin's work that are highlighted in this chapter demonstrate how the filmmaker politically used the prevailing techniques of documentary. Obomsawin has used these techniques to reinstate what Nichols sees as being central to performative documentaries – 'the sense of the local, specific, and embodied as a vital locus of social subjectivity,' because this approach to documentary 'gives figuration to and evokes dimensions of the political unconscious that remain suspended between an immediate here and now and a utopian alternative.'[34]

Furthermore, by bringing to her documentary practice a deep awareness of her own identity, she has placed her work at the service of a political and aesthetic agenda that aims at the reappropriation of an audiovisual space for Native representation. The consolidation of cultural-specific strategies in her work places Obomsawin's films within Native struggles for cultural autonomy and recognition of Aboriginal entitlement. As Loretta Todd states, 'the basis of cultural autonomy is contained within the concept of Aboriginal Title and Rights. Aboriginal Title has been described as a concept of jurisprudence that articulates a relationship of a people to their traditional lands. Traditional lands are defined by traditional use and occupancy: from Aboriginal Title flow Aboriginal Rights.'[35]

In the opening of *My Name Is Kahentiiosta* the transmutation of the National Film Board of Canada logo is a visual symbol of a transaction. A white drawing of an eye is transformed into a human figure and is placed within a larger design that incorporates Native motifs. As the cube on which the logo changes from an ocular to an anthropomorphic shape rotates, the Native eye drawing multiplies before progressively dissolving into the official image. This incorporation of Native iconography (like the Native drum sounds accompanying the NFB logo in *Kanehsatake: 270 Years of Resistance*) is a sign of institutional validation. For Obomsawin, as a documentary filmmaker, it is a recognition of her status within the National Film Board of Canada. For Canada's First Nations, it is an acknowledgment that Native artists can have equal access to existing cultural institutions in order to foster, create, and develop Native cultural practices.

NOTES

My thanks go to Peter Harcourt, Chris Creighton-Kelly, Laura U. Marks, and Brenda Longfellow, who at different points read this chapter, provided valuable feedback, and encouraged me by making useful suggestions.

1 Given the fragmented, and underdeveloped, state of Canadian film studies, the contributions of Native filmmakers have yet to be documented. I hope that the comments and interpretations presented in this article may contribute – in a modest way – to a better understanding of the politics of Native documentary.

2 'Nous étions la seule famille indienne, là-bas, évoque la cinéaste. Toute mon enfance, je me suis fait battre, insulter, cracher dessus. Après je n'ai eu qu'une envie: combattre l'injustice.' Odile Tremblay, 'Alanis Obomsawin: La douleur d'être Amérindienne,' *Le Devoir*, 19 April 1995, A3.

3 Obomsawin's talent as a singer and storyteller and her commitment to Aboriginal cultural practices were documented in *Alanis* (Ron Kelly, 1965). Incidentally, it was through the broadcast of this film on CBC's *Telescope* that she was approached by the NFB. She appeared in *Our Dear Sisters* (Kathleen Shannon, 1975), which is part of the Working Mothers series. This short film shows highlights of her participation at the Mariposa Folk Festival in Toronto and includes an interview in which she talks about being a performer and a single mother.

4 Details about the specifics of Obomsawin's work as a Native 'consultant' at the NFB are difficult to come by. Yet, her role in the salvaging of *Cold Journey* (Martin Defalco, 1972) has been documented both in Gary Evans, *In the National Interest: A Chronicle of the National Film Board of Canada from 1949 to 1989* (Toronto: University of Toronto Press, 1971), 213–14, and D.B. Jones, *The Best Butler in the Business: Tom Daly of the National Film Board of Canada* (Toronto: University of Toronto Press, 1996), 191–3.

5 The article by Maurie Alioff and Susan Schouten Levine remains the most comprehensive biographical account on Alanis Obomsawin. See 'The Long Walk of Alanis Obomsawin,' *Cinema Canada*, no. 142 (June 1987): 10–15.

6 Alanis Obomsawin, 'It Was Painful to Make, I Can Tell You That,' in Peter Steven, *Brink of Reality: New Canadian Documentary Film and Video* (Toronto: Between The Lines, 1993), 186.

7 Her films focus on children (*Christmas at Moose Factory*, 1971; *Richard Cardinal: Cry from a Diary of a Métis Child*, 1986), young people (*Gabriel Goes to the City*, 1979; *Poundmaker's Lodge: A Healing Place*, 1987; *No Address*, 1988), and women (*Mother of Many Children*, 1977; *My Name is Kahentiiosta*, 1995). Others document situations of crisis (*Incident at Restigouche*, 1984; *Kanehsatake: 270 Years of Resistance*, 1993; *Spudwrench*, 1997) or chronicle cultural history (the Canada Vignettes *The Wild Rice Harvest, Kenora*, 1979 and *June in Povungnituk*, 1980) and place this history within contemporary struggles for self-determination (*Amisk*, 1977). She has also directed short dramas such as *Walker* (1991).

8 Thomas Waugh, 'Why Documentary Filmmakers Keep Trying to Change the World, *or* Why People Changing the World Keep Making Documentaries,' in *'Show Us Life': Toward a History and Aesthetics of the Committed Documentary* (Metuchen, NJ: Scarecrow Press, 1984), xiv.

9 Brian Winston, *Claiming the Real: The Documentary Film Revisited* (London: British Film Institute, 1995), 258.

10 Obomsawin, 'It Was Painful to Make,' 177.

11 Alioff and Schouten Levine, 'The Long Walk of Alanis Obomsawin,' 13.

12 Emma LaRoque, 'Preface,' in *Writing the Circle: Native Women Writers in Western Canada*, ed. Jeanne Perreault and Sylvia Vance (Edmonton: NeWest Publishers, 1990), xv.

13 Testimonial narratives are primarily associated with the literary genre of *testimonial* but have also been linked to radical forms of Latin American documentary. Chon Noriega, 'Talking Heads, Body Politic: The Plural Self of Chicano Experimental Video,' in *Resolutions: Contemporary Video Practices*, ed. Michael Renov and Elizabeth Suderburg (Minnesota: University of Minnesota Press, 1996), 211.

14 This tension is described by Noriega in terms of an 'ethics of identity.' Doris Sommer has used this term to explain the relationship between the speaking subject and the interlocutor: 'The testimonial "I" does not invite us to identify with it. We are too different, and there is no pretence here of universal or essential experience.' Quoted in Noriega, 'Talking Heads,' 210.

15 Obomsawin, 'It Was Painful to Make,' 184.

16 Noriega, 'Talking Heads,' 210.

17 By 2 September 1990 the Canadian army advanced on the Mohawk in the Pines and set up a military barricade that prevented journalist and filmmakers from leaving the Treatment Centre. While Obomsawin remained in the Treatment Centre, her crew continued shooting material for the film on the other side of the barricades. These are the only sequences in which the point of view shifts to the other side of the military barricades. Geoffrey York and Loreen Pindera, *People of the Pines* (Toronto: Little, Brown, 1991), 375.

18 I'm borrowing the term 'interpretative frame' from Bill Nichols, who has used it to analyze the political context and ideological assumptions that surrounded the use of audio-visual evidence, and the Rodney King tape, during the first trial of four Los Angeles policemen in 1991. Bill Nichols, *Blurred Boundaries: Questions of Meaning in Contemporary Culture* (Bloomington: Indiana University Press, 1994), 19.

19 Sandy Greer, 'Mohawks and the Media: Alanis Obomsawin's *Kahnehsatake: 270 Years of Resistance,*' *Take One*, no. 4 (Winter 1994): 19.

20 Gareth Griffiths, 'The Myth of Authenticity,' in *The Post-Colonial Studies Reader*, ed. Bill Ashcroft, Gareth Griffiths, and Helen Tiffin (London: Routledge, 1995), 238.

21 Thomas Waugh, 'Words of Command: Notes on Cultural and Political Inflections of Direct Cinema in Indian Independent Documentary,' *CineAction*, no. 23 (Winter 1990–1): 36.

22 Nichols, *Blurred Boundaries*, 91.

23 Georges E. Sioui Wendayete, '1992: The Discovery of Americity,' in *Indigena: Contemporary Native Perspectives,* ed. Gerald McMaster and Lee-Ann Martin (Vancouver: Douglas and McIntyre; Hull: Canadian Museum of Civilization, 1992), 60.

24 Ibid., 59.

25 Gerald McMaster and Lee-Ann Martin, 'Introduction,' *Indigena*, 12.

26 Robert Houle, 'Alanis Obomsawin,' in *Land Spirit Power: First Nations at the National Gallery of Canada*, ed. Diana Nemiroff, Robert Houle and Charlotte Townsend-Gault (Ottawa: National Gallery of Canada, 1992), 107.

27 Alioff and Schouten Levine, 'The Long Walk of Alanis Obomsawin,' 12.

28 Houle, 'Alanis Obomsawin,' 107.

29 Loretta Todd, 'We Dream Who We Are: The Development of the Aboriginal Film and Video Arts Alliance,' *Talking Stick* 1, no. 2 (Spring 1994): 7.

30 These moments are: the pre-contact period; the migration of Mohawk to the Lake of Two Mountains – what is today Kanehsatake – during the French regime; and the two land claim petitions during the British regime – the first in 1787 and the second in 1868. For details of these events, see 'The Two Dog Wampum,' in York and Pindera, *People of the Pines*, 82–98.

31 These lines are quoted in Ronald Wright, *Stolen Continents: The 'New World' through Indian Eyes since 1492* (Toronto: Viking-Penguin, 1991), 332.
32 Quoted in York and Pindera, *People of the Pines*, 274.
33 A systematic and detailed study of television coverage still needs to be undertaken to understand the differences between CBC Newsworld's live coverage of the Oka events and Obomsawin's films.
34 Nichols, *Blurred Boundaries*, 106.
35 Loretta Todd, 'Notes on Appropriation,' *Parallélogramme* 16, no. 1 (1990): 26.

A Cinema of Duty: The Films of Jennifer Hodge de Silva

CAMERON BAILEY

Whether or not future histories of black filmmaking in Canada begin with Jennifer Hodge de Silva, they will have to acknowledge her importance. Best-known today for her 1983 documentary *Home Feeling: Struggle for a Community*, Hodge de Silva directed a number of films during the 1980s that established the dominant mode in African Canadian film culture. Working exclusively in the documentary and often on sponsored films, she staked out a set of concerns and a mode of production that might be termed black liberalism. *Home Feeling* explored relations between police and black immigrant communities in Toronto's Jane–Finch neighbourhood, but most of Hodge de Silva's films did not deal with specifically black subjects. Instead her work (and it is only since she died in 1989 that so heterogeneous a group of films has assumed the shape of a body of work) dealt with a wide range of social concerns, from anti-racist education in *Myself, Yourself* (1981) to self-help programs for ex-convicts in *In Support of the Human Spirit*. Hodge de Silva's films represent a black humanist agenda, and more specifically a black Canadian humanist agenda. Many of her sponsored films, like *A Day in the Life of Canada (The Yukon)*, *Neighbourhoods – Outremont*, and *Neighbourhoods – Kensington Market*, are precisely about Canadian cultural geography. Running through these films and the 'issue' films is this humanist agenda, this socially reconstructive program. Hodge de Silva's work does address the real nature of racism facing black people in Canada, but there's more succour than anger in her films. While *Home Feeling* and *Myself, Yourself* are critical of some elements of Canadian society, their critique is couched entirely in terms of reform rather than revolution.

But does this devalue Hodge de Silva's work? By most standards of committed black filmmaking, yes. 'Blackness does not mean that we are inherently oppositional,' cultural critic bell hooks reminds us. 'Our creative work is shaped by a market that reflects white supremacist values and concerns.'[1] However, while Hodge de Silva's films should never be misconstrued as the first alarm of a black revolution in Canadian film culture, they do occupy an important position at the beginning of a new movement. Their very status as the product of a complex set of (for the most part) institutionally defined circumstances, circumstances that continue to govern black filmmaking in Canada, makes them worthy of study. It is no accident that the vast majority of films produced by African Canadians have been firmly within the social issue, documentary realist genre, and Hodge de Silva's work is exemplary in that regard. In addition, without marginalizing this work outside of aesthetics, it is important that 'common' notions in film criticism about the category of the 'interesting' not be the first method of approach in dealing with Hodge de Silva's work. Operating entirely outside art-cinema's positive criteria of innovation and experimentation, these films' documentary realist practice seeks neither to shock nor to seriously challenge the viewer, but to reconfirm certain norms of liberal conscience and national identity. In examining something of Hodge de Silva's history and later the films themselves, I hope to articulate a way of watching her films, primarily for black viewers, that engages with them on levels both within and without their own frames of reference, but never in ignorance of what those frames of reference are, or why they exist. I hope this study will serve as a beginning in rescuing Hodge de Silva from the critical neglect (Who is she?) and critical squeamishness (Wouldn't analyzing such simple films be unfair?) under which her pioneering work has languished.

The first frame that needs to be outlined is Hodge de Silva herself. The product of a unique set of personal circumstances, she emerged from and into very particular and very divergent moments in Canadian history. Born and raised in Montreal, Hodge de Silva grew up in a class – the black Canadian urban bourgeoisie – with barely enough members to qualify as such at the time. Her mother was an accomplished figure who for years sat on the board of directors of the Canadian Broadcasting Corporation. Hodge de Silva's publicity biography boasts that, as a young woman, she attended school in Switzerland. She completed her education with a bachelor's degree from York University in 1973 and a TV Arts diploma from Ryerson Polytechnical Institute in 1979.

All of this is significant only to the extent that it establishes something of the complex and ambiguous positions from which Hodge de Silva made her films. She possessed both the class entitlement and cultural capital that her parents and education gave her, but she was also a black woman breaking into a film industry that had never been anxious to acknowledge either women or people of colour as anything but victims. She came to Toronto in the period when the relaxing of Canada's racist immigration laws began to permit thousands of black West Indian immigrants to settle in the city's suburbs. Many of them wound up in the Jane–Finch neighbourhood, just blocks from where Hodge de Silva studied Fine Arts at York University, and where she would eventually make *Home Feeling.* That rise of sudden black communities around her, with histories very different from hers, produces another frame of dissonance for Hodge de Silva. So too her mother's status at the CBC and Hodge de Silva's later work at that network and the National Film Board suggest a willingness to work inside Canada's two major image-producing institutions – accepting the limits of their liberal ideologies – even as they attempt to use the power of the institution to further a discussion of pressing political issues.

Above all, there is the simultaneous contradiction of class privilege and political solidarity that *Home Feeling* and *Myself, Yourself* try so hard to resolve. As a Canadian-born, middle-class filmmaker with roots within media institutions, Hodge de Silva could not help but come at the 'issues' her films treat so seriously – police racism, educational racism, prison rights, Native culture – from the outside. In fact, it is the variety of the subjects she treats, as well as how she treats them, that marks her work as textbook liberal documentary practice. It has historically been the privilege of (white) middle-class filmmakers to create the issue films that speak so forcefully for all the world's oppressed, and therefore define the very nature of oppression.

To better understand this history and Hodge de Silva's place in it one need look no further than one of the director's mentors, NFB veteran Terence Macartney-Filgate. A pioneer of the 'Candid-Eye' cinéma-vérité movement in Canada (he made the classic *Back Breaking Leaf* in 1959), Macartney-Filgate went on to direct in 1978 one of the first substantive films about black history in Canada, *Fields of Endless Day.* Hodge de Silva landed a job working with Macartney-Filgate as an apprentice on the project. An interview with Macartney-Filgate published just prior to *Fields of Endless Day* is instructive for the perspective from which he views his subjects. Claiming a remarkable degree of disinterest, he rejects any hint of political intent in his socially progressive body of films. About *Back Breaking Leaf,* which revealed punishing labour conditions in the tobacco industry, he says: 'Actually I loathe rural areas and farms [but] the people interested me ... People are the reason I make films, because I don't like to make films particularly about things, or work on idea films ... I have political views but they would never influence anything I did in film. This is something I think any artist has to keep apart.'[2] These were not uncommon views among a certain generation of NFB staff directors. It is without doubt an approach to documentary filmmaking to which Hodge de Silva was exposed at the Board and probably at the CBC as well, an approach which downplayed politics and ideas, even in social issue films, in favour of the emotional currency of 'people.'

There are a number of broad cultural and economic reasons for Hodge de Silva's move into social issue, documentary realist cinema that deserve closer scrutiny. If one remembers bell hooks' notion that black cultural production is shaped by a market that reflects white supremacist values and concerns, the deep structure of Canadian media culture's regimes of control becomes clearer. Hodge de Silva was not merely attracted to the CBC and the NFB because of her mother's involvement; these institutions (after short or long periods of knocking) actually opened their doors to her.

As reflections of state policy, institutions such as the NFB and the CBC have long been concerned with the nation's social well-being. Long before the capital-L Liberalism of Pearson and Trudeau, though certainly on the increase during that era, these two media institutions constructed their mandates to include the maintenance of national bonds. Acknowledging the varied ethnic make-up of the country, and more importantly controlling any social eruptions that might occur from that variety, has long been a part of the everyday work of the CBC and NFB. Broadcasting and filmmaking were designed as social cement. Given this, and the additional impetus provided by the introduction of multiculturalism as official federal policy in 1971, it made sense that black voices be encouraged within Canada's official media. But how?

It should be obvious that the size, resources, and omnipresence of the CBC and NFB within image-culture in Canada result in a breathtaking ability to control even that which takes place outside their gates. It is this element of control which is foregrounded in the interaction between these institutions and black Canadian filmmakers. Take a typical case of a first-time black filmmaker seeking to make a film about some aspect of her community. She is much more likely to receive funding from the Film Board or the federal or provincial office overseeing multiculturalism or some other wing of state social engineering than from the 'artist-driven' funding of the arts councils, which have historically considered documentary films as not art, and all black films as more or less documentary. That funding in turn determines what the resulting film will look and sound like, and, to some degree, what it will say. It is this management of dissent, this ability to channel black voices of protest or affirmation through its corridors, that has been the real race-relations success of the National Film Board.

There are of course many other factors governing the firm links that have been made between black filmmaking in Canada and institutions such as the NFB and the CBC. It is important to remember that historically all Canadian filmmaking has to one degree or another been funded by state-run agencies. It must also be acknowledged that everywhere African people have picked up movie cameras, the impulse to tell the untold 'true' stories, stories that have been suppressed or misconstrued by others, has been one of the first priorities.

There is also the question of the closed doors of the avant-garde. The network of art school and university film education, film co-ops, alternative exhibition venues and art magazines that has supported Canada's independent and experimental film movements since the 1960s has been a notoriously sealed circuit. An accusation of racism would no doubt be abhorrent to these small institutions, but the visible and persistent whiteness of the shifting power elites within these groups says all that one needs to. The white 'avant-garde' has long operated under a set of assumptions that excludes most political filmmaking, and certainly most politically engaged filmmaking by black filmmakers. As Tom Waugh notes in a discussion of the committed documentary, the criteria of bourgeois aesthetics – 'durability, abstraction, ambiguity, individualism, uniqueness, formal complexity, deconstructed or redistributed signifiers, novelty and so on' – generally do not apply to documentaries designed to motivate social change. 'How then,' he asks, 'do we talk about films whose aesthetics consist in political use-value?'[3] Pose that question to the keepers of the avant-garde and the answer surely is 'We don't.' Still, one must continue to ask, how can a movement that claims to challenge accepted perceptions of the world and of art proceed without acknowledging that those accepted perceptions are and have long been bound to sexist and racist ideologies as well? How has the avant-garde been able to continue this long without challenging the race and gender constructs of the image system it rejects and still call itself an avant-garde?

One of the unnoticed aspects of the emergence of black filmmakers in Canada during the 1980s was their work in sponsored filmmaking. These documentaries, usually made for public-service organizations or govern-

ment branches, not only provided experience and decent remuneration
to the filmmakers, but worked in a kind of shadow-economy to the output
of the Film Board. Hodge de Silva made *Home Feeling* (and a little-known
film on potato farming in Prince Edward Island) for the NFB, *Myself,
Yourself* for the Toronto Board of Education, and *In Support of the Human
Spirit* for the John Howard Society. Fellow black film pioneer Claire
Prieto has also made sponsored films. While Hodge de Silva's films
vary widely in subject, style, and conditions of production, they do each
come with an agenda, a clear, often explicit perspective on the people
and events depicted that they want to transmit to the viewer. It is this
propaganda-for-social-change method that allows her to switch easily
from 'independent' state-funded filmmaking to sponsored filmmaking. It
is also this method that she inherits from John Grierson.

Critic William Guynn notes that 'if there is one feature that characterizes documentary as institution, it is a basic dependency ... it stands outside the circuit of finance, production and consumption that defines
cinema as institution.'[4] Documentary's system of exchange, he suggests, is
based not on money-for-pleasure, as with commercial cinema, but rather
on time-for-education, or uplift. There is actually an economy of displea-
sure, or unpleasure, at work in the contract negotiated between the documentary film and its viewer. To Canadian audiences this will seem a
familiar dichotomy. It is Grierson's 'moods of resolution' versus Hollywood's moods of relaxation.

In his classic manifesto 'A Film Policy for Canada' (written in 1944 after
his policy had already been implemented, as a way of explaining it to the
nation), Grierson articulated his plan to redesign the Canadian film
industry as 'a public utility.'[5] Written in the breathless prose characteristic
of his wartime propaganda films (one wouldn't remark if he exclaimed
'Quotas have been exceeded in every sector!'), Grierson outlines his now
infamous conclusion that, given Hollywood's expertise at feature filmmaking, Canada should 'specialize' in nation-building documentaries: 'In
Canada today we may not make many feature story films, but every year
we make hundreds of short films which describe the life of the nation.
They progressively cover the whole field of civic interest: what Canadians
need to know and think about if they are going to do their best by Canada
and by themselves.' And as always Grierson was frighteningly prescient in
determining exactly what Canadians needed to know and think about:
'There are films, too, of Canadian achievements in painting and crafts-
manship, of Canadian folk songs, of the contributions of the various race
groups to Canadian culture. The instrument by which this plan is being

executed is called the National Film Board.'[6] Already the bland, leveling sweep of multiculturalism was in place, as an *effect* of the NFB. As Joyce Nelson notes in her critique of the Grierson myth, part of the Film Board's wartime nation building (i.e., propaganda) concentrated on defusing ethnic and regional differences in Canada. This was accomplished not by ignoring them, but by surveying them benignly, in films like *Peoples of Canada* (1941), from the flattening perspective of the white Anglo-Canadian. Difference was acknowledged at a surface level, only to submit eventually to the higher authority of nation, particularly the white, Anglo-ruled nation. This practice, of course, had its legacy in multiculturalism.

Through the 1960s and 1970s individual filmmakers at the NFB may have progressed beyond Grierson's vision of the Board as a cog (or perhaps a driveshaft) in the social machine, but the energy of the organization itself remained, and I believe remains today, constant. When Hodge de Silva entered in the 70s, it still functioned, though in a less direct fashion, as an instrument of state policy. It is this pedagogical imperative which turns up as Hodge de Silva's propaganda-for-social-change, a style which, given its origins in Grierson's policies, can serve independent documentary or sponsored film equally well.

So do Hodge de Silva's films participate in soliciting Grierson's 'moods of resolution'? Absolutely. But does that make them as totalitarian as Grierson's methods often were? No. A distinction, however fine, must be made between resolve in the service of consolidating national unity and resolve in the service of dismantling, or even questioning, an oppressive status quo that may in fact stem from the construction of 'national unity.' This may be allowing Hodge de Silva's films more than they intend, but it seems clear they cannot be fit easily within what Grierson meant by nation-building.

Kobena Mercer's theorizing around the limits of documentary realism is useful in shedding more light on Hodge de Silva's work. Mercer categorizes the documentary realist aesthetic as following four filmic values: 'transparency, immediacy, authority, and authenticity.'[7] When articulated from a black perspective, a film made with these values is meant to 'correct' racist and stereotypical images. 'It renders present that which is absent in the dominant discourse.' However, the 'race-relations narrative,' a system that can be engaged by either documentary or dramatic realist filmmakers, is ultimately a dead end: 'Within the logic of its narrative patterns, blacks tend to be depicted either as the source and cause of social problems – threatening to disrupt the social equilibrium – or as the passive bearers of social problems – victimised into angst-ridden submission or dependency. In either case, such stories encode versions of reality that confirm the ideological precept that "race" constitutes a "problem" per se.'[8] This is a trap into which Hodge de Silva's 'race' films fall quite cleanly, though the story doesn't end there. By nature of her training and institutional base, her films about people of colour were in a way bound to be race-relations efforts. Brian Winston, outlining what he calls 'the victim tradition' in documentary practice, finds its roots in a combination of Robert Flaherty's romantic style and privileging of the individual and Grierson's 'social concern and propaganda.'[9] But Hodge de Silva's films display a kind of frisson in this area, an oscillation between the hierarchy of filmmaker over subject of the victim-model, and a movement towards the subject, a movement actually towards identification that pushes it beyond that pattern. Particularly in *Home Feeling* there is the beginning of a new black subjectivity that surpasses the race relations notion of black as source or victim of problems. True, the problems are most definitely there, but the trajectory of the film is not *only* one of victimhood and problem-creation.

That surplus effect in *Home Feeling* may stem from what Julia Lesage, one of documentary realism's defenders, points out are the different ways in which the form can be used by members of a marginalized group: 'Realist feminist documentaries represent a use of, yet a shift in, the aesthetics of cinéma vérité, due to the feminist filmmakers' close identification with their subjects, participation in the women's movement, and sense of the films' intended effect.'[10] It may be this tentative identification with its subjects, which, given the conditions of production for the film and Hodge de Silva's own very different history, must not be an easy one, that gives the film its power. Lesage later notes that: 'If many feminist filmmakers have deliberately used a traditional "realist" documentary structure, it is because they see making these films as an urgent public act and wish to enter the 16mm circuit of educational films, especially through libraries, schools, churches, unions and YWCA, to bring a feminist analysis to many women it might otherwise never reach.'[11] Tom Waugh also stresses the importance of audience to the success and indeed the construction of the 'committed documentary,' even defining that term as 'films made by activists speaking to specific publics to bring about specific political goals.'[12] If Hodge de Silva is indeed speaking to specific publics to attain specific political goals in *Home Feeling, Myself, Yourself,* and other films, then there is some further potential for the films. Those publics, constituted at their broadest as people of colour living in Canada, subjects constructed within racism, stand outside of false, power-effacing notions of a 'general audience' under which the NFB is usually compelled to operate.

However, it is important to remember that in noting the importance of the realist style in black Canadian filmmaking, and even in rehabilitating a corner of it as acceptable under certain conditions, we cannot limit ourselves to a version of Lesage's strategic realism. That implies a choice, something that, given all that's been outlined above, black filmmakers have generally not had. The institutions within which Hodge de Silva and others made films brooked no other style but realist. These filmmakers were not schooled in various styles of avant-garde or hybrid documentary, never having been welcome in the art schools or critical journals where it was taken for granted. So by the time they were making films they were able to rationalize the 'frivolity' of such methods for dealing with black subjects, because – to return to Lesage – political urgency meant realism, but not as a choice, as an almost transparent fact of life.

But if the choice of realism was transparent, how see-through is the method itself as Hodge de Silva practised it? On the surface, *Myself, Yourself, Home Feeling* and *In Support of the Human Spirit* articulate an explicitly liberal agenda where the just and the unjust are clearly drawn categories, and empathy and understanding hold the power to solve most problems. Formally, the films appear seamlessly constructed, hard to look behind. Though Hodge de Silva's 'personality' can be found in what she chose to make films about, the films themselves resist the search for a subjective voice, a personal point of view. Of course, given the institutional origins of most of her work, notions of authorship must take a different tack. Hodge de Silva never worked in an independent film milieu that permitted (or required) reconstructing one's psyche as the point of articulation within the film text. This apparent absence of a psychological centre reinforces the films' transparency.

However, Hodge de Silva interpreted the grammar of documentary realism and the limits of sponsored films in a way that I would argue is distinct, even personal. Her films' mode of address is in fact not transparent, though what makes them particular to her is often so subtle, so slight, that one is impressed more by the implications than the direct effect. For example, both *Joe David: Spirit of the Mask* (1981) and *In Support of the Human Spirit* include establishing shots of Canadian city streets (Vancouver and Toronto) that are immediately remarkable (at least to me) for their racial mix. Black, brown, and yellow faces are prominent in Hodge de Silva's 'random' street shots – not absent and not carefully chosen tokens, but prominent. They possess the same value within the frame as white faces, which (again, to me) is much more representative of the average Toronto streetcorner than most other images we see of contemporary Canadian cities. Recent Canadian film (not to mention television commercials and public affairs broadcasting) generally constructs the urban public sphere as a uniform white space. To say nothing of the far-reaching effects this dominant image-making has, it is clear that these 'random' shots are never random at all, but the products of the individual histories of the people who framed them. It should come as no surprise that a white middle-class journalist and cameraperson assigned to do 'man-in-the-street' interviews will select predominantly white middle class (and male) subjects. The weight of ignorance, prejudice, and fear determine whom they choose to approach. In addition, the producer and editor back at the studio further winnow and refine this 'chance' representation of the population. Similarly, a documentary director, cinematographer, and editor share responsibility for constructing the views of public space that take the form of 'casual' establishing shots. Hodge de Silva's films use this tool of realist style as one avenue for interpolating alternative content. It is elements like these that suggest in Hodge de Silva's work a nascent critique, the beginnings of a restructuring of the building blocks of documentary realism that might have developed into a much more forceful political voice.

Home Feeling: Struggle for a Community is the most fully realized of Hodge de Silva's films, both in terms of its success as a liberal, realist documentary, and in terms of its subtle adumbrations to that genre. Compared to similar black British documentaries about police–black community relations (Milton Bryan's The People's Account [1986] or Menelik Shabazz's Blood Ah Go Run [1982], for example), there is very little direct critique of the police in Home Feeling. At its most pointed, the narration track notes that 'As part of their routine patrol, police walk the corridors of Ontario Housing buildings just as they do the public's sidewalks.' This is as angry as the film's overt voice gets. Nor are images of demonstrations, riots, looting, or police beatings presented as evidence of crisis, again unlike the British work. Instead, Home Feeling prefers to indict police officers and administration with a strategic use of their own words, and to counter racist image-making by constituting the police – rather than black youth – as an unspoken, ever present threat throughout.

The film begins with sound rather than image. As the National Film Board logo occupies the screen, a police radio crackles on the soundtrack (this juxtaposition may turn out to be Hodge de Silva's most subversive act). The first actual shot of the film is of a police cruiser patrolling the Jane–Finch neighbourhood. The sound of the police radio continues, soon complemented by reggae music. In these first few moments the film establishes its two primary textual domains – the police and the West Indian community, *and* brings an important extra-textual domain into play – the NFB, as represented by its body-eye logo. The only element common to these three fields, as sound, or image, or both, is the police. The film maintains this insistence on police omnipresence through constant shots of police cars and officers patrolling the area.

So while the film makes no explicit statements against the Metropolitan Toronto Police force, its tone is unmistakable enough that a film catalogue produced by the NFB for school teachers can say: 'The teacher may wish to supplement the anti-police material in the film with more analytical articles on how police think and work, and how minority youths relate to poverty, unemployment and discrimination.'[13] On its release, the film encountered open hostility from the Toronto police, who made efforts to block its public screening and broadcast.

Midway through *Home Feeling*, one of the women in a community discussion group notes that the police presence in the area 'has a very startling psychological effect on you.' This is a clue to *Home Feeling*'s second strategy. In addition to constructing the police as silent threat, the film also constructs black characters as subjects with psychology. Through the way the interviews were conducted and edited, these Jane–Finch residents are afforded a psychological complexity that goes beyond treating the black subject as an unindividuated victim of/respondent to oppression. This takes the comic form, in one case, of following a laid-off bricklayer's assistant who wants to be an interior decorator, as he looks for assistance at an employment office.

In another instance, we see an unemployed waitress search fruitlessly for work, and hear her speak of how much she missed her children before they came up from the West Indies to join her. Again Hodge de Silva takes the scene beyond one of anonymous victimhood by including the woman's confession of depression after her children arrived and hardly knew her, and her subsequent treatment in group therapy. This small moment explores psychological vulnerability as a personal reaction to economic and social conditions in a way that both race relations documentaries and West Indian communities are usually unwilling to do. The waitress's narrative within the film also marks the subtle integration of a black nationalist agenda within a liberal one. She moves from unemployment, to rejection by white corporate business (McDonald's and Burger

King), to rejection by a white-owned small business, and finally to employment in a black-owned business, the Kensington Patty Palace. The point is made, but never stressed. All of this is to point out that the black subjects in *Home Feeling* never remain at the level of mute symbols standing for either victimhood or resistance. Hodge de Silva is careful to elicit and include material that represents the contradictions and full complexity of the lives she chose to film.

In attempting to situate Hodge de Silva within a number of very difficult circumstances of production and reception, it's important to remember her successes, though small, were highly significant. Hodge de Silva was not an independent filmmaker in any sense of the term. Hers was in fact a dependent cinema, with nearly every film she made directly governed by the money that funded it. In a way she follows in a tradition of New World black artists who, at the beginning of a movement, find themselves under the wing of white liberal patrons, and sometimes employ certain white liberal forms and concerns, but whose work still results in something extra, something beyond the external forces that shaped it. This is the history of the Harlem Renaissance, and it may be the destiny of any black cultural movement created within a white power structure.

However, judged by the standards of what critics call the committed documentary, Hodge de Silva comes up lacking. Tom Waugh lists the elements of that genre as 1) ideological principle, 'a declaration of solidarity with the goal of radical socio-political transformation,' 2) 'activism, or intervention in the process of change itself,' and 3) a 'subject-centred' practice that fully involves the people engaged in these struggles.[14] All of these elements are open to much debate, but for the purposes of Hodge de Silva's work, the last category proves most interesting. Speaking directly to the film practice of bodies like the NFB, British critic Jim Pines notes that 'institutionalised "race relations" has a marginalising effect structurally and tends to reinforce rather than ameliorate the "otherness" of the subject – which documentary realism historically and representationally embodies.'[15] It's ironic that Hodge de Silva, a Canadian-born black filmmaker, chose to focus the only film she made specifically about black people on *West Indian*–born blacks, while Claire Prieto, a West Indian–born black filmmaker, has made films predominantly about established black Canadian communities. If Pines is correct, this is a direct function of the realist documentary genre, which necessarily constructs its subject as Other. But as mentioned above, *Home Feeling* demonstrates a tentative moving toward the film's subjects that provides a surplus-effect beyond the filmmaker-self/subject-other dynamic common to conventional realist documentaries.

Moving from the films' relationship to their subjects, I want to conclude by addressing how Hodge de Silva's films interact with their audience. To whom do these films speak, and how? In line with the workings of realist, social-issue documentary, most of Hodge de Silva's work constructs an ideal audience that is sympathetic to the film's subject but not directly involved – liberal outsiders reflective of the filmmaker's own relation to the material. Again without claiming too much for their powers of subversion, I would suggest that *Myself, Yourself* and *Home Feeling* problematize that unified ideal audience somewhat. Though these films also use naturalized, 'transparent' codes of cinematic address, and appeals to 'common sense' notions of injustice, both attempt to speak to outsider and insider simultaneously. The subjects in *Myself, Yourself* provide strong figures of identification for viewers who have had similar experiences of racism at the same time as they stand as objects for sympathy for those who haven't. And as outlined above, *Home Feeling* contains understated but significant messages (the waitress's story) for those with the history to read them.

At this point it becomes important not to allow a discussion of the alternative readings these films may encourage in various audiences to degenerate into the positing of a monolithic black audience capable of uniformly deciphering Hodge de Silva's secret codes. Particularly in Canada and other 'new world' sites of black populations (though not exclusively), the concept of a black community united in a common cultural background and worldview is impossible to maintain. As Stuart Hall writes, one must admit 'the recognition of the extraordinary diversity of subjective positions, social experiences and cultural identities which compose the category "black"; that is, the recognition that "black" is essentially a politically and culturally constructed category, which cannot be grounded in a set of fixed trans-cultural or transcendental racial categories, and which therefore has no guarantees in Nature.'[16] In the realm of film form, differences in 'cultural capital' also determine how a 'black' audience will be constructed. Those educated to assimilate and enjoy documentary realist cinema will read *Myself, Yourself* or *Home Feeling* far differently than those educated to hold this style in high suspicion, or even derision.[17]

One can only speculate about the films Jennifer Hodge de Silva might have made. (One planned project was a feature film called *No Crystal Stair*.) What can profitably be accomplished is a more thorough consideration of the films she did complete, a consideration that moves beyond mere joy that they exist at all. Moreover, Hodge de Silva deserves to be rescued from those who would blithely celebrate the 'truth' and 'authenticity' of her films and leave untouched any examination of how they actually work. Too often black artists are taken for mere recorders of the experience of 'their people,' with no power or ability to shape experience within the language of their chosen medium. The cinema of duty has form as well as content. We can only understand it by exploring the complexities of both.

NOTES

This essay was first published in *CineAction*, no. 23 (winter 1990–1): 4–12.

1 bell hooks, 'The Politics of Radical Black Subjectivity,' in *Yearning: Race, Gender, and Cultural Politics* (Toronto: Between the Lines Press, 1990), 18.
2 Sarah Jennings, 'An Interview with Terence Macartney-Filgate,' in *The Canadian Film Reader*, ed. Seth Feldman and Joyce Nelson (Toronto: Peter Martin Associates, 1977), 82–3.
3 Thomas Waugh, 'Introduction: Why Documentary Filmmakers Keep Trying to Change the World, *or* Why People Changing the World Keep Making Documentaries,' in *'Show Us Life': Toward a History and Aesthetics of the Committed Documentary* (Metuchen, NJ: Scarecrow Press, 1984), xxii.
4 William Guynn, *A Cinema of Nonfiction* (London: Associated University Presses, 1990), 221–2.
5 John Grierson, 'A Film Policy for Canada' [1944], in *Documents in Canadian Film*, ed. Douglas Fetherling (Peterborough: Broadview Press, 1988), 57.
6 Ibid., 64–5.
7 Kobena Mercer, 'Recording Narratives of Race and Nation,' in *Black Film, British Cinema* (ICA Documents 7. London: Institute of Contemporary Arts, 1988), 4–14.
8 Ibid., 8–9.
9 Brian Winston, 'The Tradition of the Victim in Griersonian Documentary,' in *New Challenges for Documentary*, ed. Alan Rosenthal (Berkeley: University of California Press, 1988), 272.
10 Julia Lesage. 'Feminist Documentary: Aesthetics and Politics,' in *'Show Us Life,'* ed. Waugh, 246.
11 Ibid., 225.
12 Waugh, 'Introduction,' xiii.
13 *Focus on Canada: A Film and Video Resource Handbook for Secondary Level Social Studies* (Montreal: National Film Board, n.d.), 87.

14 Waugh, 'Introduction,' xiv.

15 Jim Pines, 'The Cultural Context of Black British Cinema,' in *Blackframes: Critical Perspectives on Black Independent Film*, ed. Mybe B. Cham and Claire Andrade Watkins (Cambridge: Celebration of Black Cinema and MIT Press, 1988), 29.

16 Stuart Hall, 'New Ethnicities,' in *Black Film, British Cinema*, 28.

17 In talking about patterns of viewer response and identification, it is important to keep in mind William Guynn's suggestion that the spectator typically takes in a documentary film in a manner very different from a narrative fiction, with different psychic processes at work. Documentary, he proposes, is on one level 'a-cinematic': 'The cinematic apparatus by its very configuration [the darkened theatre, the larger than life image, etc.] tenders a promise of libidinal pleasure that the spectator here is led to refuse: the documentary film is an object inappropriate to desire' (223). Documentary requires a higher degree of vigilance from the spectator than does the fiction film. Through its apparent relation to the reality of social existence, it invokes the defence mechanisms of the ego and calls on the operations of waking thought.

Keepers of the Power: Story as Covenant in the Films of Loretta Todd, Shelley Niro, and Christine Welsh

CAROL KALAFATIC

A month had passed since I'd interviewed Loretta Todd for almost three hours. A phone call came in from the University of Toronto: would I write a chapter for a book on Canadian women's cinema? I'd been recommended as one who could write with Expertise on the topic. It took me one week to decide to accept the responsibility. Expertise? What I understand in the work of these filmmakers is only one way of understanding, informed by my particular experiences and by the layered histories that pass – or don't pass – through my family. Speaking for hours with someone whom I had come to know over months of sharing work, long meals, and stories about our lives as mixed bloods and as artists, was one thing. But words can take on undue authority once they enter the Western academic domain, where cultural inquiry serves to feed the academy's hunger to codify/quantify our Indianness; the words can get trapped there, colonized in the pages and the panel discussions if we don't look after them. Words have power, Todd said. It was a shared understanding of our responsibility to our Peoples and our stories that made it possible for me to write about the work of Loretta Todd, Shelley Niro, and Christine Welsh, three Native filmmakers who know the role of storytelling in the decolonization process.

Todd, a Cree-Métis, works primarily with documentary, bringing to light various accomplishments and struggles (such as solvent abuse, in *No More Secrets* [1996] and HIV-AIDS, in *Healing Our Spirit* [1995]) faced by Native communities. She allows the stories of individuals-as-community-members to reveal what is possible in the way of spiritual health for Native peoples. *Forgotten Warriors* (1996), in which she combines archival and interview footage with docu-fictional re-creation, examines the land rights efforts of Aboriginal veterans of the Second World War who, after mistreatment by the Canadian government and betrayal by its false land tenure guarantees, continue to seek justice for violations of individual and community land rights. Using a similar mix of techniques, *Hands of History* (1994) celebrates four Aboriginal artists – some of whom are also leaders within their communities – as carriers and caretakers of their peoples' stories. *The Learning Path* (1991) praises the resilience of those who, often by assigning muteness to their pain while keeping the voices of their peoples alive in memory, survived the brutality of the residential school system and have devoted their lives to the self-determination of their peoples and to education in their own communities. As a whole, Todd's documentary work is characterized by a complexity that (may have) caused a fellow filmmaker to suggest that she move immediately into fiction. She has been writing fiction, although not necessarily because of that individual's advice.

Fiction is what Niro prefers to create, partly because she feels there's enough documentary out there already. As a mixed-media artist she often combines visual/conceptual elements from her Mohawk culture with contemporary photographs, negatives, and mirrors that reflect us back to ourselves, but in an altered way. Her images suggest a transcendence of reality that allows a new, more dynamic understanding of reality rather than an escape from it. Whether through her artwork, or through films such as *Honey Moccasin* (1997), she reminds us of the resourceful techniques we have had to develop to maintain our sanity and strength. Her film work, which she began in 1990, reveals the significance of memory and history in our lives as Native survivors. But she also cautions us to look ahead, as in *It Starts with a Whisper* (1993). She tells us to move past the grief for our ancestors; once we honour the stories of the past, we need to make room for the humour that continues to serve us well as a survival tool in our ongoing, contemporary struggles against external as well as internal enemies.

The warrior spirit that has served Aboriginal women in their struggles against both enemies is the focus of *Keepers of the Fire* (1994), a documentary directed by Welsh. The film follows her on a journey to various regions of Canada, and through a number of women's stories of battle. In *Women in the Shadows* (1991), an earlier documentary written by Welsh and directed by Norma Bailey, she embarks on her own journey to uncover the stories that were kept silent within her family, and to provide a basis for the stories she will pass on to her children. She – like Niro and Todd – always returns to the role of words, and the power of stories, as they carry our cultures and make possible our continued survival.

Story

Little one, Shanna. Don't be afraid: the voices of the past are calling you, the
voices of the present urge you on. The voices of the dead tell you their sorrow, the
sorrow inside you and beyond you ... reading, writing, thinking – too much thinking. Tears that won't come, peace that won't come ... your grandfather had almost
forgotten this water drum ... don't be afraid, Shanna, don't be sad: we are with
you on your journey. Voices of love, voices of anger ... from the silence we speak
to you ... listen to the voices. Sing your own song ...
Shelley Niro's *It Starts with a Whisper*

'Words have power,' Niro says, explaining why she is so careful when she
speaks about other Native people's work and reflecting on the place of
oral history in the lives of contemporary Native peoples. Todd recalls a
time when, in 1967 during Vancouver's Centennial celebration of Canadian Confederation, Chief Dan George stood up and said to the crowd, 'I
have nothing to celebrate.' He then unleashed a powerful stream of ora-
tory and poetry, of *story* that mobilized the Native individuals who had
been living there together as displaced migrants to the city. He reminded
these members of perhaps fifty distinct nations *who they were to one another*:
they were tellers of stories. Story through image making then became
part of their political work, as they formed media collectives, arts alliances, and took advantage of the technology that non-Native media
missionaries[1] would bring to the reserves. From 1991 to 1992 Todd co-
founded the Aboriginal Film and Video Arts Alliance with others who
wanted to preserve that power of the storyteller.

   The cultural and geographic displacements, and the internalized anger
Todd and her intertribal family faced together, are still shared by Native
peoples throughout the hemisphere who are forced to abandon their
communities for the possibility of work in the chaotic, urban world. In
Niro's narrative *It Starts with a Whisper*, we see how the city and its media
bombardment of Indian stereotypes and bleak statistics isolate Shanna
from her family and from her own freedom/responsibility to live her life
as a young Tutelo woman. Dressed in a gloomy business suit (the city
scene is shot in black and white and has a flat quality to it), she steps into
the magically colourful car (complete with pom-pom trim along the
windshield) where her ebullient, very 3-D aunties wait for her to join
them on a journey to the New Year's Eve weekend they'd won to Niagara
Falls. Shanna takes herself very seriously as she tries to stay absorbed in a
Native news magazine instead of interacting with Aunt Pauline, Aunt Hil-

lary, and Aunt Emily, whose vintage clothing can barely contain their energy. She is jerked back to life, unwillingly at first, by her clown aunties' example ('all [they] do is just talk, laugh and eat!'). And, as a descendant of survivors of a nineteenth century epidemic, she is counselled by an elder to keep the ancestors alive in her memory and her actions.

Once in Niagara Falls, she runs from the onslaught of carnival sounds and (black and white) neon signs that blink 'MUSEUM' and flash directional arrows this way and that to tourist sights and motels. A voice says 'reservations,' and she reaches the edge of the Falls where she stands with her back to the rushing waters, holding her head as if it were about to explode with the names of Native nations crowding her thoughts. 'Tutelo,' her mind finally says, and she turns to the water as if (re)turning to a source of life. 'I don't know what to do,' she says to the voice trying to comfort her. 'I feel that my heart and my head could blow up.' 'Whatever you do, don't blow up,' Elijah (portrayed by Elijah Harper) jokes. 'We must fight these negative stereotypes ... and not let them upset us so that we doubt our own self-worth,' he says, guiding her out of her gloom. But he is not a formulaic guardian angel who speaks from a cloud. He is not merely a red version of Capra's Clarence, sent to earth on a temporary mission (although the year-end snowfall and the desperation-by-the-water's-edge are reminiscent of *It's a Wonderful Life*). He is on a permanent mission as a living member of her community whom she recognizes and trusts, and who stands with her, facing her as he listens to her story. He appears in order to remind her to feel the earth with her feet. 'Stop feeling guilty about your existence,' he says. 'You are here to live your life.'

For mixed bloods such as Todd and Welsh, internalized anger can be a double-barrelled hatred for the Indian and non-Indian selves. Welsh, in her autobiographical *Women in the Shadows*, works through and brings to light her family's historiography after over thirty years of silence that had kept her great-grandmother's story in the shadows of her Métis life. By uncovering Margaret Taylor's story through the archives of the Hudson's Bay Company (the daughter of a 'Bay man,' Taylor was the first-generation Métis wife of a director), she gives voice to a series of stories: her grandmother's, her grandfather's, and her own. She is able to understand, grieve for, and perhaps forgive the silencing of the stories and, especially, of the language. After a visit to York Factory – once a major trading post for the Bay company – she goes to the cemetery where her relatives are buried. Unnerved and saddened by her inability to speak to those relatives, she says: '*Nokum*, my grandmother; *Nosisi*, my granddaughter ... words I will never hear, never speak. Until I came here, I did not truly understand what it means to lose the language of your ancestors ... I can't recognize the voices of my grandparents because their children needed to forget. Amnesia and silence and a haunting sense of loss; these are my inheritance.'

'I'm not looking for anybody to blame anymore,' she says. 'I've grieved for a culture I never had and never *will* have.' She becomes comfortable enough in her own identity and her place within her family that she can cut the long hair she had worn for fifteen years. Newly resistant to self-imposed pressures to (dis)play herself as an Indian, she is able to say, 'All of a sudden I don't need that anymore ... I've come home.'

Her family's dependence on silence (as a survival mechanism) and story/voice (as a means to grieve and live fully) is similar to what Todd examines in *No More Secrets,* an experimental piece that combines documentary with narrative to expose the urgency of the solvent abuse crisis among Aboriginal youth. In *Healing Our Spirit,* she allows the stories of HIV-positive Native people in a Native counselling program to explain the healing value of emerging from the silence into the familiar circle of relations and tradition offered by such programs.

The films of these three women suggest that, unlike the 'primal scream,' our catharsis of expression should be a continuous activity, a way of life that should flow naturally with/from our legacy as storytellers. Once we exorcise the colonizer with our stories (almost as Catholic priests would use Latin 'story' to drive *their* demon out of their people), we are urged to continue the flow of words because, as Todd says, 'they carry the culture.'

Women in the Shadows is a spiritual journey that, for Welsh, began as an archival one. The film/story begins with her and her mother looking at an album of photos of Welsh as a young city girl, 'haunted by shadows and secrets and questions left unanswered.' It is almost painful to watch as her mother stops at one particular photo and says, 'Lord, Lord, Lord. You had *some* happy days, didn't you?' They then talk about a photo of Welsh as a young woman with long braids who wouldn't go anywhere without a beaded something-or-other around her head. The film/story ends with the now short-haired Welsh visiting her ancestors' gravesite with her son; before the final credits, we watch her as she carefully recites the names on the tombstones and tells the stories behind them. It is an act of responsibility, resistance, and love.

The same responsibility, resistance, and love fuels the incessant 'talking, laughing and eating' of Shanna's aunties in Niro's *It Starts with a*

Whisper. In a deceptively comic scene somewhere in Niagara Falls, it is their love for their niece that choreographs the aunties' singing and synchronized swimming gestures on a heart-shaped bed. Shanna joins them when, after sitting at a vanity's mirror in a dull denim jacket, she emerges from behind a screen in a bright orange party dress. She is dolled up in full colour, like her aunties, and the four women lip-synch and dance to a cathartic song-story that begins with,

> I'm pretty
> I'm pretty
> I'm pretty mad at you.
> Don't come in here, Don't call me 'dear,'
> I'm pretty mad at you ...

After some appropriately timed shimmies and shakes, the song ends with,

> You made me speak gibberish
> Instead of my language,
> But you can't control my mind ...
> I'm survivin',
> I'm thrivin',
> I'm doin' fine without you ...
> Won't waste no more time ...
> Doin' fine without you ...

Story – as witness to history, pain, struggle, and (with the help of humour) *survival* – becomes a testimony to the possible.

The Artist

As Aboriginal artists, we need to reclaim our own identities through our work, our heritage and our future.
Doreen Jensen, Gitksan artist and educator in *Hands of History*

The racism Todd and her family experienced in Canada strengthened her resolve to always speak her mind and, as one of the few Aboriginal students in a formalist film school in Vancouver, to develop a solid commitment to her vision. She was intent on making films that were relevant to her life/the life of Aboriginal peoples, work that she could 'bring home' rather than mere art-for-art's-sake portraits of alienation. 'I took up a lot of space and made sure that I wasn't just a vapor,' she said. 'I was going in there with many others "with me" ... and I had their support and love in taking the stories into the arena where they needed to be.'

As a documentary filmmaker, she draws stories out of the people in her films with painstaking deference and observance of protocol. In *Hands of History*, an homage to four contemporary Native artists and their work, her own narrative voice remains a purely visual one. Each of the four women profiled in the film is a protagonist who speaks for herself about her art and its place in the continuum of her own people's history. And in *The Learning Path*, the camera keeps a respectful distance as it follows Eva Cardinal – now supervisor of the Sacred Circle Program in Edmonton's public school system – into the harsh memories evoked by the residential school hallway. But there are other protocol details that are followed by the filmmaker.

Some might fear that filmmakers, or artists in general, limit their creative expression when they allow protocol to guide their work; protocol, as a referent to history, is seen as a cumbersome obstacle to art-making. But *as* a referent to history, and as a sign of respect for a code or form, protocol works as a cultural grid that allows the work of these filmmakers to be relevant to their peoples' lives. The colonizers' emphasis on expansion and outward momentum serves a certain kind of artistic expression. But, as Todd said after seeing a friend's painting, an artist can work with 'proud, but not arrogant innovations ... boldness without vanity, expansion without destruction [and undertake] risk with responsibility.'[2] She adds, 'Our work isn't different because it's Native; it comes out of a long history.' In *Hands of History*, Rena Point Bolton (Stolo), a master weaver of baskets and robes and an activist who helped revive the outlawed Potlatch culture in her community, says, 'I don't think of myself as an artist. I just think of myself as being obedient to the teaching of my elders, and I am passing on my teachings to the next generation.'

These three filmmakers, as Aboriginal artists, are part of a continuum of people who protect the land: their obligation to protect the land is their legacy because the land carries the culture. But within the parameters of common obligation, they each – like other Native artists – produce unique articulations: Niro balances humour and seduction-as-weapon against the necessary pain of memory, as in *Honey Moccasin*, when Mable sings 'Fever' against the backdrop of Native holocausts projected onto the surface of a tepee; Welsh is inquisitive and has a strong narrator's presence as she places herself in both of her documentaries to ask questions and untangle contradictions; and Todd carefully paints documentaries that allow multiple stories to resonate through multiple voices.

Our purpose as Indigenous peoples is guided by our historical relationship with our territories and lands that, as artists, we carry in our languages of colour, light, rhythm, and word. Todd thinks that most Aboriginal artists work with varying degrees of awareness of the covenant that is part of living on the 'red road, [where] we say, "I didn't create myself; I *was* created and need guidance" [as opposed to] "I created myself and need nothing."' She and others have been taught that, as Aboriginal artists, they hold an essential place on the series of interdependent circles that define community/nation. Aboriginal art – whether textile, song, film or basket – is 'cultural record' for our *living communities*, rather than for museums, and provides the instructions we need for life. Our role as contemporary carriers of oral traditions that are rooted in the covenant is to examine and acknowledge our relationships with others, between people and the universe, between the physical and the spiritual; we are story keepers who help acknowledge our peoples' collective responsibilities to fight, laugh, and tell stories *in order to live.* And we become warriors *by living.*

'What turns ordinary women into warriors?' Welsh asks in the first few minutes of *Keepers of the Fire.* Her camera seems to search for the answer as it scrutinizes nineteenth-century sepia portraits and twentieth-century photos of Native women on a picket line. 'Now the fire is ours to keep,' she says, wondering what kind of warriors we can be. As keepers of stories that can resonate for the community, these filmmakers take their place among the generations of warriors who have held the front lines of battle for their ancestral territories and for the right to live with dignity. As tellers of stories they wield semiotically loaded, cinematic 'madeleines' that have the power to bring layers of cultural memory to life. 'If you think about buffalo hides with the stories painted on them,' Todd said, 'or the people who could read the wampum, or the button blanket ... one button would stand for many things ... the storyteller had to bring alive that one button, that one color, that one shape ... they had to bring the *whole history* of that alive ... the filmmaker has the image, the sound ... to help *others* bring that alive in *them* ... Space and light becomes smell, touch, tears, laughter. In the same way the storyteller, when he sends words out into space, they don't just go into the ears; they also go into the *spiritual plane,* into the *basket.*'

The Land

I was thinking before, I didn't really have a story to tell my children ... I could only tell them bingo stories. But you know, I have this beautiful story to tell.
Pat Gellerman in *Keepers of the Fire*, speaking of a Haida victory against the logging industry.

'Artist,' for most Aboriginal peoples, becomes an instruction that still offers room for uniqueness. In *Keepers of the Fire*, Welsh features the warriors who have fought in their unique ways for the commonly held right to live, and for the land to continue as an inheritance that carries the culture. She travels to Haida Gwaii (Queen Charlotte Islands) to hear the stories of the Haida elders who, by blockading a logging road on Lyell Island in 1985, put an end to ninety years of logging on Gwaii Haanas ('Place of Wonders'). She also visits with the women of Anduhyaun (a Native women's shelter in Toronto), who tell stories that reveal the courage of their collective healing in the aftermath of domestic violence and homelessness. And the Maliseet women of the Tobique reserve in New Brunswick tell of their campaign in the late seventies to remove gender discrimination from the Indian Act.

Keepers of the Fire begins with footage and stories from Mohawk women of Kanehsatake and Kahnawake; they tell us that Mohawk matriarchal tradition entrusts the land to the women, and that the women have a sacred responsibility to protect the land. Welsh wonders about the forces that made certain Mohawk women link arms at Oka and face the bullets that whizzed by and the direct hits of tear gas. It seems that it could have been the instruction carried in the true name for the Mohawk nation, 'Kahniakehaka,' which means 'People of the Flint.'[3] Tribal affiliation is a responsibility; words have power. A Mohawk child is given a name that means 'The Rapids Are Dazzling Her Eyes,' and is expected one day to continue her grandmother's struggle to protect the rapids of the St Lawrence River against Hydro-Québec. 'That's who you are; that's what your name is,' her grandmother tells her. Words have power.

During our interview, Todd noted that land (in the form of landscape) permeates Canadian art. It is expressed as a limitless expanse that, she believes, is regarded with a sense of fear or even terror. 'Canadians, it is said, carry terror in their souls,' she noted. The Cartesian dichotomies that place land outside the non-Aboriginal human experience have an effect on the treatment of the land, which – through national as well as provincial policy – directly impacts Aboriginal peoples' lives. Stewardship is replaced by a form of management based on *dominion*; as such, it defers to rapacious expansion and the global market. This, together with the 'terror,' might underlie a number of contemporary events and situations: the Canadian government's 1990 siege at Oka; the 1995 armored military attacks on Mi'kmaq territory in New Brunswick and on Shushwap territory in British Columbia; the dumping of Reynold's Aluminum by-products near Mohawk waters; the recent prospector invasion of unceded, mineral-rich Innu hunting territories near Sept-Îles, Quebec.

The collective responsibilities inherent in Indigenous rights stem from our covenant with the Creator to protect the land. Non-Indigenous art, made outside such a covenant, can offer a way to outrun or escape what is of-the-earth. But for our cultures, 'the transcendental is to remind us of the sacred in the terrestrial.'[4] Story becomes a sacred trust that emerges from and returns to the land, which embodies the culture.

Frozen water was recently found on the moon; you can almost hear the bugle announce a new 'frontier.' Until the de facto colonization of celestial bodies is possible, there exists a 'Star Registry' for those who want to name stars after themselves or after loved ones. The Star Registry Vault locks the deed-like documents safely away. But, in *It Starts with a Whisper*, Shanna and her aunties celebrate New Year's at the edge of Niagara Falls. Aunt Pauline recites poetry about the river rapids ('... Dash, dash with a might crash / They seethe and boil and bound and splash ...') and they all prepare to eat a green-and-blue-frosted, earth-shaped cake. (You are what you eat?) They are Aboriginal women who – by using humour to take care of one another – protect and reaffirm life. They sing in their Native language, as Shanna plays her grandfather's water drum (a representation of the earth), and embrace as the fireworks explode over the Falls and take the shape of a turtle, sparkling with light. The turtle floats there in the dark sky, but it is a symbol of Aboriginal *land*. Land-bound and land-nourished, the women fade from view as the credits roll and a voice-over sings,

As long as the sun still rises,
As long as the rivers flow,
For as long as this land will last forever
I can see the circle grow.
Oh, I'm goin' down to the bottom of my darkest night,
I'm goin' home, where the smilin' faces make it right.
Then take my hand, and the circle again is whole,

For as long as this land will last forever
I can see the circle grow.
For as long as this land will last forever
I can see the circle grow ...

In *The Learning Path*, Todd acknowledges the healing process that continues to take place among individuals (and, as a result, entire communities) who were subject to the residential school system that forcibly
removed them from their peoples and their land. 'There was a time when
our people had their own education systems and their own knowledge,'
she says. 'Today, we are taking back our education, and our women are
again our guides along the learning path ... It's a new morning; education
is serving to empower and not oppress our children.' The women in the
film teach Aboriginal languages and all that the languages carry about
culture and the land. Among their students are future educators, future
healers, and future artists. Words have power.

NOTES

1 Unless otherwise noted, Loretta Todd's words are from an interview conducted
   on 6 June 1996 for New York University's Center for Media, Culture and History. My thanks to Faye Ginsberg and Barbara Abrash for allowing me continued use of the center's facilities, and to Loretta Todd for her stamina.
2 Loretta Todd, in 'Yuxweluptun: A Philosophy of History,' *Exhibition Catalogue*
   (Vancouver: UBC Press 1996), 45.
3 I am grateful to Kanaratitake (Lorraine Canoe) for this translation.
4 Todd, 'Yuxweluptun,' 48.

To Document – to Imagine – to Simulate

RON BURNETT

Can the documentary cinema and documentary images be thought about differently?

(Difference in the psychoanalytic sense and differences at the levels of gender, ethnicity, and the body – and so, differences in images and in what they depict, the very question of how to document the world in a different way – the structure of difference as an entry point for political claims and arguments, for ways of thinking about resistance and change, and most importantly the role of Canadian women in the production of new approaches to the documentary cinema and video.)

(To some degree, documentary films, documentary images, have lost their strength, their claim to a unique strategy of presenting issues of concern to our society. Is this the result of the massive proliferation of images that claim to represent the world in the mass media? Or could it be part of the process of simulation, which progressively layers more and more planes of the real into a 'living archeology,' segmented and sedimented sites of meaning and representation and history? Simulation is a very misunderstood term. It does not refer to a parallel reality or even a duplicate or counterfeit reality. Rather, simulation as a concept helps us understand the various ways in which reality is never a singular term and rarely describes a single moment in history. For the purposes of this essay, simulation can be thought of as a way of thinking about history in holographic terms – time and space in three dimensions, to be seen and experienced from many different vantage points, none of which provides the security of a completely knowable or predictable experience. For example, the film Mourir à tue-tête *[1979], by Anne Claire Poirier, explores simulation and raises questions about how the cinematic image can be used to identify and investigate subjectivity and gender differences. Poirier simulates a brutal rape in order to unveil the dehumanized reality of sexual violence.)*

(Simulation is one of the foundations of the real. Dreams, illusions, fantasies,

and our imaginations make it possible for us to translate our knowledge of the world into action and language. 'Without imagination, nothing in the world could be meaningful. Without imagination, we could never make sense of our experience, we could never reason toward knowledge of reality.'[1] Poirier's brilliant exegesis uses the simulated rape to unveil the brutal imaginary of the rapist. Mourir à tue-tête suggests that a rethinking of the genre of the docudrama would be in order. It also examines the role of the camera as a character.)

(Images are suggestive indicators, signs of simulation and imagination at work. Documentary images are, to varying degrees, heightened examples of simulation because they simultaneously make a claim on the real without the need to reproduce that claim in a concrete way beyond the image itself. The documentary image does not supply a simple referent from which an even simpler conclusion can be drawn about reality. On the contrary, documentary images in all media spend a good deal of time legitimizing both the simulations they have constructed and the fact that they have the right to do so.[2] And what makes documentary images so captivating is the way they move from simulation to reality, somewhat like pieces of paper being folded over into each other, while at the same time retaining the distinctive properties of illusion and fantasy mixed in with the real. The materiality of images and the popular notion that simulation is the sign of an immaterial world detract from the richness of their interdependence. We are brought in contact with the world even as space and time are altered, and it is our ability to handle this dynamic that legitimizes and sustains the experience, even though we may be puzzled by its contradictions.)

What would our society 'look' like without documentary images in all their forms and genres, without documentary images in all the locations in which we find them? To what degree have the image as document and the document as image become naturalized characteristics of everyday life? Does this question of naturalization pose a new challenge to feminist documentarians and their reflections on the reality of women's experience in Canada? (See such films as *To a Safer Place* [1987] by Beverly Shaffer and *Working Nights* [1987] by Sarah Butterfield, both of which were made at the National Film Board's Studio D.) Where are the markers that would distinguish among levels of simulation, documentation, and reproduction? Butterfield's short film examines the reality of women's work through still images and voice-over commentary. At one and the same time the stills are an evocation of the reality of women's experience and ask questions about the possibility of picturing the subjective depth of the oppression they are going through. Yet the use of the still images is also a challenge to the spectator. How can understanding be created through this use of the medium? This type of self-reflexivity is a character-istic of many feminist documentaries. The impulse is as much to explore the medium and its limitations as it is to make a point, show an event, and explore a reality.

In a world where the media inform and shape perception, the boundaries between image and reproduction, being and semblance, unique type and stereo-type are no longer distinct. Each suggests the existence of the other to such a degree that the boundaries between them disappear. It is not surprising, then, that everywhere you look in the art world there are staged fields of tension or vio-lations of 'the order of things.' Vera Frenkel turns in particular to syntheses of broken relationships in life, syntheses that allude to the contradiction between the outer and inner worlds of the viewer via material taken from reality, shown both as it is and simultaneously transposed into art.
Lydia Haustien, 'The Transformative Power of Memory'[3]

All of our oral, visual, and phenomenological experiences are open to being documented, to being transformed into images, texts and sounds. The work of Vera Frenkel moves between video, document, installation, and performance, and the very question of the real is both questioned and examined through simulation, imagination, memory, and the traces left by history on our psyches and identities. 'What interests me isn't the either/or of whether I arrive at the truth by fictional means, or at fiction through documentary, but that in the juxtaposition of the two a kind of to-and-fro traffic can keep happening where each is the interlocutor of the other, and the location of the 'real' keeps shifting.'[4]

(Judith Doyle's superb documentary Lac La Croix *[1988], on First Nations people who live in Ontario, works upon central issues of concern to First Nations people while also dealing in a self-reflexive manner with the media and with images in general. Doyle uses the documentary to comment on itself, combining the trans-formative with the philosophical. In this instance the 'real' keeps shifting ground, speaking to the past through the present, but also making the 'image' of history work in a dramatically different way. This bricolage produces a film that, like* Mourir à tue-tête *by Anne Claire Poirier, raises ideas and concerns about images as mediators of reality. It is noteworthy that Poirier's work challenges not only the conventional 'discussion' that documentaries have about the issues they are explor-ing, but also the capacity of the image to reveal and explain the truth. As a result, she creates many interlocutors who question not only memory, but the way language – cinematic, spoken, written – transforms history and our personal interpretation of it.)*

Perhaps the very notion of transformation is wrong here. If the process of simulation is itself the foundation of image creation, production, and viewing, then aren't we witnesses to stories of every kind all the time, and should they be categorized or limited according to the boundaries of genre? Anne Claire Poirier's *They Called Us 'Les Filles du Roi'* (1974) can be described as a mixed-media production. It plays with different levels of storytelling, many contrasting ways of bringing experiences into image form. What is being transformed? At which point can reality be mapped into images and at which point is reality itself an image? Are we then simply witnesses to an already constructed scene, one that has always been defined by many of the same properties that seem to be exclusive to images? [5] History always works retrospectively just as images do. Both history and the image prop each other up in an effort to find a measure of the truth even as the real recedes into the background. This is the site of an intense struggle that makes images into contingent expositions, contingent on the context in which they are shown and the discursive environment that they are placed into.

Nicole Giguère's *Histoire Infame* 'addresses the subjectivity of historical writing and reading. The tape is a rock video, replacing the traditionally sexist content with a sweeping historical overview of the interpretation of women within history and their rereading by feminism.'[6] Giguère substitutes one image for the other in an effort to find another kind of storytelling, another level of tension, even another level of contradiction. In *They Called Us 'Les Filles du Roi,'* Poirier creates a presentational/performative mode of interpreting past events through an *allegory* that uses historical and mythical characters. The allegory will not work unless we are already attuned to the allegorical as a mode of storytelling and to its possible uses for historical thought. Doyle, on the other hand, interviews the people of Lac La Croix and uses their everyday discourse as a pivot for the move into the allegorical. In this respect, the film merely accentuates the profound linkages and needs that viewers have always established among images, words, and listening. Aren't both *Lac La Croix* and *They Called Us 'Les Filles du Roi'* sites in which these problems are being worked out? As viewers we cannot at one and the same time be separate from what we watch, autonomous, and then be able to understand our experience of viewing. The attraction of simulation is precisely the ease with which distinctions *that are already dissolved* can be experienced. We are never outside of the dome of images.[7] And yet that dome is precisely what makes reality possible in the first place. Both Doyle and Poirier look for vantage points from which the real can be viewed while at the same time suggesting that the experience of images confuses location, positionality, and identity.

(These questions are an attempt to probe the very notion as well as definition of the document as image and the image as document. To what degree does the category work anymore? And if we are in a crisis of meaning as to the category's applicability and usefulness, then do we need to come up with a hybrid explanation? If the boundaries between documentary and fiction have dissolved for example, then what is the usefulness of either term, practically, theoretically, historically? Does the dissolution of boundaries suggest that images are never as literal as we presume nor as much of an illusion as we might desire?)

Man (1991) by Ann Marie Fleming and Mike Hoolboom plays with media stereotypes of gender, mixing the masculine with the feminine at the level of image to the point where the distinctions become meaningless. The brilliance of this short film is that genre is irrelevant. The filmmakers use whatever images they need to make a point. The interesting thing is that the film itself is often described as experimental, as if the genre busting somehow places the film outside of any conventional boundaries. Crucially, Fleming herself frames the main theme of the film, transvestitism, by appearing in drag as if she is a male imitating a woman. In all instances, the film never allows conventional images to mean what they usually mean. This play of signs, this play *with* signs, challenges categories of sexuality as much as it challenges the ways in which certain genres constrain images from breaking with their historical and cultural roles.

Quite aside from the factual information in ... [my] work which can be absurd enough in itself, I like reality shifts, verbal and visual puns, puzzling contradictions, coincidences, and then the devices that suggest that the play of truth and fiction is itself an invention.
Vera Frenkel, Interview with Dot Tuer[8]

The look and feel of everyday life in Western societies is governed by images and sounds. These range from billboards to shop windows, to the advertising on buses, to popular culture, mass media, and computer mediated forms of communication, to the many layers of a department store, where commodities vie for our attention in a phantasmagoria of shapes, colours, sounds, and textures. In another context, Kathleen Stewart used the phrase, 'a lived cultural poetics' as a way of describing her ethnographic research into the Appalachian coal-mining region of southwestern West Virginia.[9] I would like to appropriate the richness of this concept, the idea of a cultural poetics as lived experience in the shadows of the endless proliferation of images in all of their forms.

I cannot conceive of passing a day without at least some exposure to documentary images about the world or about my community. As a result and because images of all sorts are ubiquitous, I create as well as witness the poetics of the real through my own and other people's narratives. (Sifted Evidence *[1982], by Patricia Gruben, plays with the ambiguities of self, identity, and image and is evidence of this poetics at work. The real is unveiled as arbitrary, even as the narrative reveals itself to be the reverse. The brilliance of the film is the way it questions the real as if it were creating an anthropological sound bite on post-modern identity while at the same time declaring itself to be a failure as ethnography.)* These are the stories that both form and inform the documents that I use, watch, and create. The meaning of a lived cultural poetics is best understood as a space of desire[10] and creativity. It is the photograph in your album, that very special photograph of your child, parent, or lover. It is the images that you have used to document your life or the life of your family. All of this constitutes a site of simulation and documentation in which stories, reflections upon stories, memories of narratives, and experiences combine and fragment in an unpredictable manner. These are for the most part embodied experiences, strategies of internalizing and thinking about the world in which we live. In *Sifted Evidence* the main character is caught in a familiar bind. She has travelled to a different culture and finds it difficult to navigate through the experiences that she is having. Her solution is to imagine the place that she is in so that she can fill in the absences, precisely the position of most viewers in the cinema.

(In this way the documentary process moves from the mundane to the unique, and images are the pivot for desires that cannot be understood without reference to the personal space of the creator and the viewer, to the complex interplay of memory and knowledge. Difference in this context dissolves the boundaries of all genres and makes the place of creation and viewing the site of significance and understanding. There has never been a time in history or a culture without images, sounds, and stories. Why then do we persist with a Cartesian division between ourselves and images? Why even think of images as objects?[11] As somehow divorced from what we do to them, even if that 'doing' is a fantasy?)

The smell of burning joss sticks brings back a very specific memory for me: visiting my grandmother's house on my first trip to Hong Kong at the age of five. The smell of joss sticks has found its own particular location through the ordering and categorizing of memory that takes place somewhere within the human body. It fills the nose, seeps past the lips, enters through the pores, infuses the hair. And memory wells up from somewhere inside.
Larrisa Lai, 'The Site of Memory'[12]

Can we expand what we mean by document, by documentary, to include not only the images that we form into the shape of a film, video, photograph, or painting but the stories that accompany the media that surround us? Would this expansion dilute the extraordinary impact of recent documentaries on the crises in Bosnia? Or the way in which Michelle Mohabeer's film *Coconut/Cane & Cutlass* (1997) explores the history of Indo-Caribbean people who emigrated to Canada and are trying to find a voice as a diasporic community? Stories bring the personal into view as one of the foundations for exploring the relations among memory, image, and medium. For Larrissa Lai the memory of what happened to Chinese-Canadian labourers at the beginning of the twentieth century, *their* story, becomes the intellectual and critical framework for her exploration of two of Paul Wong's videotapes. At the same time, she clearly reveals her own heritage because that is the site within which she has developed her critical and historical method.

In *Les Filles du Roi*, Poirier produced a re-membering that simultaneously documented the history of a community and the story of her own discovery of that community. She combined a precision of narration with the ability to speak in many tongues, to engage with the reality of stories without worrying about truth or about the medium best able to recount the stories she found and invented. It is her ability to immerse herself in the experience that then brings out the richness of the stories that she hears. Poirier's ethnography turns into a voyage of discovery at all levels, from the personal to the testimonial to the descriptive. Mohabeer uses autobiography in much the same way as Gruben, as a vehicle to experiment with images, and, like Poirier and Gruben, uses testimony to explore the very meaning of discourse, language, and narrativity. All of these works question what we mean by document; they challenge us to rethink meaning with reference to history, both personal and public, and collapse the personal and the public. Perhaps this is why documentary images are now among the few remaining places for independent experimentation using film and video.

(Invention is the foundation of the document, of the documentary, of all images. Truth is more often than not an unintended consequence of the process, processing.)

For a long time, documentary images have been approached as if they have a greater task than depiction or storytelling, as if they must have a privileged voice oriented toward uncovering and displaying what the everyday hides or what conventional representations cover up. This quest for truth is really a quest for the *ideal* image, one that will transcend its creators, even its viewers, in an effort to picture a world that cannot exist unless all of the reference points have been removed. This may explain why the horror of massacres in Rwanda can exist as an image at all. It may explain why the repeated use of documentary images of death in films and in the news removes the pain of death from any concrete source. Ironically, the effort to replicate death is perhaps the greatest artifice of the documentary, the place in which simulation seems to disappear even as it explodes into existence with the power to alter our preconceptions of the world we live in.

(And yet the feelings remain. The power of the documentary still lies with its ability to 'play' with relationships of seeing and feeling, to make it seem as if the simulation can be both illusory and real. Even that most experimental of films, The Man with a Movie Camera *[1929], was critiqued for not revealing more about the reality of its time, because what it revealed was the play of image and reality, a phantasmagoria of representations and simulations of reality. Dziga-Vertov responded: 'Some said* The Man with a Movie Camera *was an experiment in visual music, a visual concert. Others saw the film in terms of a higher mathematics of montage. Still others declared that it was not "life as it is," but life the way they do not see it, etc. In fact, the film is only the facts recorded on film, or, if you like, not merely the sum, but the product of a "higher mathematics" of facts.'[13])*

Dziga-Vertov's assertion about the recording process, about facts and about the link between image and fact, about the science of images, has managed to outlive every effort at experimentation, every self-reflexive strategy aimed at delegitimizing the image. This is not necessarily a negative comment. The strength of documentary images may well be their mythic hold on an imaginary space of the real. Images that claim a documentary status are consequently about a struggle for legitimacy, for the right to use a set of conventions to create a cultural poetics of the real within a context of fantasy, projection, and desire. What must be stressed here is that fantasy provides us with a shared space of viewer and creator, so that Patricia Gruben, for example, becomes the viewer of her own history and simultaneously the inventor of her past.[14] Anne Claire Poirier uses *Mourir à tue-tête* to create a character who disintegrates in front of our eyes and then views her own trauma at an editing table as if she is both the subject and the object of the images, the storyteller, a character, and a witness to what has happened to her.

(We often forget that the legitimacy of a documentary image is based on an agreement between the spectator and the creator. This agreement evolves out of the rela-

tionships established not through one act of viewing, but through the life-long interaction of lived experiences and images. The danger is that the documentary imagemaker will overinvest in the play of analogies that are at the heart of image–viewer relations without taking the history of those relations into account.)

Analogy is about substitution. It is also about comparison. It is about metaphors designed to bring the comparative into a direct relationship with the many ways in which we interpret our experiences of reality. Over time, any number of different analogies can take on a life of their own. A great deal can be inferred from an image, but it is the *process* of inference that is the locus of creativity for the spectator. When the document is assumed to be factual the inferential disappears, ambiguity is eliminated, allusiveness is downplayed, and metaphors are transformed into reflections of and upon the real.

(This is not to suggest that documentaries about wife-battering (Gail Singer's Loved, Honoured and Bruised *[1980]) or about abortion struggles around the world (Singer's* Abortion Stories From North and South *[1984]) or about rapes of women in Bosnia (Brenda Longfellow's* A Balkan Journey: Fragments from the Other Side of the War *[1996]) fail to comment on their subjects or reveal any truths because of their devotion to the factual. Rather, images as facts are not a given; they are the site of a negotiation that can result in any number of different substitutions taking place. Gail Singer understands this, and it forms the basis of the structure of her* Loved, Honoured and Bruised. *Is the resistance of the women in the film to the documentary process legitimate? Have the image-makers failed to communicate their point of view to them outside of the context of the filming? Has the historical process disappeared through the making of the film?)*

At the heart of documentary images is a strong attraction to and an equal fear of mediation, a mix of self-consciousness (which has a distancing effect) and the desire for immediacy and closeness. Images are seen as transparent films *between* experience and thought, between events and our ability to understand and critique them.

Yet, it matters little whether mediation is opaque or transparent. In fact, it is the opposition of opaqueness and transparency (sometimes translated into mirror/window in discussions of documentary films) that keeps mediation at a distance, albeit that any image once seen and/or heard is no longer *at* a distance from the experience we have of it. The most obvious examples of this are music videos, which combine the many different elements of sound and picture into images. Not only do the videos represent the music, they picture bodies that dance – they display not only the physicality of musical creation, but the potential of audience performance. They create a space for the performance of meaning, which exceeds and often undermines the mediating layers of image projection. The recent David Bowie videos made by the Canadian video artist Floria Sigismondi are a wonderful example. The videos are like artefacts. They are snapshots of a moment in time, even as they reflect upon Bowie's music and on the cultural moment that defines him.

Arguments that join mediation, images, and experience into some kind of unity generally overlook both the inventiveness of projection and the creative influence of the imaginary. This has perhaps been one of the major faults in thinking about documentary images. For example, the notion of observational cinema, which was developed into a significant genre of the documentary in the 1950s through the work of Pennebaker, the Maysles brothers, and crews at the National Film Board, never broke with the 'idea' that, at a minimum, some aspects of screen projection *preserve* the reality being filmed. Preservation is not atemporal. Many of the films of that period retain trace elements of what made them possible. They cannot preserve history, because vantage point, subjectivity, and location will ultimately define the treatment of the images by viewers. The images, however, can trace out a relationship with the past through the very tensions that have made them possible in the first place. These are the tensions between the opaque and the transparent that no individual film ever solves, but which makes it possible to *imagine* the reality of an event *as if* we are there.

One of the most important characteristics of feminist documentary cinema, especially those films devoted to consciousness-raising or political activism, is the use of personal testimony. Voice-overs, on-screen interviews, and frontal shots try to reproduce the intimacy of a personal encounter. In 1970s documentary film and video the voice-over was the clearest expression of these efforts at work. The image becomes an exemplification of the voice that is explaining the premises of the film, and voice then brings together intention, explanation, and centrally the meaning of the images. These same traditions have carried over into eighties and nineties feminist films, although with more and more self-reflexivity built into them and less of a concern to prove that meaning and intention validate the political truthfulness of what is said. Brenda Longfellow's *Our Marilyn* (1987) is as much a meditation on the extraordinary swim by Marilyn Bell across Lake Ontario as it is an exploration of how to recover history when there are very few archival images to give a historical moment its feel and look. It is precisely because the film has to struggle with 'enactment' that the performative and theatrical reconstruction of history is effective. But for more traditional documentaries, voice brings a ring of authenticity to the film, a sense that much is being uncovered, and a reliance on the process to reveal the truth. However, what vantage point do we as viewers have on the truth of the testimony? Why would we assume that the characters in the film are not playing with their roles? What convinces us that they are not lying? To what degree is the personal testimony in front of a camera acted?

The mythopoetic place of the documentary makes it seem as if these individuals have actually found the words to speak about themselves and their situation. Is their articulateness the result of how their voices have been edited? This is precisely what Anne Claire Poirier's *Mourir à tue-tête* (1979) struggles with. As the character who plays a filmmaker discovers, truth is never simply within discourse because the character who speaks in the film has to varying degrees lost control of her identity. Testimony on the screen can flatten the contradictions and work against the best of intentions. Perhaps the less harmonious all of these relations are, the less perfect the representation, the more flawed the voice. Perhaps all of that works against the seeming directness of testimony and truth. Yet, it is often this unpredictability that worries documentary filmmakers who strive for presence, who try to convert images into a vehicle for confession and truth, for conviction and persuasion. Effectively, their images end up preventing the emergence of new and contradictory ideas. In other words, they work against the wonder of allegory, the excitement of narratives with unpredictable conclusions, the exploration of meaning without a clear intention or goal in mind.

To say that the camera 'replicates' that which is photographed is an expedient oversimplification based on a simple metaphor corresponding to the technology of the camera in the modern age. To be sure, up to now cameras could not change the image to the point it was unrelated to the object being photographed. And that's why we have the word 'special effect' which suggests there is something upon which a special effect is brought to bear; that there is an object which exists in front of the camera which is the entity being photographed. That is, there is a concrete, tangible physical object which special effects photography then effects. Now, however, special effects do not occur external to the camera but within the image itself; we are now beginning to get images for which no photographed reality exists. This is why it is impossible to discuss truth or falsehood using the object as a standard.
Kogawa Tetsuo, 'Toward a Reality of "Reference"'[15]

Tetsuo's analysis mirrors that of William J. Mitchell,[16] where the very idea of documentation ceases to be possible. But, what Tetsuo and Mitchell are both talking about and what has been taken up by many documentarists is not so much the removal of the real or its disappearance. Rather, the recognition of simulation and the imagination – their interdependence – has redefined what we mean by reality and has resulted in a flurry of inventions that have resituated the technology of image creation. Digital images extend our capacity to create more and more complex visual representations. They extend the scope and breadth of the simulations to which we have become accustomed, the simulations that have always been a crucial feature of everyday reality in Western societies. In this respect and rather ironically, we now demand even more realism on the part of images even as the technology makes it possible for those images to be produced in contexts of greater artifice than ever before. (This is the extraordinary site of the work of Vera Frenkel that has now evolved into Web pages, all of which are indebted to the videos and films that she made during the seventies.) It is clear that traditional notions of verisimilitude will have to be rethought, and this may well encourage us to redefine documentary images and our experience of them.

I began this piece by asking whether documentary images could be thought about differently. I have concluded by saying that the differences are all around us and that one of the driving forces behind the changes can be found in many of the films and videotapes created by Canadian women filmmakers and video artists. Even as we continue to think about images as objects (and keep building disciplines and traditions of interpretation to support the edifices of scholarship), our imaginations are allowing us to conquer a whole host of digital worlds and to incorporate those worlds into our lives. The new documentaries will appear on the Internet as mixed media, as a combination of the digital and the analogue. They will not only be concerned with fiction, truth, or reality within the conventional parameters of the documentary cinema. They will deal with issues of the day in whatever way possible and will allow themselves the freedom to invent and transform in the light of arguments and perspectives unbounded by genre or convention. If this sounds utopic (or dystopic, depending on your point of view), I do not intend it to be so. Rather, we have inherited a history of iconography and iconographic strategies that has always relied on an impoverished model of reality. Digital images allow us to play with reality, allow and encourage us to create images as a function of who we are and as a pivot to enhance the imaginary worlds we share. This may mean that we can finally coexist with the images we use to interpret, explain, and enhance the realities of our lives and not relegate them to an ill-defined space of illusion and untruthfulness. Perhaps we need a new term for this phantasmagoria of documents, images, and ideas. And even as we recognize the limitations of the image, perhaps the appearance of digital images will encourage us to seek new ways of creating knowledge without the need to classify that knowledge in traditional ways.

NOTES

1 Mark Johnson, *The Body in the Mind: The Bodily Basis of Meaning, Imagination, and Reason* (Chicago: University of Chicago Press, 1987), ix.
2 The best work in this area is Charles Levin, *Jean Baudrillard: A Study in Cultural Metaphysics* (London: Prentice-Hall, 1996).
3 Lydia Haustien, 'The Transformative Power of Memory: Themes and Methods in the Work of Vera Frenkel,' *From the Transit Bar*, Exhibition catalogue, ed. Jean Gagnon (Toronto: The Power Plant/National Gallery of Canada, 1995), 61–2.
4 Vera Frenkel, Interview by Dot Tuer in *Vera Frenkel*, Exhibition catalogue (Toronto: Art Gallery of York University, 1993), 55.
5 See Susan Ossman, *Picturing Casablanca: Portraits of Power in a Modern City* (Berkeley: University of California Press, 1994), esp. chapter 5, which examines the influence of television of the daily lives of people in Casablanca.
6 Sara Diamond and Gary Kibbins, 'Total Recall: History, Memory and New Documentary,' in *Video re/View*, ed. Peggy Gale and Lisa Steele (Toronto: Art Metropole and V Tape, 1996), 269.
7 See Ron Burnett, *Cultures of Vision: Images Media and the Imaginary* (Bloomington: Indiana University Press, 1995), 209–15, for further details on this strategy for thinking about images.
8 Vera Frenkel, Interview by Dot Tuer, 57.
9 Kathleen Stewart, *A Space on the Side of the Road: Cultural Poetics in an 'Other' America* (New Brunswick, NJ: Princeton University Press, 1996).
10 Ibid.
11 See the work of Bruno Latour, 'On Technical Mediation: Philosophy, Sociology, Genealogy,' *Common Knowledge* 3, no. 2 (Fall 1994): 29–64.
12 Larrisa Lai, 'The Site of Memory,' in *Video re/View*, ed. Peggy Gale and Lisa Steele (Toronto: Art Metropole and V Tape, 1996), 344.
13 Dziga-Vertov, 'The Man with a Movie Camera' in *Kino-Eye: The Writings of*

Dziga-Vertov, ed. Annette Michelson (Berkeley: University of California Press, 1984), 83–4.

14 'This is also what is so fascinating about the video work of Sadie Benning, in particular, *If Every Girl Had a Diary* and *Me and Rubyfruit*, which are stream-of-consciousness confessionals. There are really no boundaries to what Benning will say. She is very careful to make the tapes present tense, and they look as if we have accidentally come upon her talking to herself in her bedroom. She frames all of her shots as if, like a small puppet theater, the eyes of the spectator are just on the other side of the camera.' (Burnett, *Cultures of Vision*, 317).

15 Kogawa Tetsuo, 'Toward a Reality of "Reference": The Image and the Era of Virtual Reality,' *Documentary Box* 8, no. 1 (1996): 1.

16 William J. Mitchell, *The Reconfigured Eye: Visual Truth in the Post-Photographic Era* (Cambridge: MIT Press, 1992), esp. chapters 3 and 9.

AVANT-GARDE

Feminist Avant-Garde Cinema: From Introspection to Retrospection

JANINE MARCHESSAULT

If English Canada has an Experimental film tradition it is one in which efforts of women filmmakers have been largely absent. This can be attributed to the fact that with very few exceptions films produced by women have not conformed to the rigours of an international modernism. Nor can they be seen to correspond to the structural concerns generally identified with the names of Michael Snow, Jack Chambers, and David Rimmer. Indeed, the distinction between avant-garde and Experimental cinema is useful for understanding feminist film culture in this country. The Canadian experimental legacy is short in comparison with the American experimental film tradition. This discrepancy reflects not only the utilitarian influence of a state supported film industry which relegated experimentation to animation because of its affiliation to painting, but also an exhibition system monopolized by Hollywood interests. It is within the art gallery circuits of the late sixties and early seventies that experimental film practices emerged in Canada. Many of its early practitioners (Snow, Rimmer, Chambers, Greg Curnoe, Charles Gagnon, and Joyce Wieland, for example) were working as artists in other media before turning their attention to film. The artist-filmmakers would be given a place in the newly created film societies and clubs which, for the most part, were affiliated with academic institutions (McGill, University of Toronto, Western, Simon Fraser). Though marginal, the position occupied by film within the gallery and the academy reflected a drive to move away from the hegemonies and hierarchies of discipline towards new forms of interdisciplinary art and epistemology. While the motivation for this shift is arguably postmodernist, it did nothing to upset the categories of modernism. Rather than foregrounding ideological questions related to the institutions of Art, experimental films affirmed the formation of a new genre both within the academy and the gallery. These early affiliations have worked to ensure the institutional and canonical framework for the emergence of a uniquely Canadian Experimental cinema.

The difference between avant-garde and modernist impulses can be located in their relation to the institutions of art: while the historical avant-garde reacted to the commodification of art by seeking to reintegrate art into the social (Bürger), modernist art works continued to be characterized by a contradictory insistence on autonomy, on hermetic forms which could not be readily consumed. The reified tenets of modernism in Canadian Experimental cinema are derived from a Fine Art tradition and, supported by its institutions, are founded on an adversarial relationship between high art and mass culture. This hostility is what distinguishes Experimental from avant-garde films. It is expressly in their relation to popular culture, its institutional supports and the pleasures of its promise, that feminist avant-garde films are often antithetical to the Experimental tradition in Canada.

This, however, does not mean that the alliance between an avant-garde and a feminist cultural politic has ever been simple. If feminists began making avant-garde films in order to give difference expression, then the expression of difference also opened the doors to profound contradictions: to differences between women. Where historically the feminist movement in North America has depended upon a unified gendered identity as the basis for political solidarity, the historical avant-garde rejected any such identifying unity on the grounds that art must disrupt the hegemonic processes of an affirmative culture. Market forces and the forces of identity construction are often highly compatible. The union between feminism and avant-garde aesthetics has paved the way for a feminist politic that posits the solidarity of women not as natural but as historical, not as given but as something to be struggled over.

In contrast to the somewhat more consolidated aesthetic concerns of the Experimental tradition, feminist avant-garde films in Canada exceed simple delineation. From neo-narratives to experimental documentaries, from autobiographical and biographical chronicles to video hybrids, from live performance to super 8 and to feature narratives, one thing is clear, there is no normative aesthetic programme for a feminist avant-garde culture.

In their diversity, feminist avant-garde films in this country have been characterized by forms which negate the myths of creation and origin, which favour difference over unity, and which refuse the boundaries of margins and centres that patriarchal capitalism constructs. Yet more than unity in diversity, I would like to propose that across two decades of feminist film culture in the 1970s and 1980s, we can distinguish the formation of an identity politic that has shifted from feminine introspection to feminist retrospection, that has transformed the private sphere of personal rumination into a new historiography intent on expanding the public sphere to include women. This development is neither synchronous nor singularly linear, but is characterized by insistent and simultaneous calls to difference across many sites.

Feminine Introspection

Consistently employing materials and themes linked to the private sphere of women's experiences, Joyce Wieland's films introduce the identity politic so crucial to the exploration of sexual difference in feminist films of the 1970s and 1980s. Kay Armatage has argued that Wieland's insistence on the feminine as a subject worthy of artistic investigation sets her apart from her Experimental *confrères*: 'As an artist, Wieland has consistently and consciously sought out the feminine precisely as a site of potential images which have remained unexplored by her male counterparts, and in which she could construct an aesthetic based upon a tradition which she saw as belonging to women.'[1] Wieland's efforts to do this can be traced across an impressive range of work: from embroidery and quilting to hand tinted film, from 8mm 'home movies' to a narrative feature. In *Water Sark* (1964–65) Wieland films kitchen objects (crockery, rubber gloves, a tea pot) as well as her own body to discover and define a feminine space; fabric dyes are applied directly to footage, and quilting needles are used to create perforations in *Hand-Tinting* (1967–68); domestic genres such as the structural conventions of the fairytale in *Rat Life and Diet in North America* (1968) and the melodrama in her feature narrative *The Far Shore* (1976) are called upon to explore popular forms of narration generally associated with women's culture; and *Reason Over Passion*

(1967–69) according to Kass Banning is the quintessential 'girl road movie,' a trip across Canada.[2]

The aesthetic implications of women's traditional hand crafts stimulate the dialectal sphere of Wieland's investigations, providing her with the agency to explore a new feminine language. Over and again it is the artisanal 'home-made' aspects of filmmaking that are emphasized, just as some of her plastic wall hangings are made to look like film strips ('Stuffed Movie,' 'Home Movie,' 'War and Peace 8mm home movie' (1966)). Importantly, this combination does not work to reinstate the trace of the artist as divine but rather by referencing the handicraft recalls a sacral past, art as an empowering collective activity.

Wieland reclaims this history to constitute a new history of film – not as auratic high art or as mass product but as *craft* which embodies at once individual idiosyncrasy and a history of shared meaning.[3] In this sense, her project bears none of the nihilistic undertones of American Pop Art but derives from it a disregard for the boundaries of high and low art. Although her work encompasses an implicit critique of modernism's evolutionary telos, her aesthetic framework is reconstructive rather than deconstructive. Unquestionably, her approach can be seen to inaugurate the radical notions of authorship implicit in feminist appropriation strategies of the last decade. The notion of feminist authorship provides an alternative to the Great Author of bourgeois individualism, without relinquishing the rebellious subjectivity and political agency that Barthes' dead Author rescinds.

Current theorizations have related the feminine to the fragmented space of allegory where totalizing mythologies are eroded and decentered, where the whole picture gives way to many partial views and to details.[4] Undeniably, it is film's capacity to isolate and magnify details from the everyday that has served Wieland's practice. Yet in her films the feminine is more than allegorical, more than a rhetorical device of sublime negation – the feminine constitutes and is constituted through, as Lauren Rabinovitz has insisted, Wieland's experiences and perceptions as a woman.[5] Working within a prefeminist context, Wieland's films espouse a feminist sensibility by making the personal political, by seeking new ways to represent those aspects of women's lives and consciousness inconsequential to the grander narratives of history, *Water Sark* and *Hand-Tinting* being the exemplary films here. It is in the fragment and through the gaps that Wieland finds the stylistic lexicon to build on a tradition of women's culture.

Not surprisingly, the magnification of silent lips is a favourite motif in many of Wieland's films and her object art. Frozen between a yearning to speak and an unwillingness to be spoken, the magnification underscores an onerous introspection. As motif it embodies at once a parodic celebration of femininity and a desire to overcome its silence. If we trace this image across a decade of films – the silent playful lips in *Water Sark*, the muted chanting of her own patriotism in *Reason Over Passion*, and the lovers' conversation in *The Far Shore* – we detect a growing extroversion, a growing desire to move from a silent elsewhere, from the muted contradiction of a language imposed, towards a speaking. Over a ten year period, from *Water Sark* to *The Far Shore*, the category of Woman is progressively imbued with historical specificity, progressively grounded in place – from her own home to her own country.

If Wieland refuses the totalizing languages of national and imperial discourses in *Reason Over Passion*, she also insists that the unity of women be defined through an historical materialism rather than an essential femininity. Perhaps the most influential aspect of her art for feminist avant-garde practices in English Canada, is a career that spans the boundaries of short super 8 films and feature narrative filmmaking.

Making Room for Contradiction

Despite Seth Feldman's claim in the mid-1980s that a colonized silence is the chief stylistic feature in English Canadian cinema since Grierson,[6] feminist films have sought to overcome silence by forming intricate sound–image relations. In effect, the extensive use of off-screen voices and voice-over narration has become their central distinguishing mark, countering a history of images which speak for themselves. Ironically, it is via a return to Grierson, to his fervent belief in the cinema as 'hammer,' that feminists have confronted the statist authority his cinema was intended to support.

Films like *The Central Character* (1977), by Patricia Gruben, and Kay Armatage's *Speak Body* (1979) materialize two overlapping genres – new narrative and experimental documentary – that are in many ways paradigmatic of two dominant tendencies within feminist cinema of the

1980s. While Gruben's film relies on a sequential linearity (which it disrupts) derived from the fairytale, *Speak Body* grows out of the social documentary associated with early feminist filmmaking. Both films displace generic categories by combining the conventions of documentary and fiction, both films pave the way for a heterogeneous feminist body politic.

Though Wieland's foray into feature filmmaking with *The Far Shore* marks an important interface between avant-garde and popular culture, *The Central Character* extends the shattering of generic boundaries to a feminist imperative. The division between centres and margins, between inside and outside, as between avant-garde and popular culture, is shown to be part and parcel of a patriarchal order. Gruben begins by disrupting the opposition between nature and culture that the figure of Woman has always been made to mediate. Amidst ferns and greenery Gruben's character finds herself immersed in a bathtub; hair sprawled like the sprouting potatoes in her kitchen, she embodies a pun: nature as culture. Just as the female narrator comes to break down the subject/object divide by confusing 'she' and 'I,' so too does it become impossible to distinguish the inside (her kitchen) from the outside (the woods).

Indeed, the second half of the film, which has the central character (now somewhat de-centred through the voice-over narration) wandering into a petrified forest, reveals the woods to be nothing more than a domestic junkyard. Upon the ruins of history and language, a woman's voice relays a formidable tautology: 'that I would like to say that I would like to say that ...' It is because there is no outside in Gruben's universe, because desire has no origin, no centre, that her fairytale finds no resolution, there is no way out of the woods.

The Central Character, like many of Wieland's films, teeters over the abyss of the epistemic crisis – how to create new meanings with familar codes? The collapse of nature into culture suggests the creation of postmodern forms of cinema that are perhaps distinct but never separate from the representational resonances of an older order. It is not surprising, given this, that Gruben's subsequent films would, to a greater and greater degree, engage directly with the conventions of narrative cinema, steering traditional visual pleasures towards political ends.

Many films have grown out of the trajectory carved by *The Central Character*, exploring the colonization of a female imaginary by relegating feminine introspection to a sequestered imprisoning space. In stark contrast to the celebration of the endemic domestic sphere in *Water Sark*, the female protagonist in Barbara Sternberg's *Transitions* (1982) remains incarcerated within the purgatorial space of her bedroom. Between dream and reality, between sleep and waking, she is besieged by a cacophony of women's voices that keep her suspended in a reified hiatus. The filmmaker in Anna Gronau's *Mary Mary* (1988) cannot decide whether she is making a dream or a story and she too is trapped within the narcissistic expanse of her bed – speaking into a microphone, looking into a mirror, trapped within a labyrinth of doubled origins. The domestic is at best only an unhappy refuge from the perils of the outside world in Lori Spring's *Inside Out* (1988) and Ann Marie Fleming's *You Take Care Now* (1989). More than imprisoning, the private sphere has also set the stage for a parodied panopticon of phallocentric desire: the 'One Vision' in Paula Fairfield's *Fragments* (1989) and Kathleen Maitland-Carter's infamous menstrual film *Inside Upstairs* (1988) which treats scopophilic desire to a blood bath of razors and tampons. The discourses are further imploded through the parodied art history in Annette Mangaard's *The Iconography of Venus* (1987) and the commodification of black skin in Glace Lawrence's *Desire* (1990).

In the context of feminist theory, these films, and many others not mentioned here, present an important challenge. Against the essentializing impetus of French feminism's *écriture féminine*, as well as Anglo-American emphasis on experimental cinema, they displace female desire. Moving beyond idealist oppositions, ideology critique surrenders to a thinking through the body. The gaping reification of the feminine in so many of these films clears the way for the inscription of a cultured and gendered body.

Geography *is* history, and it is by representing women's bodies in spaces filled with noisy contradictions (reconstructing rather than deconstructing those spaces) that feminist avant-garde films have migrated from an introspective 'elsewhere' to a more localized space where race, class, and sexuality are among the many things that make up the politics of feminist culture and identity. From this space has emerged an elaborate politics of naming intent on exploring differences between women. That is, as Adrienne Rich has phrased it 'on seeing difference differently.'[7]

Relocating Alterity

The vast resurgence of feminist documentaries since the mid-1980s reflects the desire to define and construct women's experiences and histories in ways that offset our cultural and political marginalization. While identity formation was an essential feature in the feminist documentaries of the early 1970s, the cinéma-vérité style of these films stressed women's shared experiences. Recent avant-garde documentaries appear more intent on forging discrete identities and subjectivities to construct broader understanding of community.

Kay Armatage is a seminal influence in this respect. Armatage radicalizes the most conservative aspects of expository cinema by transforming the unitary authority of traditional voice-over narration into a discursive political commentary. The eloquent and evocative structure of *Speak Body* combines documentary and fiction to consolidate a diversity of women's experiences around abortion. Addressing topics ranging from birth control and women's wages to fear and anger, the heterogeneity of the women's voices never privileges any one experience or position. The images that accompany the testimonials are made up of fragmentary reenactments of one woman's discovery of her pregnancy through to and after her abortion. By grounding the body in many experiences, the film thwarts any unitary consolidation of female identity; by grounding the voices in one body, the film consolidates a feminist politic around gender oppression.

An analogous heterogeneity informs Gwendolyn's *Prowling by Night* (1990), a film made with the participation of several prostitutes and one stripper about police harassment. While different voices recount experiences of 'lawful' persecutions on the soundtrack, drawings made by the women are animated through lighting and camera movement. Framed as reenacted conversations between prostitutes on the street, the voices and drawings constitute a rhetorical blend of personal and factual information. Aligned with her earlier work producing women's pornography, Gwendolyn challenges a history of over determined imagery by having the prostitutes represent themselves. Relegating photographic objectification to the animated police car (which is constantly interrupting the women), she turns the empiricism of state surveillance around and in the process constructs a highly disturbing document that demands social change.

Similarly impressive is the fashioning of non-empirical epistemologies in recent biographical and autobiographical films by women. Their various hybrid forms often combine documentary and narrative with experimental techniques to suggest a subjective authorial presence which problematizes discourses of self. Many of them manage to simultaneously specify and confound an identity politic through complex formal and thematic juxtapositions. For instance, this is seen in Brenda Longfellow's exploration of the two Marilyns (Monroe and Bell) in *Our Marilyn* (1987); Marion McMahon's examination of two forms of labour (marriage and nursing) in *Nursing History* (1989); the two accidents (abroad and at home) in *You Take Care Now*; Mangaard's juxtaposition of two women artists (Spring Hurlbut and Judith Schwartz) in *Dialogue on Vision* (1990); two women recalling Hiroshima in *Clouds* (1985) by Scott Haynes and Fumiko Kiyooka; and Sally Lee's immersion into *The World of Suzie Wong* in Helen Lee's comical *Sally's Beauty Spot* (1990). While foregrounding the singularities of women's lived experiences, many of these films depend on exchanges between women, between geographies and cultures. Importantly, the intersubjective positions and cinematic pleasures they construct are directed towards women. Kathy Daymond's 'docuporn' *Nice Girls Don't Do It* (1990) brings this to the fore by providing an explicit step by step 'how to' for women who want to experience female ejaculation.

The tension between formalism and activism underlying a history of women's cinema, as Teresa de Lauretis asserts, has produced a heterogeneity that aims at expanding and creating new communities of women.[8] The political solidarity of women depends on the mutual recognition of our differences and our different needs. To this end, there is no one site of resistance, no one style or point of view that defines feminist intervention.

The critique of realism that evolved out of psychoanalytic feminism in the mid-1970s was an essential step in confronting the oppressiveness of prevailing forms of narration and representation. It has also all too often led to an over-estimation of the subversive effects of non-realist forms. The commodification of everything 'new' in corporate culture has deflated the opposition to realist forms that fuelled earlier avant-gardes. Feminists have responded to the expansionist mandates of capitalist culture by penetrating all areas of filmmaking. Several have directed their efforts towards excavating, as Brecht had put it, the *bad old pleasures* of narrative film in order to access larger audiences. Many others continue to produce work in super 8 or 8mm film as well as video, using inexpensive technologies and smaller exhibition venues to defy ever growing pressures and controls of a state funded culture.

So if feminist avant-garde films are no longer to be found in one place or under one aesthetic banner, it is not because the avant-garde is dead. It is not because the feminist movement has reached the end of the road, although ridiculous terms like 'post-feminism' would have us believe it. It is because the need to form coalitions across many sites and the corresponding urgency to construct a plurality of women's histories and imaginings to expand our participation in the public sphere, to expand the very definition of the public sphere, are clearly underway.

NOTES

This article was originally published in *CineAction*, nos. 24/25 (1991): 30–7.

1 Kay Armatage, 'The Feminine Body,' *Dialogue: Canadian and Quebec Cinema*, ed. Pierre Veronneau, Michel Dorland, and Seth Feldman (Montreal: La Cinématèque Québécoise & Media Texte, 1987), 286. It is worth noting that Wieland's emphasis on the feminine has led male critics to characterize her work as 'sentimental' and 'naive,' 'impish' and 'less complex than Snow's.' Her omittance from New York's Anthology film archives (devoted to experimental cinema) in the early 1970s reflects not only this kind of critical appraisal but her extreme divergence from the sensibilities of the New York underground.

2 Kass Banning, 'From Didactics to Desire: Building Women's Film Culture' *Work in Progress*, ed. Rhea Tregebov (Toronto: Women's Press, 1987), 175.

3 As with the acclaimed *True Patriot of Love* exhibit of 1971 at the National Gallery, the retrospective of her work at the Art Gallery of Ontario in 1987 is the result of certain liberal directives which have done nothing to unsettle the rigid foundations of art historical practices. Her presence in the gallery is somewhat disturbing not only because her work is, in so many ways, antithetical to the heroic context of Great Art but also because the most radical aspects of her practice are effectively silenced. Questions relating to the very constitution of high art and its supports, to a specificity and a typology of women's experiences which extend the possibility of a differential system of exhibition and mode of reception have formed the basis of Wieland's art since the early sixties.

4 See for example Naomi Schor, *Reading in Detail: Aesthetics and the Feminine* (New York and London: Methuen, 1987), or Christine Buci-Glucksman, 'Catastrophic Utopia: The Feminine as Allegory of the Modern,' *Representations*, no. 14 (Spring 1986).

5 Lauren Rabinovitz, 'The Films of Joyce Wieland,' *Joyce Wieland*, Art Gallery of Ontario catalogue 1987.

6 Seth Feldman, 'The Silent Subject in English Canadian Film,' *Take Two* (Toronto: Irwin Publishing, 1984), 48–57.

7 Adrienne Rich, *On Lies, Secrets and Silence* (New York: W.W. Norton, 1979), 35.

8 Teresa de Lauretis, *Technologies of Gender* (Bloomington and Indianapolis: Indiana University Press, 1987), 135.

The Scene of the Crime: Genealogies of Absence in the Films of Patricia Gruben

SUSAN LORD

Patricia Gruben's two decades of filmmaking provide us with a rich index to many of the issues central to feminist theory and practice: *The Central Character*'s (1978) recipes for women's absence from the public sphere; the archaeology of feminine discourse in *Sifted Evidence* (1982); the use of technology to invent identity in *Low Visibility* (1984); the recovery of the unconscious in *Deep Sleep* (1989); the search in *Ley Lines* (1992) through maps and archives for the father/homeland; and, most recently, the (re)turn in *Before It Blows* (1997) to questions of nature and desire.[1] Never at rest in a particular genre, moving through experimental, narrative, and documentary modes, Gruben's thematic interrogations always include an excavation of inherited forms and an interrogation of the limits of representation itself. Within this diversity of styles and subjects there are two common and interwoven elements: 'failed' quests and limited vision. There is an aura of mystery produced by a search that never arrives at the thing searched for. This apparent failure is the effect of a 'low visibility' that derails the narrative and represents a fundamental mistrust of vision's access to the 'truth.' The films thus reorient us away from the devastating effects of both master narratives and magistral vision.

In the following pages I will discuss several of these elements through a series of readings of Gruben's hybrid films.[2] I will attend most particularly to the means by which the work opens the space of representation to discontinuous temporalities. We find in Gruben's work a consistent use of non-synchronous sound: from the early work on female subjectivity, where the female body and voice are separated, to the latest films, which employ a similar technique in the investigation of relations of nature and culture, non-human and human. Intimately related to this technique is an interrogation of the means by which narrative constitutes desire and subject/object relations and produces erasures in its underlying drive toward unity and closure. Such interrogations are not performed in bad faith. Narrative and its desire are not external to the work of Gruben's films, for elements of the quest narrative can be found throughout these films, from the most experimentally informed work, such as *The Central Character*, through to the self-reflexive documentary *Ley Lines*.

This type of quest can best be understood as a critical genealogy, defined by Michel Foucault as an undertaking of a history of the present, of events that make possible various struggles. 'What is found at the historical beginning of things,' he writes, 'is not the inviolable identity of their origin, it is dissension of other things. It is disparity.'[3] Hence, the quests undertaken by Gruben's various itinerant genealogists reveal not a 'self' or a 'nation,' but rather the tension between a subject constructed through knowledge and a self apparently incommensurable with that knowledge. As this tension or disparity has been central to various aspects of feminist theory and politics of representation, I believe it important to situate Gruben's work within this project. By extension, I will be considering a question that Gruben's hybrid film practice revisits in the confounding of map and territory: to what degree can cinema register this dissension and disparity of meaning without repeating the problem that got us here in the first place – that is, without reinscribing woman as a 'dark continent.'[4] These abstract dimensions of the map/territory theme appear in Gruben's persistent use of cartographic signifiers. These signifiers are intimately linked to the mysteries pursued by her protagonists who assume the roles of explorer, archaeologist, genealogist, archivist, ethnologist, doctor, and psychic. Maps, plans, and charts – some of the tools of the filmmaker's diegetic surrogates – do not merely represent but also produce space, as do the technologies of mechanical reproducibility. As a central project of feminist politics concerns the remapping of lived and representational space, I begin with a discussion of what was (and continues to be) at stake in the distinction of public and private space, a distinction inherited from modernity by feminist filmmakers of the 1970s and early 1980s.

The history of women's occupation of public space is a long and arduous story of disenfranchisement and impropriety, given the dilemma that women's public appearance has been conditioned by codes of the spectacle. 'Public' or 'publicity' signifies the world itself, insofar as it is common to 'all' and is distinguished from any one's privately owned place in it.[5] This world is distinguished from nature and is defined in relation to the space of production and representation. It is through this distinction that subjectivity is realized. If modern subjectivity is understood as being produced in the negotiation between public and private life, in the transcendence of reason over nature, then it is no wonder that feminist film of the 1970s and 1980s is populated with internal exiles, travellers, itinerants, and interlopers – those for whom the public space of modernity offers no tangible place to live.

This reflection on the relation between women and public space was often a companion to feminist theoretical investigations into the enunciation of sexual difference. Theoretical and practical questions converged with the concern about the ethical and political stakes of representing the female body within a cultural context where economic and symbolic power pivots upon the investment, circulation, and marketing of the sexed body as a consumable entity. The structural impossibility of film and photography to not re-present the female body as already sexed, as always bound to the position of 'to-be-looked-at-ness,' was a condition that could not simply be 'overturned by a contemporary practice that is more aware, more self-conscious.'[6] On the contrary, feminist directors of the 1970s and 1980s such as Yvonne Rainer, Ulrike Ottinger, Helka Sander, Chantal Akerman, and Patricia Gruben offered new alternatives. In Gruben's hybrid films, the materiality of filmic signifying systems is treated as one discourse among others that, together and in conflict, are brought to crisis. The films simultaneously refuse the inhibiting and misleading dichotomy of presence or absence and make a space for the appearance of agency – albeit limited, contingent and subject to containment. The agent, emerges in the pursuit of that moment where the crisis of signification could be overcome: in nature; in technology; in science; in ur-history; in the father; in the unconscious; the pre-colonial. In the end, however, the quest for unity or closure is discovered to be impossible.

The Central Character ends with an incantation of the conditional ('I would like to say that I would like to say ...'). Here, the subject (of the sentence and of speech) is restricted to the degree that it has no object, and thus cannot function as a subject, even of its own speech. Without the means by which to even utter the 'if,' the conditions for speech are left unimaginable; yet, the desire for articulation, for a space of representation, does emerge through and in the midst of layers of public and private technologies, technologies that produce a space and order for 'her' absence. The voice is a tape recording 'recovered' from the garden by a female figure whose presence the camera can hardly record. It utters the only 'I' but is not the only female voice. The other voices recite shopping lists and table-setting instructions, and quote architectural theory and natural science documents. As Kay Armatage has stated, 'much of this auditory text is processed to suggest that the voice comes from a radio or broken record, from under water, or as if it were an auditory hallucination.'[7] In tracking a figure contained by a liminal space somewhere between nature and culture, the distinction between these terms – a distinction upon which public meaning depends – becomes porous: nature 'takes its dictation from science,' the blueprints for a kitchen engineered to organize flows and work against 'chaos' become over-run with plant life; dirt is on the kitchen floor, a bathtub is in the garden, etc. In investigating the conditions for the structuring absence of the central character, this film produces a critical genealogy of the conditions of publicity itself, revealing that the 'secret' of agency is not an essential or inviolable identity, but 'is fabricated in a piecemeal fashion from alien forms.'[8] While the central character recedes into the dark spaces of the garden, her discoveries become the tools of possibility.[9]

Sifted Evidence continues the quest-as-interrogation, beginning, as the voice-over states, 'from where we are at the moment.' This 'moment' comprises multiple dislocations: historical, geographic, diegetic, linguistic, visual, and auditory. Briefly, the film occupies at least two temporal registers in its narrative about a women who recounts her trip to Mexico in search of evidence of female deities at the ruins in Tlatilco. The first register is rather like an ethnologist's seminar, complete with slide-show, maps, and artefacts. The second is the memory (repressed by the space of ethnographic knowledge) of the journey itself where she attempts to learn Spanish; finds and loses her way in a 'foreign' country; meets a black, Spanish-speaking man, for whom she has an equivocal attraction; and in the dark of night arrives, finally, at the ruins, which contain merely the detritus of colonialism. This part of the film is composed of complex visual and aural elements, including front projection, which delimit realism and heighten both the artefactual and phantasmatic qualities of remembrance.

The film engages a number of issues of concern to feminist theory and politics at the time: the desire to redeem matriarchal societies into history as a counter-memory to patriarchal modernity; the appropriation of the subaltern in the search for a self; the power differentials between race and gender; and the modalities of a feminine discourse. In its engagement with these concerns, the film returns to *The Central Character*'s strategy of the disembodied voice and proliferates its registers. The non-synchronous sound technique is used here to create a multi-valent space and time, to bring a critically self-reflexive mode to the quest narrative, and to separate out the various techniques of sexual difference. The non-synchrony of voice and image has, in feature narrative film, worked to confer a unity on the text and its interpellated (male) subject. However, Gruben uses this technique as a means by which to restore a temporality to the timeless image of the female body. Also, the synchronization of female voice and image functions in mainstream cinema as a means by which to contain the feminine within the materiality of the signifier, a representation of woman as limited to and by nature. If a voice-off is used, that voice is 'submitted to the destiny of the body.'[10] Unable to see (and thus to know) beyond its restricted and fallible nature, the embodied female voice on screen signified her pre-oedipality, and thus moral inadequacy.

Given this understanding of the embodied female voice, it is no surprise to find it thoroughly interrogated in a film concerned with the evidence of women's circumscription within patriarchal history and its discourses. The synchronization occurs only twice. The first instance is in the introductory sequence, when the voice-over of an apparently disembodied female commentator 'identified with the apparatus' is revealed to be the voice-off of the central character (who, throughout the film is played by different actresses). The coalescence of body and voice is timed to an admission of failure – a failure to find, to see, and to know. In fact, at this moment the commentator/narrator/ethnologist becomes a central character – one without access to aerial shots, retrospectives, readable maps, and so on. The second occasion occurs at the moment of an ambivalent attempt to resist the physical/sexual domination of the male character. As Kaja Silverman notes, in these two scenes 'synchronization works to strip the female voice not only of discursive authority and flexibility, but of all distance from the body.'[11] In both instances, though, she is rescued 'from this bondage' of subjectification by the vocal intervention of the narrator/filmmaker. Rather than simply occupying the aural space granted a narrator in the traditional expository documentary mode, this narrator both interferes with and analyses the activities and motivations of characters within a diegesis already laced with heightened artifice. The film ends with the character now returned to the space of the narrator, a space perhaps made habitable by the recognition of its temporality and fundamental dis-unity or dislocation. But, as Armatage has articulated, '"the sifted evidence" has provided no answers to her quest. As if to assert the impossibility of resolution or escape into a finally activated alternative discourse, the woman is suspended in a freeze-frame just as she turns to the camera and opens her mouth. She is frozen in silence – about to speak.'[12]

The 'failure' to recover a 'feminine principle' – to discover a different body that could house the complex registers of the female voice (Silverman) or an 'alternative discourse' (Armatage) – is perhaps less a failure than an unanticipated discovery. What is discovered is violence at the heart of a project that seeks to unify in an inviolable identity the *imaginary* space of origins and the discontinuous time of history. What is found, after all, in the place of female deities is a crushed Coke can, the irrevocable effect of the colonial 'dream' of the world as a knowable totality. The dangers of actualizing a desire for unity (for appearance as essence) – a desire feminist theorists of psychoanalysis remind us is a foundational fantasy of the 'ego's era'[13] which manifests itself in the displacement of lack onto women – may very well be our itinerant genealogist's discovery and, by extension, Gruben's critical contribution to the dilemma's faced in Western feminism by the perceived need to recast matriarchal 'pre-history' as the origin of history. While the narrator is left 'frozen in silence – about to speak,' the viewer is left sifting the evidence of the film, 'beginning again' the work of constructing, rather than revealing, a sensate and sexuate self.

A problem revisited by Gruben's films is most readily typified as one concerned with the distinction between the map and the territory: the structurations of the subject and the experience or practice of the self. But with *Low Visibility* (1984), *Ley Lines* (1992), and *Before It Blows* (1997) the explicit concern with female subjectivity is delimited by inquiries about the limits of the human, the construction of nature, and the techniques and technologies that function not merely as a means to knowledge but as forms of containment of knowledge, the knower, and the known. As scientific and epistemological methods, genealogy and cartography reflect, among other things, the desire to reveal the historical and material ground of the self, to represent identity (national, sexual, racial) through adequation, and to limit contingency. In Gruben's critical use of these epistemologies, the coordinates for the articulation of experience are variously configured as conflicts or tensions in the temporal and spatial constituency of the subject. The narrators, investigators, doctors, psychics, and travellers that populate Gruben's films are driven by the desire to discover some first moment, a discovery that in its originality would permit the self to appear, would 'clear up' the troubles and traumas that obscured its existence under the layers of unreadable maps and invisible codes of subjectification. While the films provide a space for the representation of that desire, they also interrupt its trajectory, send it off track, by introducing some other's desire, refusal, or indifference. The search becomes troubled, indicating that we have been looking in the wrong place, that our tools are only made for specific and limited conditions.

Low Visibility and *Ley Lines* each represent this trouble both as a crisis in knowledge brought about by the intractability of the other and by the violence performed in the effort to ascertain an inviolable identity of origins. In *Ley Lines*, a self-reflexive documentary, the filmmaker's desire, enunciable only at the end of the film, is 'to find out what happened to my dad.' As we would now expect from Gruben, this is never discovered, at least not in the form anticipated. But a tremendous, almost overwhelming amount of historical and geographic terrain is traversed as she digs through archives, natural history, family memories, and sonograms, and ends up in Tuktoyaktuk where her 'voyage of discovery' for a father-land is confounded by misrecognition: 'I thought this town was a doppelganger for Spur, but it's not ...' And her coordinates are rendered useless: 'You can't get to the bottom of anything here because there is no underground.'

Her previous film, *Low Visibility*, also takes a turn away from the 'difficulties' of female subjectivity to consider the problems presented to knowledge (scientific and juridical, in particular) by an intractable other, who in this case is a male figure first seen walking out of a dense forest in the midst of a winter storm. Unlike the earlier films, the mode of representation is decidedly narrative, albeit complex and hybridized. Mr Bones, as he comes to be known, is a man suffering from Korsakoff's syndrome, a form of aphasia where speech erupts only in curses. Our male subject is barely a subject at all. Gruben's inquiry into a zero degree subjectivity allows that while aphasia may be a 'language impairment' (as Dr Korona tells us) and that language is a constitutional basis of the subject, the process of subjectification is manifold: Mr Bones is a Mr in more than his bones – the first words we hear him utter are 'fuckin' bitch.'

Low Visibility is a fascinating examination of the techniques and technologies of subject formation. As Doane discusses in her essay 'The Voice in Cinema,' speech in cinema not only functions to elaborate the phantasmatic unity of its subject, it is also confirmed as an individual property right – and, as noted in the discussion of *Sifted Evidence*, some goods are better than others. While the realization of such operations is contingent upon historical and cultural contexts of reception, a male body without speech is an improper body. Due to his linguistic incompetence, Mr

Bones is in a position traditionally occupied by women: he appears as a cipher, criminalized and pathologized (he is thought to be either a murderer or the victim of trauma) by the institutions that want to know him. The desire to reveal is intimately connected to the desire to cure or punish; and all of the visual technologies available to these institutions are deployed in order to make Mr Bones 'admit' himself, to confess. Throughout the film, his perceived emptiness is mapped over by the desires of others; his body becomes the site through which their power is circulated. However, it is precisely because he is not a woman that the etiology of the condition is sought beyond the body.

In the process of searching for causes, the mystery represented by Mr Bones is heightened. The narrative is driven by questions: Who is he? Where did he come from? How did he get this way? A variety of people want to know, and conflicting methods are employed to find out: the police, a clairvoyant, doctors and nurses, a documentary film crew, and television journalists. All but three rely upon ocular techniques for the solution of the mystery: observing him via the surveillance camera; encouraging him to watch television in order that he learn how to act; asking him to identify photographs; documenting his progress. The two nurses and the female clairvoyant, however, approach the problem of Mr Bones through different forms of knowledge. The two nurses speak with him in riddles; the clairvoyant 'sees' with her hands (the only part of her body made visible) as she passes them over a map. Later, in a helicopter over the mountains, she can't see anything and sees only blue. Perhaps, these three people and their non-ocular techniques get closer to some understanding of his condition.

For the viewer of the film, the 'low visibility' of Mr Bones's origin is intensified rather than reduced by those very technologies that, in their deployment as transparent tools of scientific objectivity, are unable to register either their effects or the off-screen space and time of its subject. The film realizes the process by which technology projects itself onto, or into, its object, and it registers the limits of such techno-logic in various ways. From our first sighting of him to the last, he is always viewed from a marked position: the point-of-view shot through the windshield of a car as it passes him by, stumbling along the side of a mountain highway; the surveillance camera (which moves to capture his image) in his hospital room; the news television camera; the documentary camera. While the heterogeneity of these views permits the audience to recognize disparity and even dissent, the film does not synthesize them into a totality by offering itself as a transparent view, for it even marks itself as a 'case-study' with the use of titles indicating the day of the treatment. We have, by the end, a series of clues that indicate that a trauma did occur (a plane crash) and that an unspeakable crime was committed (cannibalism is inferred), but any given combination of elements – any narrative inducements that could deliver identity – are not adequate to 'Mr Bones.'

Mr Bones represents to scientific and juridical knowledge that liminal space between the human and the non-human. And in order to make him the province of the human, he must be understood as having will, autonomy, and (potential) mastery of the symbolic. Hence, the police 'know what he did' and 'know that he lied'; and the doctors are convinced that he is being cured. Yet, we are left with incommensurability. His responses to treatment have moved between mimesis and parody; resistance and acquiescence. He stares at television snow, which he then draws; makes a scrambled *l'hommelette* out of the psychologist's Mr Potatohead by smashing ears, eyes, and nose into his left-over eggs; eats words given by the nurses to make sentences; curses; and repeats fragments of discourse spoken by others, though in a re-arranged and nonsensical syntax. At the end of the film, this non-sense is translated by the police detective as confession. In the final shot, we are suspended in the sky above a mountain pass with the clairvoyant who sees only blue; our apparently transcendent, aerial 'view from nowhere' obscured by the density of clouds.

The work of opening representational space to discontinuous temporalities is a constant effort in Gruben's films. As we have seen, this is interpretable as an ethical response to the dangers of actualizing a desire for unity. From the point-of-view of modernity's institutional knowledges and power, a response such as this is understood as failure: a failure to know, to see, to arrive, to confess, to identify. The 'failure' to arrive as a subject and thus to transcend nature, to distinguish oneself as a figure against the conquered and passive ground of nature, to stand over and against it and to instrumentalize it, is a condition for the possibility of becoming other than we have been. In both *Ley Lines* and *Before It Blows* the discontinuous temporalities include the time of the non-human as that which the human is along side of.

In *Before It Blows*, the time of the geyser is spatially represented in one long take without the human figure (but with a sound-track of spectators' voices that interact in various ways to the space they inhabit) and is marked as distinct from the time of technology (the Hi-8 digital clock in the bottom right of the image) and the time of the spectators' desires. As in *Low Visibility*, the heterogeneity of views is oriented not toward a total picture but rather indicates off-screen space and time relations left uncaptured by the techniques of narrativity and visuality. A number of other problems present themselves. The uncaptured off-screen space may suggest a repetition of our earlier problem regarding the 'dark continent' of the other; however, such a concept depends upon a binarism established in the name of the same. In other words, that which discourse makes absent is essentially so only for that discourse. Gruben's work is, in great part, intended to make a space for the representation not only of what has been left out but of our blindness itself. Also, if this seems to present a willy-nilly pluralism or, worse, a limitless extendability of techniques and technologies, then it must also be said that it only appears to be so from the point of view of a purposive reason that the films bring to crisis. The work of the films is to open representational space to possibilities, not to dictate in advance what the outcomes may be. The violent trajectory of knowing in advance, of dictating outcomes, of putting nature to work, and of making a total picture is stumbled upon midway through *Ley Lines* when we arrive in Nazi Germany.

A discussion of *Ley Lines* is a pertinent final section of this essay because it is the most open and hybridized of Gruben's texts in its mode of addressing many of the issues winding through the earlier work. The mode is rather difficult to describe: a self-reflexive, experimental documentary that is part autobiography, part biography, part social history, part natural history, and more. And, as these names imply, it is concerned with the past, or, more precisely, the confluence of pasts that compose various presents. It investigates the historical constitution of subjectivities in order to create the possibility of 'no longer being, doing or saying what we are, do or think.'[14] No counter-archive of Western history is established as there are no aerial views; there is instead a particular lifeline – that of the filmmaker – and a simple question about what happened to her dad. But this apparent simplicity folds into other times, spaces, and desires, much like the movement of ley lines themselves. Ley lines are invisible, imaginary lines that connect innumerable sacred or natural sites around the globe; and they are attributed to magnetic forces made by underground waterways, which surface as geysers or hot springs or even as solid forms like Stonehenge. Ley lines are playfully employed in the film as a confluence of natural and cultural geography, without centre or origin.

Within the first five minutes of the film, four unnamed, central characters are introduced: the filmmaker, a female scholar, a young girl, and an aunt (I call her this, for she has the inside story, a passion for family, and is not bothered by the filmmaker's occasional contrariness). (Much later on an elderly German-accented female voice makes a couple of appearances.) These are all trademark Gruben characters: female voices without bodies to match. Only at the end of the film, in Tuktoyaktuk, does direct synch-sound footage appear. The image register is also quintessentially Grubenesque: found, shot, and treated footage, maps, text, as well as images of eye-testing, wrist watches, magnificent landscapes, and shots of natural rock and water forms. The filmmaker introduces herself to us within moments of the film's beginning. We have just watched the last minutes of *The Incredible Shrinking Man*, the man who has reassured himself of his own existence ('To God there is no zero'). The filmmaker says: 'When I was a girl that was my favourite film. And just like him I couldn't stop thinking of myself as the centre of the universe. But, what would happen when the incredible shrinking man got too small to have a brain? It would have been too scary just to disappear. I'd already given up on Sunday School. I had to find something.' And the title *Ley Lines* appears on the black screen. Our narrator is trustworthy: she utters the personal pronoun almost immediately; she, too, was once a girl with narcissistic tendencies, with wild fears, without a god. The scholar explains what ley lines are, who used them and why. Later on she explains what a genetic code is (over an image track of a domino game); she also reads the Sartre text that appears on the screen. She is, through a good part of the film, our interpreter of archaic, 'primitive,' and natural formations, and she reads existentialism without a hitch. Her competence is reassuring, her tone bears no pedantic traces. She and the filmmaker complement each other: one public, the other private. The 'I' of the filmmaker takes from the public discourse information necessary to her search, and the private life is thus made relational and legitimate; and the scholar's work is thus made relevant to a world beyond the institutions of specialists and pedagogy.

The girl, on the other hand, is a problem – directly, for the filmmaker; indirectly, for the scholar. Her questions occasionally stymie the narrator, disturbing her self-certainty, and they disrupt the transparency of discourse delivered by the scholar. The polyvocality of these first minutes is extended by the abrupt and timely entrance of the aunt, via telephone – though she seems to have been listening in – armed with plucky family value, a list of corrections to the filmmaker's memory, and stories that date back to 1826. The 'I' that opened the film is, within minutes, part of a 'we' – which, importantly, doesn't always get along. This collaboration of the unidentical is a departure from and an alternative to the frozen 'I's that end Gruben's early films.

More than offering a question to any unified notion of identity through this 'conversation,' the film vocally maps out a space, from Texas to the filmmaker and the girl to the scholar. The filmmaker and the girl 'accompany' the images (there is an intimation that the little girl is Gruben's memory of herself) – they travel from Vancouver to Texas to Germany to Tuktoyaktuk; the scholar is in a booth reading her script or in a lecture hall interpreting the slides; the aunt is listening in from Texas. Together they produce a 'line,' of sorts, through time and space, but one that becomes increasingly incomprehensible in the singular. The discontinuous and confluent temporalities proliferate with the introduction of each voice and image. Alongside the particular time given each voice there are the times of the images: the time of petroglyphs and hieroglyphs, the time of modern technology, the time of walking the earth, the time of ice, war, watches, movies. With each passing minute of the film's time, the vertical and horizontal dimensions of the narrative complexify to such a degree that unity appears to be (happily) abandoned. Yet, after being given plenty of assurance that this engaging genealogical adventure into the filmmaker's family is to be a safe one, a line takes us to a space and time that also concerned itself with lineage: Nazi Germany.

As the 'voices' tell us, the Nazis used many of the tools at work in our narrator's quest: genealogy, geomancy, cartography. While what is to be made with these tools is radically different, incomparable, the film does implicitly question its own desire by telling us, for instance, that Himmler resurrected pagan rituals – 'earth passion' – and that Nazis used geomancy in their plans to dominate Europe. The homeland was a space 'cleansed' of difference, a map of sameness and of origin. The genealogical project of Nazi Germany tied together an inviolable identity of nature and nation; blood and soil; appearance and essence. It constructed an ur-history with its tools, and put nature to work.

The film makes its final turn, away from the line of that narrative. And this time, it is toward difference: to the Karmalut (which means 'resembling a caribou') of Tuktoyaktuk where 200 of 900 people are by birth or marriage named 'Gruben.' For the first and only time in *Ley Lines* direct synch-sound is used when the filmmaker, herself in the picture, interviews various Grubens of Inuit descent. As mentioned above, the filmmaker's coordinates fail her: there is no underground; the centre is the magnetic pole, which has migrated 400 miles since its 'discovery' by Europeans in the nineteenth century; neither can she tell day from night. As Kathleen M. Kirby has written, 'the cartographer removes himself from the actual landscape [the same could be said of the genealogist]. The mapper should be able to "master" his environment ... without it affecting him in return. This stance of superiority crumbles when the explorers' cartographic aptitude deteriorates. To actually be *in* the surroundings, incapable of separating one's self from them in a larger objective representation, is to be lost.'[15] The direct synch footage can thus be read less as the presentation of ethnographic authenticity (though this meaning cannot be completely dislodged), than as a mark of the fortuitous failure of a transcendental project of mapping the other. This argument may seem contradictory, as the unity of space and time represented by the footage is certainly the prerogative of a filmmaker/narrator, who has been searching for an origin of sorts; and this context does allow her an embodied voice without it being the sign of lack. But what is found is not at all that which motivated her search: this is not her home. It is in this dislocation, in the turn to difference from sameness, that new, uncharted relations become possibilities.

That ley lines are invisible, or more precisely, imperceptible by vision and its technological extensions, that ley lines cannot be mined and brought to light, is as significant to the film and to Gruben's overall efforts as is the suggestion that the confluence of lines functions as a kind of principle for the representation of plural worlds. This principle provides a means by which moving image practices may construct relations of space and time that signify an openness to experiences and natural processes that either exceed or are in other ways disparate from the dominant modes of cultural signification and territorialization. This is not to suggest that the films resolve ethical (cognitive, aesthetic, epistemological) problems; in our engagement with them, their questions – voiced and unvoiced – may converge with our own. In considering Gruben's work from this perspective – a perspective struggled for by various of feminism's socio-cultural practices – I am by no means delimiting the value of other, more narratively coherent work. Rather, I have tried to show that the interrogation of inherited forms and the desires they constitute is productive of an expanded and historically dynamic space of representability.

NOTES

1 At the time of writing this essay, *Before It Blows* had yet to be completed. Thanks to the filmmaker, I was able to watch a fine cut of the image track on VHS while listening to a rough soundtrack on cassette tape. My comments about the film are therefore of the most general nature.

2 I will not be discussing her feature-length narrative, *Deep Sleep*, because in this essay I am concerned with the experience of discontinuity as it is realized through a formal heterogeneity. Such heterogeneity or 'hybridity' delimits the capture of the positive sign upon which realist narrative depends.

3 Michel Foucault, 'Nietzsche, Genealogy, History,' in *Language, Counter-Memory, Practice: Selected Essays and Interviews*, ed. Donald Bouchard, trans. Donald Bouchard and Sherry Simon (Ithaca, NY: Cornell University Press, 1977), 142.

4 Behind this question is, I think, the concern with the highly volatile – and violent – effect of ascribing to identity an essence conceived in terms of biological determinism; for, in essentializing identity in this manner, not only are women contained within a concept (Woman), but nature too is humanized – that is, it is conceived as that which exists to be dominated (by concepts, technologies, and so forth) and is, thereby, merely an extension of the techniques of anthropocentrism and, considered historically, colonialism. As recent debates over essentialism have shown, the politics of 'ontological difference' (Braidotti) or 'strategic essentialism' (Spivak) offers a possibility for an ethical or situated subject. Throughout Gruben's work, she experiments with visual and auditory signifiers in an effort to represent a subject *in situ*.

5 Hannah Arendt, *The Human Condition* (Chicago: University of Chicago Press, 1958), 52.

6 Mary Ann Doane, 'Woman's Stake: Filming the Female Body,' in *Femmes Fatales: Feminism, Film Theory, Psychoanalysis* (New York: Routledge, 1991), 165.

7 Kay Armatage, 'About to Speak: The Woman's Voice in *Sifted Evidence*,' in *Take Two: A Tribute to Film in Canada*, ed. Seth Feldman (Toronto: Irwin Publishing, 1984), 299.

8 Foucault, 'Nietzsche, Genealogy, History,' 142.

9 For further discussion and contextualization of this film, see Janine Marchessault's essay in this volume.

10 Mary Ann Doane, 'The Voice in the Cinema: The Articulation of Body and Space,' in *Narrative, Apparatus, Ideology*, ed. Philip Rosen (New York: Columbia University Press, 1986).

11 Kaja Silverman, *The Acoustic Mirror: The Female Voice in Psychoanalysis and Cinema* (Bloomington: Indiana University Press, 1988), 173.

12 Armatage, 'About to Speak,' 303.

13 For an illuminating discussion of the 'ego's era,' see Teresa Brennan, *History after Lacan* (London: Routledge, 1993). She makes a very insightful connection between modernity's formation of the subject, modes of production and consumption, and the value of flesh. The discussions of nature and the spatialization of time are particularly relevant to Gruben's work. But, as space is limited, this discussion will be reserved for another time.

162   Susan Lord

14 Michel Foucault, 'What Is Enlightenment?' trans. Catherine Porter, *The Foucault Reader*, ed. Paul Rabinow (New York: Pantheon Books, 1984), 46.
15 Kathleen M. Kirby, 'Re: Mapping the Subject: Cartographic Vision and the Limits of Politics,' in *Body Space: Destabilizing Geographies of Gender and Sexuality*, ed. Nancy Duncan (London: Routledge, 1996), 48.

NARRATIVE FICTION

Gender, Landscape, and Colonial Allegories in *The Far Shore, Loyalties,* and *Mouvements du désir*

BRENDA LONGFELLOW

This paper is a major revision of an article I wrote almost ten years ago, 'The Melodramatic Imagination in Canadian Women's Cinema.'[1] That article marked a starting point from which to reconsider the thematic and theoretical frameworks we have used to talk about Canadian women's cinema. If my textual readings in that article circulated around the effort to lay claim to a unique difference of women's cinema, a subsequent decade and a half of filmmaking and theorizing has more than laid to rest the possibility of that project. As Teresa de Lauretis has pointed out, the contemporary revisioning of feminist theory is marked by a profound paradigm shift in which the binary of sexual difference (masculine versus feminine) is displaced by an investigation of the multiple differences *between* women, differences that are always mediated by specific historical and conjunctural concerns.[2]

Rather than trying to elaborate a unifying concept that would distinguish an exemplary selection of Canadian women's feature films (my original objective), my goals here are more modest and discrete. Borrowing from recent postcolonial investigations of space as a vector of power and meaning, I will explore the particular construction of space in *The Far Shore* (1975), *Loyalties* (1985), and *Mouvements du désir* (1994) as a referencing of the landscape traditions in Canadian cultural history and philosophy. As well, I shall argue that *The Far Shore* and *Loyalties* are modelled, in many ways, as allegories of colonization in which gender and race are deployed as metaphoric substitutions for each other. As the three films were produced over a twenty-year span, they mark the manner in which women's films are shaped by evolving production contexts.

The Far Shore

Joyce Wieland's *The Far Shore* opens with a title, 'Quebec 1919,' superimposed over a windswept northern landscape as a child in period costume runs into the background to join her Aunt Eulalie (Céline Lomez) and Eulalie's Anglo suitor, Ross Turner (Lawrence Benedict). While Eulalie stares wistfully into the distance, musing on the serenity of the pastoral scene, Ross points out the sites where a modern bridge and road will be built. For him, the entrepreneurial engineer, the landscape represents a functional resource to be exploited in the interests of modernity and progress. For her, the woman, aspiring pianist, and Québécoise, the landscape is a source of sublime beauty and romantic transcendence. In this first sequence, which concludes with Eulalie accepting Ross's marriage proposal, the elements of the film's meditation on the gendered spaces of landscape and nation are articulated in sharp opposition to each other.

This opposition lies at the heart of the Canadian philosophical tradition, which has been organized around a foundational opposition between technology and nature. Indeed, *The Far Shore* was originally entitled *True Patriot Love: A Canadian Love, Technology, Leadership, and Art Story*, a title that might have been ghost-written by George Grant or Harold Innis, if they had Wieland's playful feminist sensibility. Grant's *Technology and Empire* (1969)[3] and *Lament for a Nation* (1970)[4] were widely debated texts in the left nationalist movement that emerged in the late 1960s in English Canada and, no doubt, had an effect on Wieland's own particular style of nationalist art practice.[5] Like Grant, Wieland was opposed to the assumption that human progress could be measured through the technological conquest of nature. In *Rat Life and Diet in North America* (1968), she links the technological imperative with the imperialist ambitions of the American Empire, a society of death the rats (played by gerbils) must flee to find happiness in organic gardening on the Canadian side of the border. That stark national opposition takes a more nuanced form in *Reason Over Passion* (1967–9), Wieland's trans-Canada experimental road movie, in which the technological imagination is linked to indigenous political formations, notably embodied in the Cartesian stance of Pierre Trudeau. Again, like Grant, Wieland recognized the fact that official state policy in Canada, from the construction of the CPR to Trudeau's notion of rational federalism, had been characterized by its embrace of technology as a means of national defence and identity formation. In all her work, Wieland distinguishes her version of Canada from state versions of the same. Declaring 'I think of Canada as female,'[6] she saw her role as one of feminizing national symbols, of subversively aligning her sense of national belonging with emotion, the body, and passion.[7]

On one level at least, imagining Canada as female recapitulates a classic trope in which the affinity between the nation and the woman is their shared victimization. In Wieland's work, however, such affinity is related less to an overtly politicized feminism than to her own deep ecological consciousness. For her, the feminine is an elemental principle of life, fertility, and eroticism, an embodiment of all that is abjected by masculinist technological modernity. Within her archetypal consciousness, gender is powerfully related to differential attitudes toward nature and landscape.

The Far Shore is Wieland's most ambitious treatment of her long-standing nationalist passions. A 35mm feature film financed by the Canadian Film Development Corporation, Famous Players and Astral for a handsome budget (in 1975) of $435,000, photographed by Vic Sarin with meticulous period costume and set design, *The Far Shore* was expected to be a major theatrical breakthrough. By all accounts, it bombed. Gently panned for its 'blatant symbolism'[8] and its 'semi-mystical humanism,'[9] the film closed within a few weeks and was revived only within the context of specialized screenings and Canadian film scholarship.

It would be hard to argue that the contemporary critics of the film were entirely off the mark; *The Far Shore* is schematic in its articulation of philosophical and political concerns. It is also, however, a film of great beauty, and while this paper will set out to deconstruct that term, particularly as it applies to the representation of landscape, this analytic move in no way detracts from the film's subversive and generic pleasures.

While Wieland would eventually return to the experimental format, *The Far Shore* represents a flamboyant and self-reflexive embrace of melodramatic narrative conventions. Eulalie is a classic protagonist; stifled in a loveless marriage, torn between passion and propriety, she finds solace in melancholic piano playing. Replete with its quota of sighs and fuelled by the fetishistic pleasures of period costume and decor, *The Far Shore* presages the current mania for feminist costume dramas in films like *The Piano, Washington Square, Sense and Sensibility,* and so on.[10] From Jane Austen on, I would argue that the attraction to melodrama lies in the ability of the genre to give form to the repressed torrents of female longing while simultaneously (and this is crucial) critiquing the bourgeois institution of marriage and the property relations on which it is based. Rooted solidly in a heterosexual romantic tradition, melodrama pitches the spiritual values of love and sexual fulfilment against a debased material world in which the rights of patrilineal inheritance and capitalist accumulation take precedence. Within this juxtaposition of two worlds of value, the depiction of space gets over-determined by the masculine/feminine binary opposition.

In *The Far Shore*, once the couple is married the representation of space shifts from the exterior landscape of the first sequence to the austere dark interiors of Ross's claustrophobic home in Toronto. While the exterior space retains an association with the masculine world of commerce and exploration, the interior is coded as a female site of 'emotion, immobility, enclosed space and confinement.'[11] Taking up the classic posture of the 'woman at the window,'[12] Eulalie languishes in the enforced idleness and restraint of the upper-middle-class woman.

It is only through the introduction of Tom McLeod (Frank Moore), a thinly disguised incarnation of Tom Thomson, that the representation of space again opens to the exterior. Initially, however, this representation is mediated through a close-up of a charcoal drawing Tom is rendering. The camera pulls back to reveal Tom's rustic cabin in the woods where, looming in centre frame, is a half-finished painting instantly recognizable as Thomson's *Jack Pine*. Eulalie and Ross enter the cabin, and Ross proceeds to barter with Tom over the painting, which he hopes to purchase as a wedding present. While Eulalie admires the aesthetic genius of the painting, Ross's only criteria are the philistine values of the marketplace. 'How do you know how much a painting is worth?' asks Eulalie. 'Easy,' Ross responds, 'by its size, of course.'

In *The Far Shore*, however, the social critique implicit in melodrama does not remain at the level of interrogating the gendered split between public and private spaces. At issue here are the conflicting discourses of the aesthetic and the technocratic, which lay claim to the essential meanings of public space or, more specifically, the Canadian landscape. In the very schematic character distribution in the film, the technocratic is embodied by Ross and his associate Cluney (Sean McCann) and the aesthetic by Eulalie and Tom. As revealed in Ross's speech to his fellow engineers (a caricature of Sir Wilfrid Laurier's 'the twentieth century belongs to Canada'), for him the northern wilderness represents an inexhaustible means of economic development – silver mines and resource extraction. From the reverse angle of the aesthetic, the landscape is a source of spiritual transcendence, an impetus to art making, and, like Art, it is an object that cannot be quantified.

Within the series of metaphoric relays used to articulate the film's philosophy, the marriage of Ross and Eulalie stands as a microcosmic version of official state federalism, a union that is seen to be forged through relations of power and domination. This is never clearer than in the scene in which Ross attempts to force his sexual intentions on his wife, tearing off her clothes and pushing her to the ground. Here the intimation of rape mediates the metaphoric substitution, as Eulalie's body comes to stand not only for Quebec, but for the landscape itself, a landscape equally ravished by the technocratic will to power. The parallelism between the woman's body and the land is inscribed within the mise en scène, through McLeod's/Thomson's painting *Jack Pine*, which looms prominently in the background of the scene. Within this scene of ritualized violence, which condenses so many of the film's themes, an insight common to contemporary feminist theorizations of space is reiterated – that the technocratic/imperialist gaze at landscape and the masculine gaze at women share the same gendered logic. Within *The Far Shore* that gaze is a medium of destruction connected in the final sequences of the film to Cluney's gun/phallus, which results in the ultimate deaths of Tom and Eulalie.

The Tom Thomson character, of course, upsets any absolute distinctions based on essentialist ascriptions of gender. His aestheticism, taste, and gentleness redeem him as the perfect embodiment of melodrama's (and feminism's) recurring fantasy of the feminized man. He also mediates the complex and profoundly contradictory relations of colonialism and race. While ostensibly of Scottish descent, his rustic living quarters, his proficiency in a canoe, and his knowledge of natural ingredients ('Indian bark tea') position him as a surrogate Native, a character who signifies the profoundly romanticized qualities of nativeness (like Barthes's 'Italianicity'): pacifism, wisdom, and deep ecological and spiritual knowledge of the land. From this position, his gaze is necessarily tempered with difference, for while the imperialist/technocratic gaze is realized through the absolute separation of subject and object, the aesthetic/ nativist gaze implies organic connection, relation, a dissolution of the boundaries between viewing subject and landscape.

The representation of this gaze reaches its apogee in *The Far Shore* in what has to be the most sublime depiction of lovemaking in a Canadian film. Taking time off from their canoe escape from Ross and Cluney and, by extension, from the norms of Victorian sexual propriety, Eulalie and Tom embrace passionately, immersed to their necks in the northern lake. Iconographically, their lovemaking retorts to the scene of rape as an expression of the idealized relations among the tripartite figures of man, woman, and landscape. The verticality of the lovers implies an equality of relation, a reciprocity of sexual giving and taking as they stare deeply into one another's eyes. Their reciprocity extends to the representation of landscape itself. While landscape throughout the film is never simply a background for narrative action, within this scene the distinction between foreground and background is dissolved as the landscape becomes a kind of horizontal surround for the lovers, a medium of erotic touch and sight. And, indeed, at the moment of climax, Eulalie and Tom submerge completely, becoming a part of the lake. Here, in perfect symmetrical opposition to a technological gaze characterized by mastery, distance, and objectification, Wieland poses an aesthetic gaze based on proximity and intimacy, where the boundaries between subject and object, human and landscape, are dissolved in a moment of erotic surrender. This dissolution of the boundaries between subject(s) and landscape is repeated at the end of the film when the lovers' deaths are signalled by a slow pan over the water, glancing over Tom's body and coming to rest on a frame of waterlilies disturbed by the uncanny presence of Eulalie's hat, the synecdochic representation of her death. In the end, it is the woman's body that remains thoroughly assimilated into the landscape.

While the lovemaking scene condenses many of Wieland's thematic oppositions, the representation of landscape plays a central role throughout the film. A forest in the snow, the path leading to Tom's cabin, the monumental vistas of pines and Precambrian rocky shores featured in the final chase sequences function as a recurring specular lure, a vision that exceeds any diegetic mapping. The point of view in these sequences is rarely attached to any particular character, for these sequences directly represent an inscription of authorial vision and desire. They are, of course, Wieland's homage to the Group of Seven painters – the primary intertexual reference in *The Far Shore*. Within the canonical version of Canadian art history, the Group of Seven represents the first artistic movement in Canada to radically break from the colonial influence of the European 'academy' style. Characterized by their surreal, subjective interpretations of the Canadian landscape, the group developed a collective identity that stressed the distinctiveness and uniqueness of their indigenous perspective. And, clearly, whether through the deliberate visual quotation of Thomson's two most emblematic paintings (*Jack Pine* and *West Wind*) or through the prolonged contemplation of 'actual' landscape within the film, Wieland aligns herself with this tradition and with the broad cultural discourse that assumes landscape as the chief symbol and arbiter of national identity.

Ironically, the Group of Seven has recently come under scrutiny by art historians and critics who question whether their particular representation of landscape can be radically separated from the technological. For Paul Walton ('The Group of Seven and Northern Development')[13] or Scott Watson ('Race, Wilderness, Territory, and the Origins of Modern Canadian Landscape Painting'),[14] the Group's depiction of landscape as an 'empty, uninhabited, unmapped, unnamed territory'[15] in no way contradicted the aims of the business community in the first decades of the twentieth century to expand the extraction of natural resources from the North. Not only were there economic links forged between the Group and industry, through the Massey-Harris enterprise and significant patronage, but there was a smooth alignment of their joint vision of nation building. As Walton argues, the Group 'represented the wilderness as rugged enough to defy conversion to pastoral ground ... But their modernist style was meant to make it emotionally accessible in decorative terms, and they also sought to imbue it with grandeur, harmony, and a degree of poetry ... This strategy made the North seem less threatening and its resources more capable of being processed to provide aesthetic satisfaction as art expressing the national and spiritual aspirations of a culture based on resource extraction.'[16]

The North, of course, was not uninhabited, and the mythopoeic projection of landscape as virgin territory could only exist through the denial of Native presence and through the repression of centuries of racial genocide and territorial displacement. Clearly, Wieland's appropriation of the landscape tradition has to be distinguished from the contradictory legacy left by the Group. *The Far Shore*, as I have argued, constructs a radical opposition to the extractionist myth of national development. However, while Wieland's aesthetic gaze maintains an affinity to Native reverence for the land, a Native voice is present only in sublimated form through the character of Tom Thomson. This is not, in any way, intended as a critique of Wieland; her vision of nation is articulated in aesthetic and cultural terms rather than in overtly political ones. This caveat merely points out the limitations of the landscape tradition, limitations that Wieland's work both incorporates and transcends.

Loyalties

In many ways, Anne Wheeler's *Loyalties* (1985) maps territory similar to *The Far Shore* but in terms that self-consciously respond both to feminism and to Native militancy. The film was co-produced and broadcast by the CBC (and photographed as well by Vic Sarin), and its textual form is shaped by the national broadcaster's docudrama tradition, which, from the venerable series *For the Record* on, has addressed social issues through the highly conventionalized codes of naturalistic drama. *Loyalties* transcends the usual 'earnestness' of the docudrama approach, however, through its attentiveness to the regional details of characterization and setting and through the deliberate allegorical resonance of its narrative.

Loyalties opens with an archetypically gothic scene – a dark and stormy night, rain beating on the window of what appears to be an isolated cottage. A young boy in a yellow mackintosh runs up to the window and looks in, the camera aligning itself with his perspective. A man in a suit and another figure, whose identity is obscured, are struggling. The film cuts to a side table featuring a smiling family portrait of a husband and wife that suddenly, ominously, falls to the floor and shatters. All the exaggerated and overblown conventions of melodrama are brought together with a flourish: a family secret, the violence and perversion of the home, accentuated by the violence of the rainstorm and the opacity of the night. At this stage, however, the scene remains unanchored in any kind of narrative context, serving rather to introduce mood and tone, an atmosphere of darkness and a sense of fatalism drawn through the association of male violence with the uncontrollable forces of nature.

The linear pull of the narrative is only initiated in the second sequence, which begins with an extended aerial shot of the forlorn landscape of northern Alberta and introduces us to Lily Sutton (Susan Wooldridge), an upper-class British woman who has emigrated to Canada with her three small children to join her husband. Dialogue and mise en scène quickly establish that her destination, Lac La Biche, is at the furthest outreaches of 'civilization,' an isolated town surrounded by miles of 'bush.' Her eventual reunion with her husband, David (Kenneth Welsh), at the airport is stiff and formal, and his whispered remark, 'I wasn't sure you were coming,' activates narrative suspicions around the family.

Like *The Far Shore*, *Loyalties* appropriates melodramatic generic conventions to a feminist critique, but its textual predecessors are less likely to be found among romantic melodramas than among the darker gothic romances of *Jane Eyre* or *Rebecca*. Founded on the suspicion that the thin veneer of civility in the bourgeois marriage (or in the bourgeois husband: think of Rochester in *Jane Eyre*) masks a deeply malevolent brutality against women, the gothic is preoccupied with the struggle to name the source of domestic horror. Structured by an enduring tension between the said and the unsaid, between the appearance of domestic harmony and its dark foreboding underside, the gothic textually embodies the terror that women experience as targets in a patriarchal society.

The gothic carries the hermeneutic code in *Loyalties*, propelled, as it is, by the necessity of exposing the dark family secret condensed around the figure of David, a necessity that leads, inexorably, to the rape of a child. Throughout the film, suspense builds through the accretion of suspicions concerning David's past and his current and intensifying interest in a young Métis girl, Leona, whose mother, Rosanne (Tantoo Cardinal), has been employed to help with the domestic labour in the Sutton household. Scenes with Leona, in particular, carry the tension of the gothic, where ostensibly innocent gestures, such as David cavorting with Leona in the water, are lent a duplicitous quality by the aura of twisted desire that surrounds him. The gothic arc of the narrative is concluded only in the final scenes of the film, when David unexpectedly comes upon Leona babysitting at his house and proceeds to ply her with champagne. The rainstorm outside and the Bela Lugosi vampire movie on television cue audience expectations of impending violence and circle back atmospherically to the opening scene. As David rapes Leona in the sodden fields outside his house, the monster is named and the gothic mystery is resolved.

The storyline of 'male violence,' however, functions more as textual background in *Loyalties*. What is foregrounded is an alternative narrative dynamic that displaces the gothic tone of female paranoia onto the possibility of a female solidarity built across class and racial boundaries. Rooted in the developing friendship between Lily, the 'lily white' British upper-class wife, and Rosanne, the Métis, working-class woman, this storyline articulates the film's feminist politics.

What distinguishes *Loyalties* from the central Canadian preoccupations of *The Far Shore* is the way in which Wheeler's feminism is mediated through a strong regional consciousness, a trait apparent in all the director's film and television work. While *The Far Shore*'s meditation on cultural identity assumes the nation as a central category, in *Loyalties* identities arrive with the accents of specific place and location. Not only was the film actually shot in its diegetic location, Lac La Biche, using local inhabitants as extras, but the iconography of the town, the scenic shots of the lake, suburban backyards, and forest are deliberate markers of the specificity of northern Alberta.

Wheeler is never interested in landscapes in relation to the romantic sublime. Her landscapes include the grotty interiors of bars and the kitschy order of suburbia, places marked by particular class distinctions and by the dialectic of relations between metropolitan centres and margins, North and South stages of development. This almost ethnographic quality, so transparently a part of the docudrama tradition, also accounts for the very powerful Native presence in the film. It is no exaggeration to say that *Loyalties* is one of the first Canadian feature films to portray Natives, not as 'imaginary Indians,'[17] but as complex and contradictory characters who are given a progressive narrative centrality.

Indeed, while narrative focalization initially settles on the Lily character – it is her arrival at Lac La Biche that signals the initiation of the narrative – this focalization shifts with the introduction of Rosanne as a victim of her lover's drunken brawling. From that point, the film is structured around a series of alternating scenes that contrast the domestic spaces, values, and familial relations of the two women. It is through this dialectic that the film constructs its colonial allegory.

If, as I have argued, the colonial allegory in *The Far Shore* is articulated through the conflict between different discourses of landscape, in *Loyalties* spatial oppositions are rooted in social and political terms that implicate the history of white settlement in the territorial displacement of Native people. In a scene that is, perhaps, marginal to the narrative but pivotal in establishing this history, Beatrice (Rosanne's mother) informs David that the land he has built his home on used to be Indian territory. 'For one hundred and fifty years my people lived on the shore of this lake,' she says, 'until white people wanted to live here and they called us squatters.'

This history, while never more overtly articulated than through Beatrice's casual remark, is an embedded knowledge within the film, informing our understanding of the nearly apartheid conditions in which white and Native populations of Lac La Biche live. Within the geography of the film, space is distributed according to traditional class-based patterns, with the upper middle class (the Suttons) on choice property surrounding the lake, the working class centred in town, and the Native population marginalized on the farthest outskirts. In fact, the only visible spaces of integration are the bar scenes and Rosanne and Lily's improbable utopian friendship.

To be sure, there is a certain conventional pattern to their friendship, as it is the pragmatic wisdom of the racial Other that mediates the ultimate growth and consciousness of the white subject. But what rescues the film from a predictably mundane handling of interracial friendship is the manner in which the Rosanne character comes to assume a narrative centrality. Within her own domestic space she is given a narrative parity to confront her own set of issues around relationships, childrearing and work; and, increasingly, it is her attitudes that come to occupy the centre of the film's moral and political vision. As Robin Wood has astutely pointed out, 'The film's structuring strategy is progressively to transfer ... *primary* identification from Lily to Rosanne, a figure multiply alien [to a presumed white audience] as non-white, non-urban, and non-middle-class.'[18]

Let me suggest that this transference of identification marks the textual sophistication of the film, which, while using conventional naturalistic codes of narrative, engineers a subversive shaping of identification through racial and class difference. As Teresa de Lauretis has argued, the second generation of feminist filmmaking is characterized by the manner in which modes of address acknowledge the intended 'feminist' audience of the film.[19] This is distinguished, she qualifies, from earlier moves to mark the 'feminine' as a standard of difference by the deliberate political acknowledgment of shared communal values and beliefs. Clearly, *Loyalties* is very much marked by this textual inflection, positioning Rosanne, as it does, as the implicit feminist spectator, the film's moral and political centre.

Within the film, it is the white subject, Lily, who is 'othered' as upper class and British, a character whose conservative old world values, devotion to appearances and bourgeois propriety, are seen as alien to the new world – 'a real airhead,' as Rosanne caustically puts it. Rosanne, by contrast, embodies a new world subject. The inheritor of the 'metissage' of white and Native populations, she survives, free from the conventional patriarchal codes of female behaviour. From the increasing centrality of her perspective, 'whiteness' is denaturalized as a standard, and Lily's class distinction, her 'pots of money' and 'gilded upbringing' are regarded as negative values, inhibitors in the process of Lily's growth and adaptation to her new surroundings.

At the heart of *Loyalties* is an exploration of the dialectic of difference and commonality that both binds and separates the two women. Narrative syntagmas – dinner, sexual encounter, mother–child interactions – occur in each domestic space, establishing the difference of class and racial identities. In Rosanne's dinner scene, for example, the children are fully integrated, and family solidarity is conveyed through warm lighting and the crowded frame. This warmth and openness is contrasted to the stiff formal dinner endured by Lily and David where the children are absent, the china and crystal are perfect, and the meal is eaten in chilly silence. In the scenes of sexual encounter, the failure and frustration of

Lily and David's intimate life is answered by the toughly passionate reconciliation between Eddie (Tom Jackson) and Rosanne. In addition,
Rosanne's humorous and open communication with her children is set
against Lily's tense and awkward mothering.

While the film insists that the class differences between the two women
can never be transcended, in scenes where Rosanne warns Lily 'not to
start making speeches about the happy poor' or in a fragment of voice-
over where Rosanne informs Eddie that 'the only difference between her
and me is money ... but what a hell of a difference'; it also insists on the
women's commonalities and on the possibility of mutual recognition and
solidarity. But solidarity is only authentically forged through a politicization of identity. Once the rape has been discovered, Rosanne retaliates,
pulling Lily's hair and demanding, 'What kind of woman are you?' Above
all, it is an existentially feminist question, one that could be interpreted
as 'What side are you on?' a question of political affiliation and self constitution. It is the rape itself which forces Lily to break her silence and
choose her side. She acts, finally, reporting David to the police and it is
this act which allows for her reconciliation with Rosanne and her ultimate
redemption as a subject for feminism.

Mouvements du désir

While *The Far Shore* and *Loyalties* were rooted in production contexts
intended to nurture a national cinema, Léa Pool's *Mouvements du désir*
(1994) is very much a product of the international co-production economy. Pool, in fact, has been one of the pre-eminent beneficiaries of international co-production, with four of her six features produced through
international deals and intended for the commercial and art house markets of Europe. Their international destination troubles any easy ascrip-
tion of national identity to her films. And, indeed, the authorial signature
of Pool, a Swiss émigré to Quebec, is marked strongly by the influence of
European art cinema and bears a level of textual and symbolic abstraction that, in many ways, runs completely against the grain of the history of
Quebec cinema.[20]

As Robert Daudelin has argued, national cinema in Quebec is defined,
inextricably, in relation to its concrete referencing of place: Îles aux Cou-
dre, the St Lawrence, the bars and salons of Ste Catherine Street, the idio-
syncratic (and instantly identifiable) quarters of Montreal, the landscape
of northern Quebec.[21] In Pool's films, by contrast, location is rarely given
any such concrete specification. For the films set in Montreal, the city

represents a kind of anonymous postmodern urban space, viewed primarily through its generic sites of passage: a hotel, warehouse, hospital, asylum. On one level, at least, the absence of geographically specific space is related to the immigrant consciousness of her films, with their recurring thematics of wandering, exile, and diaspora. While the prevailing tone of alienation is related to the loss of a home that could root characters within a fixed sense of identity, it is also intimately related to the fluctuating sexual orientation of characters. For the lesbian characters in her earlier films and the homosexual in *A corps perdu* (1988), 'home' is often the refuge of another's body. Alienated from the national landscape of both city and country, Pool's characters remain separated from actual geographic backgrounds by their experience of otherness.

Pool's films thus resist any realist approach to representation. Signifiers, far from having any ethnographic or referential value, are always and only functions of the hermetic universe of the text itself. Densely symbolic, characters, places, and locations take on the hollow and frequently overwrought quality of figures in an existential landscape.[22] It is this level of abstraction that has enraged many Quebec critics, including Chantal Nadeau, who argues that Pool's 'existential mode of treating identity,' where women characters appear 'out of time, out of place, ahistorical, almost immaterial,'[23] repeats a mythological representation of Woman as universal, fantasized subject. While, clearly, articulating the social subject of either Quebec's national identity or feminism is not one of Pool's overt concerns, Nadeau's critical assessment needs to acknowledge the specific production and reception contexts of Pool's work – the international co-production that produces its own inherent demands and aesthetic criteria.

An elegantly produced 35mm narrative feature financed by French, Swiss, and Canadian participation, *Mouvements du désir*, on one level at least, departs from the habitual geographic abstraction of Pool's earlier films. Indeed, from the first frame to the last, its entire representational thesis is deliberately oriented around the repetition of that most reverential of Canadian national signifiers, the transcontinental landscape. Set aboard the cross-Canada passenger train, the mise en scène is constituted by the iconographical repertoire of snow-covered Canadian Shield, deserted Prairie towns, and the primeval majesty of the Rocky Mountains.

While probably the only post-referendum film originating in Quebec filmed outside the boundaries of the province, *Mouvements du désir* not only references a 'federalist' landscape but it also tropes on a central statist concept of nation, the railway. From its origin, the Canadian state and the business interests supporting it saw in the railroad a perfect technologically mediated form of identity: a national communications system that would provide an unwieldy federation with some semblance of unity. Stretching from sea to sea, across vast and diverse regions, the railroad provided the material embodiment, the concrete (and unitary) signifier of the idea of political federation. Like the National Policy, its function was to direct immigration, economic exchange, and (perhaps, most importantly) semiotic traffic[24] on an east–west bias in order to offset the relentless seductions of money and markets to the south. A more phallic symbolic embodiment of nation could scarcely be imagined.

For the most part, the signifier of the railway in *Mouvements du désir* is drained of this historical resonance. While there is a recitation of concrete place names (Winnipeg, Regina, Vancouver), these sites are only ever registered as a 'view' from the train; there is no density or depth to their representation. Regional differences (so prominent a concern in *Loyalties*) are here reduced to scenic variation within a unified specular flow. This flattening of the background certainly also distinguishes *Mouvements du désir* from the textual dynamic in *The Far Shore*, which, as I argued, consisted of the effort to transcend the antinomies of subject and object as they related to landscape, through the merging of foreground and background. In *Mouvements du désir* this textual dynamic is reversed. The landscape is always articulated as separate from the narrative foreground, a two-dimensional theatrical backdrop to the story evolving aboard the train.

Aboard, the narrative consists of a love story between two protagonists: Catherine (Valerie Kaprisky), a single mother fleeing the dissolution of a relationship with 'Ishmael,' a man who leaves her to be with other men, and Vincent (Jean-François Pichette), a computer salesman travelling to Vancouver to meet his Anglo lover. Not quite a love story like any other, it embodies a potent ratio of the conventionality of such stories. Pool has directly cited Roland Barthes's *A Lover's Discourse* as the inspiration for her film. In that text, Barthes argues that a love story is inherently banal because of its ritualistic nature, its utterly predictable repeatability. As a story, it is only alive and new at the level of experience, to lovers themselves who love 'as if for the first time.' And, indeed, the narrative of *Mouvements du désir* follows the classical trajectory of desire through its stages of repulsion, attraction, withdrawal, betrayal, and passionate consummation.

Certainly a good measure of the ritualistic aspects of the love story

stems from the heterosexual articulation of desire where the artful exposure of the woman's body is coded (almost excessively) by an imagined
heterosexual gaze and narrative trajectory.[25] The one mention of any element outside this heterosexual centre is Ishmael, Catherine's former
lover who has left her for a man. Ishmael, however, quickly disappears as
a presence in the text.

What elevates the film from its studied conventionality, however, is the
extended iconographic presentation of landscape and the use of the
train, whose own relentless passage both contains and parallels the narrative movements of desire. For the most part, the landscape shots are not
framed from the point of view of any particular character, and the characters never comment on the scenes that pass on the other side of the window. Individual perspective is always mediated (and displaced in some
sense) by the technology of the moving train, whose velocity and direction over-determine the frame with its landscape vistas. The presentation
of landscape, as such, is not bound to a body but to the externalized gaze
of the camera as aerial shots and shots taken from a crane extended out
the train window abound. Mediated by this externalized gaze, the landscape operates as an exteriorized frame outside the love story proper. Jux-
taposed to the banality of the love story, it is the landscape itself that takes
on the qualities of exoticism and otherness.

Let me suggest that this 'otherness' of the landscape is what constitutes the specular lure of the film within an international cinematic marketplace. As exotic spectacle, landscape becomes a quintessentially
exportable image, a tourist vision, where Canada comes to stand as a syn-
ecdoche of Nature, unmediated by urban blight, class struggle, or political and racial difference.[26] It is an image, as Peter Morris has observed,
with a history. Beginning with the genre of 'northwoods,' filmed in Hollywood in the 1920s with their caricatured repertoire of villainous French
Canadians and virtuous Mounties traipsing about in the snow, 'Hollywood's image of Canada,' Morris ominously reports, 'quickly became the
world's image ... and ... it might be argued, Canada's image of itself.'[27] In
this classical case of colonial misrecognition, Canada is rendered as a signifier that comes from elsewhere.

In *Mouvements du désir*, the separation between narrative background
and foreground is overcome at the end of the film, where, after a bout of
passionate lovemaking, the couple stand on an open platform between
two cars, gazing at the landscape slowly passing before their eyes, a fog-
covered glacial lake nestled at the foot of the Rocky Mountains. Within
the signifying logic of the film, the landscape becomes the displaced sig-

nifier of desire, the banality of love elevated by the transcendental beauty of the scene itself. Strictly isolated as background vista and separated from the personal narrative trajectories evolving aboard the train, the landscape can only offer itself as spectacle, as a specular embodiment of the Canadian sublime. This scene, however, offers scant reassurance of national belonging or a concrete specificity of place. The characters can only position themselves before this scene as *international* spectators, *as if they were watching a film*. There is a kind of metatextual irony here in the placement of Catherine and Vincent as surrogate spectators to a scene not at all dissimilar to those used by Hollywood's 'northwoods' genre films. Here, as in the 'northwoods,' the nation is reduced to a clichéd signifier of landscape whose function is defined as the specular seduction of an international spectator.

This chapter had been inspired by the desire to speak to the differences within women's feature production in Canada, differences that have been determined by the evolution of feminist thought, historical conjuncture, and regional location. Looking at these three films by women, produced over a twenty-year period, though, I was struck by the continuous and common interest in landscape. While the representation of landscape has a long and venerable history within Canadian culture, I've argued that the particular appropriation of this signifier in these films is profoundly shaped by the films' varying discursive and production contexts. Working during the period when English-Canadian nationalism was having a lively and kinetic effect on public debates, Wieland's vision of landscape in *The Far Shore* was deliberately aligned with the tradition in Canadian philosophy that harboured a deep suspicion of the technocratic rationalist definition of nation. Fashioning her narrative around this central debate, Wieland proffered a version of national identity (and of the landscape as the most significant aesthetic embodiment of the nation) as a feminized and erotic category. In Anne Wheeler's *Loyalties* landscape is rather mediated through the particularities of region and location just as the implicit spectator of the film is subject to a subversive shaping of identification through racial and class difference. In both of these films, the violation of the woman's body is linked, allegorically, to colonial histories that have brutally removed Native people from the land and pillaged the landscape in the interests of resource extraction and profit. Finally, the representation of landscape in Léa Pool's *Mouvements du désir* has been profoundly shaped by the international co-production environment. Articulating landscape outside of the prevailing Quebec and Canadian social realist representations, *Mouvements du désir* cites the Canadian landscape tradition, not in the interests of articulating a national social subject, but as a symbolic site of desire and specular fascination.

NOTES

Portions of this chapter have appeared in 'Gendering the Nation: Symbolic Stations in Canadian and Quebec Film History,' in *Ghosts in the Machine: Women and Cultural Policy in Canada and Australia*, ed. Alison Beale and Annette Van Den Bosch (Toronto: Garamond Press, 1998) and 'The Melodramatic Imagination in Canadian Women's Fiction Films,' *CineAction*, no. 28 (Spring 1992): 48–56.

1 Teresa de Lauretis, 'Guerrillas in the Midst: Women's Cinema in the 80s,' *Screen* 31, no. 1 (Spring 1990).
2 George Grant, *Technology and Empire* (Toronto: Anansi Press, 1969).
3 George Grant, *Lament for a Nation: The Defeat of Canadian Nationalism* (Toronto: McClelland and Stewart, 1970).
4 See Ian Angus, *A Border Within: National Identity, Cultural Plurality, and Wilderness* (Montreal: McGill-Queen's University Press, 1997) for an extended discussion on the historical impact of Grant's works.
5 Lucy Lippard, 'Watershed, Contradiction, Communication, and Canada in Joyce Wieland's Work,' in *Joyce Wieland* (Toronto: Art Gallery of Ontario and Key Porter, 1987), 2.
6 For seminal articles on Wieland see Kass Banning, 'Textual Excess in Joyce Wieland's *Hand Tinting*,' *CineAction* 5 (Spring 1986): 12–14; Kay Armatage, 'The Feminine Body: Joyce Wieland's *Water Sark*,' in *Dialogue*, ed. Pierre Véronneau, Seth Feldman, and Michael Dorland (Montreal: Mediatexte, 1987), 285–95; Kay Armatage, 'Joyce Wieland, Feminist Documentary, and the Body of the Work,' *Canadian Journal of Political and Social Theory* 13, nos. 1–2 (1989): 91–101; Kass Banning, 'The Mummification of Mommy: Joyce Wieland as the AGO's First Living Other,' in *SightLines: Reading Contemporary Canadian Art*, ed. Jessica, Bradley and Lesley Johnstone (Montreal: Art Texte, 1994), 153–67.
8 Marshall Delaney, 'Wielandism: A Personal Style in Full Bloom,' *Saturday Night*, May 1976. Cited in Lippard, 'Watershed,' 15.
9 Carole Corbeil, 'Joyce Wieland Finds Room to Bloom,' *Globe and Mail*, 2 March 1981. Cited in Lippard, 'Watershed.'
10 Julianne Pidduck, 'Intimate Places and Flights of Fancy: Gender, Space, and Movement in Contemporary Costume Drama' (PhD diss., Concordia University, 1997). I had the privilege of serving as external examiner on Pidduck's exceptional thesis.

11 Catherine Nash 'The Body and Landscape,' *Gender, Place, and Culture* 3, no. 2 (1996): 55.

12 See Pidduck, 'Intimate Places,' for a fuller discussion.

13 Paul Walton, 'The Group of Seven and Northern Development,' *RACAR* 17, no. 2 (1990).

14 Scott Watson, 'Race, Wilderness, Territory, and the Origins of Modern Canadian Landscape Painting,' in *Semiotext(e) canadas*, ed. Jordan Zinovich (New York: Marginal Editions, 1994).

15 Ibid., 93.

16 Walton, 'The Group of Seven,' 175–6.

17 Daniel Francis, *The Imaginary Indian: The Image of the Indian in Canadian Culture* (Vancouver: Arsenal Pulp Press, 1992).

18 Robin Wood, 'Towards a Canadian (Inter) national Cinema,' *CineAction* 17 (Summer 1989): 28. Emphasis in original.

19 Teresa de Lauretis, *Technologies of Gender: Essays on Theory, Film, and Fiction* (Bloomington: Indiana University Press, 1987).

20 It is this singularity that perhaps explains some of the hostile reaction to her work on the part of Québécois (male) critics.

21 Robert Daudelin, 'The Encounter between Fiction and the Direct Cinema,' in *Self-Portrait: Essays on the Canadian and Québec Cinemas* (Ottawa: Canadian Film Institute, 1980).

22 It is no surprise that Pool credits Marguerite Duras as her primary influence.

23 Chantal Nadeau, 'Women in French-Quebec Cinema,' *CineAction* 28 (1992): 13.

24 The railroad, Craig Brown noted, could never be justified in purely economic terms, as a profit-generating enterprise: 'An expensive and partially unproductive railway through Canadian territory was the price Canada had to pay to "protect" it from American penetration and absorption.' 'The Nationalism of the National Policy,' in *Nationalism in Canada*, ed. Peter Russell (Toronto: McGraw-Hill Ryerson, 1966), 161.

25 Generously pointed out to me by Thomas Waugh.

26 See Jody Berland's excellent survey of the use of this landscape imagery in 'Weathering the North: Climate, Colonialism, and the Mediated Body,' in *Relocating Cultural Studies: Developments in Theory and Research*, ed. Valda Blundell, John Shepherd, and Ian Taylor (London: Routledge, 1993).

27 Peter Morris, *Embattled Shadows: A History of Canadian Cinema, 1895–1939* (Montreal: McGill-Queen's University Press, 1978), 41.

A Minority on Someone Else's Continent: Identity, Difference, and the Media in the Films of Patricia Rozema

ROBERT L. CAGLE

A great deal of scholarship on Canadian film and popular culture has focused on documenting the terms of the ideological and economic colonization of Canada's industries of self-representation. Although Canada's entertainment industries have long been dominated by American-based images and interests, there is little scholarship on the representation of the media either as a tool of domination or as a mechanism of resistance.

The films of Patricia Rozema offer a productive model for the study of the function of communications media in Canadian cinema. *Passion* (1985), *I've Heard the Mermaids Singing* (1987), and *White Room* (1990) investigate, in different ways, the influence of the media upon the construction of identity.[1] The films offer astute observations of the subtle ways that representational norms drawn from popular film and television become behavioural norms in the social sphere and, as such, criteria for identification and alienation. They articulate the many ways that the media can be used to comment upon (and perhaps potentially reverse) these negative influences. They also depict and comment upon the conditions under which an artist, marginalized by gender, race, language, nationality, or geography, develops and produces such representations.

In 'Reversible Resistance: Canadian Popular Culture and the American Other,'[2] Frank E. Manning theorizes a set of terms of resistance for Canadian artists. Manning builds his argument around the phenomenon of what anthropologists refer to as 'cargo cults' – specific cultural movements enacted by colonized peoples that '[appear] to be an escapist attempt to mimic and achieve the "cargo" that the Europeans [have] introduced – money, goods, technology, modernity.'[3] In addition to mimicking the behaviour of the colonizer, these practices also criticize the very lifestyles and rituals that they copy. In so doing, the colonized claim agency for themselves, and thus usurp the power of the colonizer in symbolic terms.

Manning sees similarities between such practices and certain cultural phenomena in Canada: 'Canadians import and eagerly consume American cultural products but reconstitute and recontextualize them in ways representative of what consciously, albeit ambivalently, distinguishes Canada from its powerful neighbour ... The result is a made-in-Canada popular culture, played primarily to Canadian audiences, but exported to the United States in ways that create an ironic pattern of reciprocity.'[4]

Rozema's films reflect this type of ironic appropriation in their illustration, in both narrative and formal terms, of the ambivalent attitude with which Canadian consumers view American products and images. Rozema's films by and large conform to Hollywood standards as far as production values go, yet their central characters are hardly typical of such mainstream productions. Indeed, the characters who populate Rozema's films are outsiders, alienated from the world around them; their only access to happiness is through media(ted) formulas for fantasy – formulas imposed upon them from elsewhere.

Rozema has commented that this feeling of alienation is a concern that is very near to her, given the profound impact that social labels have had on her own perceptions of self and others. 'As Canadians, we're beside this big, chest-thumping, self-absorbed power – a culture that is aggressive, exciting, but kind of obnoxious at times. We've always felt a little bit like a minority on someone else's continent. So it seems like a realistic presentation of my reality to present characters who don't quite belong, who don't quite fit in, who can't pledge allegiance to the most accepted creed.'[5]

Rozema's first film, *Passion: A Letter in 16mm* (1985) deals with just such a character. Anna (Linda Griffiths) is a woman whose single-minded obsession with presenting herself 'professionally' has disastrous consequences in her private life. *Passion*, the film, becomes the medium through which Anna attempts to communicate with the lover from whom she has become alienated. 'It struck me that it would be interesting to write a love letter in the form of a film.' says Rozema, 'From that I started to think of taking other forms of expression and applying them to narrative structure.'

Passion tells the story of a successful businesswoman whose desire to conform to a certain type of accepted identity takes a high emotional toll. The protagonist finds herself time and again separated from her (nameless, faceless) lover, because of her strict adherence to an unwritten set of standards of behaviour. The viewer is presented with Anna's actions (key moments in the disintegration of the relationship) and her reactions (her direct-address pleas for understanding) not merely as realistic portrayals, but rather as the actions of a character who understands the medium and has, in her construction of a 'filmic love letter,' gained the mastery to manipulate it.

I've Heard the Mermaids Singing (1987), Rozema's first feature, takes up the themes introduced in *Passion* and runs, climbs, flies, and walks on water with them. *Mermaids* is the story of Polly Vandersma,[6] a thirty-one-year-old 'organizationally impaired' woman whose attempts to become a part of an artistic community are hindered by her social ineptness and her fear that she does not conform to stereotypical ideas about artists.

As in *Passion*, the protagonist of *Mermaids* presents a commentary on the narrative action in direct camera address; however, whereas the narrative flow of *Passion* is temporarily halted by Anna's monologues, *Mermaids* incorporates Polly's interventions into the general flow of the text. The film is framed by a videotaped 'confession' in which Polly reiterates and expands upon the events that have led up to the diegetic 'present' – the moment at which the film's action begins and, as we shall see, ends.

The film opens as Polly (Sheila McCarthy) turns on the video camera and a grainy image identified by visible lines as video appears on the screen. The film ends similarly, as Polly turns off the camera after finishing her story and the screen goes dark. Polly's role as the agent of narration is thus doubly inscribed: she is the character through whose subjectivity the narrative action is filtered, and she is the diegetic double of the filmmaker.

The structure of the narrative, framed by Polly's videotaped confession, raises a number of significant questions about the film's form and modes of address, and has prompted a number of critics to discuss the film exclusively in terms of its value as a feminist or even 'proto-feminist' text. Rozema herself hesitates to characterize this or any of her other works as 'distinctly feminist.' 'Gender is a category that doesn't interest me.' says Rozema. 'I think we're much more affected by our educational or geographical origins than by whether we're male or female.'[7] Indeed, Rozema is more inclined to discuss what she refers to as the 'distinctly Canadian' aspects of her work – the aspects that differentiate her films from typical Hollywood productions – than its gender politics.[8]

A close examination of a few key sequences from *Mermaids* illustrates how Rozema articulates this difference. The opening credits appear as Polly, in voice-over, speaks into the (offscreen) microphone of a video camera: 'Hello, hello, hello, hello. Testing ... One ... two ... three. I guess it's on ...' The film opens with a statement of discomfort, albeit an artificial one, as Polly finds herself faced with the burden of narrative authority. The appearance of the film's title – a statement in the first person – underscores the fact that one particular individual's point of view – Polly's – will structure the narrative.

The 'I' of the title – a quotation taken from 'The Love Song of J. Alfred Prufrock' by T.S. Eliot – might, in fact, refer either to the film's creator or its lead character. Eliot writes, 'I have heard the mermaids singing, each to each. / I do not think that they will sing to me.' 'Ever since I became caught by that line,' remarks Rozema, 'I have been aware of the feeling, as is my character Polly, that there is something out there beautiful beyond belief and ethereal, and I will never be able to capture it or recreate it.'[9] *Mermaids* is about the desire to create a work of self-expression and the impossibility of this task; it is about the subtle aspects of communication that become lost in the translation of experience into an existing system of representation.

Polly acts out the loss of authorial control in the fantasy sequences. For example, as she develops some of her photographs in the bathroom of the cramped apartment she shares with her cat, she daydreams about climbing a skyscraper in downtown Toronto. As she makes her way up the side of the building, holding tight to the glass and steel structure with the aid of giant suction cups, she spots a woman (Rozema) standing in one of the offices. She waves to the woman, who drops the stack of papers she is carrying and stares in disbelief. As Polly tries to reassure the startled office worker that all is well, she loses her grip and falls off the building. Then suddenly, she is no longer falling but flying through the air over the Toronto cityscape, her knit stocking cap with a large maple leaf taking the place of the (American-identified) superhero logo that one might expect to find in such a situation, and at the same time underscoring the Canadian identity of its wearer. Rozema's appearance in the diegesis at this particular moment seems to suggest that it marks the protagonist's (and narrative's) separation from the author's control.[10]

Polly is both the subject and object of her own fantasy. Her reverie is not built around an image of another, but instead, around an idealized image of herself; it is based in activity rather than simple fetishization. Rozema's appearance in Polly's fantasy (as an onlooker, no less) in effect erases the director-as-author as the driving force behind the narrative, and thus, turns the tables on the creative process. In this sequence, then, Rozema the director is reduced to playing the role of an unidentified spectator in Polly's fantasy.

This set-up writes Rozema out and Polly in as the subjective voice of the film. The narrative, framed by Polly's confession, is enunciated through Polly's point of view and by her control; after all, the story begins when Polly turns on the camera, and ends when she turns it off. Indeed, in the final sequence of the film, the presentation of diegetic reality actually switches from what could be termed a 'normal' cinematic visual presentation to one coded as different, other. The deployment of the medium of video signifies Polly's reassertion of her control of the narrative after the curator and her lover arrive at her apartment.

Up to this point in the narrative, Polly has been defined (and has defined herself) from without. She has depended upon societal norms as expressed through the opinions of others as the foundation of her own self-image. This is nowhere more apparent in the film than in the sequence in which Polly, overcome with a feeling of optimism after discussing creativity with the curator (Paule Baillargeon) of the gallery where she works, decides to submit some of her own photography under a 'pseudoname.' The curator takes one look at the photographs and summarily dismisses them, directing Polly to write a note to 'little Penelope,' the photographer, whom she assumes (incorrectly) is a child. Polly's optimism, her belief in herself, is crushed. She returns home, burns her photographs, and pushes her camera off the ledge of her balcony. It is only later when she accidentally discovers that the work she has believed is the curator's is, in fact, someone else's art, that she is able to reassess her life, her art, and the world around her in her own terms.

As the film draws to a close, we return again to Polly's video confession. As in the opening sequences, Polly is again shown seated in front of the video camera, its viewfinder exactly aligned with that of the film camera. As she finishes her monologue detailing the events depicted in the film, she is distracted by a knock at the door. The end credits alternate with short snippets of action as Polly answers the door and invites the curator and her lover, Mary Joseph (Ann-Marie MacDonald), into the room. Everything that takes place from this point onward is mediated by the 'gaze' of the video camera.

As Polly tries to explain her actions and the presence of the video camera – a piece of equipment she has 'borrowed' from the gallery – Mary Joseph notices Polly's photographs. She points out the photos to the curator, who recognizes some of them from Polly's earlier submission and apologizes. Polly shrugs off the apology and asks if the curator would like to see more of her work. The curator says she does, and Polly walks past the camera as the curator and Mary Joseph follow. Suddenly the camera's point of view shifts 180 degrees and the image changes from indistinct video to a clear filmic mode.

Polly opens a doorway onto a fantastic landscape filled with trees and grass. As the curator and Mary Joseph wander off into the forest, Polly turns and walks back toward the camera. She reaches toward the upper left-hand corner of the screen (to where the power button would be on a video camera) and the screen goes dark. The music that has begun just before the change in camera direction continues as the rest of the titles scroll over the screen.

The classical Hollywood film usually ends with the resolution of some narrative conflict that results in characters being put into their 'proper' (i.e., culturally defined as normal) places. Indeed, most Hollywood films end with the pairing of male and female characters after each has taken on traditionally established 'masculine' and 'feminine' traits, respectively, a phenomenon that has led Raymond Bellour to comment that all Hollywood films end in marriage.[11]

In the case of *Mermaids*, it is interesting to note that at the close of the film Polly is no longer the inept and bumbling character who introduced the film, but rather a calm and accomplished artist, confidently introducing the individual who has been both her role model and her harshest critic to the wonders of her creative talent. Far from being 'tamed' by the film, as is so often the case in Hollywood films, Polly rejects the limitations of the media through which she communicates (both photography and videography). As an outsider she recognizes that it is only her own acceptance of others' standards that has held her back, and not any shortcomings in her own work. Her final act, then, is a gesture of gentle yet firm defiance.

Unlike the characters in a classical Hollywood film, who are traditionally held in the narrative structure by the enunciative tactics of the director, Polly cannot be contained by the narrative in which and through which she speaks. Similarly, Rozema herself refuses to be content with the limitations of mainstream commercial film imposed upon her as a set of conventions drawn from the classical Hollywood film.

Rozema's second feature, *White Room* (1990), comments directly on these conventions. *White Room* shares many of the concerns of its filmic predecessor, but differs from *Mermaids* in its decidedly darker tone, detailing the failed attempts of a young man to communicate his desires and dreams to an uncomprehending and uncaring world. Like Polly in *Mermaids*, the protagonist of *White Room* has come to believe in the idealized images that make up the culture that surrounds him, and from which he remains somehow separated. Because of its more complex relation to narrative models and cultural standards, however, *White Room* requires a slightly different type of analysis.

'Once upon a time there was a young man who lived a very exciting life,' says an unidentified voice-over as the film opens. 'The only problem was, it was all in his head; and when he tried to put words on it, it always slipped away.' With *White Room* Rozema investigates the dynamics of identity and desire, examining how such processes as repression and representation affect the attempts of both *White Room*'s protagonist, Norm, and its enunciator, Rozema, to transmute their experiences into representations. Furthermore, it examines how each of these endeavours is threatened by the slipping away – the escape from representability – of the subjectivity that it attempts to represent. Rozema deploys a cinematic vocabulary of gaps, enunciated as narrative or formal ellipses, and appropriations – both textual disturbances of a sort – to represent a subject position that, like her own, cannot be articulated satisfactorily by the more traditional means associated with the classical Hollywood film.

With *White Room*, Rozema brings together a variety of standard narrative conventions. This strategy unites disparate cinematic and literary genres to develop a treatise on desire and repression. Rozema's multilayered fantasy is fashioned out of bits and pieces of the stories and narrative forms for which she herself is a consumer, stories and forms that reflect the values and realities of a culture other than her own. Indeed, Rozema herself characterizes *White Room*'s narrative development as 'a journey through genres. It starts out with a murder mystery and then goes into a kind of urban comedy, then, a kind of pastoral romance. It's all wrapped up in the ultimate story form, the fairy tale.'

While the storyline of *White Room* adheres to the representational standards of the fairy tale (from its costumes inspired by Prince Charming and Cinderella and its cast of fantastic characters to its final appeal to a kind of magic), its (re)interpretation of the form includes one notable exception. Rozema insists upon pointing out the constructed-ness of the happy ending, and thus rejects the closure and resolution that are the standards of both the fairy tale and the Hollywood film. 'In *White Room* I guess I wanted everything.' Rozema explains, 'I wanted the kind of closure that a fairy tale gives us, in which ill is conquered, evil is vanquished, in which effort and courage result in happiness. But, at the same time, I know that's not true. Every story [that ends happily] ends in lies.'

The (false) happy ending of *White Room* returns to the world of the fairy tale and to the images of its opening. Like *Mermaids*, *White Room* also traces a regressive narrative trajectory in which the end and the beginning not only echo one another in form and content, but, in this case, literally connect; the meaning of the film's opening images can only be understood through the (re)interpretation of the events of the final sequence. Thus, the closing of *White Room* rejoins the opening in a kind of cyclical narrative. This practice works against spectatorial reinvestment in the classical narrative form (desire for closure). Rather than creating a false suture by withholding vital information in the form of a reverse shot, like the one enacted in the famous opening and closing sequence of Michael Curtiz's 1945 film *Mildred Pierce*,[12] this representational strategy echoes Norm's failure to articulate, and thus, to experience his fantasies.

Norm's only recourse is to the world of the mass-marketed model for fantasy: the romance film, the fairy tale, the stories that give hope to even the most hopeless. Thus, the film's dependence upon a fairy tale narrative imitates Norm's dilemma. Its trajectory leads away from resolution and toward a more introspective review of the origins of cinematic fantasy, the fairy tale. The narrative of *White Room* echoes the fairy tale's role as an organizing force that eases the infant's displacement from the fantasmatic plenitude of childhood into the realities of adulthood, only in reverse.

Psychoanalytic theory suggests that what is represented in fantasy (and its literary and artistic forms) is a movement away from language into a realm in which desire does not have to be spoken, and therefore does not miss its mark in the process of (re)articulation. In such a setting, differences (sexual, racial, national, and so on) are effaced. Rozema builds her work around a character whose expression, like her own, as a Canadian and as a woman working in an industry defined by American interests and controlled primarily by males, is restricted by the system through which he must communicate. By withholding, or at least problematizing, the moment of resolution and contentment that virtually defines the classical narrative film, she illustrates the overdetermined cultural influences upon the happy ending as an unchallenged and, by extension, unrecognized-as-ideologically-determined element in the conventional Hollywood narrative structure. She draws attention to the disparity between Norm's wish for happiness and the illusion of fulfilment offered by the happy ending he (re)creates for himself out of the fairy tales and romantic movies that he has come to accept as somehow real. In so doing, she illustrates the gap of desire that separates reality from fantasy.

White Room illustrates the consequences of the American domination of Canada's industry of representation – quite literally, its industry of

fantasy[13] – for notions of culture and self, for the processes of identification and identity-formation, by illustrating the disparity between wish and
access to (illusory) wish fulfilment. Thus, while *White Room* makes use of
typical Hollywood formulas, it reorganizes these familiar themes into an
unconventional storyline. Rozema presents Norm's story in such a way
that calls attention both to the cinematic and narrative rules of representation to which her work must conform, and to the limitations and constraints imposed by these rules. *White Room* becomes an allegory of life in
the shadow of American imperialism.

Rozema explicitly addresses this in an early sequence in the film. On
their way to Zelda's home, a corrugated metal shed in the middle of a
junkyard, Norm (Maurice Godin) and Zelda (Sheila McCarthy) discuss
his career aspirations. Norm confesses that he wants to be a writer, and
that he's begun work on a story that uncannily parallels his own: 'It's
about this guy who sees a woman attacked ... by some sicko that followed
her.'

'And ...' Zelda responds.

'And it could be sort of powerful.'

'And he saves her?' she asks.

'No, he just stands there sorta paralyzed and he feels horrible about it.'

'Nope,' she insists, 'won't work. You can't have a wimp in the middle of
the story. Guys won't identify and girls won't be attracted.'

Here Rozema plays with the prevalent stereotypical image of the Canadian male as a 'born loser,' a 'wimp'[14] who consistently fails to take action
in the face of defiance or challenge. At the same time she reveals an
unwillingness to make her protagonist conform to standards that are
alien to her and to her audience.

The story that Norm tells Zelda is clearly his own (and, of course, the
story of the film). Thus, Zelda's criticism, her claim that a story built
around such an un-macho hero is destined to failure, reflects poorly not
only on Norm's tale, but on Rozema's film as well. In fact, Rozema's
choice to feature such an unconventional hero in her film caused quite a
stir among male critics at the time of its initial release. Several male critics
were uneasy with the depiction of the Norm character, and this unease,
in turn, led to quite a bit of Rozema-bashing in the press. According to
Rozema, '[One] critic told me straight out that he felt excluded as a
male ... he said [the film] made him feel so uneasy that he felt emasculated by it.'[15]

To such criticisms Rozema responds, 'I wanted to create a male character who was not the typical conquering hero and give him a kind of

androgynous quality, emotionally anyway. I wanted to create a male character that I could speak through, or that I could even imagine myself being.' It is hardly surprising, then, that Norm's desires and actions are organized, expressed, and given meaning by feminine others. 'Although the story is told from his perspective,' writes one critic, '[Norm] seems to be an invented male – a straw man in a movie where the real point of view is female.'[16]

Virtually all of Norman's contact with others in the film is with women, and, judging from the manner in which Norman's character is constructed (he is referred to as 'gentle' and 'meek'), especially in the film's final sequence in which he retreats into a world of romantic fantasy, his subject position is aligned with one culturally defined as feminine. Norm is both the catalyst that brings together the various female leads of the film and is the privileged and eroticized object of the film's (and the spectator's) gaze.

With the character of Norm, then, Rozema takes the traditional stereotype of the Canadian male as somehow less 'masculine' than the all-American male and transforms this supposedly problematic image of masculinity into a figure for both identification and erotic contemplation. Although it is Norm who 'looks' and puts the film's narrative into action, he is, all the same, watched (by Zelda, by Jane, by his mother, and by the viewer). It is Norm who wears the fetishistic costumes in the film, it is his body that is the visual focus of the film, and it is he who is nude during the film's only sex scene. Norm occupies spaces theorized as both 'masculine' and 'feminine' by critics such as Raymond Bellour and Laura Mulvey.[17] His 'dual' nature, then, problematizes the foundations of these theories of gender and representation, as well as of theories of gendered models of spectatorial desire.

In routing subjectivity through the figure of a man, *White Room* creates a cinematic environment that challenges many of the basic notions about what a feature film 'is' and how it works. This is a film that looks and feels like a Hollywood movie, but through its representation of unconventional characters and perspectives, illustrates that form or style need not necessarily dictate content.

The most masterful analysis of the limitations of language and of representation is *Desperanto (or Let Sleeping Girls Lie)* (1992), Rozema's contribution to the omnibus film, *Montréal vu par ...*[18] This short film details the misadventures of Anne (Sheila McCarthy), a meek teacher from Ontario, who hopes to find romance and adventure in mysterious and seductive Montreal.

On her final night in the city, Anne finds herself alone in a hotel room watching a Denys Arcand film on video. She decides to get dressed up in her best outfit and head out into the streets in search of a party. She stumbles into what she imagines to be a 'typical' Montreal *soirée* – an artsy gathering filled with beautiful francophones sipping wine and discussing art, dance, sex, and love. It is as though she has walked into the world of an Arcand film. Unfortunately, Anne speaks no French, and must rely on her own interpretations of entries in a phrase book that she carries with her everywhere.

A series of misunderstandings and miscommunications occur, and Anne ends up thinking that the tall, dark, and sexy man (Alexandre Hausvater) with whom she has been flirting is making advances toward her. She then realizes not only that it is the woman (Charlotte Laurier) in front of her (but out of her range of vision) who is the object of his affection, but, as if that weren't enough, that there is a large red stain on the seat of her own dress (she has unknowingly sat on a strawberry). Both the party guests and Anne herself mistake the red stain on her dress for menstrual blood. In a state of utter mortification, Anne weaves her way to the couch and there feigns a fainting spell. While she is lying silently on the couch with her eyes closed, Anne fantasizes that she is in control of her situation, able to manipulate the diegetic action of the film as would an editor on a flatbed – speeding up some sections and slowing or even stopping others – and able to understand the other party-goers by reading the subtitles that conveniently appear at the bottom of the 'screen' of the action. Anne literally steps out of the frame of the film and in front of the subtitles to read what is being said. At one point she even reaches down and picks up the titles to examine them, stuffing one ('Oh') into her cleavage, and 'dissolving' another ('marvellous') in her wine.

Anne's Cinderella-inspired fantasy is cut short by the stroke of midnight and the arrival of two paramedics (played by Denys Arcand and Geneviève Rioux, the director and star, respectively, of the film she has been watching in her room). The two carry Anne into a bedroom and try to find out what is wrong. Anne finally admits that she is not really unconscious, adding, 'I'm not on drugs or anything ...' She then explains her plight, telling how she saved up money for what she hoped would be a romantic vacation in Montreal.

Finally, she mentions the 'blood' on her dress, and at that moment, in a sequence reminiscent of the ending of *The Wizard of Oz*, she recognizes the two paramedics ('Hey, I know you.') from their video appearances. At this point the male attendant touches the stain on her dress and, much to

Anne's horror, licks his finger. 'Strawberries,' he says (in English) and smiles. The female paramedic then asks Anne what it was that she wanted to do in Montreal, to which Anne replies simply, 'To dance all night.' The three then leave the party and end up atop a Montreal skyscraper where Anne discards her stained dress. There, the three drink champagne, dance, and fly up into the morning sky over a floating subtitle translation of the words of a song playing on the soundtrack.

What is exceptional about this short film is that in addition to examining the linguistic and cultural differences that divide Canada, Rozema analyzes the *presentation* of these differences (through speech and gesture) in the media. Thus, *Desperanto* is as much about the properties of the cinematic medium as it is about linguistic and cultural difference. As in the other films, the action is structured around human emotions with strong physical resonances such as embarrassment or joy.

'I think that we are incredibly motivated by the desire to avoid embarrassment and by the need for dignity.' says Rozema. 'If you've ever been in a foreign country where you're unfamiliar with the language then you know the desire to maintain your dignity is stronger than even the desire for food. I've seen incredible examples. I just think the need for dignity is primary in all of humanity. And, the opposite of that is embarrassment. To put a character that I've set up for us to identify with in an embarrassing situation and still maintain an aura of tenderness towards that person helps me personally, and also the viewer to overcome it.'

Like Polly in *Mermaids* and Norm in *White Room*, Anne finds herself disillusioned when she fails to live up to the fantasies she has of and for herself – her 'real' identity falls somewhat short of her imagined one. Eventually, however, like the characters in the other films, she learns to negotiate the space between fantasy and reality by using tactics drawn from the discourses of representation (explicitly from media representations in the cases of *Mermaids* and *Desperanto*, and implicitly so in the case of *White Room*). In all of these works, Rozema examines how characters invest in the fantasies they have internalized from media imagery, and, then, how these same characters utilize what they have learned about the 'medium' through which they communicate to attain some level of contentment, whether that is artistic achievement, romantic happiness, or just dancing all night. These characters perfectly echo the figure of the Canadian whose ambivalent attitude toward U.S.-based products and images both seduces and excludes him/her. Rozema's films suggest that there are alternatives to passive consumerism.

Through these characters and stories Rozema channels her experiences as an outsider – a 'minority on someone else's continent' – into works that deal with subjects and subjectivities absent from Hollywood blockbuster films. Rozema's films are intriguing and complex works of cinematic art that consistently interrogate not only the limitations of a set of cinematic conventions that are foreign to her, but also the potential for using these very conventions as a means of investigating and subverting their social and cultural consequences.

NOTES

1 I have excluded Rozema's 1995 feature, *When Night Is Falling*, from my analysis because it represents a change in the tone and form of Rozema's oeuvre. Whereas Rozema's earlier works all explicitly address the role of the media in the formation of identity, *When Night Is Falling* focuses primarily upon religion and other socio-cultural institutions instead. Because of this, it offered little in terms of material for analysis in this context.

2 Frank E. Manning, 'Reversible Resistance: Canadian Popular Culture and the American Other,' in *The Beaver Bites Back: American Popular Culture in Canada*, ed. David H. Flaherty and Frank E. Manning (Montreal: McGill-Queen's University Press, 1994), 3–28.

3 Ibid., 7.

4 Ibid., 8. Like Manning, filmmaker Bruce Elder notes similarities between Canadian examples of ironic appropriation and models of colonized behaviour. Elder calls attention to the fact that the irony one finds in Canadian film closely resembles the type of irony that Frantz Fanon cites as characteristic of one of the phases of postcolonialism. However, Elder sees the irony apparent in these works as part of an unfinished project – a snag in Fanon's countdown to revolution – rather than a phenomenon deserving of study in and of itself. See Bruce Elder, 'On the Candid Eye Movement,' in *The Canadian Film Reader*, ed. Seth Feldman and Joyce Nelson (Toronto: Peter Martin, 1977), 93.

5 Patricia Rozema, personal interview with the author and Barbara L. Miller. All additional quotations, unless otherwise specified, are drawn from this interview.

6 Cameron Bailey points out the significance of Polly's last name in his review of the film for *Cinema Canada*, November 1987, 25. '"Vandersma,"' writes Bailey, 'incidentally, is perhaps the first Dutch in-joke in a Canadian feature film: it yokes together a common Dutch prefix and suffix with nothing in between.' Polly's identity, then, is articulated through a name without a substance, only a frame.

7 Peter Brunette, 'Shut Up and Just Do It!' *Sight and Sound* 60 (1991): 56.

8 Janis Cole and Holly Dale, *Calling the Shots: Profiles of Women Filmmakers* (Kingston: Quarry, 1993), 183.

9 Karen Jaehne, 'I've Heard the Mermaids Singing,' *Cinéaste* 16, no. 3 (1989): 22.

10 When asked about the significance of her appearance in this sequence, Rozema replied that she was simply the only member of the crew dressed in suitable clothes for the role and, thus, decided to play it herself.

11 Janet Bergstrom, 'Enunciation and Sexual Difference,' in *Feminism and Film Theory*, ed. Constance Penley (New York: Routledge, 1988), 179.

12 Joyce Nelson, '*Mildred Pierce* Reconsidered,' in *Movies and Methods*, vol. 2, ed. Bill Nichols (Berkeley: University of California Press, 1985), 450. Nelson outlines how the inclusion of certain visual material in the narrative supports a 'false suture' between shots, suggesting the guilt of what is eventually revealed to be an innocent character. Nelson unpacks the ideological determinants of such a process in her analysis.

13 The Hollywood motion picture industry is often referred to collectively as 'the Dream Factory.' Likewise, the prevalent fantasy that anyone can achieve his or her goals if he or she is willing to work at it (and, as is implied, occupy his or her role in the American capitalist structure) is described as the American Dream. The happy endings of the Hollywood text, too, might very well be seen as representative of this American Dream, especially in the case of films produced in Hollywood's heyday at the height of the Depression – the texts that have come to define what constitutes a classical Hollywood film.

14 The crisis of Canadian masculinity has been addressed in numerous writings. See Geoff Pevere, 'Prairie Postmodern: An Introduction to the Mind and Films of John Paizs,' *Cinema Canada*, April, 1985, 11-13.

15 Brunette, 'Shut Up,' 55.

16 Brian D. Johnson, 'Sexual Espionage: Patricia Rozema Weaves an Erotic Intrigue,' review of *White Room*, *Maclean's*, 18 March 1991, 63.

17 Laura Mulvey, 'Visual Pleasure and Narrative Cinema,' in *Feminism and Film Theory*, ed. Penley.

18 The film also features short works by Denys Arcand, Michel Brault, Atom Egoyan, Jacques Leduc, and Léa Pool. Because of the film's limited release and because of its brevity, I have included a detailed description of the plot.

Barbaras en Québec: Variations on Identity

CHANTAL NADEAU

If the issue of national identity and the process of *l'identitaire* seem irremediably tied to any film produced in Quebec, the association between sexuality, identity, and nation seems a forbidden fruit. And I am not talking strictly in terms of women and nation. For instance, very few essays have been written about the construction of masculinity in relation to the national discourse in Quebec cinema. Nation and masculinity are generally assumed to be the same – one homogeneous process of *l'identitaire*. Indeed, in their breakthrough articles on the articulation between homosexuality and nationhood, Robert Schwartzwald and Gilles Thérien have analysed the insidious links between nation and masculine and queer identities.[1] While inspiring, their analyses maintain a configuration of national space totally subsumed by issues of masculinity or male homosexuality. The Quebec national space, despite the fear of matriarchy, is still secured as the land of that male heterosexual triumphant shepherd, St Jean Baptiste.

Ironically, this lack of interest in linking constructions of nation and sexual identity to the project of *l'identitaire* with respect to Quebec cinema is even more pronounced when it comes to women's cinema. It is as if the discourses on sexuality, femininity, and desire that clearly map a substantial trajectory through the films made by women in Quebec could in no case be visibly informed by a reflection on national identities. This seems to me even more peculiar because most of the films directed by women were developed under the explosion of nationalist discourses in Quebec that began in the early 1970s. The discrepancies between how 'films by women' and 'Quebec cinema' (i.e., films by men) are talked about become even more acute in the division between a so-called imaginary cinema, which is necessarily analysed in terms of the imaginary nation, and the 'cinema by the girls,' where personal crisis can never be a question of national silence, which is seen as a cinema of the body.

In this essay, I propose to revisit some very important documents of Quebec women's film production of the 1970s and the 1980s in order to offer a way to explore them through a critical articulation of narratives of the nation and sexuality. By revisiting productions such as *La Vie rêvée* (Mireille Dansereau, 1972), *La Cuisine rouge* (Paule Baillargeon and Frédérique Collin, 1979), and some of the films directed by Léa Pool, I argue that, beyond their so-called absence of national concern, these films allow us to consider how the representation of sexuality closely informs the ways that the narrative of the nation circulates. If films like *La Vie rêvée* and *La Cuisine rouge* have allowed a strong critique of the exclusion of women and desire from the national scene, others such as those of Léa Pool have, on the contrary, contributed to the persistence of the distinction between desire, body, and the nation. But beyond their differences, most of the films discussed here manage to address questions of identities outside the parameters of nationalist rhetoric, exploring instead the borders of the domestic and subjective territories and spaces as a strategy of marking differences. By taking on the necessity of questioning the common grounds and common sites of the relations between territory and subjectivity, I open up the debate by looking briefly at some works of the late Esther Valiquette in order to bring a different angle to a too often claustrophobic debate.

In this sense, the films I address here allow us to think through the production of cinema in terms of nation and representation, and not necessarily within the constraints of a concept of 'national cinema.' Through their paradoxes and contradictions, the women portrayed in the films analyzed below participate in a broader reflection of the process of *l'identitaire* in Quebec.

The Cultural Context of Women's Cinema in Quebec: or, the Life and Death of Barbara

One of the first images that comes to mind when I think of 'women and cinema in Quebec' is inspired by a hallmark of the Quebec cinéma-direct culture of the sixties, *Le Chat dans le sac* (Gilles Groulx, 1964). In this black and white feature, which officially deals with the change in social consciousness at the core of the Quiet Revolution, there is a woman, Barbara, who for ninety minutes desperately attempts to convince her Québécois *pure laine* lover that her difference lies in being at once anglophone, bourgeoise, intellectual, frivolous, idle, and dilettante. Against the unconsciousness of the Westmountish rich anglophone woman to *le Québec en éveil* is the desperate quest of Claude, whose true identity is neatly presented as being Québécois in a society beginning to emerge from a long darkness. For Claude, Barbara embodies exactly the curse of a too-long-exposed double identity in Quebec, her sensuality and desire shamelessly blurring the boundaries between sexuality and nation. Henceforth, his predictable separation from Barbara-the-Other at the end of the film emerges as the future nation's true condemnation of both feminine lust and traditional English domination.

Clearly, the 'love'/'sexual' relationship between Claude and Barbara is haunted by the linguistic and cultural duality that arose between the francophone and anglophone communities in Quebec at the dawn of the 1960s, a decade shaken by the decline of the subjugating influence of the Catholic Church and the emergence of a new nationalist consciousness. Through the eyes of Claude, somber and stiff with a sense of his own destiny, Barbara represents the prerogative of disinterest, the non-investment of the stranger, the satellite attitude of the privileged; Barbara-the-English-Woman-from-Westmount evolves in parallel with the 'real' society, the francophone one that stirs up nationalism and the imperatives of a dream about to come true. Barbara serves as a counterpoint to Claude's ghosts in the measure that *she* is the one who will allow him to speak as *he* is creating himself. While Claude's inertia becomes the metaphor for an awakening Quebec, Barbara's incessant babbling chatters away the investment of women in 'la chose publique.' She, Barbara, is therefore the loudspeaker of his conscience; she will be called upon, sooner or later, to disappear. She, the other woman, does not exist; because he, through their break-up, appropriates the processes of identity formation, of *l'identitaire*, empowered through the absence of the other's voice.

Why bring up this film, now more than thirty years old, to discuss contemporary Quebec cinema? Quite simply because *Le Chat dans le sac* constructs the relation to alterity that is mirrored by current Quebec film production. Contemporary Quebec cinema, I would argue, obliterates the territory of sexual difference and renders it anonymous in such a way that the entire space of difference, of identity and otherness, is occupied by the masculine subject. In Groulx's film, the couple acts as a window on the world, where illusion becomes the shock of a palpable reality through the dislocation of relations with the other; the other seen here as the embodiment of the traditional figure of otherness, English, and the sublimated portion of otherness, the woman. The other, the different and the specific, are hence consolidated in one reference: Him/He. One slight exception though: in *Le Chat dans le sac* the marks of identity are metaphorically embodied in the relationship between him, the Québécois, and her, the Jewish anglophone. Today, however, these marks are barely visible, and do not include 'her,' i.e., Barbara, but only him/Claude as he engages with 'them,' where 'them' is most of the time reduced to a pale white figure of the masculine self.

There is another reason for inscribing my argument in relation to *Le Chat dans le sac*. Secretly, I believe that most of Quebec women's films have been produced in response to Groulx's film, in an effort to give voice to all these Barbaras who are lost in the cracks of the national imaginary. If Groulx's Barbara offers a kaleidoscopic representation of female positionalities, most of the Barbaras portrayed in French-Quebec women's cinema, alas, have lost this touch of plurality. However, they have displaced the national preoccupation with the nationalist discourse onto the potentialities of representing and addressing the nation from a subjective and intimate point of view. In this sense, from Barbara I to Barbara III, the trajectory followed by these female subjects unveils the complexities and paradoxes of thinking the sexual other and nation together. Interestingly enough, removed from the tightness of the necessary nationalist agenda that seems to contaminate of lot of male-buddy movies produced in Quebec over the same period, the discourses emanating from Barbara's chameleon performances become a rich site from which to look at the nation with a different eye.

Barbara I

We are at the end of the 1960s and the 1970s are well on their way. Barbara now speaks in voice-off. She speaks of oppression rather than the *Fleurdelysé*, of diapers and marriage instead of the Constitution and paper tigers. *De mère en fille* (1967) by Anne Claire Poirier offers a first glimpse of what would be Barbara's destiny. The filmmaker then consolidates her inaugural efforts further with the series En tant que femmes, produced by the French division of the National Film Board (NFB). The new series will be the point of departure for a whole string of documented stories about patriarchal oppression in all its guises: abortion (*Le Temps de l'avant*, Anne Claire Poirier, 1975); obviously marriage (*J'me marie, j'me marie pas*, Mireille Dansereau, 1973); but also a critical interpretation of our colonial history (*Les Filles du Roi*, Anne Claire Poirier, 1974).

But Barbara also dreams of independence and of freedom. This will be encapsulated in *La Vie rêvée*, the first independent film (with private subsidies) to be produced by a woman in Quebec, followed a few years later by the devastating and difficult *La Cuisine rouge*. While *La Vie rêvée* speaks ironically of dreams built on advertising and of two women's emancipatory detachment from a male world, *La Cuisine rouge* is an iconoclastic celebration of male–female relations in the domestic sphere.

Looking at how the films were received by critics and historians, one can easily measure the ideological tension that divided Quebec film production of the 1970s and 1980s. On the one hand, there is the celebration of authentic Quebec cinema, which embraces the spirit of nationalist discourse. On the other hand, there is a discrete nod to 'girlie-girl' cinema, a practice that is marginalized in the context of the so-called grand political issues of the time: the national question as seen, conceptualized, and 'mise en scened' by the 'big brothers' of French-Quebec cinema – Denys Arcand, Gilles Groulx, Jacques Godbout, Gilles Carles, and later on Pierre Falardeau. From that very specific, narrow, gendered representation of the specifics of film practices in Quebec, *La Vie rêvée* and *La Cuisine rouge* testify to the difficulty of engaging with women's strategies that do not necessarily mount an economic or political critique of the 'feminine condition' in Quebec society. Louise Carrière captures the ambiance of the era in the following terms: 'It was a real dialogue of the deaf between certain male filmmakers and women directors. The former accused the latter of not being *political*, for being disconnected from the Québécois reality. But on their side, members of the boy's club were directing political films which completely ignored the participation of women in calling that society into challenge.'[2]

Ironically, Carrière is among those critics who reproached Dansereau's film for its satire, judged too transient in respect to the 'greater' (read important) social concerns that animated both the feminist and the nationalist movements at that time.[3] But beneath the apparent insouciance of the love dreams of Virginie and Isabelle in *La Vie rêvée* lies the urgency of a generation in turmoil to affirm the need for change, to think of change in more subjective and personal terms. For instance, one can't forget the great scene in which Virginie invites Isabelle to her mother's house for coffee. Just for the record, the film takes place in 1972 – the events of October 1970 are still fresh in memory, and neo-Marxist movements of all kinds are burgeoning. We witness a row between Virginie and her brother Paul about what troubles, or rather does not trouble, 'the girls.'

PAUL: You women, all that interests you are your love affairs and your asses.

VIRGINIE: 'We don't care whether it [the form of government] is good or not. We want it to change.

La Vie rêvée, while betraying a certain *naïveté* about dreams of independence, still offers a treatment in which the address to the spectator is significantly skewed in favour of the female spectator. The tone and the gaze privileged by the film do not seek so much to convince as to pull the women away from a traditional representation that confines them to roles as either mothers or whores. Beyond the playful tone and the dilettantism of the two female characters, *La Vie rêvée* offers a powerful diatribe against a Québécois society that is full of its masculinity and where the other is constantly relegated to a deceptive space, a no-man's land.

In fact, upon closer interrogation of the criticisms of Dansereau's film, it is interesting to note that the exploration of subjectivity as a strategy of referral for a feminine gaze was never raised. It is true that the historical, economic, and political context of the era was more in tune with engaged reflection and concrete, collective solutions rather than individual outpourings on the possibilities for women in 1970s Quebec. And yet, Quebec at that time was marching to the beat of the sexual revolution (including gay and lesbian movements) and exploring the avenues for women to redesign private space in the most public way. In fact, for those who identify the film practices of the 1970s with the years of mobilization and activism, *La Vie rêvée* might sound a discordant note. However, upon closer inspection, Dansereau's film heralds a concern with creating compositions specific to the experience of women, a concern that will be fully exploited in the following decade, most notably with Léa Pool's cinema.

La Cuisine rouge is another film that operates in the margins of the film practices traditionally associated with women's documentary and interventionist works. An allegory on the breaking of sexual spaces correlated to daily rituals, the film is less important for its 'documentary' quality than for its exploration of clichés. With *La Cuisine rouge*, the intimate space of male–female relations is exposed to the tectonic shock of distance between men and women. But the space that separates the sexes is made apparent not only in the banality of daily ritual, but also in the construction of a dreamlike and fantasized female space. In *La Cuisine rouge*, the women play at being, in turn, the invisible Other and the ones who perpetuate the harshness of being 'there,' in that carnivalesque and claustrophobic space within which women have been portrayed and displayed as a form of amusement and entertainment. The film takes on the potentially disruptive narrative of *La Vie rêvée* to sug-

gest that there is no real possibility of reconciling the gendered territories occupied by women and men. On the contrary, *La Cuisine rouge*
plays constantly on the growing and ridiculous impossibility of conflating
male and female spaces. As the men wait constantly for things to happen, even in their most banal expression – i.e., the banquet and being
fed by the women – the women build on an imaginary world where
Sapphic desire and Amazonian dreams dominate their quite inoffensive
retreat from the men's world. The kitchen becomes a public bath, where
ethereal interludes are interrupted constantly by the contingencies of
the real male world. Some scenes in the kitchen/bath-house seem
directly inspired by *The Smiling Madame Beudet* (Germaine Dulac, 1924),
to the true joy of the female spectators. Following Madame Beudet's
inoffensive dream, the film darkly ends with the women accomplishing
the rituals and routines of the so-called gendered positionalities orches-
trated in the dining room.

In these early feminist films, the female space is mostly defined in relation to issues of oppression and states of silence. If some critics refer to
the battle of the sexes to describe a film like *La Cuisine rouge*,[4] from my
own perspective I see, above all else, an effective strategy to map the
social and political territory through the female gaze. The other sex (read
male) doesn't exist in *La Cuisine rouge* or in *La Vie rêvée*. These films refuse
to acknowledge a gendered space, privileging on the contrary an all-
female world. Moreover, what they solicit first and foremost is a complex
set of references that address the female subject through a political reading of male–female relations where men are actually displayed rather
than represented. *La Vie rêvée* and *La Cuisine rouge* speak primarily to the
spaces of positivity where the women can probe their own difference.
This episodic discourse makes the plurality of the feminist position suddenly appear, as much by the position of enunciation that it advocates as
by the liberating happy endings that both films suggest.[5] The enunciative
construction of the two films seems even more obvious when compared
to a film such as *Mourir à tue-tête* (Anne Claire Poirier, 1979), whose fictional strategy of appropriating the male position/gaze was heralded as a
brutal but nevertheless challenging means to confront male spectators
with the horror of their own disgust for and mistrust of women. However,
if to a certain extent *Mourir à tue-tête* cared about 'educating' the male
subjects, proposing a reconciliation, *La Vie rêvée* and *La Cuisine rouge* obviously couldn't care less. The women in these films would rather maintain
separation than offer a reconciliation. They coexist with their significant
others; they don't share. Their independence is informed by their capacity to set their own rules, even imaginary ones. Their unique way of

expressing and shaping their desire and fantasies is the only authentic and legitimate space they will ever belong to.

Barbara II

The 1980s emerge with gaping social wounds and pulsing memories. Barbara has also become a contrite and prescribed body. Some women's films that had abandoned the problematic of male–female relations emerge to look into the issues of relations to the female body. The themes oscillate around marriage and maternity but are treated in much more ambiguous ways than in earlier films, particularly by contesting the traditional schemes associated with the couple (*Le Plus beau jour de ma vie*, Diane Létourneau, 1981) and biomedical power over women's bodies via childbirth (*Depuis que le monde est monde*, Sylvie Brabant, Louise Dugal, and Serge Giguère, 1981). Control over the body is also the subject of a shock film about anorexia, *La Peau et les os* (Johanne Prégent, 1988). *Sonatine* (Micheline Lanctôt, 1983) and *Marie s'en-va-t-en-ville* (Marquise Lepage, 1987) treat the despair of a misunderstood and schizophrenic generation in a silent society. In contrast to the biting tone of an earlier generation of women, there is a more intimate, retreating, almost lost voice. Against a vision of the possible comes a darker representation where dead ends and pitfalls loom. The treatment is often voluntarily pessimistic, the quest for an identity still linked to the strange feeling of *le mal d'être du corps*: that of the norm, that of a generation of women who refuse, or simply do not recognize themselves in, a body that is not theirs.

Hence, alongside the collective but also individual solutions explored in the works of Dansereau, Baillargeon, and Collin for example, films such as *Sonatine* and *La Peau et les os* stress the profound identity crisis that afflicts a younger generation of women. The models of emancipation proposed by their mother's generation find no takers among these young women, such as the girl who becomes obsessed with the figure of the sex-worker in *Marie s'en-t-en-ville*. On the contrary, these films delineate escape (rather than emancipation) in terms of an eccentric other, a position that articulates the tensions between the representation of difference and the self-representation of identity. Denise Pérusse has described this shift in Quebec women's productions: 'A new trajectory is drawn at the beginning of the 80s at the heart of feminist film practices. The cinema of denunciation loses feathers to the benefit of a self-reflexive, creative, poetic cinema. While feminist cinema of the 70s initiates a radical questioning of male-female relations in a changing society, that of the 80s adopts a more intimate attitude, more introspective, branching off towards the imaginary, the poetic or the quest to create.'[6] Thus, in these films the conditions of possibility for woman as the other subject suddenly cease to be conceptualized solely in terms of gender. Issues of generation and sexuality also come into focus.

Just as women filmmakers in Quebec begin to complicate their approach to women's identity, their presence in the feature film industry shrinks away. From the mid-1980s, the domain of fiction is more than ever the privilege of just a few women. Some persist, of course, but the time is no longer ripe for the titillation of the collective memory; the tendency leans more toward introspection. The propensity to construct the relation to identity, even to difference, under the neutral mode of an internal exile maps most of the French-Quebec production of the 1980s. From Jacques Leduc to Jean-Claude Lauzon to Denys Arcand, the tone is necessarily self-indulgent, and, rather than recognizing the other as a concerned party in the *identitaire* process, filmmakers fall back upon the internal universe to express the impossible collective quest for identity. The other, more than ever, has a ceremonial mask, almost banal, covering the figure of a forgotten self, hidden, but rarely uncovered and asserted. On those rare occasions that French-Québécois cinema allows a woman to appear and speak, she is most often caught in the trap of her own absence, constrained by her own silence.

In this vein, Léa Pool's cinema fleshes out a discourse on the internal *identitaire* where the space of the other is returned to the dimensions of an imaginary, a space where difference seems impossible to judge. With Pool, women's cinema in Quebec explores the spaces of paradox between social indifference and sexual difference, thus forcing the gaze to realign the relation between a position of enunciation and a feminist gaze.

Barbara III

Historically, few women directors can claim a 'commercial' visibility in the film industry in Quebec as much as Léa Pool. Pool is the woman filmmaker who has received the greatest amount of support from the organizations that subsidized Quebec's film industry in the 1980s. She is the only woman filmmaker in Quebec to win acclaim on commercial screens and festival circuits. In fact, Pool occupies a privileged position in feature film production: six feature films,[7] two documentaries, and a coproduction in a film of sketches, *Montréal vu par ...* (1991). In fact, as regards Québécois fiction films of the 1980s, Pool's productions stand out.

This incredible visibility might partially explain why certain feminist critics as well as certain film historians have been quite keen to have Pool carry the torch as the harbinger of the feminist/feminine cinema in Quebec. On the one hand, for historians, Pool's films are somehow reassuring. Her films, safely anchored in the intimate universe, voluntarily non-engaged and non-confrontational, diffuse any connotation of politics or ideology traditionally associated with feminist discourses. On the other hand, for feminist scholars, Pool's films have been seen as a cinema of the other fused to a universe defined as feminine, a cinema that represents the actualization of women's cinema as a practice by, for, and with women.[8] Pool's works come to signify in this sense the perfect match between female aesthetics and film production.

This double recognition is one of the points of interest of Léa Pool's cinema for a feminist approach to cultural and sexual identity in Quebec. But Pool's cinema, rather than being a counter-vision, echoes in many ways a vision of Québécois society in the 1980s that is also characteristic of the works produced by male filmmakers such as André Forcier, Jean-Claude Lauzon, and Denys Arcand. In other words, her films do not run counter to the social order within which the other can hardly speak.

Pool's films, both the first wave – *La Femme de l'hôtel* (1984) and *Anne Trister* (1986) – and the second – *A corps perdu* (1988), *La Demoiselle sauvage* (1991), and *Mouvements du désir* (1994) – develop female characters while paradoxically defining women in terms of alterity; they address women but do not construct a feminist subject. In this sense, I would describe Pool's cinema in terms of paradox. That is, as I have argued elsewhere,[9] it is a cinema that privileges a discourse oscillating between the desire for sexual difference and the representation of (lesbian) sexuality as socially indifferent. But in retrospect, even if I still think that this description is quite accurate, I would be more precise in saying that Pool's representation of women is both sexually and socially indifferent. She disengages the possibility of addressing women as sexual subjects struggling with the complexities of identities. She denies the materiality of sexuality as constitutive of representation. What her films emphasize is women as politically and sexually neutral. This is accomplished by providing a representation of women as universal and asexual (i.e., disengaged subject).

In other words, with Pool's films, we are back to the Barbara of *Le Chat dans le sac*. Confined to the most infinitesimal of intimate spaces, the voice of the other is barely audible, a whisper that seeks less to speak for than to be heard. The 1980s clearly mark a move toward subjective positionalities within which the female subject as sexually and politically different is erased. In this sense, the strategies of representation privileged by Pool express a complete capitulation to the intimate disengaged subject. This figure of Barbara betrays the masculinity of a society and a culture that exalts the romanticization of the Other. One could argue that behind this blurred screen of indifference, we witness the indestructible imprint of a feminine subjectivity. The question then remains: how does this subjectivity challenge the apolitical other? How does this subjectivity avoid constructing a sexuality with no identity? In fact, subjectivity is possible in Pool's films only as long as it never confronts the materiality of the other-woman and the significance of this alterity for a feminist position.

My reading of Pool's films is informed by a larger critique of a Québécois cultural context within which the project of *l'identitaire* continues to evolve in an atmosphere wherein the issues around identities are barely distinguishable from questions of subjectivity, sexuality, and ethnicity.[10] In most of French-Quebec films, the coexistence between differences is still silent; when the nation dares to speak the sexual other, any allegory to the nation is, ironically, obliterated. To say the least, there is a sustained consensus among artists, filmmakers, and critics to avoid mixing sexuality and nation, sexuality and identity, gender and nation. And for the few who dare to suggest such articulation, the debate is usually quite marginalized.

Part of the difficulty seems to stem from the fact that there have been few attempts in the 1990s to explore the relations between identity, ethnicity, and nation from different spaces and positions simultaneously. The province of Quebec has never felt so small, nor the female voice so little – barely a sigh in the commercial enterprise of identity. Curiously enough, it is by looking at more independent work, or more allegorical work, that one can rediscover a sense of the other in women's cinema. For instance, Esther Valiquette's stunning production, *Le Singe Bleu* (1993), though traditional in its aestheticization of AIDS and science, powerfully displays a sensibility about the female body that seems to have been absent from more ambitious works. Moreover, her intense desire to see the world outside the frontiers of Quebec reactivates the possibility of reconciling both history and memory through autobiographical traces. As a conclusion, I would like to offer a brief analysis of Valiquette's *Le Singe Bleu* in the context of a reflection on territory, identity, and gender.

Blue Barbara

Historically, a central issue for feminist theory has been the interrogation of the legitimacy and authority of science in the construction of the gendered subject. Politically denounced, culturally revised hundreds of times, the relation of knowledge to science is still at the core of many feminist works; in the AIDS era, science and knowledge are more than ever political and controversial in the ways they (re)trace the boundaries of identities and sexualities. Grounded in the quest to bring science close to home, to reappropriate science as the ultimate mark of autobiography, Valiquette's innovative works constitute a way to interrogate the limits of representation for the female body in a context of chosen invisibility.[11]

Le Singe Bleu is the second film directed by Valiquette, after her first video work *Le Récit d'A* (1990).[12] Winner of a Genie Award for the best documentary in 1994, *Le Singe Bleu* (16 mm., col. 29 min., 1993, prod. ONF) represents a journey through catastrophe and death, a journey within which the once feared other becomes a site of recognition. Beyond its arty scientific representation and sometimes difficult narrative construction, *Le Singe Bleu* delicately unpacks the different moments that lead to the final encounter of the self and the other. Through a poignant reflection on the specificity of the universal within which the infected body is clinically marked, Valiquette's film offers an allegorical approach to the debate on representation and self-representation. Stressing the aesthetic possibilities raised by a set of discourses intertwining autobiography, genetics, archaeology, and history, her works clearly construct medical images as both the stigma of Otherness, and as the only site of representability for herself. The place of the 'I' (herself) becomes then the site of a growing curiosity regarding the scientific imagery of the retro-virus as well as a quest for historical similitude and coincidences.

This encounter between a body reduced to scanner iconography, CD4 T-cells count, the sanitized spaces, and the ruins of the lost Greek paradise of Santorini Island is amazing, though never decentred. By refusing to be seen, only heard, Valiquette makes clear that the materiality of her own identity is quite accessory. Reappropriating for herself the body of the blue monkey – the master of time – Valiquette makes the elsewhere a place where she truly belongs. In this metaphoric illustration of marginality, her work hardly makes room for discourses on sexuality or national space. Henceforth, Valiquette's voice becomes, *a contrario*, the territory through which the encounter with the Other will be materialized.

In *Le Singe Bleu*, archaeological traces and medical records are the only references that make sense of the accident, an accident that would actually give Valiquette both a new identity and a new invisibility. By refusing to be seen according to the conventions of the documentary portrait, choosing rather the safety of the scanners and the mythical figure of the blue monkey, Valiquette questions the limits of representation that traditionally have given access to the subject's identity. In *Le Singe Bleu*, Esther Valiquette as Blue Barbara has fled the homeland. Blue Barbara is now represented by the most condensed, complete, unique representation of human being: a ruin, a statue, an artefact of the past. In the most destabilizing way, Blue Barbara embodies the perfect identificatory process: the complete immateriality of the female subject. In her last production, *Extenderis* (1993), an experimental five-minute video that could be seen as an afterthought to *Le Singe Bleu*, Valiquette reaches the sublime perfection of the uniqueness of the self. The blue monkey/Blue Barbara is now reduced to its simplest representation: the DNA structure. With *Extenderis* Valiquette accepts herself again and uses the most distinguishable biological reference as the perfect representation of her brief passage in this end of millennium. Constructed as postmodern psalm, the video offers a striking quest for the origins of humanity and the incredible archivist possibilities of DNA. Henceforth, reduced to an identificatory code, a simple genetic configuration, the representability of Valiquette's body is completely unquestionable: she can now be perfectly visible.

If some might see in Valiquette's unusual dissolution of the female body/subject a depoliticization of the feminist narrative, I argue that in the most traditional way, she revisits the conventions of women's cinema where the voice, the other, and, to a certain extent, traces that belong to others all contribute to recording the history of the absent female subject. Through this struggle with her own representability as a woman with AIDS, Valiquette manages with *Le Singe Bleu* and *Extenderis* to offer a very subjective representation of disease/herself, where the notion of identity cannot be reduced to a matter of surface.

NOTES

1 See Gilles Thérien, 'Cinéma québécois: la difficile conquête de l'altérité,' *Littérature* 66 (May 1986): 101–14; and Robert Schwartzwald, 'Fear of Federasty: Quebec's Inverted Fictions,' in *Comparative American Identities: Race, Sex, and Nationality in the Modern Text*, ed. Hortense, Spillers, (London: Routledge, 1991), 175–95.

2 Louise Carrière, *Femmes et cinéma québécois* (Montréal: Boréal Express, 1983), 151; my emphasis.

3 Louise Carrière defines Dansereau's film as one of 'self-analysis and self-consciousness,' a bit inhabited by, after all, very 'bourgeois' problems. (Later, the qualifier 'bourgeois cinema' would also be applied to Pool's films; see Manjunath Pendakur, *Canadian Dreams and American Control: The Political Economy of the Canadian Film Industry* [Toronto: Garamond Press, 1990].) Furthermore, Carrière denounces the independence of filmmakers such as Dansereau in regard to the women's 'cause' (read movement): 'As contradictory as it may seem, women filmmakers, while criticizing the ignorance of their masculine counter-parts in regards to women's struggle, do not themselves associate with the feminist movement' (Carrière, *Femmes et cinéma québécois*, 151).

4 Carrière, *Femmes et cinéma québécois*; and Denise Pérusse, 'Analyse spectrale autour de la représentation de la femme,' in *Dialogue: Cinéma canadien et québécois/Canadian and Quebec Cinema,* ed. Pierre Véronneau, Michael Dorland, and Seth Feldman. Canadian Film Series 3 (Montreal: Mediatexte Publications/ Cinémathèque québécoise, 1987), 22–37.

5 And this, even in the suicide at the end of *Mourir à tue-tête*. The structure of the film emphasizes the need for change rather than the tragedy of suicide. Certainly it is a bewildering and depressing ending for the female viewer, yet Poirier couples moments of possibility overall. The individual 'failure' is in fact the anchoring point to the need for women to act collectively. For a detailed discussion of *Mourir à tue-tête*, see Pérusse's article 'Mise en espace – temps des femmes dans le cinéma québécois: *Mourir à tue-tête* comme point d'ouverture,' in *Le Cinéma aujourd'hui: Films, théories, nouvelles approches* (Montreal: Les Editions Guernica, 1988), 81–96.

6 Denise Pérusse, 'Bilan d'un cinéma féministe au Québec,' *L'Incontournable* 9 (April 1991): 12.

7 Pool's newest project, a feature documentary on the life of the famous Canadian writer Gabrielle Roy, premiered on 14 March 1998 at Radio-Québec.

8 See Brenda Longfellow, 'The Melodramatic Imagination in Quebec in Canadian Women's Feature Films,' *CineAction*, no. 28 (1992): 48–56; Mary Jean Green, 'Léa Pool's *La Femme de l'hôtel* and Women's Film in Quebec,' *Quebec Studies* 9 (Fall/Winter 1989–90): 49–62; Janis L. Pallister, 'Léa Pool's Gynefilms.' in *Essays on Quebec Cinema*, ed. Joseph I. Donohoe Jr. (East Lansing: Michigan State University Press, 1991), 111–34; and Lizzie Thynne, 'The Space Between: Daughters and Lovers in *Anne Trister*,' in *Immortal Invisible: Lesbians and the Moving Image*, ed. Tamsin Wilson (London: Routledge 1995), 131–42.

9 See Chantal Nadeau, 'Women in French-Quebec Cinema: The Space of Socio-Sexual (In)difference,'" *CineAction*, no. 28 (Spring 1992): 4–15; 'La Représen-

tation de la femme comme autre: L'ambiguïté du cinéma de Léa Pool pour
une position féministe,' *Quebec Studies* 17 (1994): 83–95.

10 Martin Allor argues that over the last few years in Quebec, there has emerged
a public discourse that configures in a global way the relation between ethnic
and linguistic identity and the people of Quebec. Allor's theoretical position is
interesting in regard to a theory of alterity in the sense that he recognizes that
effect has a fundamental dimension in the construction of the subject other, a
subject other that he links to the perception that the Québécois have of themselves. Thus, he explains: 'I call this broader public discourse structuring in
the sense that its terms underpin a complex network of (sometimes contradictory) statements ranging from the pragmatic and public (is Quebec a nation-
state) to the affective and personal (am I, are we, fundamentally American or
something different; neither traditional nor simply modern or postmodern,
something different: étrange à nous-mêmes).' See Martin Allor, 'Cultural
Métissage: National Formations and Productive Discourse in Quebec Cinema
and Television,' *Screen* 34, no. 1 (1993): 65–73.

11 For a discussion of Valiquette's work, see my article 'Esthétique scientifique et
autobiographie dans l'œuvre d'Esther Valiquette,' *Protée* 24, no. 2 (1996):
35–43.

12 Esther Valiquette directed two videos and one film over a period of three years
before she died from complications related to HIV/AIDS in September 1994.
In 1990, Valiquette directed, edited (in collaboration with René Roberge),
and co-produced with Vidéographe her first video *Le Récit d'A* (VHS, col. 20
min., French and English), a documentary/travelogue that explores the traces
that one leaves. A true poetic essay, the video received numerous awards,
and is now part of the permanent collection of Musée d'art contemporain,
Montreal.

Mourning the Woman's Film: The Dislocated Spectator of *The Company of Strangers*

CATHERINE RUSSELL

The Company of Strangers (1990), produced by the National Film Board's Studio B and directed by Cynthia Scott, is a documentary that takes a 'detour' into fiction. It is a film on aging, with seven elderly women as its subject, that takes the form of a narrative precariously balanced between ethnography and performance, history and pathos. The delicate inter-weaving of documentary and fiction through the thematics of mortality and female bonding produces a very unusual spectatorial effect. As cine-matic and photographic realisms become encounters with death, the spectator is drawn into the 'pathetic' histories of the film's ethnographic subjects. The fictional detour produces a fictional spectator with a very specific history: traces of 'the woman's film' persist in *The Company of Strangers* as the ruins of lost desires, the traces of other spectators.[1]

Reaching its zenith during the Second World War, the woman's film was a mainstay of classical Hollywood cinema. Starring actresses with 'independent' pedigrees – Davis, Crawford, Stanwyck, Hepburn – the melodramatic genre made a direct appeal to female audiences. Often based on women's romance literature, narratives of maternal pathos and romantic longing addressed the female viewer's contradictory desires and sacrifices in highly emotional terms. Production of women's films dropped off in the 1950s as melodrama became more male-centered and as soap operas began to appear on TV. With the advent of feminist film-making in the 1970s, the term 'women's film' became synonymous with the tearjerkers that our mothers and grandmothers used to watch.[2] By the 1990s, however, the rift between 'women' and 'feminists' has begun to disappear as women filmmakers reach wider audiences, and as 'femi-nism' has diversified into a range of cultural discourses. *The Company of Strangers* represents women's diversity and generational rift directly, and in its simplicity the film manages to produce a very complex spectatorial position, one which is at once fixed and shifting.

Seven women between the ages of 67 and 88 are stranded in the Quebec countryside along with their bus driver, a 29-year-old woman of colour. A plot device as thin as that of *The Exterminating Angel*, without the surrealist edge, brings the women together to make a film about themselves. The spectator is in a sense 'used' by fiction to be drawn into a documentary on seven women whose lives are really rather banal. If the film has an ideal spectator, it is not me, or anyone else who can see through its occasionally awkward staging, its tokenist selection of women,[3] and its shaky narrative premises. Perhaps my grandmother, who saw the film in the final, 92nd year of her life, is the ideal spectator, although I don't think she and her age-group are alone in empathizing with the characters. Neither an art film, nor a feminist film, *The Company of Strangers* offers a disjunctive, dislocated form of address.

The Female Spectator

The notion of the ideal spectator hypothesizes an ideal convergence of a spectator-position produced by a text and a real ethnographic/historical spectator.[4] Feminist film scholarship has turned to the woman's film as an historical instance of this convergence, as a site – especially in the 1940s – where a textual spectator-effect might be played off historical configurations of gender roles.[5] Ideal spectatorship implies the 'transcendental' subject of apparatus theory, positioned within the interplay of camera and character gazes, and notoriously gendered as male.[6] Mary Ann Doane has theorized the organization of the gaze in the woman's film most thoroughly, to conclude that the contradictory impulses of the genre engage women's desire only to secure her position within a patriarchal system. '"The woman's film" thus functions in a rather complex way to deny the woman the space of a reading.'[7]

Doane, like many of the contributors to the special *Camera Obscura* issue on 'The Spectatrix,' insists that the female spectator does not in fact exist. The vanishing point of the ideal viewing position, even – or especially – of the 'woman's film,' is precisely the point of her disappearance. Joan Copjec argues that the problem of the female spectator is interchangeable with the nonexistence of Women, because it is only a 'problem' on the level of theory: 'It is only in the unconscious that the signifier for woman is lacking.'[8] Feminist film theory reaches a certain point of exhaustion with the question of spectatorship because it must at once confirm and deny the ethnographic heterogeneity of actual female spectators. The spectator produced by a film text can never be entirely aligned with the differences between race, age, sexual orientation, and class that exist in a non-essentialist conception of women. Equally vital is the difference between feminist and feminine spectators that a genre such as the woman's film produces.[9]

The empirical spectator resists theorization, and has emerged within film-critical discourse partly as a challenge to psychoanalytic models of spectatorship.[10] Maureen Turim claims that in fact the empirical spectator does not exist either: 'only empirical methods for measuring and assessing the individual women who leave the movie theatre' exist.[11] Ethnography is itself an abstraction of otherness. In other words, my grandmother is no more 'representative' of all older middle class English Canadian women than I am representative of younger middle class women. My grandmother and I may have quite different responses and readings of the film, but we are also united to some extent by the film's pathos – for personal as well as generic reasons. My grandmother's impending death affected my viewing of the film as I'm sure it affected hers.

The 'real' spectator resists theory in other ways as well. She resists the 'positioning' of the narrative apparatus and potentially reads 'against the grain' of the text. The feminist reading of the woman's film as the textual inscription of woman's repressed desire within the patriarchal logic of Hollywood, Doane's own 'position,' is made possible only by such a resistance. Thus the woman's film constitutes an ideal point of contact between the theoretically real women of the past and the theorizing women of the present. In *The Company of Strangers* this privileged point of contact is accessed through the oblique recovery of the lost genre of the woman's film.

The lack of anger in the film, the lack of resistant or subversive discourse, may alienate the feminist spectator, and yet the film is undoubtedly a 'woman's film.' Its signs include the de-dramatized, domesticated pace of the film, its appeal to the emotions, and the thematics of female bonding. But the gaze of the viewer who sees 'through' *The Company of Strangers* is halted with the inserted photographs of the actresses as younger women. By disrupting its own fictional premises, the film supplements its sentiments about aging and companionship with a certain fascination with character and history. If the women in the film are both actresses and historical subjects, the spectator also oscillates between an empathy with character and an observation of character.

While *The Company of Strangers* is generically estranged from the Hollywood productions of the 1930s and 1940s, the notion of spectatorship may provide a link. In the first place, the women in the film would have been in their 20s and 30s during the 1930s and 1940s. They are the ideal original audience for films like *Now Voyager, Stella Dallas, Imitation of Life,* and the many other, lesser-known films of the period. Most strikingly, archival photos inscribe the seven women into the film in generic terms. The photo-bios of the women include a number of poses and fashions familiar from the genre. With two striking exceptions, glamour shots from the 1930s and 1940s are combined and followed by images of weddings, children, and couples in each series of images.

The narratives of the women's lives, produced through the fragments of biography as well as the photographs, are somewhat sad tales of sacrifice and loneliness. The fictional waiting game of the plot becomes a vehicle for intimate revelations about the women's different lives. Devotion to family, or, in the case of Catherine, to the Church, has constituted their chief joys in life. In little mock-interviews, framed as conversations but filmed in long-take documentary style, each woman talks about herself on-camera. Constance gave up her art when her first child was born; Cissy is afraid of losing her only son; Beth's son died as a young man; Alice hates her ex-husband now as much as she once loved him. The film wants to redeem these women's lives, and does so through the metaphor of Catherine's spirituality (she walks 20 miles and miraculously returns on a sea-plane to rescue the group), but also through the act of filmmaking.

The Company of Strangers differs from the generic woman's film not only formally, but in its inclusion of women who remain outside the genre's definition of the feminine altogether. Michelle Sweeny, the African-American younger woman, has a sassy presence that serves in the film as the benchmark of 1990 against which the older women's ages might be read. We learn very little about her biography (she has no photomontage of her own) and she seems to be acting, playing the part of the bus driver, while the other women act as themselves. She also acts as interviewer, the director and spectator's surrogate within the text. When she belts out a few notes of a soul tune, it is clear that her cultural orientation is quite unlike that of the film. And yet, because of her gender, Michelle 'fits in' to the company of strangers, expanding the sense of 'company' beyond the senior citizens.

Because it is a woman of colour who embodies the film's 'other' position – of generational difference – identification as a form of mirroring is further complicated for the white Canadian 'feminist' spectator. The 'other' position is effectively dispersed across a multiply determined spectator. Judith Mayne suggests that the model of spectatorship which has been established and revised in film studies has been a specifically white model, and that the 'facile oppositions between "subjects" and "real people" that have characterized film theory' might be left behind by a consideration of racially determined spectatorship (p. 156). In fact her analysis of *Ghost* doesn't quite prove this hypothesis, leaving the irreconcilable poles of spectatorship firmly in place: the analyzable text and the hypothetical spectator(s).

No theory of spectatorship can ever adequately account for all determinations of textuality, ethnographic specificity, identification, and address. And yet if women and racial and ethnic minorities are ever going to be able to 'find themselves' on screen, it remains a pressing issue for film theory and criticism. Race figures in *Company* as an axis of identification that cuts across those of gender and generation, and Sweeny escapes the 'mammy' stereotype[12] only to the extent that she is perceived by the spectator as a 'subject' of identification, of equal status as the older white women.[13] The ideal spectator is effectively coded as pluralist and heterogeneous, and while not *fixed* in either gender or racial terms, she is positioned within a textual system in which these terms determine possible subject-positions.

Realism, Loss, and Pathos

Michelle hoots and hollers when Catherine tells her she is married to God. The photograph of Catherine in her nun's habit, following a shot of her as a young woman, is perhaps the most disturbing of all of the pictures. The tightness of the costume around her face seems particularly cruel, despite her smile. The building behind her, presumably a convent, seems cold and institutional despite the pastoral setting. No commentary is offered for any of the photos, and this one in particular invites a reading of repression and sacrifice. At the same time, one respects this woman's strength of character to have chosen to be a nun. The contradiction produced within the text is very close to that produced in a film like *Stella Dallas*. *The Company of Strangers* is 'like' the classical woman's film as seen by the 'feminist' spectator who is both sympathetic to and angered by female characters' struggles within social institutions.

The photo-bio of Mary Meigs, the single lesbian in the film, is the most unremarkable of the seven. Its lack of narrative clues either about her coming out, or her success as a writer and artist, elides any counter-narrative to the other women's more conventional lives. Meigs has written a book about the production, which is illuminating on several counts.[14] She makes it clear just how much of the film was scripted, designed, and rehearsed, from costumes to dialogue. But she also describes what it meant to the seven women to be actresses, to undergo the physical ordeal of the shoot, to be pampered and attended to by a crew of professionals, to learn how films are made, and to be taken seriously. She describes the friendships that developed between the women during the production and she fills out the fragmentary biographies, all in the same deadpan, slightly distanced, tone of her performance in the film. In a sense she has been luckier than the others to have been able to resist the prescribed fates of so many women her age. And yet her age also links her inexorably to the group, of which she is very much a part.

Meigs quotes 80–year-old Beth as saying, 'The film was the best thing in my life' (p.58). In the local hotel where the cast stayed during the shoot in the Laurentians they continued to be movie stars. According to director Cynthia Scott, there was some initial disappointment among the women when they saw the final film and realized just how far from Hollywood they really were. After seeing the rushes, Meigs comments, 'for the first time we are separated from our mirror-images, the ones we can control, and have become Others' (p.75). She is surprised at how old she looks. 'We have to learn to let go of all our pre-conceived ideas, both about how we look and about the nature of the film. "Nothing happens," says Winnie. I tell her that *we* are happening. The film is about seven semi-old women and a young woman happening' (p.78).

The women of the cast, to whom Cynthia Scott dedicates the film, may be the film's ideal spectators, but, as Meigs suggests, any potential narcissistic relation is dislocated by their age, and by the genre of the film. What they see on the screen does not sustain the fantasy of the movies. Watching the film, the seven women lose their youth, but also their stardom. They become ethnographic subjects, identified only with themselves, not with anyone they might have wished to be. Such an aesthetic of loss is in fact fundamental to the woman's film. Mary Ann Doane describes the vanishing point of the Hollywood woman's film: 'Spectating becomes an affective rather than cognitive activity, and it is infused with the negativity of longing and mourning. The films activate a pathos which embraces and celebrates loss, reconciling the spectator to the terms of the given social order.'[15]

The reconciliation of *The Company of Strangers* is to mortality, which effectively displaces the ideological resignation of the woman's film. In contrast with Michelle Sweeny's dynamic presence, the older women represent the passing of a repressive history which they have survived. Classical music and painterly landscape provide the excessive signifiers of melodramatic pathos fundamental to the genre's indulgence in loss and resignation. At the same time, this expressivity signifies the 'triumph of desire' of 'virtue' in all its spiritual and moral senses, a triumph over the 'reality principle' of mortality.[16]

The photographic interruptions are equally important though, in the film's discourse of loss. If the fantasy of 'the movies' is eternal youth, this film offers eternal age posited over and against the lost youth of the photographs. The women's identities as historical subjects are authorized through this documentation, but, at the same time, the spectator's identification with them as characters undergoes a significant change. They become historical characters who are no longer stranded by a broken-down bus, but who have been brought together for a film. The documentary conventions trigger what Bill Nichols calls an 'epistephilia' – a desire to know.[17] Especially after the first photomontage about half an hour into the film, one wants to know who these women are, and how the film was made: Are they acting? Is this 'really' Constance's childhood home? What can we believe in this film? The loss of one kind of 'fictional' realism is not fully answered by the fragmentary traces of documentary realism. In this loss of authenticity and documentary authority the photographs shine through as the sign of historical truth, ironically stranded outside the present-tense of the film.

Comparing *Company* to the social Darwinism of Michael Apted's *28-* and *35-up* films underlines its different generic premises. For Apted's subjects, the filmmaking process has become a kind of curse of unfulfilled ambition; for Scott's the filmmaking process is a mechanism of redemption. This is partially accomplished by the references to historical events and institutions that have affected the women's lives: the London Blitz, the Mohawk reservation, the religious education, coming out as a lesbian, etc. It is the way in which the film links lived history with the pathos of mortality on one hand, and with the documentary on aging on the other, that gives the generic narrative of the woman's film a radical edge. If Apted's subjects live out their fates of class, gender, and race, the women in *The Company of Strangers* seem to rise above theirs. They do this in part through a humanist discourse of 'meaningfulness' or redemption through representation in true Bazinian style, but the film also has an ethnographic specificity which remains in place despite the aesthetic ideals of realism.

The fictional premise dislocates the women from their ethnographic characters, and then lets documentary seep in from the edges. In a sense the fiction opens up a space for a documentary on a generation of anglophone Montreal women from an extremely intimate perspective. The woman's film encodes intimacy as the pathos of loss as it is bound to the institutionalization of gender roles. Evoking these codes within the context of documentary realism pulls the spectator into the text on the level of affect, but only within the limits of ethnographic performance. The women do not perform characters so much as subjects struggling to achieve identities at the end of their lives.[18]

The concept of the woman's film suggests that the implied vanishing point of a film's spectator is less a formal than a generic construct. *Company* uses very little point-of-view editing, often framing the women through architecture, mediating the gaze, and situating the viewer outside the action of the film. In this way the film aligns itself with documentary, observing the actions of the cast and making them 'other.' The numerous landscape shots punctuating the narrative are unsutured, specularizing the location and aestheticizing the narrative predicament. Far from a hostile wilderness, the natural setting is romantically pacifying. It becomes a virtual extension of the domestic space from which it is so frequently viewed, even if it is rarely sutured to the women's gazes. The landscape interruptions represent the gaze in the film as pensive, distracted, and, above all, taking place in time.

In the absence of narrative codes of sutured (fictional) realism and/or documentary codes of transparent (authentic) realism, the spectator is not necessarily 'positioned.' And yet the iconographic representation of impending death, along with the pathos of the pastoral, restores a transcendent mythology on the level of the film's content – one which is overtly feminized. The ideal spectator-position is one which the film dreams of in its fantasy of immortality, a fixed mirror for the film's real subjects, whose images are rapidly slipping away from them. In the fictional detour to Constance's childhood home, time becomes tangible, but does not stand still. The shifting gaze through history, across the photo-montages, enacts a discourse of memory that guarantees the irreversibility of history. Within the specificity of the women's very different lives, the spectator is ironically 'affected' and positioned within a textual address.

Women's Cinema

Both Judith Mayne and Teresa de Lauretis have described 'women's cinema' as the common ground of films for women, by women *and* film-critical discourse. For Mayne, it is characterized by the recasting of voyeuristic and fetishistic desires 'so as to open up other possible pleasures for film viewing.'[19] For de Lauretis, women's cinema 'cuts across any easy division or opposition between high and popular culture' and 'destabilizes the criteria by which film-critical categories have been set up.'[20] I would argue that insofar as *The Company of Strangers* answers to both of these definitions, it may be exemplary of a textual production of a female spectator, which is neither to say that it is necessarily *for* women, or that it is a feminist film. The spectator produced by the text is in some ways similar to that of the Hollywood woman's film. But she is also beside herself, as a spectator of the construction of identity, as it is traced historically in the photo-montages, and as it informs the performances of character.

No doubt the male spectator is equally affected by the pathos and intrigued by the film's fictional instabilities. The nonexistence of the female spectator confirms the flexibility of the concept and enables it to be inclusive rather than exclusive. The idea of female spectatorship is, nevertheless, an important one to retain precisely because of the continued prevalence of the gendered gaze of mainstream filmmaking. The narratives of sacrifice, loss, and fatedness that lurk within *The Company of Strangers* are reminders of the need to theorize female subjectivity as a function of representation. If the woman's film inscribed that subjectivity under the sign of repression, woman's cinema potentially re-visions and reworks that subjectivity as a discourse of desire.

The dramatic changes that the seven women in *Company* have seen the world go through in their life-times culminate in their own performances as film-stars. From ideal spectators, positioned firmly in their youth outside the text and indeed outside history,[21] they finally find themselves on-screen. That they have become the center of attention in an NFB film produced in Quebec is not entirely coincidental. *Company* is on several levels a highly successful realization of the 'integrated feminism' mandate of Studio D,[22] where Scott worked at one time. Woman's cinema finds a uniquely institutionalized form in Canada, although it has struggled to find a mode of address suitable to a wide spectrum of women. Indeed the pressures on the studio to meet the diverse demand for women's cinema have been detrimental to its existence.[23] Perhaps, like the female spectator, it is a necessary fiction, a vanishing point of women's diversity of desires as they are represented by women filmmakers working outside the ghetto of the woman's studio.

In fact, *The Company of Strangers* was produced as an 'Alternative Drama' in Studio B, and the film can perhaps be more clearly located within a tradition of documentary-fiction hybridity which has characterized a great deal of Quebec cinema.[24] The NFB 'Alternative Drama' series, which includes some well-known films by John Smith and Giles Walker, is characterized precisely by the use of non-professional actors performing themselves in loosely scripted dramas, a technique pioneered by the cinéma direct filmmakers of the 1960s. Scott's mastery of cinema verité techniques enables her to pull off a very unlikely film, but it is crucial that it does not slip into the nostalgia of an ethnographic 'salvage paradigm.'[25] Its different spectatorial address is part and parcel of a redemptive realism mobilized by the discrete referencing of a lost fictional genre. In other words, it is not *any* fiction that is mixed with documentary, but the specific fiction of the woman's film.

The feminine and feminist spectators are momentarily brought together through the fantasy of immortality provided by filmmaking. The epistephilic desires of documentary displace narrative desires and expectations, while the pathos of mortality displaces feminist historiography. *The Company of Strangers*, like many documentaries, is therapeutic in its discourse of 'acting out,' but the performances here are neither re-enactments nor confessions. The act of being in a film brings the women together offscreen and onscreen; and while the togetherness may be highly contrived, the brevity of their time together is not. In the summer of 1989, when the film was shot, the seven women looked like that and moved like that. In contrast to the unchanging pastoral setting, their bodies are decaying, as the constant pill-taking reminds us.

When the mortifying discourse of photography interrupts the cinematic fantasy of realism, the body itself becomes an historical signifier. The spectator of *The Company of Strangers* is also addressed as mortal, as transgressing certain expectations of cinematic pleasure and identification. These strangers are also, on some level, ourselves. It is this overlapping of feminine and mortifying discourses that produces such an unusual spectatorial address, an address which is at once broad enough to incorporate all mortal spectators, and yet remains inscribed within a discourse of pathos that is highly coded in gender terms. The older women are themselves the female spectators who are vanishing, and in mourning their passing we can understand the magnitude of their desires and pleasures.

NOTES

This essay was originally published in *Canadian Journal of Film Studies/Revue canadienne d'études cinématographique* 3, no. 2 (Fall 1994).

1 The notion of 'ruined desires' is drawn from Walter Benjamin, as is the related theory of cultural redemption that informs this paper. See *The Origins of German Tragic Drama*, John Osborne trans. (London: New Left Books, 1977); and Craig Owens, 'The Allegorical Impulse: Towards a Theory of Postmodernism,' Part I *October* 12 (Spring 1980): 67–86; Part 2 *October* 13 (Summer 1980): 59–80.

2 The 'woman's film' or the 'woman's picture' is discussed extensively by Molly Haskell in *From Reverence to Rape: The Treatment of Women in the Movies* (Baltimore: Penguin Books, 1974), and by a number of authors in *Home is Where the Heart Is*, ed. Christine Gledhill (London: British Film Institute, 1987). The most thorough analysis of the genre can be found in Mary Ann Doane, *The Desire to Desire: The Woman's Film of the 1940s* (Bloomington: Indiana UP, 1987).

3 By 'tokenism' I mean the deliberate selection of women with a range of class and ethnic backgrounds for the film, which forces the individual women into the ethnographic convention of 'representativeness.'

4 Janice Radaway introduces the notion of ideal spectatorship in *Reading the Romance: Women, Patriarchy and Popular Culture* (Chapel Hill: University of North Carolina Press, 1984). Judith Mayne, in *Cinema and Spectatorship* (London: Routledge, 1993) is highly critical of the conception of ideal spectatorship, but even she concludes that 'it may be difficult to do away entirely with the notion of an ideal reader, since we all live this culture's fictions and institutions and participate in them to some extent.'

5 Linda Williams, 'Feminist Film Theory: *Mildred Pierce* and the Second World War,' in *Female Spectators: Looking at Film and Television*, Diedre Pribram ed. (London: Verso, 1988).

6 Laura Mulvey, 'Visual Pleasure and Narrative Cinema,' *Screen* 16:3 (Autumn 1975): 6–18.

7 Mary Ann Doane, 'The Woman's Film: Possession and Address,' in *Home Is Where the Heart Is*, 296. See also Mary Ann Doane, *The Desire to Desire: The Woman's Film of the 1940s* (Bloomington: Indiana UP, 1987).

8 Joan Copjec, *Camera Obscura* 20–21 (May–September 1989), 125.

9 Diane Waldman, *Camera Obscura* 20–21 (May–September 1989), 309.

10 Mayne, *Cinema and Spectatorship*, 60–61.

11 Maureen Turim, *Camera Obscura* 20–21 (May–September 1989), 306.

12 Michelle Sweeny's role may in fact be seen as a 'recycling of the mammy role.' Judith Mayne notes that Whoopie Goldberg is really not so far in *Ghost* from Hattie McDaniel in *Gone with the Wind* as 'nurturer' for white leading actors (Mayne, 142).

13 Mayne notes that theories of spectatorship are inherently bound to theories of 'the subject' for an account of the 'positions constructed by the various and interconnecting institutions of the cinema.' 'The subject should not be confused with the individual,' (33) and yet subjectivity remains the key mechanism by which individuals are signified as consciousnesses within discourse.

14 Mary Meigs, *In the Company of Strangers* (Vancouver: Talon Books, 1991). Meigs says that she resisted being cast at first because she didn't want to be the token gay. She complied only after she was sure that Scott and writer/associate director Gloria Demers (who passed away in 1989) were interested in her because she was 'not *only* a lesbian' (17).

15 Mary Ann Doane, *Camera Obscura* 20–21 (May–September 1989), 144.

16 Peter Brooks, *The Melodramatic Imagination* (New York: Columbia UP, 1976), 41.

17 Bill Nichols, *Representing Reality: Issues and Concepts in Documentary* (Bloomington: Indiana UP, 1991), 178–180.

18 A film with a similar task of constructing an identity through a discourse of mortality is Wim Wenders' *Lightning Over Water* (1980), a documentary-fiction about Nick Ray dying of cancer. See my *Narrative Mortality: Death and Closure in New Wave Cinemas* (Minneapolis: University of Minnesota Press, 1995). In that film Nick valiantly attempts to bring himself together, while the film records his physical deterioration.

19 Judith Mayne, *The Woman at the Keyhole: Feminism and Women's Cinema* (Bloomington: Indiana UP 1990), 5.

20 Teresa de Lauretis, 'Guerrilla in the Midst: Women's Cinema in the 80's,' *Screen* 31:1 (Spring, 1990), 9.

21 Of *Stella Dallas* Doane notes that Stella (Barbara Stanwyck), like the ideal spectator of the film, is situated 'in her "proper" place, as contented and passive spectator, weeping but nevertheless recognizing and accepting her position on the margins of the social scene, in a space outside' (*The Desire to Desire*, 57).

22 Gary Evans, *In the National Interest: A Chronicle of the NFB from 1949 to 1989* (Toronto: University of Toronto Press, 1991), 211.

23 Chris Sherbarth, 'Why Not D? An Historical Look at the NFB's Woman's Studio,' *Cinema Canada* no. 139 (March 1987), 9–13.

24 Paul Warren, 'The French Canadian Cinema: A Hyphen Between Documen-

tary and Fiction,' *Essays on Quebec Cinema,* Joseph J. Donohoe Jr., ed. (East Lansing: Michigan State UP, 1991), 3–14.

25 'Beyond the "Salvage" Paradigm,' by James Clifford, Virginia Dominguez, and Trinh T. Minh-ha, in *Discussions in Contemporary Culture* #1, Hal Foster ed. (Seattle: Bay Press, 1987). Pierre Perrault and Michel Brault's *Pour la suite du monde* (1963) is perhaps the most famous example of the *cinéma direct*'s version of the salvage paradigm, in which a rural community play out the activities of their ancestors.

Fragmenting the Feminine: Aesthetic Memory in Anne Claire Poirier's Cinema

JOAN NICKS

The Early Years

Je suis une femme et le serai toujours. Je suis cinéaste et tiens à le rester.
Anne Claire Poirier (1980)

Anne Claire Poirier has been a politicized and influential Québécoise film director, editor, and writer, one of the pioneers[1] of modern film production and feminism at the Office national du film du Canada (ONF, the French branch of the National Film Board) with roots as a producer in the French Unit and the Société nouvelle program (established in the 1960s to effect social change by putting the means of production into the people's hands). Poirier locates her cinema's political engagement in the most important liberation movement of the era, women's liberation, and belongs to that generation of francophone filmmakers in the ONF informed by Quebec's Quiet Revolution (the post-Duplessis era, beginning in 1959). She laid ground in Quebec cinema both as a Québécoise and a woman in a fertile period of the arts, literature, and popular culture – speaking of and to her culture and to patriarchal institutions – and was instrumental in Quebec's new wave of filmmaking.

In her early years as a filmmaker, Poirier was the exception not the rule: 'Je devins donc cinéaste à une époque où "être femme" n'était pas à la mode. Unique de mon espèce, j'était l'exception non menaçante.' She testifies that, in keeping with the board's ideology and tradition of the non-personal documentary, NFB filmmakers did not use a personal filmmaking voice ('moi') or speak of 'mes films.' Underlying this effective suppression of the filmmaker's voice and vision is the board's mandate of social and national-purpose documentary film. Poirier does not attribute this deferral or denial of the personal solely to deep-seated patriarchal thinking, but cites the very difficulty of making films: 'Le cinéma est un métier dur, qui s'apprend, qui demande beaucoup de travail, des connaissances techniques et humaines. On ne fait pas du cinéma comme on fait du camping ... en avoir envie n'est pas suffisant.'[2]

Poirier has referred to herself unequivocally as a feminist, one whose cinema speaks in the feminine: 'Mais quels que soient les sujets que j'aborderai, que je parle de vieillissement, d'amour ou de guerre, mon cinéma sera toujours au féminin. C'est comme ça, ce n'est ni mieux, ni moindre, je suis une femme.'[3] From an individuated voice culturally grounded in Quebec society, her films speak the feminine in a practice that takes up issues of maternity, women's work, creativity, visual representation, and inferior or emerging social positions. But, what makes her work stand out from other women's filmmaking at the board is the reflexivity and subjectivity of her formal aesthetic, in which memory codes are a central strategy. Poirier made an aesthetic of formalizing questions that address not only who controls and constructs gendered voices, but also how these voices effect, shift, and reassert narrative control and ideological positions. Poirier's formal practice and assertion of an aestheticized feminine voice might be termed 'process art,' which reveals its methods, dialectically and in collaboration with other women as subjects and as spectators, and so departs from the 'masterful' artist (male-centred creator) of modernism. Such work falls within the domain of poststructuralism, as interpreted by Chris Weedon: 'poststructuralism proposes a subjectivity which is precarious, contradictory and in process, constantly being reconstituted in discourse each time we think or speak.'[4] This well describes the structures of De mère en fille (1968) and Mourir à tue-tête (1979), the focus of my analysis of Poirier's formalism.

Early in her work as filmmaker and producer in the French Unit, Poirier was directly involved in issues concerning Quebec women. Laurinda Hartt explains that the impetus and research for the NFB's En tant que femmes series (1975–8) aimed not just for statistics, but for clear information on these women's experiences.[5] This series, under the Société nouvelle umbrella, was criticized for being too aesthetic, unlike the vérité-style documentaries of the parallel English program, Challenge for Change, and, later, the conventional documentary approaches of the women's unit, Studio D (created in 1975), both of which produced realist documentaries with a social and political agenda of feminizing the NFB through woman's-issues film. Yet Poirier has asserted, 'I don't believe that because a film is good it is less effective as a means of social intervention.'[6] The term 'good' indicates the aesthetic formality of Poirier's work. She values and asserts the formal power of cinema to be artful as well as committed, following in the traditions of the French Unit, a revolution in film form beyond cultural lessons, and a postwar European art cinema involved in creative and critical change as well as social effect. Poirier has admired Agnes Varda, François Truffaut, Michelangelo Antonioni, and Madeleine Gobeil as filmmakers.[7] Her discursive non-linear structures shift between documentary, narrative subjectivity, and theatrical alienation, as in dramas of formal and critical Brechtian detachment.

De mère en fille (Mother-to-be) (1968)

We can look to early 'proof' of Poirier's aestheticised feminism in her mannered first feature film.[8] The black and white *De mère en fille* sometimes makes sharp formal distinctions between its documentary and dramatic modes, and sometimes theatrically blurs them. In its documentariness, this film centres on one woman's pregnancy, delivery, and the aftermath of maternity. In its subjective aestheticization of this material, the film constructs imaginary flights for the central woman. As memory codes, these flights fragment the documentary-narrative order and lend the woman the doubleness of experiencing the feminine as part of her domestic construction, and of mentally contesting its constricting codes. Michèle Lalonde, a woman with three children, composed the dialogue and voice-over, based on a personal journal written by Poirier when she was pregnant with her second child.[9] The formalized voice-over indicates two levels of aesthetic interpretation: from the actual to the artful, and from Poirier's experience to the construction of female subjectivity as film discourse.

De mère en fille is structured as a physical and mental movement of the central woman into maternity and its imaginary, domestic, and cultural contradictions. This movement is marked by studied images of her caressing her pregnant body, stationed before a mirror to absorb this pleasure; intimate scenes of her husband kissing her belly and their love making; the paranoia of a fantasy of entrapment on a beach; the solitariness of another woman's Caesarean section; and the mind-numbing routines of motherhood. Poirier both documents and dramatizes the shifts between the feminine body and mind in private and public spaces; she thus aesthetically fragments how maternity prompts colliding desires, imagery, and experiences.

De mère en fille critiques the social and domestic codes of motherhood that endured amid the 'swinging 60s' in a sophisticated Montreal, where the film's central couple dances in a club typical of the period. A pregnant woman of the day could play, be her husband's date, smoke a cigarette, have a drink. That is, she could participate within the cultural and ideological limits and freedoms of this ethos.

The domestic cameos of the central couple's life are sometimes romantic (pregnancy appears to be no barrier to sex or tenderness), but pivot around the pregnancy and, later, the unbroken business of the woman at home with a young daughter and newborn son. This is bourgeois life in the late 1960s, initially played out by the young mother (a model? an actor?) and her pre-school-age daughter as a charmed suburban existence that appears to revolve around the family's pool. In the routines and ritualized mental escapes that Poirier constructs out of her documentation and dramatization of this family, sharp gender distinctions emerge. The wife-mother is a constant presence, the husband-father a sweetly romantic but mostly absent figure. The wife-mother does not complain, but indulges in voice-over reveries that drift through the film with her as she wanders the city, observing. Her subjective looking is rendered in highly stylized imagery and dramatized mental escapes, in contrast to the unvarnished scenes of childbirth (both a natural birth and a Caesarean section).

The stark excesses of the constructed beach fantasy have the central pregnant woman trapped in a large round cage, looking out at stony-faced models and plastic mannequins. Posed in balloon-shaped garments that pass for fashion, they are a travesty of femininity's excess. From the trapped mother and glamour's static 'lookers,' the scene cuts to a close up of the film's other pregnant woman alone in labour. This is woman's work indeed, and this scene is as stark in its documentation of actual labour and birth as the prior scene is absurdly surreal in its fabrication of femininity's traps. In a period of Quebec culture not yet changed by the modern women's movement, Poirier highly values women's bodies.

With the birth of the central woman's second child, she acts out another surreal reverie, which begins with her pushing a bassinet down a long unmarked passage lit with only intermittent spotlights. Through this theatrical shadow-and-light interplay, she appears to move in and out of consciousness as if with blind purpose. She enters an empty room, opens the window, feels the snow against her face, then pushes the bassinet out the window. In a reverse shot, angled upward from the bottom of a long elegant staircase, the bassinet tumbles downward in slow motion. This scene pointedly recalls the Odessa Steps sequence in *Battleship Potemkin* (Eisenstein, 1925) where the baby carriage careens downward, signifying the momentum of the revolution, as the wounded mother dies at the top of the stairs. Poirier's scene prompts Quebec audiences of the period to think aesthetically and referentially, and to place her central woman and *De mère en fille* within the scope of revolutionary cinema and women. Her fabrication of a woman's non-maternal imagination ironically questions the sacrificing mother within film history. Yet Poirier's structuring does not retain only an imaginative, expressive position on this woman. The next scene returns the film to the woman's maternal pleasure and domestic order, as she explains to her daughter the images and stages of fetal life depicted in a pictorial feature in *Life* magazine. However, even this documentary return concentrates on the mother and daughter's reflection on photographic imagery, which is structured into an ideal visual narrative of the embryo's development.

Earlier, this woman's imagined scenario, while being prepared for her Caesarean section, formally overdetermines a traditional feminine fear expressing maternal responsibility and guilt: if she dies her children will be orphaned (from her subjectively wandering perspective, the camera pans sleeping children in a dorm). This mental drama (like the 'bad mother' reverie) is hived off from the husband's minimal experience in the hospital, through a sharp structural juxtaposition that maintains Poirier's focus on the distinctions and paradoxes of feminine experience. He is the smiling father gazing at his new son from the corridor of the glassed-in nursery, physically incapable of his wife's experience and unaware of her fear of dying (the orphanage dream, albeit one induced by the anaesthetic). Poirier does not 'blame' the father for his biological difference and, therefore, his minimal role; rather, she lets the camera linger on the pleasure of his spectator's position as admiring parent. But, in the short bedroom scene depicting the couple's mutual interest in post-natal sex, she carries forward his spectator's position as husband more formally. The loving couple is framed so theatrically – from behind the husband (his back to the camera) propped on the bed – that they appear to be cued by Hollywood's construction of the male gaze in scenes of sexual intimacy. The woman disrobes, the man watches, admiring spectator of the feminine. The tableau-like formality doubly pitches us into his viewing position and distances us from his passive watching. The gender-coded performances – his and hers – that frame heterosexual desire are destabilized. Through formal framing and detachment from the husband's posed watching, as well as from the wife's mannered gestures, Poirier deconstructs the male look at feminine striptease. At once, we are placed inside and outside the fourth wall of the bedroom scenario, and thus inside and outside the camera's reflection on voyeurism at work. This scene, indeed the film itself – Quebec's first feature by a woman –

predates the first wave of feminist film as well as Laura Mulvey's claim that 'mainstream film and the pleasure it provides can be challenged,' but only by breaking down 'the cinematic codes [that] create a gaze ... an illusion ... cut to the measure of desire.'[10]

In part, Poirier's developing style can be seen as a retort to the NFB's Anglo tradition of 'the picturesque,' which goes back to the institution's upbeat wartime propaganda films committed to cultural wholeness. Centrally, her style was a feminist re-visioning of her culture's depiction of women. Though, like her male peers, Poirier absorbed the regional consciousness of cinéma direct into her film practice,[11] she prominently invested herself in Quebec women as film and social subjects, simultaneously critiquing the maleness of Quebec nationalism in the 1970s.

She takes a historical view of this maleness in the powerful *Les Filles du Roi* (*They Called Us 'Les Filles du Roy'*) (1974). In the film's coda, set in a studio space, Poirier appears on screen to unwrap a 'mummified' woman of her symbolic bandages, a powerful sign of returning humanity to the forgotten woman in Quebec's Quiet Revolution and of reconfiguring *la québécoise* in feminist terms. Unveiled by Poirier, the naked woman remains standing in well-lit view of the camera, as the female voice-over dismantles the hitherto male look at *la québécoise* as a 'porno' figure:

Let's have our very own striptease, one that won't hurt for once ...
You call me Valérie
One day they dreamed up a Valérie ...
It was our first skin flick
At last, the uncensored body of *la québécoise*, as if all those old lies were about to be unmasked
But there is no real Valérie, except perhaps inside your own head.[12]

As the camera tracks back slowly and the light fades, Poirier's revealed woman remains visible in the opaque whiteness. No longer a *fille du roi*, her image appears to be impregnated into the screen, and her presence imprinted in a re-visioned québécois cinema.

Mourir à tue-tête (*A Scream from Silence*) (1979)

Once in a while my mind slips and I think I am back in my dream and that I have shut the door, the one without a handle on the inside. I imagine that tomorrow I will be pounding and screaming to be let out, but no one will hear, no one will come.
Marilyn French, *The Women's Room* (1977)

Mourir à tue-tête (U.S. title, *The Primal Fear*) is the most central of Poirier's films. It belongs to that first wave of Canadian women's production addressing cultural, human, and legal topics such as rape and domestic abuse, for audiences well prepared by feminism and ready to debate the confrontation evoked by the film, particularly around the long opening rape scene and the ironic sense of injustice with which the film ends.[13] The film's formality, which is key to the rape scene, as to the whole, needs to be understood within this multiple frame of aesthetics, spectatorship, confrontation, and 1970s feminism. This integration continues the core of my argument on Poirier's fragmentation of the feminine through memory codes. *Mourir à tue-tête* never allows itself an unqualified realist look or narrative linearity, existing instead on the aesthetic edges that understand realism without employing its seamless devices and ideology. It is propelled by ruptures that remember the aestheticized dialectical processes of its own narrative form through a recall-and-recover structure.

Poirier's structural manner and irony in *Mourir à tu-tête* are close to postwar European cinemas and the rethinking of film practices and narrative forms within national cultures fractured by war. She looks in the direction of Godardian didacticism, ideological commitment, and the materiality[14] of film composition in aestheticizing content. *Mourir à tue-tête*'s discursive structure de-familiarizes patriarchal dogma, beginning with the rapist's discontinuous dramatic monologue that expresses a dark, parochial culture. Here, as in three other interjections, the diegesis is broken by simulated documentary sequences in which the director and editor (Monique Miller plays the director and Micheline Lanctôt the editor) comment on the fiction that begins with the lengthy rape scene. In these shifts from fiction to documentary-like debate on issues of narrative construction, women's collaboration becomes an aesthetic and ethical necessity in Poirier's feminizing voice and vision. The symbolic tableau-scene of women's testimony against patriarchy works similarly, with different women (played by a cast of well-known Quebec actresses) speaking and unmasking before an unseen judge identifiable only by his judicial rhetoric. The church-like setting, bathed in shafts of light that illuminate the women, becomes a paradoxical site of patriarchal orthodoxy (the judge's off-screen voice) and polyphonic feminist heresy (a literal and figurative chorus of protesting women). These devices assume interior and exterior listeners; that is, the women hear each other, but speak directly to the screen, implicating us in analytical spectatorship, similar to the function of the on-screen fictive director and editor debating representational and narrative control and spectatorship.

The film's initial shots of a male director at work in a studio establishes cinema, not society, as the pertinent source for Poirier's feminist filmmaking. Poirier acknowledges that all filmmaking works within the shadows of whatever aesthetic practices are adopted. Cinematographer Michel Brault's lighting – expressionistic underexposure and impression-istic overexposure – plays off its extreme pallet to strip colour of its trans-parency and the film object of its seduction. Like the male director in the prologue, even Poirier's sensitized female director and editor operate within dimly lit spaces (a production studio and an editing room). But the film's intermittent return to the editing room codifies a space that women artists must occupy to redirect film discourse.[15]

In this vein, Poirier opens up the aesthetic and historical dimensions of feminist film with formal interpolations of black-and-white stock-shot and constructed footage dissolving in and out of the narrative at key points. The inserts include images of Vietnamese war victims, an actual clitori-dectomy, and French women collaborators in the Second World War hav-ing their heads shaved as a form of public humiliation. Structured as media memories emanating from within and without the nurse's percep-tual disorientation following her rape, and during examination by the male doctor, they show the resonance of the historical victimization of women. I am inclined to term this referential strategy the persistence of feminist vision, mindful that Poirier's use of archival footage is always bracketed by tight and medium close-ups of the nurse (Julie Vincent) in a waking nightmare state. In other words, Poirier not only contextualizes the rape narrative, but the nurse's fictional condition mentally seeks the intervention of women filmmakers in constructing stories of women's devaluation in global histories.

Two related examples of the historical-memory links between the nurse's story and the archival and non-archival footage further illuminate this strategy of women's interventions. The newsreel footage of Vietnam, wherein wandering women are peripheral silent subjects of war, is inter-woven with Poirier's coded close-ups and group-shot tableaux of Asiatic women. Sometimes they look outward past the frame, sometimes upward toward the screen, as if formally seeking supportive, creative, and social sources – arguably, women filmmakers and spectators. This insert follows the stark close-up of the nurse-victim's mirror reflection in the aftermath of her rape. Her overdetermined scream continues into the archival and constructed imagery just described and is attached to overdubbed African throat chanting. Thus the nurse's lingering scream becomes an aesthetic sign: the voice that carries the remembered imagery of damaged spirits within women's histories. But the dissolve that returns the film to the nurse's story finds her virtually silenced, lying in an examining room before a doctor who faces the screen. In other words, the damaging of women's spirits persists without closure or recourse in patriarchal structures. However, as with the rape scene, the camera takes the nurse's perspective from the foreground of the film frame. From this vantage point, over the spatial plane of the nurse's body, the male doctor and medical photographer become problematized as woman's scrutineers.

Yet, Poirier does not allow women viewers to escape her cultural critique. Archival footage of a ritual clitoridectomy, performed on a girl by unspeaking female handmaids in unnamed African territory, is inserted between the scenes of the nurse's examination by the doctor and her questioning by the policeman. The notion that female empathy is universal is thrown into stark disarray in this anthropological example of martyrdom facilitated by women, underscored by the humming lament of a female voice on the soundtrack. The wounding clitoridectomy, painful to view, is remembered symbolically in the nurse's story in the three stigmatic bruises marking her forehead, mouth, and neck, after her rape. Women's martyrdom (akin to the sacrifice of female desire in the clitoridectomy, and the nurse's wounding in the rape) runs through myth and women's history, a view Poirier aesthetically embeds both in the church-set testimonial scene and the Catholic codification of the nurse's eventual suicide. Here, Silvia Bovenschen's general commentary on 'a feminine approach to art' captures an emphasis on the eternal victim in 1970s feminism: 'The hidden story of women, which reveals itself to us as primarily one of suffering and subjugation ... is the dark side of cultural history – or better, the dark side of its idealised version.'[16]

Screening Rape's Expressionist Face

Mourir à tue-tête addresses some of the deepest dilemmas for feminist filmmaking and film culture in a period of much theorizing (including Mulvey's work). The opening rape scene, some fifteen minutes long, is a paradigm of the gender politics confronting feminists in the 1970s. The unflinching camera, positioned from the woman's point of view,[17] maintains its perspective on the rapist (Germain Houde) as if privileging a documentary subject with a story to tell. With her back to the camera, the nurse is positioned in the space 'occupied' by the viewer, a space that also marks the feminist screen through which we see and hear the rapist's confessional monologue. We learn at the end of the scene that it is undergoing editing by the watching filmmakers. The film's conceit is that a working cut of a narrative is being re-screened in progress and in retrospect by the director and editor, crucial to Poirier's own discursive shaping of memory as an aesthetic practice. The rapist's right to determine the nurse's speechlessness in the van accrues from his phallocentric authority over the woman and, seemingly, over the film frame. But Poirier's narrative and analytical separations evolve out of the scene's simultaneously victimized and feminized point-of-view, as control shifts (through a freeze frame of the rapist's contorted face, and a cut to the darkened editing room) to the two women who constructed the scene. They stop the rapist's voice and control with the flick of a switch. Their technical control will determine the aesthetics and ideology of re-presenting rape in and as film. This overriding reflexivity emerges out of the viewing and working space of Poirier's two stand-ins. In the editing room, women's work involves structuring and repositioning spectatorship through an interrogation of image-making processes. Here lies Poirier's inscription of feminist creativity and analytical control that takes the subversive text and informed spectatorship as norm.

Mourir à tue-tête's studied compression of aestheticized feminist gestures alters formulaic patriarchal habits. Its strategic operation is rooted in the project of 1970s feminism to reform film discourse. For Poirier's internal director and editor, the melodramatic victim, who ultimately loses even her ability to scream at the seizure of her composite emotional, cultural, and aesthetic voice, must be rewritten. Re-screened. Re-framed. Thus the ubiquitous rapist is rendered as specimen cutting across type – guru, protector, husband, boss, stranger, spectator, with a male director as the 'prime suspect' – all caught in the film's prologue through freeze framing, for various women's extra-diegetic identification ('Yes, that's him'). Why, the film challenges, is this specimen under examination capable of playing extremes, antagonist as well as protagonist? Why do his institutionalized forms (artist, doctor, policeman, judge) abstract woman into a benign hostage tied to an alien frame, as with the narrative's victim in the rape scene? Deploying the same actor (Germain Houde) in the prologue, in familiar settings, cultural roles, and professions, Poirier isolates the potential rapist as a schematically recollected anyman.[18] This distinction of anyman, as opposed to everyman, is important for male viewers to understand in retrospect, given some of the early male outrage at this film.[19] Anyman is culturally, not personally, accusatory, and, in the scene's duration, viewers can come to understand the film's rapist as a cultural victim who victimizes.

The prologue frames the narrative establishment of a worst-case rape scenario, the lone woman randomly attacked. After working a night shift, a young nurse is abducted by a stranger and thrown into his van. Making the victim a nurse identifies the vulnerability of the female care-giver who, theoretically, might be deemed capable of surviving rape. The man's aggression ('I'll hit you if you scream') suspends the victim's speech. His now familiar face recalls for us the male director at work in the dimly lit studio. The stranger's old van suggests anyman's 'Black Maria,' site of contemporary blue movies, perhaps a travesty of Quebec's 'maple syrup porno' films[20] and an allusion to the 1970s infatuation with customizing vans for sexual conquest.[21] The dramatic action is from the rapist, though the scene's emotional and structural weight is determined by the victim's framing. From the victim's captive positioning, we are privileged witnesses of the rapist's processes, psychology, and rhetoric – his anti-heroic performance. Poirier's trust in the stationary camera's revealing eye, and the scene's temporal unfolding in what seems like a single manipulated shot, conjoins the Lumière and Méliès traditions at the roots of film history. This replication of 'primitive' screen space through the stationary camera, trained on the rapist's assault forces empathetic and critical feminized spectatorship against masculine domination, for we only view the rapist from the nurse's sightline. The male viewer is not excluded from this aestheticized sightline (similar to other alternative positionings, such as 'queer looking'), for no viewer could identify with Poirier's rapist. The rapist imitates the gaze and command of the looka-like male director of the film's prologue, providing us with a sharp distinction between identification and critical understanding of the scene's dynamics.

With this critical framework in mind, the rapist's (direct address) monologue of angry despair sits both outside and inside the victim's captive purview. Through flashing intercuts in which the screen turns red whenever the victim is struck, Poirier establishes a digressive colour field for both the woman's pain and the rapist's rage. Theoretically, the rapist's attacks on the woman can be read as attacks on Poirier's feminist camera and, simultaneously, as her diffusion of Hollywood's voyeuristic pleasure and the shot–reverse shot system. After the rapist ties up his victim, ordering that he wants to hear her fear, the screen goes black each time he strikes her. Lacking light, the image dies, anticipating the narrative closure of the nurse's suicide at the end of the film, which is defined by the leaching of light and thus her passing image.

The rapist's verbal abuse is self-directed as well as accusatory: a soliloquy of indeterminate duration, paced by internal dissolves. Sitting on a beer case, he speaks to his captive, though his manic glances are also directed outward to the female space inhabited by Poirier's camera and by us as receivers of his look. He is fixed within the film frame, yet seems capable of crossing over into the spectator's private space as he speculates about the nurse's sexuality with her 'nice doctor' (fiancé). We recognize something culturally familiar in his unkempt appearance and chronic beer drinking, a clichéd figure resentful of the Canadian or, more pointedly, the Quebec society that has failed him, and very like Denys Arcand's rampaging rural gang in *Gina* (1974), depicted as rapists of *la québecoise*, embodied in the stripper. In the van's low light, Poirier's archetypal rapist is a shadowy, unshaven persona with a mentality born of deep hate, arrested development, and helplessness. He conveys a confessional need to expose his emotional lack within a closed, dark setting – employing the rhetoric of a sinner or an analyst or a director, who names his sins in order to repeat them against a spectator rendered incapable of stopping him. The victim's loss of speech as she cowers in the foregrounded lower corner of the van is the sign of her conditioned silence. She connotes a terrorized listener condemned to inaction, central to the rape scenario and, symbolically, to captive spectatorship.

With the camera's perspective over the victim's shoulder, Poirier enters a composition of rape, a site of trespass and extreme visual distortion. Poirier's theatrical training comes to bear here (and variously throughout the film). The film frame is effectively 'broken,' much as stage actors are said to 'break' the proscenium arch and the boundaries of their playing space to pull the live audience into the processes or conditions of the stage 'world.' In close proximity, with her sprawled legs and her arms pinned in the foreground of the frame, the victim's position is formally alienating, as the rapist cuts off her 'disguises' (her white uniform and pantyhose suggest her 'virgin ways') to dismantle her image ('fucking little slut') – Madonna and whore. The closer the rapist is to his victim, and to the camera, the more contorted is his persona and the greater the distance from his hysterical melodrama. Tight shots detail the rapist's shaky mentality, along with his victim's quivering body, yet the scene pivots on the problems of cinematically gazing at rape, enforced by the rapist's comment that his bound and undressed victim looks 'stupid.' This access – Laura Mulvey's notion of the audience's 'passionate detachment'[22] in practice – positions us as critical spectators to detach our gaze from the rapist and, more complexly, from the nurse's experience as narrative. Unlike the rapist, however, our sentiments as female spectators are summoned by her very subjugation as screen victim.

I want to recircle briefly the rape scene's aesthetics to cite the anthropological implications of the rapist's ritualized emanation of phallic failure and gender supremacy ('When you can piss standing up we can talk'). The rapist laments his failure with women, then in turn spits beer and urinates on his victim. And on the screen. In its primitivism, this travesty of ejaculation reveals the rapist's emotional and cultural projection. From his perspective, the woman before him is mere surface, for his manipulation and framing, as with cinema's common coding of the female. From our perspective, we are privy to formal and ideological problems: the female is fixed at the surface of the image, while the male seems to occupy spatial depth. In his violent penetration of the woman (extremely foregrounded in the frame), the rapist loses all visual and spatial characteristics of depth.

The closing of the scene is cued formally by a freeze-frame close-up of the rapist's twisted face. Reminiscent of the boxed subjects of Francis Bacon's paintings (grotesque male figures melting under their very plasticity), the rapist's face is his narrative summary. He is the deferred subject of the fictional women filmmakers' analytical gaze. In the interests of feminist discourse, the woman director identifies the rape scene as a 'point of reference.' It is also a signifier of formal narrative departure from the rapist-victimizer's control of the image, not only of his narrative victim, flagged in the director's remark that 'rape forms no couple.'

This conjunction of reference and deferral obtains in Poirier's appositional endings, which serially split off into a triad rupturing narrative, aesthetic, and authorial absoluteness. Ending One involves the female subject's narrative stasis (the death throes of the nurse's will). Ending Two involves problems of discourse regarding the nurse's narrative condition (the third dialogue between the internal director and her editor). Ending Three involves the aesthetics of mythic closure (the nurse's death state). The ironic coda thrusts the film outside itself into the cultural space that women occupy, the social arena. This echoes the strategies of informed spectatorship that shape and drive the rape scene beyond narrative incident.

Ending One: The Victim Silenced

The nurse's inability to re-experience love inflects the testimonial-church scene, which Poirier has called 'the affidavit.'[23] When he leaves both the bed and the house without a word, the fiancé, Philippe, abandons Suzanne to the devices of the lost victim. Named only late in the film, the character has her identity and victimization merged. The camera tracks back from her fetal curl to reveal her resting on her bed as on a sacrificial alter, a freeze-frame pietà. In the bathroom, Suzanne rehearses her responses following the rape, mimicking, as if through aesthetic reflex, artist Edward Munch's androgynous otherly figure in his painting *The Scream*. Art provides neither solace nor solution, only the potential of comprehension through aesthetic memory. Ritually, the woman summons up the nurse within to prepare to die. She slips on a fresh white nightgown then looks blankly into the mirror. Putting hand to mouth before the mirror, she appears to sanction the reflected image of the detached woman about to take the pills. We are left to ponder momentarily her reflection upon a mirror reflection of herself as an aestheticized doomed victim.

Ending Two: The Victim Restored

A discursive rupture, Ending Two structurally parallels the women filmmakers' initial analysis of the rape scene. The two women informally discuss narrative closure (Suzanne's preparation for death) as a problem in representation. Ever challenging, the editor is uneasy about a suicide ending, offering that love (a romantic ending with Philippe as rescuer) would be preferable. In their conversational debate, the director's authorial will undercuts the editor's plumping for a happy ending. She accepts her collaborator's belief in women's capacity to survive, but insists that Suzanne's character be restored on behalf of rape victims, especially the actual victim (Francine, still a pseudonym) who inspired Suzanne's character. Yet the director's admission that neither her research nor her deconstructive film could save the actual person implies that feminist film practices mean discourse, not social solution. Hence, the film's serial endings dialectically eschew easy reconciliations, which must occur outside film discourse.

Ending Three: The Victim Redeemed

In long shot, laid out in white, Suzanne's mythic repose within the theatrically 'holy' mise en scène, evokes what Linda Nochlin describes as art history's classical 'Aesthetic Woman par excellence ... conceived of ... as a kind of visual poetry.'[24] Redeemed in death by saintly posture, Suzanne is no longer herself, but rather Poirier's aesthetically distanced up-bringing of a particular subject position. The shot's formal immaculateness restores the violated woman from victim to martyr to light – in Catholic terms, a process of spiritual rehabilitation. This redemption of the rape victim is enhanced by the soft focus lens and the illuminated lighting streaming through an upper window, and so functions as art process. Bathed in an impressionistic halo-lighting effect, reminiscent of a convention of 'holy pictures,' the victim exists in a suspended state of grace for the duration of the shot. The white-out then transposes her mythic presence into pure light, recuperating the film screen for women as subjects, filmmakers, and spectators. This screen is not blank so much as opaque with cinematic memory.

The Coda: A Call for Never-ending Noise

The coda's ideological weight is carried by its evocative soundscape, featuring a strong female narrator who refers to society's 'wall of silence' regarding rape. At once she speaks to us and to the visual collage of empty urban spaces (streets, alleys, parks), dispassionately mocking the only weapon society offers to mothers whose offspring have vaginas. A token whistle. The cacophonous whistles and sirens turn this absurd advice into a political call to women, to ferret out and mark the many places where female bodies are unsafe. As such, the coda echoes the second of the serial endings (the filmmakers' intervention), dialectically pulling women's spectatorship into moral and cultural dilemmas, triggered by the formal processes of aestheticizing memory.

Inconclusions

My interest in giving substantial critical weight to the formality, cinematic historicity, feminist voice, and theoretical awareness of *Mourir à tue-tête* arises out of the film's aesthetic 'permission' to indulge in the pleasurable headache of analysis, rather than to suffer the film's supposed victimization or non-solutions, or even the empowerment that an initial viewing sometimes evokes. Rape is a crucial social issue, at once horridly personal and public, whatever women's status on political agendas before or since Poirier's film. Certainly *Mourir à tue-tête* is deeply serious about the human and cultural dimensions of rape, but it is not an easy topic film that settles for social consciousness and good intentions, or for minimal film form.[25] The allusions to topical research by the internal director in *Mourir à tue-tête* work formally, in the manner of process art. Because of the victim's narrative demise, Poirier's nurse must become a 'maker of meaning,'[26] though briefly, in the aestheticized pseudo-research interview with the narrative's internal director. As a 'bearer' of a female victim's identity, 'Suzanne' is named only once in the film, suggesting the insufficiency of film practices given to simple feminist, or nationalist, identification.[27]

In *Mourir à tue-tête*'s narrative frame, the two women filmmakers are positioned in a concrete space (the editing room) where technical control and analysis become a committed practice of questioning art-making processes and vision – the very basis of Poirier's aestheticized feminism. In Poirier's and Marilyn French's comparable feminist narrative texts of the 1970s,[28] such speculation and imaginative practice may be rooted in middle-class self-examination and privilege, but pivot on larger ideological concerns with changed aesthetic and narrative forms and historical 'scripts' for women. The focus of such change is cultural re-formation. In the context of the period, it entails calling up memories of suppressed or unheard screams that trouble women's unspoken stories, to be formally aestheticized as feminist discourses.

NOTES

The section dealing with *Mourir à tue-tête* is an expansion and revision of a shorter paper on this film that appeared in *Responses*, ed. Blaine Allan, Michael Dorland, Zuzana M. Pick (Kingston, Montreal, Ottawa: Responsibility Press/Les Editions la Responsabilité, 1992), 168–82.

1 In editing *Jour après jour* (1962, director, Clément Perron) Poirier's structuring of the cinéma-direct footage is fluid, surreally poetic, and mannered. Her voice-over commentary effects a haunting, often ironically resonant reading of the images of paper-mill workers in a Quebec town. Poirier has referred to her editing experience on *Jour après jour* as pivotal in her decision to pursue filmmaking: 'c'était la première fois que j'assumais la responsabilité entière de ce miracle qu'est montage ... et que je fait le choix de faire du cinéma mon métier, pour toujours.' Pierre Véronneau and Pierre Jutras, 'Anne Claire Poirier de A à Z: Bio-filmographie commentée par l'auteure,' *Copie Zéro* 23 (1985): 4. Piers Handling, 'The National Film Board of Canada: 1939–1959,' in *Self Portrait: Essays on the Canadian and Quebec Cinemas*, ed. Pierre Véronneau and Piers Handling (Ottawa: Canadian Film Institute, 1980), 52, observes that *Jour après jour* was among the early Québécois films

'made by people who would provide the backbone of the Quebec film industry for years to come.'

2 Anne Claire Poirier, 'Paroles et variations,' *Copie Zéro* 6 (1980): 18.

3 Ibid.

4 Chris Weedon, *Feminist Practice and Poststructuralist Theory*, 3rd ed. (Oxford: Basil Blackwell, 1989), 33.

5 Laurinda Hartt, 'En tant que femmes,' *Cinema Canada* 15 (Aug.–Sept. 1974): 53.

6 Ibid.

7 Francine Prévost, 'L'Itinéraire cinématographique d'Anne-Claire Poirier,' *Séquences* 116 (April 1984): 15.

8 *De mère en fille* was shown on late-night television (due to the adult subject matter, nakedness, and birthing images) on Radio-Canada in the fall of 1968. Poirier has lamented that, despite its success, her profile at the board was not raised by this institutional and personal venture: 'mais pas à l'Office national du film où, pour le lui faire expier, on lui refuse en cinq ans trois autres projets de longs métrages dramatiques basés sur des personnages féminins.' Prévost 'L'Itinéraire cinématographique,' 18.

9 Ibid., 16.

10 Laura Mulvey, 'Visual Pleasure and Narrative Cinema,' *Screen* 16, no. 3 (Aug. 1975), reprinted in *Feminism and Film Theory*, ed. Constance Penley (New York: Routledge, 1988), 67.

11 David Clandfield, 'From the Picturesque to the Familiar: Films of the French Unit at the NFB (1958–1964),' in *Take Two: A Tribute to Film in Canada*, ed. Seth Feldman (Toronto: Irwin, 1984), 114, has defined the picturesque as 'the view of the outsider,' specifically the English-Canadian view of Quebec, in the documentary tradition that was eclipsed by the cinéma-direct practices of Quebeckers filming Quebeckers.

12 Subtitle, English film print. *Valérie* (1968), directed by Denis Héroux, has been identified as 'the first of the "maple syrup porno" films and the prototype for the many that followed in its apparently outspoken sexuality, its sentimentality and its echoes of Jansenist Catholic morality. It was a huge box office success ... and established Cinépix as a major force in Quebec's commercial film industry.' Peter Morris, *The Film Companion* (Toronto: Irwin, 1984), 305.

13 Seeing *Mourir à tue-tête* in the year of its release (1979–80) at the National Film Theatre, Ottawa, with a mixed audience of women and men, was memorable. While the post-screening discussion, notably on the rape scene and the connotations of the ubiquitous male rapist, was earnest and tempered, I suspect that most people, particularly women, left the theatre as I did (alone): feeling con

templative, acutely aware of the night-time city streets and the power of Poirier's film.

14 See Zucker, 'Les oeuvres récentes d'Anne Claire Poirier et Paule Baillargeon,' *Copie Zéro* 11 (Oct. 1981): 52. Zucker notes the Brechtian origins of the post-Godardian influences in Poirier's film, specifically the shifting poles of analysis and narrative.

15 See *Femme du Québec* (Sept.–Oct. 1979): 7. Poirier describes her long collaboration with writer Marthe Blackburn as working 'on the level of thought.' 'But ... Michel Brault, for example, being a man absolutely does not handicap me in my cinematographic development: on the contrary, he is a very respectful man, deeply respectful of the ideology that I convey in my films' (translation).

16 Silvia Bovenschen, 'Is There a Feminine Aesthetic?' in *Feminist Aesthetics*, ed. Gisela Ecker (London: Women's Press, 1985), 31.

17 See Jutras, *Copie Zéro* 23 (Feb. 1985): 24. Michel Brault explains that filming from the victim's point of view was Poirier's idea, 'moreover like the one to film in a van.' 'I added to this choice by suitable lighting, by light coming from the exterior and shining through the window at the rear of the van' (translation).

18 Dan Georgakas and William Starr, 'The Primal Fear: An Interview with Anne-Claire Poirier,' *Cineaste* 10, no. 3 (summer 1980): 21.

19 *Mourir à tue-tête* is a confrontational film, particularly the rape scene, and I have found that students need to vent their viewing experience before they can work through the film's deconstructive manner and feminized aesthetics. But, the gap between 1970s production and 1990s reception has narrowed.

20 Morris, *Film Companion*, 141.

21 The 'Black Maria' was the first motion-picture studio, built by American inventor Thomas Alva Edison's assistant, William Kennedy Laurie Dickson, in 1893. David Cook, *A History of Narrative Film*, 3rd ed. (New York: W.W. Norton, 1996), 5–9, explains the derivation of its name, 'after contemporary slang for what was later known as a "paddy wagon."' In an unpublished paper, I have analysed the legacy of the Black Maria's imagery in Atom Egoyan's television drama, *Gross Misconduct*, where the central character (a declining hockey hero of the 1970s) customizes a van to serve as his masculinized site ('The Hulk') of video surveillance and sexual conquest.

22 Mulvey, 'Visual Pleasure,' 68.

23 Georgakas and Starr, 'The Primal Fear,' 24.

24 Linda Nochlin, 'Visions of Languor,' *House and Garden*, April 1983, 129.

25 The film's first television broadcast (Radio-Canada) was followed by a reaction poll of its large viewership (two million, according to the report) on the film's content and treatment. For excerpted responses, including some differing

views between men and women on the film's narrative style, not only its subject matter, see 'Anne Claire Poivier de A à Z,' *Copie Zéro* 23 (Feb 1985): 16–17.

26 Mulvey, 'Visual Pleasure,' 58.

27 Ibid., 58; Rhona Berenstein, 'As Canadian as Possible: The Female Spectator
and the Canadian Context,' *Camera Obscura* 20–1 (May–Sept. 1989): 40–52.
Berenstein makes some sweeping assumptions (as if forgetting the numerous
qualifications that thread her article) about women 'writing, teaching and creating in a patriarchal society.' She writes, 'More specifically, in film studies the
ratio of men to women is high, and despite the work being done by Canadian
feminists, most courses continue to concentrate on Hollywood narrative cinema as both the standard and model for film analysis. When Canadian film is
addressed, it is primarily in the context of the National Film Board or internationally acclaimed experimental work; if Canadian women are discussed, it is
through the work of the NFB's women's studio, Studio D' (47). Berenstein's
remarks have become historical, and miss the scope of change and differences
despite patriarchal institutional habits, among academic programs (film studies course models; gender, women's, cultural, communications, and media
studies) and creativity.

28 Marilyn French, *The Women's Room* (New York: Summit Books, 1977).

Two plus Two: Contesting the Boundaries of Identity in Two Films by Micheline Lanctôt

PETER HARCOURT

I'm surely very naive and provincial and my way of approaching cinema is too idealist. But I belong to a generation when, if you wanted to make a film, you rolled up your sleeves and got on with it.
Micheline Lanctôt (1995)[1]

There is a moment toward the end of *Deux actrices* (*Two Can Play*, 1993), an improvisational 16mm feature by Micheline Lanctôt, that might stand for the film as a whole. Marginal to the narrative – a 'bracket syntagma,' as we might once have described it[2] – it is central to the theme of the film. After Fabienne, the indomitable sister, has tried to commit suicide, Solange, the domitable one, is waiting for a bus when she is confronted by a strangely huge woman. S/he is, in fact, a male transvestite, seeking reassurance that s/he looks feminine enough, that s/he hasn't overdone the disguise.

The theme of disguise, of masquerade, of performance is at the heart of this film as, to a degree, it is at the heart of all of Lanctôt's work. In *Deux actrices*, the sense of perpetual performance is crucial not just for the construction of gender (as Judith Butler has argued), but also for the construction of self. 'Gender ought not to be construed as a stable identity or locus of agency from which various acts follow; rather gender is an identity tenuously constituted in time, instituted in an exterior space through a *stylized repetition of acts*.'[3] In the scene in *Deux actrices*, at what must be for Solange her moment of greatest ontological uncertainty, she is asked to reassure another person that 'he' genuinely resembles that which he is not.

Who does Solange now resemble? Her former self, whom she has carefully constructed by a 'stylized repetition of acts' at her day care with the children and at home with her caring husband? Does she now resemble her sister, who, abandoned by Solange, finally turned her frustrations with the social world against herself, attempting to take her own life? Or does she resemble her mother, another 'bracketed' presence in the film, whose lack of love for Fabienne had driven the daughter from home when still a young girl? Indeed, the theme of the mother, if equally marginal to the narrative, is central to the psychology of the film, as it must now be to Solange's life.[4] Experientially, however (as we will examine in a moment), the film operates at another level.

I write like a woman. My projects are more contemplative, more lyrical, more introspective. It's not a weakness; it's a difference.
– Micheline Lanctôt (1990)[5]

All of Lanctôt's films are more theoretical than they appear. As actress, animator, teacher, musician, screenwriter, cultural agitator, and film director, Lanctôt has a strong sense of self that refuses received assumptions – as much in her work as an actress and in her commissioned pieces as in her more personal productions.[6] Even her deceptively simple first feature, *L'Homme à tout faire* (*The Handyman*, 1980) confronts theoretical issues. Made during the peak of cinematic feminism, when so much theory addressed itself to the disempowering effects of the male gaze upon the woman,[7] Lanctôt creates Armand (Jocelyn Bérubé), a timid character from Gaspésie, whose shy glances are insubstantial when compared with the flirtatious looks that the women in the film bestow upon *him*. Indeed, in all of Lanctôt's films, even in those in which she is an actress, women are as much the initiator of the gaze as the recipient of it.

Although Armand's love affair with a rich housewife, Thérèse (Andrée Pelletier) – the 'performance' of this love together – liberates them for a time from their inherited roles, it cannot endure. Issues of class intervene and drive them apart – he back to his marginalized status as a handyman from the provinces, she trapped within the moneyed expectations of her husband's career.

Sonatine (1983), Lanctôt's second film and, arguably, her most intricate, is (as its name implies) musical in form, a film in three movements. Appropriately, it employs sound in innovative ways. In the first two movements, through the device of diaries that the girls in the film have recorded on their Walkmans, Lanctôt establishes different relationships of sound to image, implying different references to time. Although scarcely noticeable when experiencing the film, this dialogic structure is, on analysis, strangely disorienting. Which element constitutes the present tense, images or sound?

Conventionally, the image *always* constitutes a present – a sense of this-is-happening-now. Structurally, however, the device of the spoken diary might seem to relegate it to the prior, to a sense of this-has-already-taken-place. Or, indeed, do these tape-recorded diaries that *precede* the images actually *follow* them within the narrative order? How can spectators situate themselves in relation to these temporal dislocations? This device of dis-location lends itself to an inverted Lacanian analysis. As Kaja Silverman has argued about acoustic space in film: 'When the voice is identified ... with presence, it is given the imaginary power to place not only sounds but meaning in the here and now. In other words, it is understood as clos-ing the gap between signifier and signified.'[8] In *Sonatine*, because of the *refusal* of temporal identification, the gap between signifier and signified is widened, conveying through these dislocations a sense of adolescent fantasy – a separation from the social more akin to dream.

If the technology of the Walkman is central to the girls' experience in the film, technologies of transportation dominate their social world. Buses, boats, and subway trains form the backdrop of all three move-ments. Designed for transportation, to make connections between peo-ple, to be outward-looking, these technologies form part of the male surround of the film. Within Montreal, however, they are in a state of stress. Masculine communication systems are breaking down. Transporta-tion workers are about to go on strike.

Although it performs a number of narrative functions in the film – bridging ellipses, destabilizing time – the Walkman, which is inward-looking, suggests interior monologue, the recipient of the girls' private fantasies and dreams. It represents their private world, sometimes receiv-ing from them, sometimes giving to them messages and sounds, often indecipherable to others, like the acoustic game on tape that opens the film. For instance, the first movement charts the teenage infatuation of Chantal (Pascale Bussières, in her first screen performance) with Lam-bert (Pierre Fauteux), a driver of the bus that she catches every Friday.

In this movement, her Walkman serves simultaneously both as source and receiver of sound, disturbing the temporal sequencing of the narra-tive by troubling the distinctions between listen and record. At a crucial moment when Chantal has been listening to her Walkman (possibly in radio mode), Lambert avows that he finds her pretty. Since she has appar-ently recorded these words on her Walkman, she plays his voice over and over again– 'Tu es belle pareil' – the words finally expanding on her tape (as if in her imagination) from what he actually said.

In the final sequence of this movement, she is listening to a love poem obviously recorded for Lambert, only to discover that her driver has been replaced, leaving her with just the sounds associated with his memory. The acoustic disjunctions in this opening movement serve to destabilize the boundaries between the real and the imaginary, establishing Chantal's identity more in her imagined than in her social world.

In the second movement, comparable acoustic dislocations occur. As Loisette (Marcia Pilote) is on her way to the docks, before she has even met her sailor, we hear her voice, as from her Walkman, stating her declaration of purpose: 'I'm not sure exactly why I left. I wanted adventure, life, something intense. I knew I had to find it right away or I never would.' She wants to be a stowaway. When she is discovered by her Bulgarian benefactor, the exchanges between them are tender in the extreme. He is warmly solicitous but also desirous. At one point, they exchange coats and caps, she sniffing his out of curiosity, he inhaling hers out of need. But in ways similar to Chantal's relationship with Lambert, Loisette's response is more an adolescent crush, transformed by the fantasy of interior monologue. 'I had so many plans for us. I wanted to run away with him. I wanted us to travel together, to love each other, without speaking, just watching the sky.' Whether these words anticipate or follow the images, they destabilize the temporal sequence, disorienting spectators within the narrative space of the film.

For the final movement (a kind of tutti) although the Walkmans are still present during the opening sequences, the diary form is abandoned. The girls are now living in the present tense. We see them travelling on the métro, laughing through the corridors of their school, roller skating through the streets of the petit bourgeois district in which they live – apparently two normal, carefree teenage girls. Fed up with the preoccupations of their parents, however, and with the perceived hostility of their inhabited world, they decide to kill themselves, to perform their discontent through the public spectacle of suicide. Since the film eschews psychology and only presents its politics as a backdrop to the action, the *reasons* for this suicide are not at all clear. Their parents have no time for them, and the girls do complain of an indifferent world; yet with their Walkmans always plugged into their heads, they might themselves seem indifferent, preferring fantasy love relationships to social engagement.

Finally, these two young women are always exquisitely dressed. Indeed, their sense of fashion deserves special comment because their clothes are part of an intricate colour-coding that is one of the film's many accomplishments in design. For their suicide trip, they are dressed to the nines. Loisette sports red shoes and matching leather gloves; Chantal wears pale pinks and blues and a tiny mini skirt. They descend into the métro, their intended purpose announced by a sign that they prop up behind them on their seat: 'In an indifferent world, we are going to die, unless you stop us. Do something!'

They have left their Walkmans behind, as if now, at last, they are open to the world. The world that they encounter in the métro, however, is not open to them. Most people don't even notice the sign, and the one guy who does thinks it is a joke. They clink together their little cartons of chocolate milk that they had almost forgot to purchase, pop their pills, and sit there, getting drowsy, smiling at one another and holding hands as if they were on their way to their first communion. We never see them grieving or seriously upset: they are just fed up. On one level, the project seems a lark – psychologically implausible, possibly engendering in spectators a constrained or awkward sympathy. The formal achievement of the film, however, renders these issues of plausibility temporarily irrelevant.

In essence, *Sonatine* is an exercise in rhythm and movement and in the evocative potentialities of sound, properties frequently rendered unnoticeable by the psychologized nature of conventional narratives. Like the early films of Robert Bresson, it is a celebration of the formal properties of cinema. It is Bressonian as well in its final concentration of purpose. *Sonatine* is a film that displaces response from reason, the affective from the plausible, the structural from the representational. As (in another context) Christine Ross has suggested, 'Representation ... is no longer so much the site of a complete and total recognition of the world, as it is an image that *impresses* and acts upon the spectator, an impression that takes on the value of meaning.'9

Sonatine becomes a site in which narrative is subsumed within structure, the mimetic within the iconic, the political within the aesthetic. The sign usurps the referent. Perhaps on another level, Silverman is right: the signifier *becomes* the signified. More than any other film in the cinematic repertoire, *Sonatine* enacts that aesthetic ideal put forward over a century ago by the Victorian art critic Walter Pater: 'All art constantly aspires towards the condition of music.'10 By the end of *Sonatine*, the exhilaration that we feel at its formal achievement suspends any judgment we might make concerning the narrative plausibilities of cause and effect.

Finally, however, a politics remains. The aftertaste of *Sonatine* returns us to the story – to the girls, to the men, to the uncaring world. It is *after* we have seen the film that we might want to talk about its assumptions concerning class and gender. While we are watching it, we simply marvel at the intricacy of the achievement of its form.

Deux actrices is without a doubt the most feminine of my films.
Micheline Lanctôt (1994)[11]

Although less abstractly organized, *Deux actrices* also troubles any simple response. Full of the casualness of an improvisational work, its episodic structure builds up a complex picture of, again, two women. Structurally, *Deux actrices* consists of two films: the 16mm footage, the 'fictional' film, about two sisters, Solange and Fabienne; and the video footage, the 'true' film, where the actors sit around a table and talk about their characters.

Initially, the video footage comments on the film footage, presenting the actors' plans for constructing their roles. Very soon the video takes on a life of its own, creating another set of characters, destabilizing the simple binaries that the film footage implies. Through the process of reiteration and of internal digression, this supposedly profilmic event becomes a *contestational* filmic event. 'Performativity' (in Judith Butler's sense) is problematized in that the female characters, when switching from film to video, also switch roles.[12] *Deux actrices*, the film, establishes a system of binary oppositions between anarchy and stability, courage and fear, unreliability and reliability. However, *Deux actrices*, the video, overturns these oppositions.

In *Deux actrices*, the film, Solange (Pascale Bussières) lives with Charles (François Delisle). She works in a day care and he studies medicine. They are nice, clean, caring, ordinary people who, apparently, take few risks. Into their lives bursts Fabienne (Pascale Paroisien), a woman so demanding that her own mother threw her out while she was still a teenager, disowning her so thoroughly that Solange had no idea that a sister existed.

Fabienne fills their place with rock 'n roll; she spies at their love making through the keyhole of their bedroom door; she creeps into their bed at night; and after a number of rows, the last of which escalates into violence, she drives Charles from the apartment.

But Charles is scarcely important to this story. The relationship between the sisters dominates our attention, along with their different relationships to their mother. Indeed, the visit to their mother (Louise Latraverse) provides perhaps the one awkward moment in this film, making needlessly explicit what we have already inferred.[13] The mother obviously behaved monstrously to her first child, however difficult Fabienne might have been. Fabienne, in turn, has had her daughter taken away from her because of inadequate parenting. Having desperately sought recognition from her mother throughout her life, she experiences great pleasure when, finding herself in prison after kidnapping her own daughter, she was recognized by her child.

In *Deux actrices*, the video (on the other hand), we have Pascale Bussières, an actress, recently the star of *Blanche*, an on-going television series, at ease in her own body, speaking freely about AIDS, edible condoms, and the exhilaration given to her by her periods. In contrast, we have Pascale Paroisien, a film editor by trade, diffident in speech, uncertain of her abilities as a performer, asking Micheline what she wants her to say.

Thus the differences between the two sisters in the film text of *Deux actrices* are contested by the reversal of roles that we experience in the video text. This dual exegesis emphasizes the extent to which not just one's gender but one's entire personality is an active performance, confirmed through repetition. As Judith Butler has suggested, 'Paradoxically, the reconceptualization of identity as an *effect*, that is, as *produced* or *generated*, opens up possibilities of "agency" that are insidiously foreclosed by positions that take identity categories as foundational and fixed.'[14] However, when looked at closely, the film contests the optimism of Judith Butler's politics. According to Butler, a recognition of performativity opens up possibilities for the construction of gender and identity; yet, in *Deux actrices*, whether within the fiction-film text or the film as a whole – *except at the level of theatrical performance* – agency seems elusive. The twin texts suggest that the act of performance may just as easily lead to a kind of assumed inauthenticity, like the inauthenticity of the transvestite in the scene described at the opening of this essay.

In the film text, the two women are trapped within their matriarchal inheritance. For Fabienne, a declension is established from unloving mother to unloving daughter, a declension that Solange has managed to side-step by being perpetually willing to sympathize and to please, to attempt at every moment, as Lanctôt as an actress tried to do in *La Vraie nature de Bernadette* (1972), to annul aggression through love.[15]

Although the declared sense of performativity does inflect the confidence of our response to the observed performativity in the film text, finally *Deux actrices* as a whole operates more on the level of an unresolvable irony. As Donna Haraway has explained, 'Irony is about contradictions that do not resolve into larger wholes, even dialectically, about the tension of holding incompatible things together because both or all are necessary and true.'[16] In *Deux actrices*, the unresolvable contradictions involve the two texts of video and film that run parallel through the work, each challenging the perceived authority of the other. Furthermore, performativity itself operates in a double space: the space of the film text, of the fictionalized world, and the space of the video text, where 'performance' is both discussed and enacted in the theatrical sense of the term, where safety can be found within the comforts of theatrical representations.

In neither text, however, is the sense of agency enhanced. In the video text, apparently naturally, the characters simply are what they are – including François Delisle, who plays Charles, the marginalized male in this film, and Micheline Lanctôt, who acts out her own role as director of the project. In the film text, while the boundaries of identity are certainly challenged – especially Solange's when faced with the insistences of Fabienne – by the end, the 'stylized repetition of acts' is as much the product of cultural conditioning, returning the characters to the possibly self-deceiving attitudes that they held about themselves at the opening of the film.

For me, the cinema will always represent a wonderful defiance.
Micheline Lanctôt (1995) [17]

The films of Micheline Lanctôt offer a variety of pleasures. Agreeable on the surface, lively in execution, pleasant to look at, they are more complicated than they appear. Though Lanctôt herself is innocent of theatrical intention, her films both pose theoretical problems and overturn received theoretical positions. *Sonatine* problematizes the relation between image and sound and their temporal order within narrative space. *Deux actrices*, with its twin texts, also confronts head-on the nature both of performance and of performativity and the permeable boundaries of identity that hold one's sense of self in place. At the end, however, the film places these contestations in context by suggesting that once these boundaries have been extended through 'performance' or 'masquerade' in the effort to escape the conditionings of class and gender, they are quite likely to snap back into place.

NOTES

1 Micheline Lanctôt, *Micheline Lanctôt: La vie d'une héroïne*, Collection entretiens par Denise Pérusse (Montreal: l'Hexagone, 1995), 13. All translations from the French are my own.
2 Christian Metz, *Film Language: A Semiotics of the Cinema*, trans. Michael Taylor (New York: Oxford University Press, 1974), 150–1.

3　Judith Butler, *Gender Trouble: Feminism and the Subversion of Identity* (New York: Routledge, 1990), 140.

4　As it also is in Lanctôt's life: 'A strong mother is hell for a daughter; and the stronger the mother, the more violent the dissociation has to be.' Personal interview, Montreal, May 1996.

5　Micheline Lanctôt, 'On ne voit bien qu'avec le coeur,' *Lumières* 22 (1990): 16.

6　For a more detailed discussion of her life work see Peter Harcourt, 'Micheline Lanctôt: A Woman in the World,' *Descant* 98 (1997), 109–29.

7　Largely owing to a most germinal article by Laura Mulvey, 'Visual Pleasure in the Narrative Cinema,' *Screen* 16 (1975): 6–18.

8　Kaja Silverman, *The Acoustic Mirror: The Female Voice in Psychoanalysis and Cinema* (Bloomington: Indiana University Press, 1988), 43.

9　Christine Ross, 'The Lamented Moments/Desired Objects of Video Art: Towards an Aesthetics of Discrepancy,' in *Mirror Machine/Video and Identity*, ed. Janine Marchessault (Toronto: YYZ Books & CRCCII, 1995), 130.

10　Walter Pater, 'The School of Giorgione,' *Fortnightly Review*, October 1877; reprinted in Richard Aldington, ed., *Walter Pater: Selected Works* (London: William Heineman, 1948), 271.

11　Micheline Lanctôt, 'De l'accouchement comme métaphore,' *La Revue de la cinémathèque* 26 (1994): 5.

12　'Performativity must be understood not as a singular or deliberate "act," but, rather, as the reiterative and citational practice by which discourse produces the effects that it names.' Judith Butler, in *Bodies That Matter: On the Discursive Limits of 'Sex'* (New York: Routledge, 1993), 2.

13　In part, Lanctôt agrees. At the same time, this film began as an acting exercise, and, through the performance of Louise Latraverse, she wanted to display another style of acting for the screen. Personal interview.

14　Butler, *Gender Trouble*, 147.

15　Directed by Gilles Carle, *La Vraie nature de Bernadette* remains Lanctôt's most outstanding acting achievement.

16　Donna J. Haraway, *Simians, Cyborgs, and Women: The Reinvention of Nature* (New York: Routledge, 1991), 149.

17　Lanctôt, *Micheline Lanctôt*, 184.

Cowards, Bullies, and Cadavers: Feminist Re-Mappings of the Passive Male Body in English-Canadian and Québécois Cinema

LEE PARPART

Although until recently feminist film theory has shown little interest in the male body as a site of social meaning or as an object of the cinematic gaze, it has been a different story on the domestic production side: our own women filmmakers in English Canada and Quebec have made masculinity and its embodied forms an intermittent focus of interest for over thirty years.[1] Beginning with Joyce Wieland's satiric exploration of phallic nationalism in *Patriotism, Part One* (1964), taking on a distinct new form in the early Québécois films *Mourir à tue-tête* (1979) and *La Vie rêvée* (1972), and extending most recently to Lynne Stopkewich's debut feature, *Kissed*, women directors have been stealing unauthorized glances at the male body and generally imagining masculinity on their own terms since the mid-1960s. And while this phenomenon is still marginal in comparison to the more pronounced feminist focus on 'women's images of women' that has given us such films as *Water Sark* (1966), *Speak Body* (1979), and *Sifted Evidence* (1982), it is worth noting that Canadian women working on the edges of an already marginalized cultural site have, at times, felt free to unveil, inscribe their own messages upon, and (re)figure the male body in distinctive and provocative ways.

In the mid-1990s, this treatment takes the form of a small but distinctive cycle of 'female gaze' films in which the male body is either frozen in states of erotic availability or singled out for sexualized forms of abuse. Caught up in a version of contemporary feminism that is largely won over to the causes of anti-censorship and anti-essentialism, a certain corner of recent feminist filmmaking puts the Love back in *Not a Love Story* (1981) by exploring raunchiness as a form of political engagement (Cynthia Roberts's *Bubbles Galore* [1997]), defining female desire and the feminist problematic in diverse and taboo ways (*Kissed* [1996]), and embracing not only the approved activity of women representing women,[2] but the less immediately acceptable one of women representing men.

It is this last phenomenon – the proliferation of sexual images of men in films by English-Canadian and Québécois women – that I want to focus on in this essay by looking at a number of texts that seem to inscribe the male body from ambiguously defined positions within the margin of the margin that is feminist film in this country. Through discussions of work from different regions and periods – Wieland's *Patriotism,* Karethe Linaae's 1994 short, *off Key,* and Stopkewich's *Kissed* – I explore some of conditions that might make such patterns of male sexual representation possible, asking what it has meant for women filmmakers to turn their camera-look on the male body at various moments in time, and how different approaches to representing the male body might be interrogated as both feminine/feminist and Canadian.

Marginality and the Male Body

The links between various forms of marginality and approaches to representing the male body are hardly self-evident, but have been dealt with by implication in recent theories of masculinity and representation. With the male body now starting to come under the same kind of cultural and academic scrutiny previously reserved for women, a number of theorists, including Peter Lehman, Maxine Sheets-Johnstone, and Kaja Silverman, have addressed the links between 'dominant' culture and attempts to preserve the male body as a site of unassailable stature and power. One of the many ways this protective function is carried out, Sheets-Johnstone argues, is by keeping the material reminder of phallic power (the penis) out of the public eye, so as to suppress knowledge of the gap between material and symbolic registers of masculine authority.[3] In his related work on the sexual representation of men in film and other forms of popular culture, Lehman goes so far as to argue that 'dominant representations of phallic masculinity in [American] culture *depend* on keeping the male body and the genitals out of the critical spotlight,' since the sight/site of the penis has a way of drawing attention to the humble material foundations of phallic power.[4] Kaja Silverman, in a more strictly psychoanalytic context, suggests that certain films challenge the 'dominant fiction' that sustains sexual difference by representing the male body in ways that upset widespread cultural assumptions about the commensurability of penis and phallus.[5] In all of the above arguments, then, 'dominance' is associated with a cultural imperative to limit or carefully control sexual representations of the male body, while 'marginality' (at the level of gender, sexual orientation, class, race, or nation) is thought to provide the conditions for alternatives which 'say "No" to [phallic] power'[6] (Silverman) or provide new screens through which to view the male body and think about masculinities.

Despite the sometimes axiomatic tone of such arguments, the idea that various forms of marginality may have a role to play in allowing for alternative or non-patriarchal[7] views of the male body helps shed light on a range of cultural products by English-Canadian women. If Lehman is correct about dominant representations of phallic masculinity *needing* to keep the male body and particularly the genitals out of sight, then it is worth considering what motives or possibilities might exist for *revealing* the male body from the feminist margins of an already industrially marginalized national cinema such as that of English Canada. Could there be something about the 'Canadianness' of English-Canadian feminist film, in other words, that is especially conducive to foregrounding the vulnerable, mutable foundations of phallic authority?

(Post)colonial Masculinities in English-Canadian Film

One of the key assertions made about masculinity in English-Canadian cinema is the idea that our own films tend to imagine masculinity in distinct ways that are related to Canada's colonial past and its culturally and economically marginalized position relative to the United States. While critics in the 1960s and 1970s often viewed the absence of empowered male film heroes as signalling a crisis in Canadian masculinity, the same conditions have been re-read in the 1990s as symptoms of a Canadian talent for tolerance and heterogeneity. In her influential 1992 essay about *Goin' Down the Road* (1970),[8] for example, Christine Ramsay overturned a generation of worried writing about the beleaguered male subject in Canadian film by pointing out that he's not merely a 'coward, bully, or clown,' in Robert Fothergill's famous phrase,[9] but a complex and contingent subject with qualities to be admired. Arguing that dominant masculine gender identity and the modern nation are both 'product[s] of imagination' linked by a common metaphoric impulse to power and mastery, Ramsay points out that English-Canadian films have tended to imagine 'the nation' and the ideal of omnipotent, empowered masculinity from the position of the margins. Such minority discourses carve out a '"performative space" for the representation of our social self' that should be 'celebrated and studied ... for what it offers as a lived text that makes intelligible to us, as English Canadians, from the position of the margins, the unique way we have historically faced the problems of social and personal identity through the Western concepts of "the nation" and omnipotent masculinity.'[10]

Although Ramsay's essay is not concerned with feminist filmmaking or representations of the male body per se, her work raises the possibility that some of the strategies and approaches found in films by English-Canadian women may be simply 'doubled' or more gender-specific versions of a gaze or look at the male body that is already to some extent on offer in male-authored products of English-Canadian cinema. If the 'alternative aesthetic' shaping English-Canadian film includes the potential for what Ramsay has elsewhere termed 'phallically limp' models of masculinity,[11] then films by English-Canadian women may add another layer of 'limpness,' analysis, or opposition, along with new textual strategies and aesthetic models for refiguring the male through non-phallic screens. Thus while a surprising number of male-authored Canadian films have managed to de-centre the phallus by centring the penis'[12] – the key to Lehman's formula for a progressive and non-patriarchal approach to the male body in cinema – women have explored Barbara de Genevieve's related axiom (that 'to unveil the penis is to unveil the phallus is to unveil the social construction of masculinity')[13] from strategic positions and within narrative and aesthetic contexts all their own.

Joyce Wieland: Flag Jobs and the (Pre-)feminist/national Gaze

Although it is only one part of a large body of work that has been enormously important to Canadian feminists,[14] Joyce Wieland's consistent attention to the male body (as a source of playful imagery, erotic inspiration, and fuel for satiric explorations of phallic sexuality) raises important questions about the potential for a female gaze at the male within an English-Canadian context. As the so-called mother of the Canadian feminist avant-garde, Wieland was the first to launch a sustained analysis of the male body in relation to Canadian landscape and national identity, and her work still provides some of the clearest juxtapositions of masculinity and nation in English-Canadian film. Despite the immense variety in Wieland's approach to male embodiment, however, this aspect of her work has not received the close attention it deserves. While her overtly women-centred works have been analysed in detail, a lack of conceptual models for including a gaze at the male within the range of activities thought of as feminist has at times led to the collapse of Wieland's multiply-positioned, complex looks at the male body into the general terms of a 'pre-feminist' absorption with 'phallic pleasure.'[15] On the contrary, Wieland's early stain-painted and Pop art versions of the penis (i.e., *Penis Wallpaper* and *Balling*), her numerous Tiepolo-inspired paintings of nude male angels, her explicit 1983 painting *Artist on Fire* (a self-portrait with Wieland, hoofed like Pan, putting the finishing touches on the erect penis of her male model), and at least two early films dealing with the corporeal effects of colonization (*Pierre Vallières* and *Patriotism, Part One*), call to be read as instances of a simultaneously Canadian and female gaze that reads, constructs, and imag(in)es male bodies to its own ends.

One early example can be found in her 1964 stop-motion film, *Patriotism, Part One*. Wieland once called this her 'hot dog film' and downplayed it as a 'technically bad' experiment in animation.[16] But as an early product of her New York years (1963–71, during which Wieland says she became increasingly politicized as a Canadian nationalist and as a woman faced with the often overt sexism of her male colleagues in the avant-garde), the film gestures toward a view of the male body as a complex, vulnerable site, criss-crossed by power and inscribed with the marks of gendered national identity. Shot in New York and finished in Canada in the mid-1980s, the film features a young man (David Shackman) sleeping fitfully under a white sheet while a small army of hot dogs advances up his body in stop-motion, to the strains of a Sousa military march. Stopping near his chest, some of the animated wieners receive what appear to be 'flag jobs' from a miniature version of Old Glory, then slip under the sheet to take sexual advantage of their snoozing object of desire. When Shackman's character wakes up, he pulls several of the franks off his body (from the area near his bottom) and holds them next to his face as his look of discomfort gradually turns into a sheepish smile.

Although in some ways it's just a trifle, the film's approach to macho American masculinity can be read against a backdrop of Wieland's emerging Canadian nationalism and gradual discovery of a women-centred artist's territory. *Patriotism* has been described as a parody of phallocentrism, which seems appropriate, but it is worth remembering that only one of the masculinities held up in the film is phallic, in the sense that it's succeeding at being 'top dog.' The other is lying in bed, playing the receptive role in an ambiguously sexualized cross-cultural exchange, and in fact sleeps through the whole experience of being colonized/sodomized. By placing her male character under a white sheet, which could be taken to signal death or surrender, and by staging what amounts to a simultaneously camp/homoerotic and American imperialist attack on his body, Wieland seems to be referring to a passive (perhaps even Canadian) masculinity that is both 'in bed' to some extent with the Yankee Doodle wiener and that may even find that there are pleasures to be had from the colonizer's attentions, as long as one remains asleep.

The problematic conflation of colonization and sodomy that I'm detecting here may be a by-product of Wieland's particular, anthropomorphizing version of a pan-Canadian nationalism that increasingly defined itself in opposition to American culture in the 1960s and 1970s. Years after making this film, Wieland would state that she sees Canada as 'female' while its de facto colonial ruler, the United States, is best thought of as 'male' – a construction that may have allowed her, by extension, to distinguish between 'feminized' national masculinities, which are 'penetrated,' and those that primarily 'penetrate.' But as Kass Banning points out,[17] Wieland's true patriot love for Canada has never been of the facile, flag-waving sort, and her analysis of the interplay of dominant and subordinate masculinities is anything but straightforward either. In keeping with her tendency to foreground 'the inherent contradictions underlying our engraved national consciousness'[18] rather than engage in simple celebrations of national identity, Wieland leaves the door open for a certain amount of complicity on the part of the colonized/penetrated male in *Patriotism*.

In one sense the film is recognizably 'Canadian' in that it takes up the matter of how dominant and subordinate masculinities function and interact through tropes of national identity – a preoccupation that shows up in dozens of male-authored Canadian films dealing with the way in which socio-economic marginality and the humiliations of neocolonial rule are visited upon the male body and masculine subjectivity.[19] But *Patriotism, Part One* substitutes satire for anxiety and marks itself off as an early (literally 'pre-feminist')[20] instance of female writing through its willingness to deflate the phallic accoutrements of national identity to hot dog proportions and probe colonized masculinities for signs of complicity. The film's would-be phallic-colonial oppressors are, after all, just tube steaks. One could not, as Randi Spires notes in another context, conflate them with 'the mighty phalluses of myth.'[21] And even a receptive, 'subordinate' masculinity gets playfully interrogated for signs of collusion with the colonizer. Passive – in some senses perversely inviting victimization – and caught up in a complex circuit of power plays and semi-pleasurable submission, the colonial male body in *Patriotism* is one that not only benefits to some degree from its own seduction by the imperial American Other, but that is, in a progressive sense, also *capable* of enjoying a passive role. At roughly the same time that male critics were raising a hue and cry about weak masculinity in Canadian cinema, then, Wieland was finding something to celebrate (and, of course, gently satirize) in a vision of the vulnerable, colonial male.

'I've Seen Bodies Shining Like Stars': Late Feminism's Look at the Male

Some three decades later, male sexual representation in work by English-Canadian women takes a different form in a small cycle of 'female gaze' films depicting male bodies suspended in states of erotic availability or subjected to sexualized forms of abuse. The nude male model in Karethe Linaae's critically praised 1994 short, *off Key*, sits at the benign, Chippendales-inspired end of this spectrum while, at the other extreme, Cynthia Roberts depicts a bad-guy pornographer being twirled around by his penis in the otherwise pro-porn, proto-feminist feature *Bubbles Galore*. But it is Vancouver director Lynne Stopkewich's 1996 debut feature, *Kissed*, that stands as something of a limit text within the cycle by positing the nude male body as an irreversibly passive site of sexual interest for a female necrophile. Utterly rejecting the psychoanalytic doxa that says women 'lack the means to represent lack'[22] and are therefore less likely to hold objects at a distance from themselves in a manner resembling voyeurism, the female protagonist in *Kissed* insists on the ultimate distance from her male sexual 'partners': they have to be dead, or she's just not interested.

One can begin to make sense of both *off Key* and *Kissed* as part of a general trend toward an overt concern with desire, sexuality, and the inscription of the body in English-Canadian cinema after about 1992. On the surface, both films accommodate the critical category: *off Key* revolves around a middle-aged, female photographer who seduces her young male subject (a concert pianist played by David Lougren) into posing nude during a standard portrait session; *Kissed* relates the tragicomic story of a female necrophile's sexual interest in young male corpses. Like many of the male-authored films in this 'perversion chic'[23] cycle – David Cronenberg's *Crash* (1996), Atom Egoyan's *The Adjuster* (1991), and Peter Wellington's *I Love a Man in Uniform* (1993) – *Kissed* and *off Key* investigate the strange carnalities of desire and take part in an inflationary trend that seems to be constantly upping the ante of allowable (perhaps even mandatory) eroticism in English-Canadian cinema. What signals a difference, however, is their explicit focus on female desire for the male body, their insistence on specularizing the male, and their recognizably 'late feminist'[24] tendency to disrupt, rewrite, and relativize the gendered terms of psychoanalytically defined categories such as voyeurism and fetishism.

On the surface, both *off Key* and *Kissed* reassign these traditionally 'masculine' scopic positions to female characters who are ostensibly in control of the circuit of looks within the diegesis. Hence Gabrielle Rose's character in *off Key*, the famous portrait photographer Agnes L., has turned her voyeurism into a career behind the lens, while the female necrophile in *Kissed* transcends routine voyeurism by wielding a 'dissecting' or 'anatomic' gaze that permits her to peer into the bodies of dead animals and, eventually, human corpses. In opposition to Raymond Bellour's axiom about the 'extreme condensation of sexuality in the woman's body-image'[25] as a defining component of the enunciative work of classical narrative cinema, both films work to avoid objectifying and fetishizing their female characters, while turning their scopic attention to male bodies coded for 'to-be-looked-at-ness.' Rather than simply reversing the scopic rules that conventionally position woman as the object of the gaze, however, *off Key* and *Kissed* go further and in various ways try to challenge the whole structure of looks by which subjects are conventionally turned into objects. In Linaae's film, this includes two striking instances of a 'free-floating fetishism' unattached to any male look or attempt to disavow lack, while in *Kissed* the female voyeur uses her control of the look in ways that lead directly to a *loss* of control, as she empties herself out to accept the corpses' alchemical energy.

Since *Kissed* and *off Key* were both made by young women fresh out of graduate programs in film and theatre,[26] it is not surprising that they are also to some extent 'theory films' that interact in some cases directly with recent projects geared to breaking down fixed notions of power, gender identity, and access to an eroticizing look. Made two years apart in similar production circumstances, they emerge out of a cultural moment in which gender identity, sexual preference, and bodies themselves are increasingly perceived as fluid, performed, and unfixed; in which the binaries of active/male looking and passive/female to-be-looked-at-ness are profoundly called into question; in which old Oedipal narratives are interrogated as positing a too-linear route to normative sexuality; and in which the gaze and the look are no longer assumed to be either 'male' or 'female' but prone to oscillating between, and at times transcending, both terms. Mobilizing a gaze that is neither historically static nor automatically aligned with masculinity, *off Key* and *Kissed* suggest a fluid range of possibilities for the operations of power and spectacle, and deal directly with questions of how much control the female look can, or should, be made to bear.

The ambiguity surrounding this issue of gendered looking surfaces about halfway through *off Key*, when Rose's character asks her portrait subject, Vladimir (the impossibly gorgeous grand concert master of the St Petersburg Symphony Orchestra), to remove his remaining clothes. Having already convinced him to strip down to the waist, Agnes L. suddenly announces that he 'should be naked,' since she needs an 'uninterrupted curve from [his] head to [his] feet.' As she makes the request, Linaae clarifies what is at stake here (the violation of a sacred prohibition against libidinal female looks at the male) by cutting to a high, wide shot in which Agnes L. physically turns away from Vladimir to stare at the camera in her palm. Her expression of chop-licking anticipation says it all: she's dying to look at him, if only to see if she has managed to get away with her request, but for the time being she will look at him with her imagination rather than her eyes – a time-honoured technique for ensuring that women in classical narrative cinema 'recognize and desire [the male] only through the mediation of images of an unimpaired masculinity,' according to Silverman.[27] What this juxtaposition of shots seems to do is raise the idea that, under different circumstances, in a film organized by masculine desire, Agnes would very likely not be *allowed* to look at the spectacle of male nudity that's unfolding before her. Almost as soon as this suggestion is made, however, it is redirected by two disturbances within the film's circuit of looks: an instance of free-floating fetishism, in the form of an unmotivated close-up of Agnes's black boots (at a moment when the only man in the room is looking down at his *own* feet and getting ready to reveal his 'lack' rather than cover it over through disavowal), and a shot of Agnes suddenly pointing her camera at Vladimir as he silently consents to her request.

This pattern repeats itself a little later at the end of a funny scene in which Vladimir helps Agnes L. scare off some pigeons that have been roosting on the skylights. Unable to get the 5.6 f-stop she needs to complete the shoot, Agnes suddenly breaks the erotic tension that has been building for several minutes when she runs off to swing a broom at the birds' nesting spot, in an attempt to bring in more sunlight. Vladimir, who is now fully nude, offers to help and spends the next minute or so flailing about in the altogether while Agnes takes an opportunity to lay on the floor and snap some photos. The result is a montage of black-and-white stills of the pianist leaping through the air, swinging a standard symbol of domesticity (doubling, in this case, as a phallic referent) in order to help an openly desiring and professionally voyeuristic older woman better objectify him on film. Having managed to obscure Lougren's genitals throughout all of this, *off Key* then draws attention to its own coy cinematography by suddenly confronting the viewer with the pianist's penis, during a playfully sensuous scene in which Vladimir performs Eric Satie's *3eme Gnosienne* while standing up with his back to the keys. Sending a smouldering look in Agnes L.'s direction and telling her that 'at the academy, we used to play games,' Vladimir is, at this moment, both the subject of his own desire and the willing object of desire for a female voyeur. By raising the idea (dealt with so thoroughly by Lehman) that 'men don't appear nude in films,' then abruptly cancelling that thought with a cut to an instance of full frontal nudity, *off Key* poses a new erotics of vision in which the woman is free to look and the male is free to offer himself up to the look, each according to their own desire.

Not surprisingly, given the subject matter, Stopkewich's approach to the nude male body in *Kissed* is less playful and more chilling. Based on Barbara Gowdy's short story 'We So Seldom Look on Love,' Stopkewich's feature centres on the sexual awakening of a necrophile, Sandra Larson (played by Molly Parker), who becomes involved with a (live) young man only to realize that she can desire him sexually only after he is dead. The short story was reportedly inspired in part by the true account of a Sacramento, California, woman who hijacked a young male corpse en route to its funeral and made love to the cadaver in a motel for several days before being caught by the police.[28]

One of the many intriguing production details that relates to this discussion is the fact that Stopkewich required her actors to sign a 'nudity parity agreement,' committing them to equal amounts of exposed flesh throughout the film. Explaining her reasons for the agreement, Stopkewich evoked the terms of a common sense feminism, saying she was 'sick and tired of seeing naked women on screen while the men always seemed to get out of it.'[29] Despite the possibility of attracting a kiss-of-death NC-17 rating in the United States and of encountering resistance from Canadian censor boards,[30] she went ahead with one prolonged scene of full frontal nudity and several other semi-nude scenes involving her willing male lead, Peter Outerbridge.

While the film remains somewhat vague, or perhaps just understated, on the details of how a woman might engineer a sexual encounter with a corpse (the story specifies that Sandra sits on top of the body and gets it to 'perform' cunnilingus), *Kissed* nevertheless stages several fairly graphic yet surprisingly 'tasteful' scenes of necrophilia, which consist of Sandra dancing around the embalming table, stripping down and then climbing on top of the corpse in preparation for the act. The film's climax occurs when the boyfriend, Matt, hangs himself in the nude while Sandra kneels paralysed at his feet, unable or unwilling to prevent his death.

Throughout these events – vaguely situated in the recent past and handled as a narrative with occasional self-reflexive moments – Sandra's vision is emphasized in ways that place viewers in radically new territory with respect to the capacity for a female gaze at the male body. While *off Key* features a woman taking partial command of the gaze and using it to construct the male body to her own artistic ends, the lead character in *Kissed* wields a more overtly controlling look in order to produce a compliant male body marked to the ultimate extent by lack. At the same time, this look leads Sandra to *divest* herself of power as she participates in a *loss-of-control* that mimics the 'chaos of disintegration' experienced by the corpse.

There is a sense of role playing in all of Sandra's sexual encounters. With the cadavers, Sandra is the phallic lover, performing a ritualistic dance around the embalming table, crawling up on their bodies, and somehow affecting a form of cunnilingus. With Matt, she is, ironically, the virginal one who has 'never done this before' when they go to his apartment and shyly make love for the first time. As their relationship progresses, she is determined to be the passive one, the corpse who deliberately toys with a receptive, stereotypically feminine role in preparation for her trips to the funeral home, where she satisfies the other, more assertive and, in normative language, 'masculine' pole of her oscillating desire. This leads to a kind of vaguely homoerotic sexual relay between the embalming room and the bedroom, as she stages indirect exchanges of energy between the one live man and the many dead men in her life. And although it might sound like a rather thankless job, her dividend from the arrangement is a kind of auto-erotic ecstasy that coincides with a blast of white light whenever she takes part in what she terms 'crossing over.'

One striking aspect of the relay involving Matt, Sandra, and the corpses is the resemblance it bears to Gayle Rubin's description of the Oedipal complex as an expression of the circulation of the phallus in intrafamily exchange. In the shared conceptual set underlying the work of both Lévi-Strauss and Lacan, Rubin argues, 'the phallus passes through the medium of women from one man to another – from father to son, from mother's brother to sister's son, and so forth ... [so that] women go one way, the phallus the other ... In this sense, the phallus is more than a feature which distinguishes the sexes; it is the embodiment of the male status, to which men accede, and in which certain rights inhere – among them, the right to a woman ... *The tracks which it leaves include gender identity, the division of the sexes.*'[31]

Like women in this patriarchal model, Sandra serves as a medium for an exchange of value between men. But it is obviously a non-normative version of this model that is proposed in the film and the story, since the woman is seen to *choose* her role as a conduit and enact the transfer on her own sexual terms, while the energy blazing between the corpses and Matt is of a death-star variety – briefly thrilling for all involved (with the possible exception of the corpses) but not much use as a source of masculine empowerment for the only living male subject involved.

I have dwelled on this point because it seems to encapsulate much of what the film and the story do, which is make use of a shocking sexual subject (one that has been turned into a commodity with somewhat unsettling ease by agents and distributors sniffing out a hot new talent)[32] as a pretext for rewriting the rules of sexual conduct and the gendered binaries of active and passive, masculine and feminine, controlling and compliant, penetrating and receptive. The film's final target is the mother lode, that base structure that Rubin describes as the primary residue of the circulation of the phallus: gender identity and the division of the sexes. What *Kissed* offers in its place is a vision of fluid gender and sexual identities, preferences, and positions that is in keeping with a range of recent theoretical projects geared to revealing gender as a 'tenuous identity constituted in time and external space through a stylized repetition of acts.'[33]

Obviously when one is in the territory of a necrophile, the desire associated with that character is being reshaped from the norm in important ways. Not surprisingly, much of the desiring difference signalled in *Kissed* takes place at the level of the gaze or the look, where we find a constellation of issues around 'masculine' and 'feminine' access to the gaze, the role of libidinal looking in the formation of the object, and the shifting, provisional nature of scopic control. In keeping with its status and possibilities as a visual medium, the film makes more of Sandra's transgressive deployment of the look than the story does, to the point of adding several lines of dialogue related to her vision and emphasizing the motif of the bright white light mentioned more peripherally by Gowdy. Stopkewich describes her approach to the circuit of looks as an overt decision, based on her familiarity with feminist film theory, and describes Sandra's access to the gaze as a reversal: 'I wanted to empower her gaze from a sexual

standpoint, which is why whenever it's her point of view, she's always looking at a dead guy ... You see [scopic rules] in courtship rituals, where the
man is always the one with a "penetrating gaze" while the woman "averts
her eyes in a coquettish way." ... It's embedded in the language we use
about looking. I wanted that to be completely turned around.'[34]

On one level the film enacts a stark reversal of the medical or anatomic
gaze that conventionally reserves a 'masculine' right to peer into female
bodies. Just as 'necrophiles aren't supposed to be female,' as Sandra at
one point observes, the female look is rarely thought of as extending *into*
the body, least of all the male body. Women, according to scopic regimes
in effect until recently in arenas ranging from the cinema to the operating theatre, do not *dissect* things, visually or otherwise; they exist in order
to be dissected, literally or as spectacle for 'the [masculine] desire to
explore mapped onto "the lust of the eyes."'[35] Yet Sandra's subversion of
this rule starts early. As a child, she is fascinated by death, and performs
ritualistic burial services for sparrows and mice, complete with popsicle-
stick crosses, wild circular dancing in her white underwear, and chillingly
innocent mantras about 'shrouding the body' and 'burying the body.'
Her one childhood friend, Carol, gets involved in this for a while, but
finally jumps ship when she realizes – during a somewhat bloody funeral
for a family of chipmunks – that all of this means more to Sandra than
she realized; that Sandra is, in fact, erotically interested in death. The
large black patch on Carol's wandering eye seems to suggest that her failure of will is somehow tied to her *lack* of access to a focused and penetrating gaze – a type of defect that makes it impossible for her to inhabit
Sandra's world or share her wide-eyed look into the beyond. In order to
be a necrophile, the film seems to suggest, one has to be able to gaze
directly at things that for everyone else are considered 'unsightly'; one's
vision must be unwavering, penetrating, and, in a sense, anatomical. For
Sandra, this involves increasingly taboo encounters with the spectacle of
death, beginning with the interior organs of mice (which she removes,
cleans, and returns to the body, licking the seam like an envelope) and
eventually moving on to human corpses.

This reversal of the conventional gender associations of the dissecting
gaze is underlined by the fact that Matt is 'taking some time off' from
medical school, which seems readable as code for his failure at, or lack of
commitment to, the type of 'masculine' scopic penetration involved in
the study and practice of medicine. Whereas Sandra 'sees it all' (Matt's
words to her on their first meeting) and actively pursues her goal of
becoming an embalmer, Matt is recoiling from the requirements of an

active gaze at the medicalized body, in a sense leaving a space for Sandra to occupy in a scopic arena historically off-limits to women. But Sandra's particular deployment of the look holds profound consequences for Matt, who becomes less and less capable of performing a coherent masculine identity as their relationship deteriorates. Her unwillingness or inability to look at him in the manner classically offered to women in narrative cinema – her inability, that is, to deny his lack by gazing at him with her imagination rather than her eyes – unsettles his already tenuous hold on exemplary male subjectivity and sends him into a spiral of self-doubt and eventual self-destruction. He becomes obsessed with understanding her behaviour in all its macabre detail, believing that by taking a systematic approach to it he can somehow explain it away and help Sandra return to a normative feminine identity that would, in turn, lead her to look at him with love and affirmation. What he's faced with, instead, is a woman of such frightening independence and utterly non-normative erotic tastes that she would rather 'stare directly into the sun without going blind' (her own metaphor for the necrophilic act) than gaze on a live male body.

It is arguable that Sandra's commitment to a radically dispersed, non-normative gaze affects Matt by undermining his connection to what Silverman, adapting a term coined by Jacques Rancière, calls the 'dominant fiction.' In Rancière's terms, the dominant fiction is that reservoir of images and stories through which a society figures consensus, and within which members of the social formation are asked to identify themselves.[36] Silverman adds a gender element to the concept, arguing that a key function of the dominant fiction lies in supporting '"exemplary" male subjectivity' by encouraging 'a kind of collective make-believe in the commensurability of the penis and the phallus'[37] – that is, a belief in the fiction that the symbolic power and privilege associated with the phallus should or does adhere automatically to those subjects possessing its 'representative,' the penis. Because of the pivotal status of the phallus, Silverman explains, more than sexual difference is sustained through alignment of that signifier with the male sexual organ: 'within our dominant fiction the phallus/penis equation occupies absolute pride of place ... Our entire "world," then, depends upon the alignment of the phallus and penis.'[38]

Sandra's refusal to stay within the scopic regime laid out for women by the dominant fiction (or to cooperate with Matt's requests for a clear-cut, temporary reversal of the gaze through sexual role playing) is a major part of what marks her as a dangerous female subject with the ability to destabilize masculine identity. Largely unmoved by the sight of live male flesh, and addicted to the dispersed blast of light energy that results from her ritualistic couplings with the corpses, Sandra remakes the (heterosexual) female look in ways that directly threaten the dominant fiction by falling *outside* the binaries of active and passive, feminine and masculine, controlling and compliant, that serve as the dominant fiction's points of reference.

It is this 'vision' of destabilized gender categories that helps to explain Matt's full frontal nudity toward the end of the film, when he hangs himself in his apartment with Sandra looking on. Summoned there by a cryptic phone call, Sandra arrives to find Matt standing nude on top of a chair with a noose around his neck. A close-up of her eyes as they glaze over and blink in slow motion brings us directly to the source of Matt's 'problem': a woman's inability to gaze at him with conventional female desire. Suspended there on his suicidal perch, bathed in warm yellow light that makes him look like a Caravaggio figure, Matt is doing the only thing he can under the circumstances: prostrating himself, and submitting his body as further evidence that the penis is *not* commensurate with the phallus, that there are alternate masculinities (and femininities) that function in ways that are at least implicitly antagonistic to the dominant fiction. The fact that his penis is flaccid in this scene seems all the more appropriate when we consider how *little* Sandra Larson's erotic tastes depend for their satisfaction on the erect, conquering, or penetrating penis. In fact her sexual preferences bypass the penis altogether, in favour of the dead male tongue, and it may be this knowledge that leads Matt to offer himself to her in a detumescent state.

On the surface, Matt's decision to hang himself in the nude reflects his desire to be ravished by Sandra after death. 'You don't [love me],' he tells her from atop the chair he's about to kick away, 'but you will.' He is offering himself to her on the only level that she can finally appreciate, guaranteeing one last great roll in the morgue with the object of his obsession, and perhaps even sparing her the bother of undressing him.[39] In another sense, however, his nudity might be seen to literalize Sandra's refusal of the dominant fiction. Her sexual modus operandi involves *freezing* the male body in place with her look, choosing men who can never break free of the voyeuristic relationship in which they are held as absolute objects of her desire, then, on her own terms, loosening her control over the situation. By denuding Matt in this scene, both Gowdy (who wrote the scene this way) and Stopkewich (who filmed it essentially as written) seem to be clarifying what is at stake in Sandra's refusal to wield the look in ways that will uphold Matt in his phallic identification: in challenging the gendered basis of the scopic regime, Sandra is challenging gender division per se, while holding out the possibility for a fluid oscillation between active and passive aims.

Interestingly enough, in a significant departure from the classical Hollywood pattern of killing or otherwise punishing the woman for gazing inappropriately at the male, it is Outerbridge's character who dies while Sandra continues, unrepentant, as an occasional necrophile who cherishes the memory of having ravished her dead boyfriend: 'His star was the brightest I've ever seen, exploding and surrounding us,' she says in the film's closing voice over. 'I still work in a funeral home. I'm still compelled to cross over. But now I see Matt when I look into the centre.'

Cowards, Bullies, and Cadavers: Nation and Masculinity in the Mid-90s

Having looked at three very different approaches to the male body, it remains for me to show how *Kissed* and *off Key* interact with an earlier work like *Patriotism, Part One*. While there is little in *Kissed* or *off Key* to suggest the kind of overt interest in national dimensions of masculine embodiment that I've identified in *Patriotism*, it seems relevant that both later films emerge out of a cultural moment in which many of our theories about masculinity and the nation are being simultaneously redefined. They emerge, that is, out of a moment in which the increasingly fractured and heterogeneous character of Canadian social life (along with the current popularity of theories stressing Canada's inherent postmodernity and its refusal of 'a monolithic meta-narrative of nationhood')[40] are coinciding with a broadly based rediscovery of the male body's erotic potential and a simultaneous rethinking of once taken-for-granted ideas about what it means to 'be a man' in any particular setting or historical period.

As Ramsay points out, dominant masculine gender identity and traditional concepts of the modern nation share 'a common metaphoric impulse to mastery over margins,'[41] in the sense that both have been geared to shoring up 'the ideal, ordered stability of the centre in order to contain the threats of difference, disorder and death' from the outside. Like nation, she writes, 'masculinity is about the drawing up of borders and the myth of complete independence from others, while asserting complete rights, sovereignty and freedom for itself in dominating and mastering others.'[42] But in an English-Canadian setting, where the narrative Canada tells about itself is increasingly one of margins triumphing over centre, traditional scripts of empowered masculinity lack interpellating power. In keeping with the imagined community of Canadian nation-hood that, Howells tells us, 'focuses not on unity but on disunity, highlighting individual difference through regionalism, bilingualism, [and] multiculturalism,'[43] masculinities in English Canada lean toward a spectrum of 'subordinate' varieties. Individual Canadian men are undoubtedly still able to exert power over other groups internally (women, Indigenous peoples, and children, for example), but Canada's colonial history and ongoing neocolonial relationship with the United States have, arguably, made it difficult to sustain an imagined community of empowered masculinity in English Canada.

In both *off Key* and *Kissed*, this refusal of a meta-narrative of nationhood (and the correspondingly weak access to empowered masculinity that I'm suggesting is a part of the same package) are written on the male body by means of an active and overtly desiring female gaze. Both films display confidence in the right to assertive female looking, and offer fresh approaches to a familiar subject: what used to be considered (and still is, by some) the 'problem' of beleaguered, passive, inadequate, English-Canadian masculinity. Instead of revolving around the 'cowards, bullies and clowns' that Fothergill saw as symptomizing the sorry state of Cana-dian masculinity in films of the 1960s and 1970s,[44] however, these two late feminist films bring us buffed concert pianists and well-lit male cadavers – objects of desire for women in control of the look. Substituting female desire for anxiety about the vulnerable, colonial male body, these films celebrate subordinate masculinity as an aspect of Canadian heterogeneity rather than viewing it as a problem in need of a solution.

NOTES

I would like to thank Brenda Longfellow, Peter Morris, Blaine Allan, Peter Har-court, and Peter Lehman for their insightful comments about earlier drafts of this article. Funding for the larger project of which this is a part was received from Telefilm Canada, the Ontario Film Development Corporation, and the Film Stud-ies Association of Canada through the Gerald Pratley Award.

1 The pattern is more pronounced in the visual arts, where low production costs, individual working methods, and an established life-drawing tradition have made it easier for artists such as Charlotte Hammond, Badanna Zack, Jennifer Dickson, Tanya Rosenberg, and Diana Thornycroft to paint, sculpt, and photograph the male nude. Maria Tippett, *By a Lady: Celebrating Three Cen-turies of Art by Canadian Women* (Toronto: Penguin, 1992), 174–7.

2 Dot Tuer, 'Mirages of Difference, Dreams of the Body,' in *Film Portraits of Women by Women* (Toronto: The Funnel, 1986), 17–18.
3 Maxine Sheets-Johnstone, 'Corporeal Archetypes and Power,' *Hypatia* 7, no. 3 (Summer 1992): 69.
4 Peter Lehman, *Running Scared: Masculinity and the Representation of the Male Body* (Philadelphia: Temple University Press, 1993), 28.
5 Kaja Silverman, *Male Subjectivity at the Margins* (New York: Routledge, 1992), 15.
6 Ibid., 2–3.
7 This expression obviously begs the question: What does a non-patriarchal view of the male body look like? There are no 'hard and fast' rules, but I'm generally in sympathy with Lehman's idea that patriarchal culture needs to keep the penis out of sight in order to uphold phallic privilege. According to this thinking, a non-patriarchal view of the male body might be one that draws attention to the humble material foundations of phallic power, either by revealing the penis (though it's never this simple) or by taking some other approach that foregrounds the relationship between the symbolic and material bases of male privilege. Having said that, though, individual cases are always more complex than this schema implies, and female artists cannot be automatically expected to produce non-patriarchal views of the male body.
8 Christine Ramsay, 'Canadian Narrative Cinema from the Margins: "The Nation" and Masculinity in *Goin' Down the Road*,' *Canadian Journal of Film Studies* 2, nos. 2–3 (1993): 27–50.
9 Fothergill's 1973 paper, 'Coward, Bully, or Clown,' focused on a variety of complaints from the late 1960s and early 1970s about so-called weak masculinity in Canadian cinema. He concluded that the primary version of *la condition canadienne* reflected to Canadians by their own films is 'the depiction, through many different scenarios, of the radical inadequacy of the male protagonist – his moral failure, especially, and most visibly, in his relationships with women.' Robert Fothergill, 'Coward, Bully, or Clown: The Dream-Life of a Younger Brother,' in *Canadian Film Reader*, ed. Seth Feldman and Joyce Nelson (Toronto: Peter Martin Associates and Take One Film Book Series, 1977), 235–6.
10 Ramsay, 'Canadian Narrative Cinema,' 47.
11 Ramsay used the term during a panel discussion about 'Why Canadian films are weird.' *Benmergui Live*, Canadian Broadcasting Corporation, 13 Sept. 1996.
12 Lehman, *Running Scared*, 5 and 28. The following is a partial list of male-authored, Canadian and Québécois films featuring full-frontal nudity or prominent images of artworks depicting the penis: Darrell Wasyk's *Mustard Bath* (1992); Gerard Ciccoritti's *Paris, France*; David Wellington's *I Love a Man in Uni-*

form; Atom Egoyan's *The Adjuster*; Richard L. Lewis's *Whale Music*; John Greyson's *Zero Patience* and *Lilies*; various Mike Hoolboom films; Bruce Sweeney's *Live Bait*; Bruce LaBruce's *Super 8½*; Bill MacGillivray's *Life Classes*; Robert Lepage's *Le Confessional*; Mort Ransen's *Margaret's Museum*; and Roger Frappier's Quebec–Argentinian co-production, *La Côté obscure du coeur*. Gregory Wild's 1994 feature, *Highway of Heartache*, assaults the viewer with what seems like dozens of images of grotesquely oversized 'puppet penises,' and the group production *Pink Komkommer*, an animated short that includes characters drawn by Alison Snowden and David Fine, revels in the graphic depiction of animated phallic objects dreamed up by a snoozing (and otherwise very proper-looking) elderly woman. Two more Québécois films that flirt with revealing the penis but ultimately don't are *Un Zoo, la nuit* and *Jacques et novembre*.

13 Barbara de Genevieve, 'Masculinity and Its Discontents,' *Camerawork* 18, nos. 3–4 (Summer–Fall 1991): 4.

14 This is not to exclude American feminists who have written about Wieland and find her important to their work, but to acknowledge Kass Banning's point that Wieland has things to say of particular importance to Canadian women. See Banning, 'The Mummification of Mommy: Joyce Wieland as the AGO's First Living Other,' *C Magazine* 13 (March 1987): 32–8.

15 Kay Armatage, 'The Feminine Body: Joyce Wieland's *Water Sark*,' in *Dialogue: Canadian and Quebec Cinema*, ed. Pierre Véronneau, Michael Dorland, and Seth Feldman (Ottawa: Canadian Film Institute, 1987), 283–95. Armatage describes the films *A Salt in the Park*, *Larry's Recent Behaviour*, *Patriotism II*, and the 1961 stain painting *Balling* as examples of 'an approach to sexuality which is clearly prefeminist, particularly in its absorption with phallic pleasure.'

16 Lauren Rabinovitz, 'An Interview with Joyce Wieland,' *AfterImage*, May 1981, 8.

17 Banning, 'Mummification of Mommy,' 33.

18 Ibid.

19 It would take another paper to explore this assertion fully, but I'll venture a few titles here: *Goin' Down the Road*; *Un Zoo, la nuit*; *Jacques et novembre*; and *Perfectly Normal*.

20 In the sense that it predates feminism's arrival as a widespread movement in North America.

21 Randi Spires, 'True Matriot Love: Joyce Wieland's One-Woman Show,' *Canadian Forum*, Aug.–Sept. 1987, 31.

22 Parveen Adams, 'Representation and Sexuality,' *m/f* 1 (1978): 66–7.

23 Brian D. Johnson, 'The Canadian Patient,' *Maclean's*, 24 March 1997, 44.

24 By late feminism, I mean a version of it inflected by poststructuralist and postmodern critiques of the unity of the subject and debates into the nature and problems of late capitalism. Judith Butler, Donna Haraway, Rosi Braidotti, and

Diana Fuss are a few practitioners of this approach, which tends to emphasize differences among and between women.

25 Raymond Bellour, 'Hitchcock: The Enunciator,' *Camera Obscura 2* (Fall 1977): 86.

26 Both attended the University of British Columbia.

27 Silverman, *Male Subjectivity*, 42. See also Lehman's discussion of *Beauty and the Beast* narratives and *Cyrano de Bergerac* in *Running Scared*, 12–13.

28 According to Stopkewich, Karen Greenlee was an embalmer who fell in love with a corpse and kidnapped it rather than let it be buried. 'She was driving the hearse to the cemetery, but when she saw the family standing there she did a big donut with the hearse and took off. She spent the next three days in a cheap hotel room getting high on Tylenol and codeine and doing the deed.' Author's notes of Stopkewich addressing the Directors Guild of Canada after a 4 November 1996 screening of *Kissed* at the Deluxe Laboratory on Adelaide Street, Toronto. Today Greenlee, who is also a poet, tours North America with her writing and speaks to groups about necrophilia and sexual liberation.

29 Telephone interview with the filmmaker, 1 Oct. 1996. Stopkewich said she had no trouble getting Peter Outerbridge to sign the contract. Outerbridge, who bared it all in Gerard Ciccoritti's 1992 feature, *Paris, France,* joked during the film shoot that he wanted more male nudity.

30 *Kissed* avoided an NC-17 rating in the United States by signing with Samuel Goldwyn, which screened the film unrated in its own theatres.

31 Gayle Rubin, 'The Traffic in Women: Notes on the "Political Economy" of Sex,' in *Toward an Anthropology of Women*, ed. Rayna R. Reiter (New York: Monthly Review Press, 1975), 191–2. Cited in Teresa de Lauretis, 'Through the Looking-Glass,' in *Narrative, Apparatus, Ideology: A Film Theory Reader*, ed. Philip Rosen (New York: Columbia University Press, 1986), 364. My emphasis.

32 Stopkewich was able to parlay the film's festival success into a twenty-four-screen deal with Samuel Goldwyn in the United States, a minimum six-the-atre Canadian run with Malofilm, and a contract for representation with the Los Angeles talent agency William Morris. As Brenda Longfellow pointed out to me, it's unlikely that the film's commitment to 'subversive female desire' had anything to do with these commercial successes. While the film's market appeal does not negate Stopkewich's feminist intent or alter the film's formal debt to an earlier feminist avant-garde, it does serve as a sobering reminder that the film industry is capable of engaging in its own 'oppositional reading' strategies, handily converting feminist intent into high finance.

33 Judith Butler, *Gender Trouble* (New York: Routledge 1990), 140.

34 Interview with the filmmaker, 19 Nov. 1996.

35 Giuliana Bruno, 'Spectatorial Embodiments: Anatomies of the Visible and the Female Bodyscape,' *Camera Obscura* 28 (Jan. 1992): 239.

36 Silverman, *Male Subjectivity*, 30.

37 Ibid., 15.

38 Ibid., 16.

39 This is Stopkewich's view: 'Basically, he's trying to make very clear to her what he's doing, what kind of offering this is, and he's saving her some work.' Interview, 19 Nov. 1996.

40 Carol Ann Howells, 'No Transcendental Image: Canadianness in Contemporary Women's Fictions in English,' in *Canada on the Threshold of the 21st Century*, ed. C.H.W. Remie and J.M. Lacroix (Philadelphia: John Benjamin Publishing, 1991), 318.

41 Ramsay, 'Canadian Narrative Cinema,' 45.

42 Ibid., 46.

43 Howells, 'No Transcendental Image,' 318.

44 Fothergill, 'Coward, Bully, or Clown,' 234–51.

Querying/Queering the Nation

JEAN BRUCE

I believe that feminine artistic production takes place by means of a complicated process involving conquering and reclaiming, appropriating and formulating, as well as forgetting and subverting. In the works of those female artists who are concerned with the women's movement, one finds artistic tradition as well as the break with it.
Silvia Bovenschen[1]

You can only read against the grain if misfits in the text signal the way.
Gayatri Spivak[2]

'Women's cinema' is not just a set of films or practices of cinema, but also a number of film-critical discourses and broadly cast networks of cinema-related practices that are directly connected with the history of feminism.
Teresa de Lauretis[3]

In rethinking a definition for women's cinema while reflecting on 1980s cinema by and/or for women, Teresa de Lauretis concludes that women's cinema has emerged historically as both a practice and an attitude, a relationship between text and context. She suggests that there are any number of 'guerrilla tactics' – discursive possibilities, specific textual strategies, and counter-cinema audiences – that contribute to the ambiguity of the term 'women's cinema.' She cites some of the contributing factors that help to create a women's film community as being the 'mutual support and interchange between feminist film critics, scholars, festival organizers, distributors, and filmmakers'[4] who together constitute a critical mass. Likewise, changes within these groups have been signalled by ongoing challenges to the predominantly white, middle-class, and heterosexual character of the feminist movement, notably from women of colour and lesbians. They were among the first to provide more subtly nuanced critiques of patriarchy that foregrounded the interconnected-ness of racism and homophobia as discourses of oppression. It is within this history of both stylistic and political challenges to mainstream forms of representation, and the critical mass that supports it, that the elusive and unruly notion of the 'lesbian postmodern' can be seen to develop.

After I attempt to sketch out some of the features of what might be characterized as 'the lesbian postmodern' in cinema, I will discuss two films that I think rely on the relationship between postmodern aesthetics and lesbian identity politics in order for their subversive 'messages' to be 'read.' I hope this discussion will be a useful method of textual analysis that helps to situate the films in a larger theoretical and discursive frame-work at the same time as it addresses the accountability of the spectator for what might be deemed her textual interventions. My discussion of *La Vie rêvée* (Dansereau, 1972) foregrounds the slipperiness of viewing strate-gies that allow the unruly/lesbian spectator to make the film her own. The historio-critical conditions for re-reading this film as lesbian are derived from its counter-cinema conventions as well as from the history of feminism; that is, in the ongoing discursive relationship between text, context, and spectator. Feminist critiques of patriarchy claim that if women's place is always as a cultural outsider, then her pleasures must be gotten 'against its grain,' a practice of conflicting or inappropriate read-ings of culture that, over time, has produced unruly cultural consumers. It might be further suggested that these conditions provide a discursive space in which a film such as *Forbidden Love* (Fernie, Weissman, 1992) is (only) the logical outcome. *Forbidden Love* is ironic and unusual; the film foregrounds postmodern artistic practices such as pastiche and parody, and, notwithstanding the complexities of the screen–spectator relation-ship, it addresses the lesbian spectator directly.

Defining the Lesbian Postmodern in Cinema

Spectators who are particularly marginalized within socio-political dis-courses (perhaps because they are part of a sexually subordinate group such as lesbians) arguably make especially astute cultural analysts and 'wilful' spectators. This tendency may be due to the fact that we must engage in an ongoing process of (re)negotiating our tenuous positions as cultural consumers of representations that tend to exclude us. This marginality or alterity invites us to 'perform complex manoeuvres when watching films that make it possible to gain pleasure against the grain of representational and narrative structures.'[5]

It could be argued that lesbian spectators, in particular, manoeuvre with a high degree of agility within and outside the dominant discourses of gender and sexuality. This manoeuvring presents at least two – sometimes competing, sometimes complementary – positions for the lesbian spectator. One acknowledges the exclusive nature of heterosexual romance upon which much of mainstream cinema rests; another admits that in order for any film to be understood, the lesbian spectator must be familiar with those very modes of social discourse and cinematic address. A third position results from the relationship between these two that acknowledges her adept skills as cultural negotiator and survivor as a marginal subject: the lesbian spectator is in some ways always a cultural guerrilla. She is constrained by cultural exclusion, but can take pleasure in the wilful act of reworking scenarios to include her. Films about sexuality and gender – in other words most, if not all, films – are thus susceptible to unruly lesbian readings.

Postmodernism tends to valorize multiplicity, reflexivity, parody, and textual and sexual ambivalence. In those texts that are postmodern and directly involve sexuality and gender, the availability of lesbian readings is especially highlighted. However, as Robyn Wiegman suggests, a merely 'facile embrace of contradiction, multiplicity and flux'[6] is insufficient for claiming a politics of postmodern lesbian aesthetics. Thus, films can and do exist along a continuum of political engagement to the degree that they 'enable an interventionist or transformative politics.'[7] They foreground the complexity and instability of the categories of gender and sexuality by employing defamiliarizing cinematic strategies.

These films achieve the 'goal' of destabilizing or intervening into and multiplying sexual subjectivity, but do not stop there. It is not as though you can take lesbian sexuality and postmodernism and place them side by side to get the lesbian postmodern. When you put them together, the first kind of transformation that occurs is between them. Both lesbian sexuality and postmodernism are changed by their association with the other. Together, they do not simply provide spectatorial experiences that please everyone, *even* lesbians. Rather, the lesbian postmodern marks an opportunity for the politicization of postmodernist practices. As an implicit example of cultural querying, lesbianism becomes a means to both anchor and unmoor the relationship between politics and culture in a manner consistent with, but also deviant from, either 'mainstream' feminism or 'facile' postmodernism.

La Vie rêvée

La Vie rêvée, the first feminist feature film directed by a woman in Quebec, is a film that offers sexuality as a utopia for women at the same time as it argues strongly against its own utopic view of sex. The topic of sex – of heterosexual sex – is one of the film's main focal points, but sex is so pervasive in *La Vie rêvée* that the idea itself becomes excessive. This excess is one of the ways in which the film critiques gender relations. The two main female characters, Isabelle and Virginie, discuss the topic constantly, and are often presented in situations in which sex and gender roles are at issue. The film's loose narrative structure revolves around their discussions of sex, relationships, and their fantasies about men, although there is nothing like a conventional 'plot' in *La Vie rêvée*. Male sexuality, as seen through their eyes, is made strange; this functions as a critique of heterosexuality as male sexuality, and, as Brenda Longfellow has pointed out, is an inversion of the classic psychoanalytic question, 'what do women want?' The film implicitly asks 'what do men want?' although this question is never really answered.[8]

The film's discourse on female sexuality and gender are examined, in part, through *La Vie rêvée*'s dialectical structure. Its combination of cinematic collisions invites comparisons among the ideas it presents. Specific examples of this structure can be detected in the pre-credits portion of the opening sequence. The imagery, which is presented first in slow motion and then at normal speed, is used as a means to explore the relationship of fantasy to reality. This exploration establishes a comparative premise that extends beyond this sequence and informs other kinds of arbitrary divisions in the film such as the split between mind and body, the personal and the political, the public and the private, and the hetero and the homo.

The first image or 'establishing shot' is a medium close-up of a man and a woman on a downtown street (later identifiable as Montreal) depicted in slow motion. They look like tourists posing for a photo, an idea that is conveyed by their friendly direct smiles and Hawaiian leis. This image is replaced by the disturbing home movie–like shot of a little girl lifting her nightgown and exposing her genitalia, also presented in slow motion and with her direct address gaze. Next, young women are depicted twirling around, laughing, and playing with young men outdoors; the sound and the image track are out of sync. Finally, a woman is seen beating her fists against a closed door at the top of a staircase.

Since all of these images have been presented in slow motion without a clear establishing shot as such, their status as imaginary is highlighted. As spectators we are thus invited to try to make sense of the relationship of the images to each other perhaps in a more overt manner than if the sequence were presented in a classic realist fashion with its location in time and space (and its narrative purpose) firmly established. Only later does it become clear that these images are possibly Isabelle's mindscreen, but it is never completely clear whether they are her memories, her fantasies, or her dream projections, or some combination of all of these.

A close-up of a toilet flushing in the women's lavatory at B&C Films (the film company where Isabelle and Virginie are employed) is one of the first images in *La Vie rêvée* that is presented at a normal speed. Such a shot is still a rather unusual way to introduce the film's 'real' setting, and in fact not much time is spent at the film company after the sequence ends. However, this brief sequence is noteworthy, partly because it is quite unconventional and precisely because it does not appear to serve any obvious narrative function. Yet its purpose, even though the shot is repeated once more, is more than simple scatological 'excess.' It underscores the public–private blur that the preceding images have first suggested about the relationship of fantasy to reality and that will later be more overtly linked to sexuality.

The credit and opening sequences may not contribute much to the establishment of 'setting' per se, but they do clearly establish that spectatorship is usually an exercise in voyeurism, a relationship to film images that is here subtly contested. The opening suggests that this film intends to deviate from that norm to the extent that it will get closer to the characters' subjective points of view rather than farther away. This excessively close view disrupts the voyeuristic pleasure that might otherwise be offered by a more classic play between distance and proximity. These counter-cinema strategies are both dislocating and confrontational; moreover, their very ordinariness begs the question of what usually constitutes a 'narrative event' at the same time that they expose the spectator's basic scopophilia. From the opening sequence onward, spectatorial complicity is attached to cultural critique, an idea that is foregrounded by linking two kinds of transgressive looking: sexual (inappropriate and potentially incestuous with the little girl's lifting of her nightgown) and confrontational (in conjunction with her direct address gaze), with the digestive or scatological (the flushing of the toilets). The blurring of public and private spaces is achieved by making visible the invisible of private bodily functions and connecting them to the spectator's look. The clearly marked boundaries of the public and private continue to be blurred at a number of junctures within the film.

The 'function' of social and ideological border controls, conversely, becomes more apparent as the women grapple with their own personal and social relationships, including the discourse on the relationship of feminine (and masculine) behaviour to appearance developed throughout the film. Social and cinematic conventions become particularly evident when 'propriety' is transgressed. What the women say and do is often at odds with the film's position on the topics it deals with: *La Vie rêvée* uses cinematic point of view to underscore ideological critique. By depicting several possible takes on an issue, cinematic point of view becomes a discursive strategy that encourages debate on the topic of sexuality and gender in a patriarchal society. This is perhaps what Seth Feldman is referring to when he describes *La Vie rêvée* as an exploration of the relationship between 'the subjective experience and the larger social context.'[9]

The most striking effects of the blurring of boundaries in the film are its tendency to destabilize sexual identity and its implicit invitation to renegotiate the relationship between film and spectator. Nowhere in the film is the notion that Isabelle and Virginie are or might be lovers mentioned; in fact they spend considerable time fantasizing about men. Yet, in *La Vie rêvée*, one could say that lesbianism is the disruptive discourse that dares not speak its name. Its irruption may be achieved, in part, through the excess of sexual desire circulating in the film with no appropriate object to fix upon. It may also be that the circulation of desire is partly due to the erotic charge of the suppressed – but not unarticulated – lesbian subtext of the film, which is available to the film's 'readers' independent of their sexual orientation. In the context of all of its other destabilizing strategies, this becomes one more unbalancing act.

The sequence that best raises the issue of the lesbian subtext occurs when Isabelle has just been told that her contract with the company will not be renewed because of a lower demand for the Montreal company's services based on the uncertain political climate in Quebec. Isabelle is introduced almost literally as 'a piece of ass': she appears as a fragmented image with her buttocks and upper thighs forming the establishing shot for this sequence. The next shot locates the point of view with her Anglo boss. He tells her, partly in English, and partly in very poor French, that 'for a woman this is not so important' (separatist politics or having a job?), and that she 'should have no trouble finding a man to marry' her. As Isabelle storms out of his office and races down the hall, images of her crying are replaced by her smiling and having sex with Jean-Jacques, the man of her dreams. Her ideal man, it appears, will rescue her from economic crisis and provide satisfying sex to boot. This *rêve* is abruptly interrupted by a low-angle shot of a woman, presumably J-J's wife, who breaks the spell of Isabelle's fantasy fuck by saying, 'he always comes back to me.'[10] Isabelle is left alone on the bed, jolted from her reverie (as are we by the abrupt edit) in what now appears to be her masturbation fantasy. When, at this point, a disembodied female whispers, 'You have to go all the way,' Isabelle sits up on the bed, and says – or rather thinks, in voice-over – 'I would not have gone near this far without her.'

Another ambiguous reference, probably to Virginie since the voice-over/mindscreen is followed by a medium close-up of her, is thus made in a highly sexually charged context. The voice-over also raises the very question the film has so far been suppressing: if heterosexual romance and the (hetero)sexist context of work have so far provided unsatisfying experiences for Isabelle and Virginie, lesbianism (and escape) must be the logical next step.[11] And, although the film ostensibly critiques patriarchal social structures and not heterosexuality, the two have become blurred by the excess of attention devoted to sexuality, and connected through the cinematic techniques I have mentioned. This blurring signals the film's duplicity or ambivalence about heterosexuality, even though the belief our identification figures express regarding heterosexual romance remains relatively secure until the film's end.

At this point, the two women conspire to get Isabelle's love object to meet her for an afternoon tryst. A series of still photos of the couple engaged in 'lifestyle activities,' which are echoed in the posters on Isabelle's bedroom wall, provides the evidence that the image of heterosexual romance is important. The myth that these images carry is soon overburdened by the impossibility of the image becoming a reality, underscored by Jean-Jacques's inability to maintain an erection. The film reasserts heterosexual sex as male-active, with the object of the penis entering the vagina as the defining feature (at least for J-J) of a 'complete' sexual encounter.

La Vie rêvée organizes its discourse on the relations of gender to sexuality by linking the social and political problems it raises to cinematic point of view and the film's dialectical structure. The film offers several complex narrative and visual points of view that link the dilemmas in which Isabelle and Virginie find themselves to the social structures of the family and politics, to personal and cultural memory, and to rampant consumerism. In short, the film 'levels' the competing and complementary discourses on female sexual subjectivity. This is accomplished cinematically by introducing a series of what J-F Lyotard has called '*petits récits*,' which are dialectical and impure. According to Lyotard, the complexity of exchanges in the story-telling matrix is made more problematic – that is, harder to nail down ideologically – with the introduction of multiple narratives typical of postmodern texts.[12] However, Andreas Huyssen adds an important proviso to this claim by arguing that 'it is certainly no accident that questions of subjectivity and authorship have resurfaced with a vengeance in the postmodern text. After all, it does matter who is speaking or writing.'[13]

That the two women in this film, together, cooperatively attempt to recreate their subjectivities in relation to the images that constitute their personal and cultural histories is both aesthetically and politically significant. Their courage is exemplified by rejecting some mythic images and reclaiming others. The closing of the film has them tearing down the lifestyle posters and advertisements from the wall in an almost manic montage sequence. Isabelle claims that she is now free, but of what? These images suggests that the 'dreamlife' of patriarchy provides no real options since it is based on romantic promises that are meaningless, impossible to achieve, or exploitative. *La Vie rêvée* rejects patriarchy as an unfinished history of women's struggles. This is signified by the layering of sounds that end the film, and it suggests a more complex history of which these women are also a part. In an ending that again blurs the distinction between fantasy and reality – by referring to off-screen spaces aurally that cannot be confirmed as either diegetic or non-diegetic in origin – we hear references to Quebec cultural history (the musical spoons), as well as perhaps to women's biological history (the joyful sound of children playing). We also hear the sound of their Volkswagen bug as they drive off into an open and rêvé future.

Susan Rubin Suleiman reminds us that to conceive of art as a strict political platform rather than as a forum for debate locates the notion of resistance firmly within texts (or films) and 'not in their readings.'[14] Suleiman cites Stanley Fish's argument that 'every reading of a text, no matter how personal or "quirky," can be shown to be part of a collective discourse and analysed historically and ideologically as characteristic of a group, or what Fish has called "an interpretive community."'[15] Suleiman also challenges the hierarchy of the 'correct reading,' which she claims valorizes certain readings at the expense of others. She sees this valorization as operating hegemonically to block new interpretive and discursive strategies by seeking to define what a thing *is* (in this case postmodernist culture), and then naming what it can *do*.[16] This approach to culture ignores the long history of women as cultural consumers who have 'stolen' pleasures from a variety of cultural sources and used them for their own purposes, but it does raise the issue of wanting representations that address us directly.

Forbidden Love

The problem of negotiating a satisfactory relationship between personal and cultural notions of identity (which I have so far been raising in relation to *La Vie rêvée*) is a central problematic of *Forbidden Love*. In *Forbidden Love* the criticism, and, indeed, much of the pleasure, comes from placing two styles of filmmaking – the documentary and the melodrama – side by side and by playing with identification strategies in the film. These techniques are a part of a self-reflexive, postmodern pastiche of both cinematic genres that are here attached to the sometimes contradictory formations of identity. The interview-style documentary favoured by feminist filmmakers in the 1960s and 1970s is intercut with a filmic version of the lesbian pulp melodrama of the 1950s and 1960s to create a new, hybrid style. This particular stylistic treatment of the subject matter makes the film both 'playful' and 'serious.' The parody it engages in permits a wide-ranging critique of the ideology that historically has informed these representational strategies. At the same time, the film valorizes the historical struggles and celebrates the pleasures of lesbianism. The tension between the two forms is a technique the film exploits in order to carry its political message.

'Full' is, I think, an appropriate word to describe the style of *Forbidden Love*. From the opening credits sequences to the post-credits coda, *Forbidden Love* is a visually sumptuous and witty film. It is loaded with in-jokes and astute commentary. The film's opening plays knowingly with the conventions of the institutional style of the NFB by satirizing both the Board's logo and its tendency to warn viewers in writing about the contents of its films, despite their general tameness. Both of these devices help to convey the National Film Board's image as 'nice and inoffensive,' but the logo of the fluidly moving figure, who presumably represents the ideal, non-gendered, and multicultural Canadian, is the first image to take a 'shot' from the filmmakers.

The familiar NFB logo is accompanied by the sound of hot electric guitar riff, followed almost immediately by a honkin' sax and drums. Together they suggest that the film already offers two, perhaps contradictory, positions for its spectators. On the one hand, the image briefly conforms to the opening of any NFB film, and to its political (if not aesthetic) mandate of correctness – to interpret Canada to Canadians, no matter how diverse we may be. On the other hand, the musical style of the soundtrack suggests that this film may be 'hotter' than expected, and, in retrospect, it serves to remind viewers that some of the people who were groovin' to that sexy urban music known as R&B were also dykes.

The spinning logo is followed by an intertitled disclaimer stating: 'Unless otherwise stated the people who appear in this film should not be presumed to be homosexual ...' The music then fades as one intertitle is replaced by another: '... or heterosexual.' In the first half of the intertitle, the form and message are consistent with the middle-class liberalism that it could be argued, given the style and subject matter of the documentary films it often produces, is the board's overriding ideology. However, the second half of the intertitle, with its obvious playfulness, acts as a corrective that also situates *Forbidden Love* within a selectively subversive tradition that is also part of the legacy of the NFB. The opening intertitle is thus connected to the film's title of 'forbidden love,' which suggests that the film will be a serious (albeit vicarious) look at 'perverse desire.' *Forbidden Love* is, after all, an educational film.

This immediate instance of the give-and-take character of the film is also a good example of the film's rhetorical strategies employed for political and educational purposes. It is a device first introduced in the opening that the film exploits throughout to surprise spectators and then 'correct' any misperceptions they may have about the subject matter. The pattern is consistent, and the surprise is not usually given away in advance unless a greater jolt is in store for the audience. The overall structure works something like this: first, the film raises certain expectations based on the familiar conventions associated with melodrama or documentary. These expectations are then modified, undermined, or completely discarded by mixing the two styles, or interrupting one with the other. In other words, the subversion often occurs as a result of mixing the expectations of one genre with the outcome of the other. The tension created between the different modes of address is directly related to the presumed identity of the viewer (as suggested by the opening disclaimer intertitle), but these cinematic techniques are also made visible by the overtly shifting identification strategies of the film. As a result, the homophilia of this film becomes explicit, and the implicit heterosexism in traditional positions of spectatorship is also subtly challenged.

Such a contestatory position is offered, for example, in the sequence

following the opening, which is introduced by a long shot of a truck travelling in a vast landscape. The 'washed out' almost sepia quality of the
sequence gives it the character of overexposed film stock; it is literally an
'outdated' image. It thus locates the scene firmly in the past, and, judging
by the costumes and music, the setting is likely the late 1950s or early
1960s. On the now explicitly diegetic soundtrack, the song 'Tell Laura I
Love Her' is announced by the D.J. The relationship of the image to the
sound track might suggest that the song refers to the heterosexual
romance of the couple in the image, since 'the couple' acknowledges it
with a knowing look. The song (by Paul Peterson) is referred to by the
D.J. but not performed in the film. As the young woman gets out of the
truck, her boyfriend gently cautions her about the woman on the train
platform.

In this context, it might be safe to assume that the conflict has been
between the two women, and that they have perhaps been vying for the
young man's love, particularly as the woman at the station is quickly identified as 'Laura.' The song itself recalls a fairly typical conceit of the melodramatic modes both from film and music genres of the 1950s but
represents a rather atypical development within them: the masochistic
male torch singer.[17] Because the song is not actually performed in the
film, its status as a secure marker of heterosexual love is questionable.
Given the song's new reference within the context of the film, the heterosexual presumption upon which the 'joke' relies is completely undermined. The affair, which has ended, is clearly revealed to have been
between the two women, and one of them, heartbroken, must now leave
town. This sequence demonstrates that heterosexual romance is a reference point, not something to be taken for granted. In retrospect, the couple's anxious reaction to the song's title – their 'knowing look' – indicates
the fragility, *not* the stability, of their union. By extension, their status as
the only heterosexual couple depicted in the film – and one whom we
never see before or after this sequence – suggests that heterosexuality
itself is a social fiction that requires the constant cultural propping up
that the song ostensibly provides. The suggestion that the song as a cultural product and an ideological apparatus could be read against the
grain, or 'consumed' by both lesbians and heterosexual men, however
differently, is underscored by the revelation that Laura and the woman
were romantically involved.

The narrative trajectory of this sequence is quite conventional, but its
participants and the outcome are not. The film undermines this reversal
of the realist reference even further by resolving the narrative of this

sequence in a somewhat realistic but not completely satisfactory manner. The women bid their tearful goodbyes, but these are also artificially and excessively emotional, even for melodrama, particularly since we have been thrust into the action, as it were, and the film has yet to invite us, as spectators, to become invested in the film's narrative resolution, or to identify in any way with these characters. To further complicate matters stylistically, the sequence ends with a close-up on a locket that the other woman has just returned to Laura. Laura protests, but eventually waves goodbye with the locket in her palm. The gesture appears very wooden, and the image then becomes highly saturated with colour. The camera tracks out while it freeze-frames Laura's direct-address gaze, effectively shrinking the image to create the effect of a paperback book. The long shot is then digitally altered as it dissolves into the cover of the lesbian pulp novel, *Forbidden Love: The Unashamed Stories of Lesbian Lives.*

The 'hot' and 'cool' emotional temperatures, or the push and pull of the narrative and the subject matter that the film so far offers, underscore the tension of the melodramatic mode. And while it does so playfully, the film also conveys an anxiety that something unforeseen may yet happen. Everything, however amusing, is not all fun and games for lesbians. This nagging sense of ill- or unresolved tensions in the film has at least two purposes, both of which are at once potentially subversive, serious, and playful. First, the tension foreshadows the interview featuring Ann Bannon, a writer of lesbian pulp novels, who acknowledges the difficulties of writing for the often tragic narrative resolution that lesbian pulp tradition imposed. Second, it embues the film with a tension that is later expressed as an erotic charge taken up in the revised 'pulp fiction' sequences. While Ann Bannon claims that 'some of her women survived,' the film's ending goes much further. It suggests that our protagonist, Laura, has not only survived but will actually flourish, judging from her 'successful' entry into lesbian subculture – a success that the film depicts (and that is under-scored by the playfully romantic commentary of the female voice-over narrator and signalled by Laura's affair with the woman she meets at the bar).

There are at least two purposes for revising the pulp formula in *Forbidden Love* itself: identification and distanciation. The happy ending of the pulp romance in the film can be seen as a means to reconstruct the aesthetics of melodrama for lesbian political revision.[18] The utopic revising of the fictions thus becomes a marker of the 'progress' of the real history of lesbians and lesbian culture. However, the parodic mode that these portions of the film engage does not completely allow the spectator to forget that this is indeed a conscious revision, a fiction we as spectators agree to participate in for the duration of the film. The tension that results from these competing strategies makes identification problematic. The most overt of the techniques is the previously mentioned direct-address gaze combined with the freeze-frame that ends each section of the pulp melodrama parody of *Forbidden Love*. This strategy both invites spectators in and keeps them out by making visible the processes of identification; the direct-address gaze thereby undoes the voyeurism of spectatorship with one hand while offering it with the other. This gaze is the gaze of the lesbian/protagonist. Her desires and ours are aligned, thus our mutual voyeurism is 'outed' and made complicitous in a tentative erotics of identification.

Forbidden Love is an example of postmodern parody that re-examines ways of knowing knowingly and takes issue with those forms (documentary and melodrama) stylistically. Thus the film works in the way critics such as Robyn Wiegman suggest is true of postmodernism generally. Following Lyotard, Wiegman proposes what I think is an important way of considering the critical elements of identification/distanciation of postmodernism when she claims that 'the postmodern doesn't transcend the modern; it rereads the modern, not from beyond but from within.'[19] Examples of postmodernist cinema such as *Forbidden Love* thus contribute to a confrontation between discourses – Lyotard's *'grands récits'* – that, however embedded within a history of unequal power relationships, are aesthetically challenged in the films. Such films rely also upon a tradition of political/feminist filmmaking, like *La Vie rêvée*, as well as the work of critics, and a leaping critical mass of lesbians who together, and in excess, challenge the *grands récits* of culture with exemplary *'petits récits.'* The cinematic strategies of identification thus resonate outside the film as a politics of identification, though not as a strict identity politics. *Forbidden Love* demonstrates that there is both strength and pleasure in identifying with a community of like-minded/desiring women. However, the film imposes a critical distance between the pleasure of identification and the spectator through the various strategies it sets up, such as the structural layering of the melodrama and the documentary, and the selective use of irony and parody.

In the documentary portion of the film, the women's lives are presented as being both ordinary and extraordinary. The women are depicted in conversation with the offscreen, pro-filmic world represented by the space of the filmmakers. Their conversations with the filmmakers are sometimes edited together so as to create links among the women interviewed, but the situations they face are also shown to be unique to them individually. At the same time, it becomes clear that these lesbians are constrained by many of the same issues that affect other (heterosexual) women's lives at the same historical moment. The new conversation that emerges from this layering of conversations through editing connects the women's stories. This functions as a rhetorical strategy, a common feature of documentaries, which Bill Nichols suggests is 'the means by which the author attempts to convey his or her outlook persuasively to the viewer.'[20] Nichols explains that strategies such as these are based on Aristotelian rhetoric; their success or failure is achieved through evidence and artistic proof, or 'factual material recruited to the argument' and 'the quality of the text's construction.'[21] In this case, however, to get caught up in these 'recruitment' or rhetorical strategies is to align oneself overtly with these lesbian women, to identify with their struggles *and* their desires. Since the women remain individuals, neither their stories nor their desires can be contained en masse and dismissed or excluded from the overall historical and larger cultural context in which they exist. These devices are employed within, and not outside, more familiar representational forms of documentary, which also have historical resonance and relevance to both lesbian culture and feminist filmmaking. Thus, these rhetorical strategies operate in conjunction with the pulp romance parody to consciously hover between persuasion and refutation.

Together the combined styles of melodrama and documentary exceed the constraints of either modernist mode taken individually. The film is thus stylistically 'queered,' since the juxtaposition of the two styles is neither delivered nor can be taken as 'straight.' The cinematic address of one spills over into the other. 'Queerness' itself is expressed (or 'outed') as an excessive, unruly aesthetic value: excessively sexual and, in this case, excessively woman-centred. *Forbidden Love* also includes many references that are directed to many audiences simultaneously. This audience is not only an 'ideal' or general Canadian audience (whatever that may be); in some cases the references are quite specifically addressed to lesbian spectators. Thus, sometimes non-lesbians are initially excluded, and some of the references are never explained. The pay-off for the lesbian spectator is in seeing something of her desires and history represented on-screen.

Conclusion

According to Linda Hutcheon[22] and Gayatri Spivak,[23] 'in-jokes' such as those found in *Forbidden Love* and *La Vie rêvée* can function to redress the 'lost' history of the 'ex-centric' while voicing a complaint about the way things are now. The films are thus metaphors for different modes of cultural salvaging processes that are differently locatable as both lesbian and Canadian. *Forbidden Love*, like *La Vie rêvée*, performs a kind of double coding – double-voicing/double-imaging – to both connect and dissociate itself from the mainstream of culture through the use of dialectical and hybrid film styles. The complexities of a politics of identity and postmodern aesthetics are thus related, in part through various textual and contextual identification strategies, but are not identical to one another. However tempting it may be to conflate feminism and anti-homophobia in acknowledging the many things they share in common, their relationship is not, as Craig Owens has reminded us by quoting Eve Sedgwick, 'automatic or transhistorical.'[24]

In both of my examples, the relationship between the aesthetic and political hybrids has a different range, tone, and impetus (and therefore effect). These can also be related to the social context in which the films have been released, particularly the changing political climate regarding feminism and sexuality, postmodern culture, and the loose framework of women's cinema. I have concentrated on the interpretive site of these films, which I consider to be constituted, in part, by the relationship of the spectator as a strategic viewer of culture, on the one hand, and the vulnerable film text, on the other. The exploration of their conjunction with the lesbian postmodern is an example of an unruly reading located at the margins of film culture, but available across cultural forms.

By examining the 'queer' aspects of cultural discourse – those instances of de Lauretis's 'film-critical discourses and broadly cast networks of cinema-related practices'[25] that raise but do not settle issues of (lesbian) sexual politics – notions of both film textuality and potential viewing situations are inevitably opened up. A queer reading, against the grain, to steal pleasure is also an implicit politics of interpretation. This is one place where the politics of identity and the aesthetics of resistance coincide in textual analysis. Together they point toward – as the closing intertitle of *Forbidden Love* suggests – 'another fragment, another telling, as we break the silence of our lives.'

NOTES

This paper is dedicated to Laura, and the dream-life of a younger sister.

My thanks to the Ontario Film Development Corporation and Telefilm Canada for the 1994 Gerald Pratley Award. This is a *revised* version of the paper I presented at the 1995 Film Studies Association of Canada Conference at the Learneds (UQAM, Montreal) and published in the *Canadian Journal of Film Studies* 5, no. 2 (Fall 1996). Many thanks to Joan Nicks, Brenda Longfellow, Zuzana Pick, and Katie Russell for their helpful comments and encouragement.

1 Silvia Bovenschen, 'Is There a Feminine Aesthetic?' trans. Harriet Anderson, in *Feminist Aesthetics*, ed. Gisela Ecker (Boston: Beacon Press, 1985), 47–8.

2 Gayatri Chakravorty Spivak, *In Other Worlds: Essays in Cultural Politics* (New York: Routledge, 1988), 211.

3 Teresa de Lauretis, 'Guerrilla in the Midst: Women's Cinema in the 80s,' *Screen* 31, no. 1 (Spring 1990): 9.

4 Ibid.

5 Penny Florence, 'Lesbian Cinema, Women's Cinema,' in *Outwrite: Lesbianism and Popular Culture*, ed. Gabriele Griffin (London: Pluto Press, 1993), 127.

6 Robyn Wiegman, 'Introduction: Mapping the Lesbian Postmodern,' in *The Lesbian Postmodern*, ed. Laura Doan (New York: Columbia University Press, 1994), 13.

7 Doan, *The Lesbian Postmodern*, x.

8 Brenda Longfellow, 'The Feminist Fiction Film in Quebec: *La Vie rêvée* and *La Cuisine rouge*,' in *Take Two*, ed. Seth Feldman (Toronto: Irwin Publishing, 1984), 153.

9 Feldman, *Take Two*, 149.

10 It is also significant in context with the film's references to 'lifestyle imagery' that she looks suspiciously like a model. Independent of whether she actually is Jean-Jacques's wife, or some other 'ideal' woman, her image seems to haunt their encounter.

11 This may explain why student discussions of the film, in my experience, repeatedly raise the issue of the lesbian-feminist link in conjunction with the film's critique of patriarchy. As a neophyte film student, and later as a teaching assistant, I was willing to acknowledge this reaction only as the paranoid delusions of ultra-conservative, anti-feminist university students, most of whom (I consoled myself by thinking) are not even film studies majors! I presumed that these students were enrolled in a course that continually confronted their conservatism in a number of areas, while, I further speculated, the reality of their lives was likely in complete conflict with the leftist leanings of such cultural analyses. However, as desirable as it may have been to dismiss these responses on those grounds (I admit I was being snobbish about my own marginal existence), it was sheer numbers that led me to take their 'ravings' seriously. What I then confronted was my own wish to contain the film within a 'perfect' analysis that valourized the preferred feminist reading while it dissed

the more radical lesbian one. In my own internalized lesbophobia, I wanted to make the film *palatable* not only to the students, but to myself.

12 Jean-François Lyotard, *The Lyotard Reader*, trans. David Macey (Oxford: Basil Blackwell, 1989), 132–3.

13 Andreas Huyssen, 'Mapping the Postmodern,' in *The Post-Modern Reader*, ed. Charles Jencks (London: Academy Editions; New York: St Martin's Press, 1992), 64.

14 Susan Rubin Suleiman, 'Feminism and Postmodernism: A Question of Politics,' in ibid., 324.

15 Fish as quoted by Suleiman, ibid.

16 Ibid., 325.

17 The not quite falsetto voice of Paul Peterson is reminiscent of other male torch singers of the day, notably Canada's Paul Anka. In this film, it could be argued that the boyfriend fills the role of the male masochist suggested by the song's generic reference since he sits anxiously (and idly) by while his girlfriend actively deals with Laura.

18 This idea is in keeping with the socially critical 1950s Hollywood melodrama analyzed by Thomas Elsaesser, 'Tales of Sound and Fury: Observations on the Family Melodrama,' in *Movies and Methods*, vol. 2, ed. Bill Nichols (Berkeley: University of California Press, 1985), 165–89.

19 Wiegman, 'Introduction,' 14.

20 Bill Nichols, *Representing Reality: Issues and Concepts in Documentary* (Bloomington: Indiana University Press, 1991), 134.

21 Ibid.

22 Linda Hutcheon, *A Poetics of Postmodernism* (New York: Routledge, 1988).

23 Spivak, *In Other Worlds*.

24 Eve Sedgwick as quoted by Craig Owens in Scott Bryson et al., eds., *Beyond Recognition: Representation, Power, and Culture* (Berkeley: University of California Press, 1992), 219.

25 Lauretis, 'Guerilla in the Midst,' 9.

Playing in the Light: Canadianizing Race and Nation

KASS BANNING

We're Canadians. [*Sam and Me*] is not about Indians, Jews or multiculturalism. This is about people as human beings.
Deepa Mehta[1]

I was hoping [*Double Happiness*] would transcend cultural barriers and it has. The difficulty of leaving home is something everyone has gone through. It feels like the film is therapeutic for many people.
Mina Shum[2]

Although separated by the speakers' ethnic and generational differences, these quotations illustrate two filmmakers' attempts to steer the reception of their films away from a limited racialized reading. The entreaty that their work be considered beyond chromatics – that crossover and universal themes be recognized – is motivated by more than market considerations. It indicates a shared, tacit understanding that ethnicity brings an attendant particularism that annuls the possibility of making allegorical statements. The justifiable concern about being pegged by 'race,' and its inherent operations of racial prejudice, is not uncommon. In the dramatic case of African-American writer Anatole Broyard – who was, in addition to various writerly roles, once editor of the *New York Times Book Review* – so acutely did he perceive that his blackness would limit his career and life-chances, that he chose to pass as white 'in order to be a writer, not a black writer.'[3] Operating, of course, within distinct racial and historical contexts, contemporary Canadian filmmakers such as Mehta and Shum can nevertheless experience related apprehension regarding categorization.

In what follows I briefly sketch the fragile operations of 'race' in *Sam and Me* (1991) and *Double Happiness* (1994). I do not intend to ignite fears of classification or to endorse ethnic absolutism by designating culture as an essential property of different ethnicities. Rather, my purpose is to extend consideration beyond normative discussions of films by 'emerging' directors by insisting that marginalized groups participate in what Stuart Hall calls 'the racialized regime of representation.' While self-representation is a much anticipated and desired practice, situating these works within a narrow anti-racist rhetoric would lead to distinctions that further reinscribe dominance. It would also do them an injustice. Transcending the role of native informant, both films actively construct and contest racial meanings while taking on issues that are close to the bone for their communities.

The title of this chapter draws from Toni Morrison's *Playing in the Dark*,[4] a work that irrefutably confirms the enduring *présence Africaine* in America's white literary imagination. I perversely invert Morrison's racial subtext to suggest how playing in the light – interactions with dominance[5] – can produce both dissonance and accommodation in works by 'emerging' filmmakers. Through this transposed optic, *Sam and Me* and *Double Happiness* can be reconfigured to transcend the elementary badge of multicultural artefact. Seemingly simple immigrant or struggles-with-assimilation tales, they nevertheless labour under the designation minoritarian.[6] Yet, like state multiculturalism itself, these films render complex and contradictory effects. While acts of transformation and accommodation from marginalized communities, they also serve to further diffuse the notion that Canadian identity is principally white, dismantling earlier sedimented, centrist discourses of Canadian identity evinced in the well-trodden themes of landscape imagery, victimology, and miserabilism.

Yet, minoritarian films simultaneously perform a corresponding mutuality with the state and can bear the marks of that encounter: Canada requires them for self-definition. As Timothy Brennan maintains, 'nations ... are imaginary constructs that depend for their existence on the apparatus of cultural fictions in which imaginative literature [film] plays a decisive role.'[7] In addition, Canadian films are engineered, to some degree, to reflect evolving national policies and, accordingly, are representative of a desired cultural ideal.[8] Principally since the refurbished Multiculturalism Act of 1988, the combined rhetorics of nation, identity, and progress have supplanted the founding multiculturalist grandiloquence of racial harmony: among other attributes, Multiculturalism now means business.[9] The discursive shift from ethnic accord to the language of capital, nonetheless, has not altered the underlying function of a state-sanctioned multiculturalism to manage diversity.

The trope of playing in the light suggests also an implicit comprehension of how Manichean forms of thinking inform the ways that the dominant positions 'other' texts. It is beyond the scope of this short chapter to review the racialized reception that attends 'emerging' culture,[10] but emphasizing ethnic origin can lead to the inscription of racialized constructs. While the celebration of cultural diversity that routinely greets emerging work in both the popular and more scholarly-inflected press may produce worthwhile reassessments of certain racial and cultural stereotypes, simple endorsement has a levelling effect with limiting consequences.[11] Against the dangers of minoritarian celebration, Abdul JanMohamed and David Lloyd caution that 'unmediated by a theoretical perspective, the mere affirmation of achievement lends itself too easily to selective recuperation into dominant culture.'[12]

Although inflected by the requirements of multiculturalism, *Sam and Me* and *Double Happiness* are reciprocally rewritten by the politics of difference, a difference expressed in their representative ethnoscapes.[13] Relatedly, they illustrate Stuart Hall's suggestion that working '*inside* the notion of ethnicity itself'[14] potentially challenges the essentialist formation of group boundaries. Yet the ethnic excavations of *Sam and Me* and *Double Happiness* are realized through very distinct representational strategies. Tracing their unique aesthetic approaches will perhaps offer the theoretical traction necessary to more fully conceptualize Canadian minoritarian film.

Same and Me?

Signifying the promise and the perils of cross-cultural dialogue, *Sam and Me* both validates and negates the multiculturalist utopian myth of inter-ethnic cooperation. An allegory for the thorn in the nation's side, *Sam and Me* particularizes Canadian ethnic conflict as a nation of dramatized 'others.' Bearing the marks of the burden of representation,[15] multiple forms of difference are compressed into its short ninety minutes. *Sam and Me* thematizes the mantra of 'race,' sexuality, and class[16] (with age completing the circle), signalling the film's propitious emergence. Racial display, however, takes precedence, fleshing and structuring its narrative. Through its representative epidermal mosaic, *Sam and Me* embodies correctness while at the same time avoiding smugness. Risking offence, it casts off the veneer of 'multiculti' exhibition, dwelling instead on the uneasy relations between ethnic groups, and thereby setting the distinct particularities of 'South Asianness' and 'Jewishness' (often humorously) into relief.

Herein lies *Sam and Me*'s atypical nature, its strength, and, paradoxically, its weakness. Most 'emerging' films are habitually structured in relation to a white dominant, and, as such, are defined by negativity. An ancillary, but no less significant, accomplishment is the film's intra-ethnic slice-of-life sketch of a conspicuously male South Asian community not yet having acquired a hyphenated identity, almost ethnographic in its unflinching perspicuity.[17] What fascinates is the way, in spite of the film's cross-cultural juxtapositions – the traffic in parallelisms between South Asians and Jews – 'race' sneaks in through the back door. Confounding the film's relational approach to ethnicity, hierarchy emerges in spite of the two groups' manifest equivalence. The film's tight ethnic binary implodes, emphasizing the claim that ethnicity is not corporeally fixed or genetic but something mobile and fragile, that race is indeed 'the floating signifier.'[18] And it is the unassimilable 'fact of blackness,'[19] the necessary corollary to whiteness, that is displaced (once again) onto the narrative of ethnicity, driving and extending *Sam and Me*'s un-anticipated explication of 'race.'

The achievement of *Sam and Me* is frustrated by its production context: a pervasive faux, chipper tone buttressed by a musical score, the constraints of a televisual aesthetic, relentless tableaux of bonding buddies blossoming into interracial brotherhood, the extensive use of strategic essentialism, and the underlying familiar theme of 'pity the poor immigrant.' In spite of these limitations, which situate it as a 'minor'[20] work, the film generates an unprecedented space where a series of different social developments and a set of related discourses – 'race,' ethnicity, migration, male homosociality,[21] and Toronto – intersect.

Premised on a *Driving Miss Daisy* tale with no back seat, *Sam and Me* is 'about prejudice.'[22] Sam (Peter Boretski), seventy-five and Jewish, and Nikhil (Ranjit Chowdhry), twenty-five and a recent South Asian arrival, develop an unlikely friendship in the face of different class, ethnic, cultural, and generational identities. Alienated from their respective Jewish and South Asian communities, disassociated from the demands of family, they bond over the liberating and displacing corollaries that accompany the 'enigma of arrival.' Although they are lured, as Sam puts it, by 'peace, freedom and money – the usual,' Canada is prison to one, reform school to the other. Anxious to end his days in the Promised Land, Sam schemes for his departure to Israel against the strict wishes of his son, whereas Nik tries (unsuccessfully) to follow his Uncle Chetan's five-year plan for success: work hard and a triumphant financial return to India awaits, with 'the cricket pavilion's scoreboard shouting [Nick and Chetan's] story loud and clear.' Additionally forged through Oedipal longing, this interethnic adoption enables each to find in the other what they lack: the good son and the good father.

Arriving from India with high expectations that he would launch a career in the new land of opportunity with his uncle at Cohen's Hospital Supplies, Nik is hired instead by its owner, Morris (Heath Lamberts), to care for his ailing father, Sam. In a stroke, Nik is demoted to nurse's aid, part servant, part babysitter. Administering to Sam's precious white body, Nik is subjected to the historically colonial conditions of racialized labour exploitation, recalling the fact that many immigrants (especially women) began their 'careers' in Canada as domestics. Nik's indebtedness to his Janus-faced uncle, for sponsorship and the cost of his airfare, similarly resembles that of an indentured servant, extending the master–slave relation that Morris and Nik enact.

In spite of Sam's and Nik's desire for one another, the imperative of ethnicity dominates, as intercultural 'misunderstanding' dismantles pluralism's mandate, the logic of ethnic equivalence. At the same time cultural misconceptions do serve a purpose. As George Lipsitz puts it, '"misunderstandings" allow people of colour to see "families of resemblance" that reframe their separate experiences as similar, although not identical.'[23] Distinct from Sam and Nik's association, and the odd suggestion of homosexual filiation at the Toronto boarding house where Nik lives, interethnic alignment falters.

Sam and Me is built upon a series of symmetrical differences and similarities, with Sam and Nik's ethnic border crossings helping to highlight the rigid contours of their specific ethnic groups. Two domestic settings, for example, throw class and cultural difference into relief: the raucous, cramped, lived-in, warm-hued, boarding house that the group of South Asian men inhabit contrasts vividly with the sterile, suburban, bourgeois Cohen household. On the other hand, a succession of parallel syntagmas serve to sketch the two groups' likeness regarding religion. The prayers to Krishna correspond to the company of men who sit shiva for Sam at the Cohen household, and Xavier's playful signing of the cross before a neighbour's statue of the Virgin Mary resembles the scene in which Nik describes Sam sending a flying kiss to a mezuzah on the Cohen's door. An extended categorical instance suggesting commonality occurs when Sam dances the hora nude in the rain (with Nik later joining in), and when

Xavier (Javed Jafri) performs (in drag) a lip-synched rendition of a popular Hindu song for his housemates.

Race, the Floating Signifier

Linked to a series of racialized (and sexualized) signifiers that crisscross the film, this last instance of transgressive equivalence suggests what Sander Gilman identifies as 'the interrelationship of images of difference.'[24] Sam's lack of inhibition and presumed mental incapacity, Xavier's cross-gender excess, Nik's and Sam's infantalization, their general expressiveness and 'loose' behaviour combine to suggest attributes usually associated with 'the primitive,' affiliated with the pejoratively inflected instinctual, rather than the rational. Morris's inability to feel tenderness, to even touch his father, coupled with his will-to-capital, secures his hierarchical position, whereas Nik's diligent tending to Sam's body, and the many acts of bodily contact – from massage to tickling to dancing to playing cricket – indicates Sam and Nick's 'lower order' position. Such distinctions dramatize the cost of assimilation, with Morris principally paying 'the price of the ticket.' Sacrificing the sensual, Morris embodies what, according to Slavoj Žižek, white Western societies demand: that one give up the unspeakable powers of enjoyment, that pleasure become prohibited and dirty, imagined only within the realm of racial Others.[25] Whereas Morris has crossed over and bears the marks of loss and alienation, his father can still get down with the 'natives' and thus shares the code of authenticity.

The feel-good parallels between the two ethnic groups, evinced through the mythic, interracial buddy charm[26] of Sam and Nik's ability to transcend caste and class, are achieved at the price of further racial suggestiveness. Moreover, the representation of blackness corroborates and extends the elusive but consistent metaphorical character of racial definition. One could argue that *Sam and Me* has nothing to do with blackness.[27] Yet the centrality of the black racial trope is neither abstract nor forced. The reggae-inflected soundtrack of the opening credits, Sam's constant application of the epithets 'schwartzer' and 'brown boy' to Nik, Nik's internalization of the words, leading to his entreaty to Sam to don a pair of sunglasses so he will appear 'more like a *real* schwartzer,' and the extensive references made to race and chromatics at large all signify the enduring codes of blackness in the racial imaginary.

Black presence, however, is neither exclusively metaphoric nor discursive. The bodies of peripheral black 'characters' support and authenticate the racial metaphors that circulate. The spatial and racial configurations of the rooming house, for example, illustrate an oppositional racial logic that, once grounded in the black figure, is relayed to the brown body, further inflecting and, hence, racializing ethnicity. When Nik first arrives, his housemates are in the midst of a game of cricket in the yard. But, as C.L.R. James so deftly contends in *Beyond a Boundary*,[28] cricket is much more than a game. Cricket's dual function, serving to police the colonial subject through normalizing the codes of Englishness and to foster indigenous expression or neocolonial nationalism, is suggested in *Sam and Me*. That is, the hierarchical social practices of the heated history of the sport (the exclusion of black players on white teams, the enduring presence of the white captain on black teams, intense national rivalries) inform *Sam and Me*'s hierarchical ethnic expression. Greeted by shouts of 'new man in' (an invitation to join), Nik looks up at a black man on the third floor quietly observing their game. Xavier asks, 'Falling in love or what?' Baldev quips, 'He's not one of us.' Nik replies, 'He might be a good cross baller.' Baldev retorts, 'Exactly. Want your head broken?' An unmotivated shot of the same man at his window pumping iron appears after a short interval. He resurfaces once again to save the day, resuscitating Sam after his collapse, literally breathing life into Sam's fading white body. (The maxim that whiteness equals death is unavoidable here.) Divorced from his prior physicality, he nurses Sam, placing his racial alterity temporarily in check. While serving to frame and amplify ethnicity (in this case, South Asian), the surplus corporeality of blackness is denied particularization. Supporting the differential racial logic of outsiderism, the black 'character' is neither named nor ethnicized; he occupies the habitual contradictory social position of black men, as threat and emasculated servant. This anonymous man is simply 'black.' At the same time, however, blackness simultaneously shares South Asian discursive affiliations (neither voluntary nor fixed) that maintain and inform South Asian–Jewish relations.

The black figure's radical exteriority additionally heightens and extends Jewish ethnicity. When Lucas, a large black man, delivers copious amounts of patties and goat curry to Morris's home (initiated as a prank by Sam and Nik), a frightened Morris pays the bill for food that he neither ordered nor can eat. Analogous to the South Asian dis-associative acts, this racialized reaction, and other displays by Morris of abjection towards the South Asian household, demonstrates how, historically, immigrant groups distanced themselves from blacks to adopt the privileges that accrue from white skin.[29] (This generated distance is also necessary to the master–slave relationship that Morris and Nik play out.) At the same time, however, the figurative presence of blackness invokes historical white-and-black antagonisms that are then, in turn, displaced onto 'Jewishness' and 'South Asianness.'[30]

The minute representation of a specific South Asian bachelor culture remains *Sam and Me*'s notable achievement. Despite the near absence of women characters, the performance of gender, like that of race, is complex and contradictory. Conjoined to the metonymic operations of race that crisscross the film, gender and sexuality discursively shape the male homosocial habitus of the rooming house. Bodies of women, nevertheless, frame the film: the opening scene where a man and woman initiate sex (the background reggae music linking blackness and lasciviousness, again suggesting the 'interrelatedness of difference') is answered near the film's end when Xavier indoctrinates Nik into the 'joys' of normalized masculinity at a strip club. Significantly, this entertainment was mustered by Xavier to help Nik take his mind off Sam, his real object of desire. Heterosexual desire, however, is somewhat forced: ruse-like, it works to contain the threat of homosexuality flagrantly embodied in the landlord's nephew, the film's 'genuine' homosexual. His presence, nevertheless, is absolutely necessary to the production of positive heterosexual identity. Yet the slippages between homosociality and homosexuality are perhaps aided by the near omission of women, thus making room for Nik and others to take up a feminine position. Coded as non-phallic, Nik is 'feminized' through his labour and sensitivity, qualities that throw the more blatant masculinist behaviour of Sam's son and Nik's uncle into relief. This gender position is highly inflected by race, as the denial of masculinity to the black male and man of colour is constitutive of the dominant white social imaginary.

In many ways, *Sam and Me* suggests both Frantz Fanon's demonstration of the power of the racial binary to *fix* and Homi K. Bhabha's claim that all binary systems are troubled by disavowal and ambivalence.[31] While *Sam and Me*'s rehearsal of the Manichean (black–white divide) allegory[32] dramatizes power relations, these interchangeable oppositions bring an attendant web of conventional associations that are difficult to shake, as they hinge on the ontological reduction of the black figure. Although these racialized slippages are in flux, they are subject to the return of the logic of ethnic equivalence, evinced in Baldev's comment to Nik that his Jewish employers are 'like us, only a little bit coloured.' Morris's interpretation of a policeman's query, if *Le Shana Haba BeYirushalem* was a Jewish name, as anti-Semitic, similarly attempts to balance the prejudicial scale, but it comes off as paranoid shtick. Yet the implication that both groups equally inhabit a not-white and yet not-quite-black status[33] works against the discursive operations of 'race' in the film. Attempts to parallel suggested anti-Semitism with racism ultimately fail, partially because Jewish ethnicity is occluded by whiteness, which is in turn produced by blackness. That is, the goals of multiculturalism to represent and manage ethnicity – what *Sam and Me* works so hard to achieve – paradoxically shifts the film into the unexpected discourse of 'race,' thus simplifying what it seeks to describe. While acknowledging multiculturalism's concerns, the film's use of the repressed racial binary aids the recirculation of ethnic hierarchies. Just as the state cannot control the excess of multiculturalism, difference exceeds *Sam and Me* through the unassimilable black signifier, which acts back in the film, shading ethnicity as it bumps up against whiteness.

Negotiating *Double Happiness*

While *Sam and Me* lives up to its promotional material as a 'black comedy,' producing an unforeseen spin to the genre, *Double Happiness* eschews the tragic, offering another up-beat illustration of the decidedly negotiated nature of diasporic life. The films are further distinguished by differing aesthetic and formal approaches, which stem from generational influences, as well as different political milieux and distinct production contexts.[34] Both works, however, slyly acknowledge how the Canadian dominant translates Others. While neither film engages with the majoritarian head-on, each self-consciously nods to ethnic placement. Recognition, if not resigned acceptance, usually follows the 'givenness' of a racialized encounter. Over-attention to ethnic particularisms by outsiders is generally rendered ludicrous. *Sam and Me*'s cabdriver Baldev, for example, recites a comic litany of lines from white Canadian fares who have attempted to place him by talking 'Indian.' Many similar confrontations populate *Double Happiness*. Jade Li (Sandra Oh), the central character, continually rubs against white and Chinese Vancouverites who are driven by the will to ethnically locate and, at times, circumscribe. White efforts are graciously lampooned, while attempts by Chinese Canadians are generally tempered with more tolerance.

While both films foreground the ethnic markers of 'South Asianness,' 'Jewishness,' or 'Chineseness,' utilizing strategic essentialism to plumb ethnic particularity, *Double Happiness* adopts exaggeration further as its strategy, pushing the limits of Chinese specificity. Eschewing the relational, minority–minority economy of *Sam and Me*, *Double Happiness* positions ethnicity from further within, affectionately riffing on 'Chineseness.' Accentuating difference, the film exercises what Manthia Diawara suggests as the appropriate response to the complex and ambiguous minefield of racial representation for the minority artist, 'that it's important to embrace the stereotype first in order to find a reflexive position *within* the stereotype.'[35]

Double Happiness visits the familiar 'caught between two cultures' genre that aestheticized migrant tales often rehearse. This film, however, revitalizes expectations of the 'struggle for happiness' – cultural conflict between traditional parents and their modern 'Canadianized' children – and combines it with a coming-of-age tale. Situated between the sweet *My American Cousin* (Sandy Wilson, 1985) and the raw *Sonatine* (Micheline Lanctôt, 1984), *Double Happiness* playfully surpasses the sincerity of both, traversing the site of teenage-girl passages without the self-conscious cuteness-and-Kleenex requirements of the genre.

It is a truism that first efforts milk the autobiographical. As Shum confided, 'It's my story.' At the film's centre stands the young aspiring actor Jade Li. Like director Shum, Jade shares an intimate understanding of how coming to adulthood in the 'New World' under the watchful eyes of 'Old World' parents can exacerbate the crisis of adolescence, fanning nascent Oedipal flames. *Double Happiness*, however, imbues its autobiographical impulse with technique, rather than realism, subverting the perilous baggage of authenticity that often inflects works by emerging directors. From the vibrantly hued mise en scène, to the perspicaciously blocked choreography, which lends an ensemble effect to family encounters, to the pyrotechnics that punctuate the narrative, a playful formalism[36] prevails. Seamless yet almost episodic, *Double Happiness* proceeds with a narrative drive strong and familiar enough to sustain its expressionistic techniques. With the mechanics in place, there is a springboard for Shum to trope on specific details: the fetishes of 'rice kings,' the cult of opportunity (and food) in immigrant families, the role of luck and feng-shui spirits for good fortune, the burden of filial expectation and the gift of parental sacrifice, the humorous horrors of racist typecasting and tokenism, the perils of concealing a white boyfriend (Collum Rennie), and hyphenated identity blues in general.

The film, however, balances these bittersweet experiences with a double-edged treatment of its treatise on identity. Like its central character Jade, *Double Happiness* is simultaneously irreverent and resonant, heartfelt and ironic. While Sandra Oh delivers an irresistible character, combining youthful optimism with an I-will-survive practicality, minor characters conjoin to provide chorus-like effects. The chemistry between the members of the Li family, the 'girl-stuff' with Jade and her sister Pearl in particular, similarly infuse the film's formal constructions with moments of seeming transparency. If the Li family quotidian and ritual encounters and aversions mark the film's rhythm, the sometimes self-reflexive, often non-diegetic, direct address tableaux punctuate its narrative. Calls upstairs for supper or the visit of an 'appropriate' (Chinese) potential suitor abruptly interrupt Jade's constant 're-her-zing' (Mom Li's [Alannah Ong] pronunciation) of the lines of Blanche Dubois or Joan of Arc. While playing out plot requirements – Jade is indeed a budding actor – her auditions for different parts and the parade of possible roles suggested by friends and family help to thematize how identity is doubly fluid and circumscribed.

Rewriting the Oedipal drama in female terms, *Double Happiness* dramatizes the common generational conflict of teen will-to-power against father-knows-best. Yet this is subtly expressed in the frisson-layered lingua franca codes particular to the Li family. Jade's offer of buns to Dad Li (Stephen Chang), with their proverbial exchange (Dad: 'What kind of buns?' Jade: 'Red bean.' Dad: 'Good.') is shorthand for peace, if not communication.[37] Although Jade and Dad Li visit the master narrative of conflict between Chinese-born first generation and North American–born second generation, *Double Happiness* at times surpasses the ideological limitations of this strict familial dualism. As many Asian-American scholars contend, representing Asian–American culture exclusively in these privatized oppositional terms essentializes it. Lisa Lowe similarly maintains that this first generation-second generation struggle reduces and obscures 'the particularities and incommensurabilites of class, gender and national diversities among Asians.'[38] While Jade and Dad Li's interactions might invoke the dialectical stance of traditionalism versus modernity and their attendant Eurocentric designations of negative and positive value, countervailing forces intervene, and thus widen the possibility for more multiple and diverse articulations of Chinese-Canadian identity.

Characters like Mrs Mau and Ah Hong, for example, interrupt the binarism of nativism and assimilation set up in the Dad–Jade dyad. Friend-of-the-family Mrs Mau, while just as eager as the rest to see Jade married off, adheres to the joint world of amour and career and encourages Jade to seek both. Shum's brief cameo as a smoke-breathing Hong Kong dragon-lady director similarly expands traditional Chinese gender roles. While she exceeds any Hollywood 'Asian businesswoman' stereotype, her interrogating quip to Jade, 'Are you really Chinese?' offers additional commentary to Jade's up-for-grabs identity. Ah Hong, Dad Li's visiting childhood friend from China, dismantles the fusion of patriarchal conservatism and tradition with Chineseness. Direct from the new China, Ah Hong destabilizes any singular definition of the category. Speaking English fluently, he warmly offers Jade advice through shared dialogue and example, not patriarchal dictation. Like Jade, Ah Hong carries his secrets, also living a life that deviates from Dad's 'Li family values.' Both take the risk of excommunication from family, of becoming 'white ghosts,' if their concealed lifestyles are disclosed. Yet the disruption of tradition here is not necessarily conceived as loss. In contrast to Dad Li, guardian of Chinese group definition, Ah Hong is paradoxically the more 'modern' of the pair. Serving to de-essentialize notions of Chineseness, his presence re-inforces the notion that hegemonic ethnic categories are indeed false and unstable, that the syncretic effects of diaspora flow both ways.[39] His line of dialogue soon after his arrival in Canada, 'I will become a new man in this country,' underlines how place indelibly shapes identity, but it also underscores how cultural identity is a process that denotes a position, not an essence.

With Dad Li, however, the marks of migration helped to solidify his rigid definition of 'Chinese' identity. Although portrayed as somewhat paranoid and tyrannical, his hoe-in-hand direct address tableau contextualizes his metamorphosis in class terms. Employed in Canada as a security guard, he relates a prelapsarian past before the Chinese Revolution. The use of tableau here offers further dimensions to his character, engendering understanding, if not empathy, which thus defines his 'traditional' behaviour as residual, not necessarily essence-driven. In this manner, the direct address 'interruptions' provide insight into characters, throwing the sedimented traditionalist position temporarily off balance.

While direct address furthers a character's profile, it simultaneously calls attention to normalized representations. With other techniques such as slow motion, difference is similarly accentuated. Extended moments, such as when the family group watches and waves to Jade as she embarks on a date, emphasize the situation's faux superficiality. Instead of correcting stereotypes, these techniques humorously accentuate and attempt to refute them. Paradoxically, these and similar acts of self-subalternization,[40] exhibited in the rich display of exaggerated ethnic markers of Chineseness – from the grandmother who is outfitted in an overly traditional manner, to the wide-angle lazy susan shots, which underscore the exquisite and plentiful Chinese food dishes, to speaking Cantonese and using

subtitles – help to dismantle exoticism by heightening it. The ethniciza-
tion of gender is similarly satirized and de-familiarized through the
embellished performance of 'traditional' (i.e., feminine) Chinese man-
nerisms, exploiting the fetishism that attends exotic placement. These
aesthetic and acting strategies, however, are not employed to simply jive
up a story. As Sau-ling Cynthia Wong writes, 'in showing an intense interest in the "playful" and seemingly gratuitous aspect of artistic creation,
Asian American authors are not, as a mechanical analogy with universalis-
tic Western ludic discourse would suggest, promoting a rarefied aestheticism. Instead, they are formulating an "interested disinterestedness"
appropriate to their condition as minority artists with responsibilities to
their community but also a need for room to exercise their creativity.'[41]
The stylistic inflections of *Double Happiness* thus expand the range of
racial representations and the complexity of what it means to be Chinese
Canadian. Coupled with the thematized play on roles (and models) that
foreground the variegated nature of subjectivity, technique here serves to
capture identities in movement.

At the film's beginning Sandra Oh says directly to camera, 'I said I
would never make a big deal out of being Chinese ... But I want to tell you
about my family. They are very Chinese. You know what I mean. But for
the moment, just forget they are a Chinese family. Just think of them as
any old family, any old, you know, white family.' This opening statement
points to the multisituated nature of *Double Happiness*.[42] Ambivalent,
these words assert but at the same time deny difference – perhaps a residue of self-representation, of 'telling our own stories,' in this present
moment of post-identity politics.

Almost the Same but Not Quite, or No Guarantees

Both *Sam and Me* and *Double Happiness* exhibit, with varying degrees of
effectiveness, distinct representational strategies for handling racial resonance. To presume similarities would ultimately reproduce what this chapter attempts to redress – the customary response of sameness. While *Double
Happiness* often eludes multiculturalism's grasp, *Sam and Me* seems to
inscribe itself as multicultural artefact. The paradox of *Sam and Me* is that
it seeks more extensive representation through its relational, minority–
minority perspective. Although *Sam and Me* adopts the rhetorics of state
equivalence, the stubborn categories of white and black persevere, with
the insistent trope of blackness serving to mediate and sustain ethnic categories, helping to define the 'differential racialization'[43] of South Asian

and Jewish identity. This discursive sliding, however, does not reduce its achievements: the film troubles the paradigmatic construction of kinship as the central trope in immigrant culture, offering an unsurpassed representation of South Asian–Canadian diasporic experience. While *Double Happiness* also utilizes a counterposing cultural perspective – similarly constructing its subjects as Others – it employs the tactics of transcoding to aid the circulation of identity within the category of Chineseness.[44]

Both *Sam and Me* and *Double Happiness* coincidentally end with their young protagonists, Nik and Jade, sitting with their thoughts, alone, at a window. Occupying the position of Fanon's 'new man,' they have disengaged from their roots in order to renew themselves, to inhabit and express their 'new ethnicities.' On the one hand, these acts of closure accommodate the state's concealed multiculturalist legacy, unobtrusively thematizing its extended narrative of national belonging. On the other, they are acts of intervention that displace the narrative of white ethnicity undergirding multiculturalism's formation and continuing practice. As I have attempted to demonstrate, films by women from communities like Mehta's and Shum's similarly enact this double-edged position, while serving to extend the ongoing project of gendering the nation.

NOTES

1 Chung Wong, 'Movie Breaks Barriers in Immigrant Experience,' *Toronto Star*, 21 August 1990. E1.
2 'Happy Endings: Peter Broderick on Mina Shum's *Double Happiness*,' Filmmaker 3, no. 4 (Summer 1995): 46.
3 See Henry Louis Gates's insightful discussion of the manifold implications of Broyard's choice in 'White Like Me,' *New Yorker*, 17 June 1996, 66–81.
4 Toni Morrison, *Playing in the Dark: Whiteness and the Literary Imagination* (Cambridge: Harvard University Press, 1992). Morrison joins a long line of black writers, from Frederick Douglass to James Baldwin and Ralph Ellison to bell hooks, who have commented on whiteness. The emerging academic whiteness studies 'craze' generally neglects this tradition, betraying its political efficacy. Suggestive of late capitalist white supremacist practice, it could be charged that whiteness studies seize and re-name an extant rich tradition, active since the beginning of the slave trade, in order to resuscitate the recent poverty of theoretical work. For a comprehensive selection of black writers on whiteness see David R. Roediger, ed., *Black on White: Black Writers on What It Means to Be White* (New York: Schocken Books, 1998).

5 Dominance here is equated broadly with whiteness and nationhood to include
   the state's interpretation and practice of multiculturalism.
6 I use the term advisedly, in all its applications, emphasizing Deleuze and
   Guattari's understanding that the minor is characterized by negation, that it
   deterritorializes the dominant language, is political in nature, and represents
   collective value. See 'What Is a Minor Literature?' trans. Dana Polan, in *Out
   There: Marginalization and Contemporary Cultures*, ed. Russel Ferguson, Martha
   Gever, Trinh T. Minh-ha, and Cornel West (New York: New Museum of Contemporary Art, 1990), 59–70.
7 Timothy Brennan 'The National Longing for Form,' in *Nation and Narration*,
   ed. Homi K. Bhabha (London: Routledge, 1990), 49.
8 See Michael Dorland, *So Close to the State/s: The Emergence of Canadian Feature
   Film Policy* (Toronto: University of Toronto Press, 1998.)
9 'Multiculturalism Means Business' provided a fitting name for a conference in
   1987 where Prime Minister Brian Mulroney stressed the economic benefits of
   multiculturalism. 'We, as a nation, need to grasp the opportunity afforded to
   us by our multicultural identity ... Our multicultural nature gives us an edge in
   selling to that world.' Quoted in Jean Elliot and Augie Fleras, 'Immigration
   and the Canadian Ethnic Mosaic,' in *Race and Ethnic Relations in Canada*, ed.
   Peter Li (Toronto: Oxford University Press, 1990), 67.
10 *Sam and Me* and *Double Happiness*, nevertheless, are indeed 'firsts'; both broke
   the feature film glass ceiling for women-of-colour directors, signalling the
   emergence of the South Asian–Canadian and the Chinese-Canadian woman
   feature director. My point is that this fact often pre-empts further analysis of
   the works themselves.
11 A related danger resides in the transference of early rhetorics that typified
   Canadian film in the 60s and 70s to 'emerging' Canadian filmmaking. The discourses of oppositionality evinced in the outsider, victim, or loser trope, which
   served to validate and drag the study of Canadian film into critical arrival, are
   seeping into critical commentary on minoritarian Canadian film. Although
   the generalized victim or landscape analogy has been replaced by contemporary discourses of outsiderism – framed, at its crudest, by paradigms of exile or
   immigrant experience and, at its most sophisticated, by the postcolonial or the
   diasporic – similar allegories are rehearsed through the inherent structural,
   hence oppositional, nature of engagement.
12 See 'Toward a Theory of Minority Discourse: What Is To Be Done?' in *The
   Nature and Context of Minority Discourse*, ed. Abdul R. JanMohamed and David
   Lloyd (New York: Oxford University Press, 1990), 7. Salman Rushdie, in a different context, similarly claims 'celebration makes us lazy.' See 'Songs Doesn't
   Know the Score' in *Black Film: British Cinema* (London: ICA Documents 7,

1988), 17. Rinaldo Walcott has also recently implored that critical reception of black Canadian work 'move beyond celebration.' See *Black Like Who: Writing. Black. Canada* (Toronto: Insomniac Press, 1997), xiv.

13 The term is Arjun Appadurai's. See *Modernity at Large: Cultural Dimensions of Globalization* (Minneapolis: University of Minnesota Press, 1996).

14 Stuart Hall, 'New Ethnicities,' in *Black Film, British Cinema*, 29.

15 The phrase 'burden of representation' indicates how marginalized groups experience the desire to cover manifold aspects of racialized experience because another opportunity to produce might be a long time coming. In addition to limited access to resources, the term also implies that work is burdened with a range of extra-artistic concerns because artists are 'accountable' to their communities. For a fully considered account of the dilemma see Kobena Mercer, 'Black Art and the Burden of Representation,' in *Welcome to the Jungle: New Positions in Black Cultural Studies* (New York: Routledge, 1994), 233–58.

16 It is noteworthy that *Sam and Me* skirts one prerequisite of the mantra of race, gender, and class. Women are scarcely present here. In her two subsequent 'women's films,' *Camilla* (1994) and *Fire* (1996), Mehta extends the themes of *Sam and Me*, but redresses the imperatives of gender with a vengeance; these are unabashed 'girl films.' Unlike *Sam and Me*, Oedipal desire is sexually (and stunningly) realized in *Fire*. The film stretches the shifts between homosexual and homosocial relationships between women, realizing Adrienne Rich's 'lesbian continuum' – the manner in which women slip from maternal and sisterly forms of love into same-sex sexual relationships. See 'Compulsory Heterosexuality and Lesbian Existence,' in *Women: Sex and Sexuality*, ed. Catherine Stimpson and Ethel Spector Person (Chicago: University of Chicago Press, 1980), 62–91. *Camilla* also sketches intergenerational filial amour, of the non-genital variety. It is critical to note that both films were made outside of Canada, and *Fire* was made without traditional funding sources (Telefilm, OFDC). *Camilla* was a Canadian–British co-production. *Sam and Me*, similarly, was initially backed by England's Channel Four and later some publicity and distribution support was provided by local Canadian agencies (CBC and OFDC, for example). In this regard Deepa Mehta's films exemplify the transnational film genre. See Hamid Naficy, 'Phobic Spaces and Liminal Panics: The Independent Transnational Film Genre,' in *Global Local: Cultural Production and the Transnational Imaginary*, ed. Rob Wilson and Wimal Dissanayake (Durham: Duke University Press, 1996). Ironically this transnational aspect has worked against Mehta's ability to secure support from Canadian funding agencies.

17 Drawing attention to the film's power of observation does not intend to validate an 'authentic' depiction of immigrant experience. The use of actors direct from India, however, heightens an accented verisimilitude. Rather, I

comment here on the elision of an air-brushed portrayal – the attempt to register the differences within a specific community with such meticulous regard for the minutiae of domestic life. Prior to the release of *Sam and Me* in 1991, exacting representation of this nature was unprecedented in the Canadian feature film. Space restrictions unfortunately prohibit a discussion of the relevant debates around racialized representation and realism. For an early discussion of the paradoxical effects of realism in select racialized Canadian film, see Kass Banning, 'Rhetorical Remarks towards the Politics of Otherness,' *CineAction*, no. 16 (May 1989): 14–19.

18 I borrow this phrase from the title of an educational videotape 'starring' Stuart Hall.

19 The phrase, of course, refers to the title of chapter 5 of Frantz Fanon's *Black Skin, White Masks*, trans. Charles Lam Markmann (New York: Grove Press, 1967).

20 Again, I use the term advisedly. See note 6.

21 See Eve Kosofsky Sedgwick, *Between Men: English Literature and Male Homosocial Desire* (New York: Columbia University Press, 1985).

22 Deepa Mehta, Press kit for film, 11.

23 See 'It's All Wrong, but It's All Right,' in *Dangerous Crossroads: Popular Music, Postmodernism and the Poetics of Place* (London: Verso, 1994), 164.

24 Sander L. Gilman, *Difference and Pathology: Stereotypes of Sexuality, Race and Madness* (Ithaca: Cornell University Press, 1985), 35.

25 Slavoj Žižek, 'Eastern Europe's Republics of Gilead,' *New Left Review*, no. 183 (Oct. 1990): 50–63.

26 Two classic interracial bonding films come to mind: *The Defiant Ones* (Stanley Kramer, 1958) and *In the Heat of the Night* (Norman Jewison, 1967). Distinguished by different production contexts and ideological conjunctures, the Hollywood films were informed by the civil rights movement and integrationism, *Sam and Me* by the dynamics of multiculturalism and diaspora. Although each film responds to its individual 'racial time,' all represent and contain the black figure.

27 Suggesting how blackness is relayed here in no way pre-empts what *Sam and Me* is actually 'about,' the interplay between two ethnic communities that are not of African descent. My emphasis does not intend to displace the lived specificity of either group, but to demonstrate the film's metaphoric and discursive use of blackness.

28 C.L.R. James, *Beyond a Boundary* (London: Stanley Paul, 1963) remains the classic reference to the dynamics of cricket and colonialism. For related discussions of the indigenization of cricket and decolonization see Manthia Diawara, 'Englishness and Blackness: Cricket as Discourse on Colonialism,'

Callaloo 13, no. 2 (1990): 830–44; and Arjun Appadurai, 'Playing with Modernity: The Decolonization of Indian Cricket,' in his *Modernity at Large: Cultural
Dimensions of Globalization* (Minneapolis: University of Minnesota Press, 1996),
89–113.

29 See Noel Ignatiev, *How the Irish Became White* (London: Routledge, 1995), for a
discussion of how distance from blackness was a *necessary* process of 'American-
ization' for ethnics, the Irish in particular, and Michael Berman, ed., *Blacks
and Jews: Alliances and Arguments* (New York: Delacorte Press, 1994), on the
evolving black–Jewish encounter and its relations to whiteness. For an astute
overview of this shifting association, see Julius Lester, 'The Outsiders: Blacks
and Jews and the Soul of America,' *Transition* 68 (1995): 66–88. For a consistent opposing view that insists on the historical affiliations between 'blackness'
and 'Jewishness' – how blackness explicates 'Jewishness' through the trope of
pathology – see Sander L. Gilman, 'I'm Down on Whores: Race and Gender
in Victorian England,' in *Anatomy of Racism*, ed. David Theo Goldberg (Minneapolis: University of Minnesota Press, 1990) 146–70.

30 This observation supports the view of Angela Davis, among others, that the
politics of 'race' have revolved around black–white relations, which inform
relationships among communities of colour, where interracial relations 'are
crowded into this [black–white] paradigm as the objects of multiculturalism's
reconciliation.' See Angela Y. Davis, 'Gender, Race and Multiculturalism:
Rethinking "Race" Politics,' in *Mapping Multiculturalism*, ed. Avery F. Gordon
and Christopher Newfield (Minneapolis: University of Minnesota Press, 1996),
47. Canadian racial antagonisms, of course, must be distinguished from
American ones. Although different racial histories obtain, black–white
relations discursively migrate north, especially through the vehicle of popular
culture with its schizophrenic deployment of blackness as both fetish and
denigrated object.

31 For an explication of how these two impulses are negotiated, see Stuart Hall,
'The After-life of Frantz Fanon: Why Fanon? Why Now? Why *Black Skin, White
Masks*?' in *The Fact of Blackness: Frantz Fanon and Visual Representation*, ed. Alan
Read (London: Institute of Contemporary Arts, 1996), 27.

32 See Abdul R. JanMohamed, 'The Economy of Manichean Allegory: The Function of Racial Difference in Colonial Literature,' *Critical Inquiry* 12 (Autumn
1985): 59–87.

33 See Homi K. Bhabha, 'Of Mimicry and Man: The Ambivalence of Colonial Discourse,' *October* 28 (Spring 1984): 125–33. I refer here to his play on colonial
mimicry as 'the desire for a recognizable Other, as a subject of difference that
is almost the same, but not quite ... almost the same but not white.'

34 Written and directed by Shum, *Double Happiness* could be conceived as more

conventionally auteurist than *Sam and Me*. Although initiated from a story idea by Mehta, the script for *Sam and Me* was written by Ranjit Chowdhry (Nik of *Sam and Me*), an actor and writer for Indian television, and the film demonstrates these influences. Financed by Telefilm, the National Film Board, and the province of British Columbia's New Visions, *Double Happiness* was additionally produced by Multiculturalism Canada and the Canada Council and developed at the Canadian Film Centre and Praxis. New Views was founded to give emerging filmmakers an opportunity to direct their first film. In addition to the extensive workshopping of her film, Shum – and many filmmakers of her generation – has been nurtured on a hearty diet of independent film and critiques of representation, emphases that generally accompanied a university film education in the 1980s. These conjunctural differences influence the production, look, and ultimate meaning of the two films. On the other hand, *Fire*, written and directed by Mehta, is decidely auteurist.

35 Manthia Diawara, 'Homeboy Cosmopolitan,' *October* 83 (Winter 1998): 66. Attempts to subvert stereotypes from many contexts date the cinema's conception. Black actors, for example, have historically compensated for their stereotyped roles by spinning them, acknowledging their circumscribed nature while taking them to a different level. See Donald Bogle, *Toms, Coons, Mulattoes, Mammies, and Bucks: An Interpretive History of Blacks in American Film* (New York: Viking Press, 1973). Artists of Shum's generation, however, have taken up the strategy of transcoding stereotypes with a vengeance. The practice of foregrounding negative stereotypes has fomented somewhat of a generational war of representation among artists of colour. See 'Roland Jones on "Black Like Who?" Crimson Herring,' *Artforum International*, Summer 1998, 17–18, for an apt description of these tensions.

36 Shum's previous mock documentary, *Me, Mom and Mona* (1993) similarly deploys a minimalist formalist structure. Shot like a game show, it offers a dry run for *Double Happiness*. Family participants recall their childhood exploits, but they mostly relate dealing-with-Dad tales.

37 For an intriguing account of the significance of food symbolism in Asian-American narratives, see Sau-ling Cynthia Wong, 'Big Eaters, Treat Lovers, "Food Prostitutes," "Food Pornographers," and Doughnut Makers,' in *Reading Asian American Literature: From Necessity to Extravagance* (Princeton: Princeton University Press, 1993), 20. She writes: 'alimentary images ... symbolize Necessity – all the hardships, restrictions, deprivations, disenfranchisements, and dislocations that Asian Americans have collectively suffered as immigrants and minorities in a white-dominated country.'

38 Lisa Lowe, *Immigrant Acts: On Asian American Cultural Politics* (Durham: Duke University Press, 1996), 62.

39 Two-way cultural traffic – designated as syncretic, hybrid, or creole – has been advanced by scholars in diverse fields. See in particular, James Clifford, 'Travelling Cultures,' in *Cultural Studies*, ed. Lawrence Greenberg, Cary Nelson, and Paula Treichler (New York: Routledge, 1991), 96–116; Trinh T. Minh-ha, 'Difference: "A Special Third World Women Issue,"' *Discourse* 8 (Fall–Winter 1986–7): 11–37; and Paul Gilroy, *The Black Atlantic: Modernity and Double Consciousness* (Cambridge: Harvard University Press, 1993).

40 Rey Chow disparagingly applies the term to a wider category of individuals who claim outsider status. I purposefully extend its use here. See *Writing Diaspora: Tactics of Intervention in Contemporary Cultural Studies* (Bloomington: University of Indiana Press, 1993), 13.

41 Wong, *Reading Asian American Literature*, 13.

42 Ambassador-like, it also functions as a form of justification to a non-Chinese audience. Although a Chinese audience might make very different sense of the same phenomenon presented in *Double Happiness*, I hesitate to claim that racially differentiated audiences differ in *absolute* terms from white audiences.

43 The term is Avtar Brah's. See 'Difference, Diversity and Differentiation,' in *'Race,' Culture and Difference*, ed. James Donald and Ali Rattansi (London: Sage, 1992), 126–45.

44 While their approaches, determined both by generation and by production contexts, have borne different effects, it would be misguided to delegate one film more successful than the other simply based on their varying degrees of engagement with realism. Privileging *Double Happiness* as progressive because it problematizes realist aesthetics through deconstructive play and *Sam and Me* as flawed because it employs more conventional techniques is woefully wrong-headed. Such a view not only rehearses the monolithic proscriptions of 1970s film theory (feminist and not) but it negates the possibility of oppositional readings. For a related conjunctural study that explains the prevailing accommodating response of Canadian feminist film to 'foreign' theory, see Kass Banning, 'The Canadian Feminist Hybrid Film,' *CineAction*, nos. 26–7 (Winter, 1992): 108–13. Stuart Hall's views on documentary photography are also applicable here: 'the current orthodoxy has somewhat trivialized the argument about documentary realism by assimilating all "realisms" (which one ought to be at pains to discriminate and differentiate) into one great essential so-called "realist discourse."' Stuart Hall, 'Reconstruction Work: Images of Post War Black Settlement,' in *Critical Decade: Black British Photography in the 80s* (*Ten 8* Photo Paperback, 2:3, 1992), 111.

Selected Bibliography

Alioff, Maurie, and Susan Schouten Levine. 'The Long Walk of Alanis Obom-
  sawin.' *Cinema Canada*, no. 142 (June 1987): 10–15
Anderson, Elizabeth. *Pirating Feminisms: Film and the Production of Post War
  Canadian Identity*. Ann Arbor, MI: UMI, 1996
Armatage, Kay. 'About to Speak: The Woman's Voice in Patricia Gruben's *Sifted
  Evidence*.' In *Take Two: A Tribute to Film in Canada*, edited by Seth Feldman,
  298–304. Toronto: Irwin, 1984
– 'The Feminine Body: Joyce Wieland's *Water Sark*.' In *Dialogue: Cinéma canadien et
  québécois / Canadian and Quebec Cinema*, edited by Pierre Véronneau, Michael
  Dorland, and Seth Feldman, 285–95. Canadian Film Series 3. Montreal: Media-
  texte/Cinémathèque québécoise, 1987
– 'Joyce Wieland, Feminist Documentary, and the Body of the Work.' *Canadian
  Journal of Political and Social Theory* 13, nos. 1–2 (1989): 91–101
– 'The Silent Screen and My Talking Heart.' *Journal of Social and Political Theory*
  14, nos. 1–3 (1990): 12–17
Asper-Burnett, Martha. 'Des cinéastes québécoises anglophones.' *Copie Zéro* 6
  (1980): 32–4
Banning, Kass. 'The Canadian Feminist Hybrid Film.' *CineAction*, nos. 26–7
  (Winter 1992): 108–13
– 'Engendering the Nation: *Gerda*, "A Girl's Own Story."' *CineAction*, no. 30
  (1992): 87–9
– 'From Didactics to Desire: Building Women's Film Culture.' In *Work in Progress:
  Building Feminist Culture*, edited by Rhea Tregebov, 149–76. Toronto: Women's
  Press, 1987
– 'The Mummification of Mommy: Joyce Wieland as the AGO's First Living

Other.' *C Magazine*, no. 13 (March 1987). Reprinted in Jessica Bradley and
Lesley Johnstone, eds. *SightLines: Reading Contemporary Canadian Art*, 153–67.
Montreal: Art Texte, 1994
– 'Rhetorical Remarks towards the Politics of Otherness.' *CineAction*, no. 16
(Spring 1989): 14–19
– 'Surfacing: Canadian Women's Cinema.' *Cinema Canada*, no. 167 (Oct. 1989):
12–20
– 'Textual Excess in Joyce Wieland's *Hand-Tinting*.' *CineAction*, no. 5 (Spring
1986): 12–14
Beale, Alison, and Annette Van Den Bosch, eds. *Ghost in the Machine: Women and
Cultural Policy in Canada*. Toronto: Garamond Press, 1998
Berenstein, Rhona. 'As Canadian as Possible: The Female Spectator and the
Canadian Context.' *Camera Obscura* 20–1 (May–Sept. 1989): 40–52
– 'Quoting Women's Bodies: *Our Marilyn* and Cultural Mediations.' *Canadian
Journal of Political and Social Theory* 14 (Nov. 1990): 40–52
Bradley, Jessica, and Lesley Johnstone, eds. *SightLines: Reading Contemporary
Canadian Art*. Montreal: Art Texte, 1994
Burnett, Ron. *Cultures of Vision: Images Media and the Imaginary*. Bloomington:
Indiana University Press, 1995
Carrière, Louise. 'A propos des films faits par des femmes au Québec.' *Copie Zéro*
11 (1981): 44–51
– *Femmes et cinéma québécois*. Montreal: Boréal Express, 1983
Chisholm, Elspeth, and Patricia Thorvaldson. 'Women in Documentary: The
Early Years.' *Motion* 4, no. 5 (1975): 14–19
Clandfield, David. *Canadian Film*. Toronto: Oxford University Press, 1987
Cole, Janis, and Holly Dale. *Calling the Shots: Profiles of Women Filmmakers*. Kingston:
Quarry Press, 1993
Crossman, Brenda, ed. *Bad Attitudes on Trial: Pornography, Feminism, and the Butler
Decision*. Toronto: University of Toronto Press, 1997
Dandurand, Anne. 'Cinéma et femmes: Une réalité.' *Canadian Women's Studies* 2,
no. 3 (1980): 91–7
Denault, Jocelyne. 'Le cinéma féminin au Québec.' *Copie Zéro* 11 (1981): 36–44
– 'Cinquante ans de cinéma des femmes au Québec: Une Recherche difficile.'
Canadian Woman Studies 7, no. 3 (Autumn 1986): 35–8
Diamond, Bonnie, and Francine Fournier. *Equality and Access: A New Social
Contract*. Montreal: National Film Board of Canada, 1987
Dorland, Michael. *So Close to the State/s: The Emergence of Canadian Feature Film
Policy*. Toronto: University of Toronto Press, 1998
Doyle, Judith, ed. *In a Different Voice: Conversations with Women Artists and Film-
makers*. Toronto: Funnel Experimental Film Theatre, 1986

Evans, Gary. *In the National Interest: A Chronicle of the National Film Board of Canada from 1949 to 1989.* Toronto: University of Toronto Press, 1971

Fetherling, Douglas, ed. *Documents in Canadian Film.* Peterborough, ON: Broadview Press, 1988

Feldman, Seth, ed. *Take Two: A Tribute to Film in Canada.* Toronto: Irwin, 1984

Feldman, Seth, and Joyce Nelson, eds. *The Canadian Film Reader.* Toronto: Peter Martin, 1977

Francis, Daniel. *The Imaginary Indian: The Image of the Indian in Canadian Culture.* Vancouver: Arsenal Pulp Press, 1992

Gale, Peggy, and Lisa Steele, eds. *Video reView.* Toronto: Art Metropole and V Tape, 1996

Georgakas, Dan, and William Starr. 'The Primal Fear: An Interview with Anne-Claire Poirier.' *Cinéaste* 10, no. 3 (Summer 1980): 20–49

Gever, Martha, Pratibha Parmar, and John Greyson, eds. *Queer Looks: Perspectives on Lesbian and Gay Film and Video.* New York: Routledge, 1993

Green, Mary Jean. 'Léa Pool's *La Femme de l'hôtel* and Women's Film in Quebec.' *Quebec Studies* 9 (Fall–Winter 1989–90): 49–62

Harcourt, Peter. 'The Canadian Nation: An Unfinished Text.' *Canadian Journal of Film Studies* 2, nos. 2–3 (1993): 5–26

– 'Introduction: The Invisible Cinema.' *Cine-Tracts* 1, no. 4 (Spring–Summer 1978): 48–9

– 'Micheline Lanctôt: A Woman in the World.' *Descant*, no. 98 (1997): 109–29

– *Movies and Mythologies.* Toronto: CBC Publications, 1977

Hartt, Laurinda. 'En tant que femmes.' *Cinema Canada* 15 (Aug.–Sept. 1974): 52–4

Jaehne, Karen. 'I've Heard the Mermaids Singing: An Interview with Patricia Rozema.' *Cinéaste* 16, no. 3 (1989): 22–3

Kiss, Ibranyi. 'Women in Canadian Films.' *Cinema Canada* 5 (Dec. 1972–Jan. 1973): 26–7

Lamartine, Thérèse. 'Du cinéma et de-ci de-la, des femmes.' *Copie Zéro* 6 (1980): 30–2

Lanctôt, Micheline. 'De l'accouchement comme métaphore.' *La Revue de la cinémathèque* 26 (1994): 5

Larouche, Michel, ed. *Le cinéma aujourd'hui.* Montreal: Les Editions Guernica, 1988

Lerner, Loren R. *Canadian Film and Video: A Bibliography and Guide to the Literature.* Toronto: University of Toronto Press, 1997

Lippard, Lucy. 'Watershed, Contradiction, Communication and Canada in Joyce Wieland's Work.' In *Joyce Wieland.* Toronto: Art Gallery of Ontario and Key Porter, 1987

Loiselle, André. 'Scenes from a Failed Marriage: A Brief Analytical History of Canadian and Québécois Feature Film Adaptions of Drama from 1942 to 1992.'

Theatre Research in Canada / Recherches théatrales au Canada 17, no. 1 (Fall 1996):
38–58

Longfellow, Brenda. 'Un Cinéma distinct: Stratégies féministes dans les films
canadiens.' In *Les Cinémas du Canada*, edited by Sylvain Garel and André
Paquet, 221–33. Paris: Centre Georges Pompidou, 1993

– 'The Feminist Film in Quebec: *La Vie rêvée* and *La Cuisine rouge*.' *Cine-Tracts* 4,
no. 4 (Winter 1982): 62–73

– 'Feminist Language in *Journal Inachevé* and *Strauss Café*.' In *Words and Moving
Images: Essays on Verbal and Visual Expression in Film and Television*, edited by
William Wees and Michael Dorland, 77–95. Montreal: Mediatexte, 1984

– 'The Melodramatic Imagination in Quebec and Canadian Women's Feature
Films.' *CineAction*, no. 28 (1992): 48–56

– 'The Search for Voice: *Le Femme de l'hôtel*.' In *Dialogue: Cinéma canadien et
québécois / Canadian and Quebec Cinema*, edited by Pierre Véronneau, Michael
Dorland, and Seth Feldman, 269–81. Canadian Film Series 3. Montreal: Mediatexte Publications/Cinémathèque québécoise, 1987

McHugh, Kathleen. 'The Films of Patricia Gruben: Subjectivity and Space.' *Jump
Cut*, no. 35 (1990): 110–16

McMaster, Gerald, and Lee-Ann Martin, eds. *Indigena: Contemporary Native Perspectives*. Vancouver: Douglas and McIntyre; Hull: Canadian Museum of Civilization, 1992

Magder, Ted. *Canada's Hollywood: The Canadian State and Feature Films*. Toronto:
University of Toronto Press, 1993

Marchessault, Janine. 'Is the Dead Author a Woman? Some Thoughts on Female
Authorship.' *Parallélogramme* (Feb. 1990): 6–15

– 'Wieland's Reason into Passion.' *Border/lines* 1 (1985): 35–6

– 'Writing Feminist Histories: *The Burning Times* and *The Company of Strangers*.'
CineAction, no. 23 (Winter 1990–1): 47–51

Marchessault, Janine, ed. *Mirror Machine/Video and Identity*. Toronto: YYZ Books,
1995

Martineau, Barbara Halpern. 'Leading Ladies behind the Camera.' *Cinema
Canada*, no. 71 (Jan.–Feb. 1981): 17–32

Meigs, Mary. *In the Company of Strangers*. Vancouver: Talon Books, 1991

Morris, Peter. *Embattled Shadows: A History of Canadian Cinema, 1895–1939*.
Montreal: McGill-Queen's University Press, 1978

– *The Film Companion*. Toronto: Irwin, 1984

– 'In Our Own Eyes: The Canonizing of Canadian Film.' *Canadian Journal of Film
Studies* 3, no. 1 (Spring 1994): 27–44

Nadeau, Chantal. 'La Représentation de la femme comme autre: L'Ambiguïté du
cinéma de Léa Pool pour une position féministe.' *Quebec Studies* 17 (1994): 83–95

– 'Women in French-Quebec Cinema: The Space of Socio-Sexual (In)difference.' *CineAction*, no. 28 (Spring 1992): 4–15

Nash, Teresa. 'Images of Women in National Film Board of Canada Films during World War II and the Post-War Years, 1939–1949.' PhD diss., McGill University, 1982

Nelson, Joyce. *The Colonized Eye: Rethinking the Grierson Legend.* Toronto: Between the Lines, 1988

– 'Through Her Eyes: The Time of Sweet, Sweet Change – Changes in Feminist Film Practice.' *Cinema Canada*, no. 116 (March 1985): 20–3

Nichols, Bill. *Representing Reality: Issues and Concepts in Documentary.* Bloomington: Indiana University Press, 1991

Pallister, Janis L. 'Léa Pool's Gynefilms.' In *Essays on Quebec Cinema*, edited by Joseph I. Donohoe Jr., 111–34. East Lansing: Michigan State University Press, 1991

Pendakur, Manjunath. *Canadian Dreams and American Control: The Political Economy of the Canadian Film Industry.* Toronto: Garamond Press, 1990

Pérusse, Denise. *Micheline Lanctôt: La vie d'une héroïne.* Montreal: l'Hexagone, 1995

– 'La Mise en espace: Temps des femmes dans le cinéma québécois de 1976–1989.' PhD diss., Laval University, 1989

Pérusse, Denise, ed. *Cinéma et sexualité: Actes du septième colloque.* Quebec: Prospec, 1988

Pietropaolo, Laura, and Ada Testaferri, eds. *Feminisms in the Cinema.* Bloomington: Indiana University Press, 1995

Poirier, Anne Claire. 'Paroles et variations.' *Copie Zéro* 6 (1980): 18–19

Prévost, Francine. 'L'itinérnaire cinématographique d'Anne-Claire Poirier.' *Séquences*, no. 116 (April 1984): 12–26

Rabinovitz, Lauren. 'The Development of Feminist Strategies in the Experimental Films of Joyce Wieland.' *Film Reader*, no. 5 (1982): 130–7

Rich, B. Ruby. 'In the Name of Feminist Film Criticism.' In *Multiple Voices in Feminist Film Criticism*, edited by Diane Carson, Linda Dittmar, and Janice R. Welsh, 27–47. Minneapolis: University of Minnesota Press, 1994

Sherbarth, Chris. 'Why Not D? An Historical Look at the NFB's Woman's Studio.' *Cinema Canada*, no. 139 (March 1987): 9–13

Shipman, Nell. *The Silent Screen and My Talking Heart.* Boise: Boise University Press, 1987

Stukator, Angela. 'Hags, Nags, Witches and Crones: Reframing Age in *The Company of Strangers*.' *Canadian Journal of Film Studies* 5, no. 2 (1996): 51–66

Thérien, Gilles. 'Cinéma québécois: La Difficile conquête de l'altérité.' *Littérature* 66 (May 1986): 101–14

Todd, Loretta. 'Notes on Appropriation.' *Parallélogramme* 16, no. 1 (1990): 27–34

Tregebov, Rhea, ed. *Work in Progress: Building Feminist Culture.* Toronto: Women's Press, 1987

Véronneau, Pierre, Michael Dorland, and Seth Feldman, eds. *Dialogue: Cinéma canadien et québécois / Canadian and Quebec Cinema.* Canadian Film Series 3. Montreal: Mediatexte Publications/Cinémathèque québécoise, 1987

Véronneau, Pierre, and Piers Handling. *Self Portrait: Essays on the Canadian and Quebec Cinemas.* Ottawa: Canadian Film Institute, 1980

Véronneau, Pierre, and Pierre Jutras. 'Anne Claire Poirier de A à Z: Bio-filmographie commentée par l'auteure.' *Copie Zéro* 23 (1985): 4–21

Walcott, Rinaldo. *Black Like Who: Writing. Black. Canada.* Toronto: Insomniac Press, 1997

Walz, Gene, ed. *Flashback: People and Institutions in Canadian Film History.* Montreal: Mediatexte, 1986

Wieland, Joyce. 'North America's Second All-Woman Film Crew.' *Take One* 1 (1968): 14–15

Wood, Robin. 'Towards a Canadian (Inter)national Cinema.' *CineAction*, no. 17 (Summer 1989): 23–35

Zucker, Carole. 'Les Oeuvres récentes d'Anne Claire Poirier et Paule Baillargeon.' *Copie Zéro* 11 (1981): 52–5

Contributors

Karen Anderson earned her doctorate in (North) American Studies at the University of Minnesota. Currently, she lives in Chicago where she manages research for E-Lab, a research-design consultancy. Continuing her interest in documentary, she uses video ethnography and other visually based techniques to understand human behaviour and end-user experience.

Kay Armatage is an associate professor of cinema studies and women's studies at the University of Toronto. Her academic work concerns women filmmakers and contemporary film theory. She is currently working on a study of Nell Shipman, Canadian director/writer/producer/star of the silent era. She has directed seven films, including *Artist on Fire: The Work of Joyce Wieland.*

Cameron Bailey writes and broadcasts from Toronto. He reviews film for *NOW* magazine, and contributed to the anthologies *Immersed in Technology* and *Territories of Difference.* He is the founder and former programmer of the Toronto International Film Festival's Planet Africa section, and past head of the festival's Perspective Canada series.

Kass Banning teaches cinema studies at the University of Toronto. Banning has written extensively in the areas of Canadian, feminist, and 'emerging' cinemas and is at present completing a study of race and nation in recent minoritarian Canadian film.

Jean Bruce is PhD candidate in the Humanities Doctoral Program at Concordia University, Montreal, and teaches part-time in the cinema department. Her interests include ethnographic and early cinema, melodrama, early communications technology, film, and cultural theory.

Ron Burnett, author of *Cultures of Vision: Images, Media and the Imaginary*, president, Emily Carr Institute of Art and Design, and former director, Graduate Program in Communications at McGill University, is the author of over fifty published articles and the founder of one of Canada's first theoretical journals devoted to film, communications, and cultural studies, *Cine-Tracts*. He was recently appointed to a UNESCO advisory committee on the role of new technologies in learning for developing countries and is presently completing a new book entitled *How Images Think*.

Robert L. Cagle writes about film and popular culture. He is currently at work on a study of cult films, tentatively titled *Cinematic Compulsions*.

Peter Harcourt is currently an adjunct research professor at Carleton University. He has published articles in *Sight and Sound, Film Comment, Cinema Canada, Canadian Forum, Film Quarterly, CineAction*, and, more recently, in *POV*. He is the author of the following books: *Six European Directors: Speculations on the Meaning of Film Style* (Harmondsworth: Penguin Books, 1974), *Movies and Mythologies: Towards a National Cinema* (Toronto: CBC Publications, 1977), *Jean Pierre Lefebvre: Almost a Chronological Survey* (Ottawa: Canadian Film Institute, 1981), and *A Canadian Journey: Conversations with Time* (Ottawa: Oberon Press, 1994).

Carol Kalafatic is a New York–based cultural activist, artist, and writer whose work has appeared in Native American periodicals and in the anthology *As We Are Now: Mixblood Essays on Race and Identity*. She is currently the Latin-American media specialist at the Film and Video Center of the National Museum of the American Indian, and is at work on a contribution to the new edition of *Cinema and Social Change in Latin America*.

Brenda Longfellow is currently co-chair of the Department of Fine Arts, Atkinson College, York University, where she teaches film studies. She has written extensively about women's cinema in *Screen, Cine-Tracts*, and the *Canadian Journal of Film Studies* and is an award-winning documentary filmmaker whose films include *Our Marilyn, Gerda, A Balkan Journey*, and *Shadow Maker*.

Susan Lord is an assistant professor in the Department of Film Studies and is cross-appointed to the Institute of Women's Studies at Queen's University, Kingston. She is on the editorial board of *Public.*

Janine Marchessault is an assistant professor in the Department of Film and Video at York University. She is the editor of *Mirror Machine: Video and Identity* (1995). Her writings have appeared in *CineAction, Screen, Public,* and *New Formations.*

Chantal Nadeau is an assistant professor in the Department of Communication Studies, Concordia University, where she teaches film criticism, cultural studies, and feminist theory. She has published on women's cinema, postcolonial theory and national cultures, and lesbian representation. She is currently working on a book on the sexual and colonial economy of fur in Canada and Quebec.

Joan Nicks is an associate professor in the Department of Film Studies, Dramatic and Visual Arts, Brock University. Her essays and reviews have been published in *Cinema Canada, Canadian Journal of Film Studies, Texual Studies in Canada, Postscript,* and *Documenting the Documentary.* She is the co-editor of a forthcoming anthology on Canadian popular culture.

Lee Parpart has worked as a freelance film and visual arts critic and is now pursuing doctoral studies in social and political thought at York University, with an emphasis on feminist film theory and 'borderline' contributions to the canon. She has written about Canadian and feminist cinema and the visual arts for the *Kingston Whig-Standard,* the *Globe and Mail, POV* magazine, *C magazine,* and *Canadian Art.*

Zuzana Pick is a professor of film studies in the School for Studies in Art and Culture at Carleton University. She is the author of *The New Latin American Cinema: A Continental Project* (1993) and is currently researching reception practices of Canadian feature documentaries.

B. Ruby Rich writes on film, sexuality, and popular culture. Her book, *Chick Flicks: Theories and Memories of the Feminist Movement* (1998), has been published by Duke University Press. She reports on films for American and Canadian public radio and writes for the scholarly press as well as *The Advocate,* the *San Francisco Bay Guardian, The Village Voice,* and other papers. She is an adjunct associate professor at the University of California, Berkeley.

Catherine Russell teaches film studies at Concordia University. She is the author of *Narrative Morality: Death and Closure in New Wave Cinemas* (1995) and *Experimental Ethnography: The Work of Film in the Age of Video* (forthcoming).

Index

A corps perdu, 177, 206
A qui appartient ce gage?, 5
Aboriginal Film and Video Arts Alliance, 111
abortion, 68, 144
Abortion Stories from North and South, 50, 128
Access Resource Catalogue (ARC), 45
Adjuster, The, 259
adventure films, 26–7
African-Canadian women, 7, 51–2, 94–107, 215–16
AIDS, 109, 207–9, 250
Akerman, Chantal, 150
Alanis, 90
allegory, 140
Amisk, 76, 91
Anne Trister, 206
anthropology, 81
anti-pornography, 58, 62–75
apparatus theory, 24, 153
Apted, Michael, 218
Arcand, Denys, 193, 196, 201, 236
Armatage, Kay, 60, 139, 141, 144, 151, 152–3
Around 1981, 18
Atwood, Margaret, 64

authorship, 20–2, 140, 281, 309
autobiography, 23, 47, 144
avant-garde, 9, 25, 98, 137–47

Back to God's Country, 4, 20–1, 25, 26, 28–34
Bacon, Francis, 237
Bailey, Norma, 110
Baillargeon, Paule, 8, 198, 204
Baldwin, James, 304
Balkan Journey: Fragments from the Other Side of the War, A, 128
Ball of Yarn, The, 20
Banning, Kass, 43, 108, 140, 179, 258, 271
Baree, Son of Kazan, 20, 26
Barling, Marion, 45
Barnard Conference, 73
Barry, Kathleen, 64, 72
Barthes, Roland, 178
Battleship Potemkin, 228
Bear, the Boy, and the Dog, The, 30
Before It Blows, 148, 153, 156–7, 160
Behind the Veil: Nuns, 50
Bellour, Raymond, 188, 192, 260
Bhabha, Homi K., 298
Bissonette, Sophie, 6

Bjerring-Parker, Gudrun, 4, 5
Blaché, Alice Guy, 19
Black Mother, Black Daughter, 7
Blackburn, Marthe, 5
Blanche, 250
Bovenschen, Silvia, 233, 276
Brand, Dionne, 7, 53, 56
Brault, Michel, 196
Brecht, Bertolt, 8, 146, 227
Brennon, Timothy, 292
Bresson, Robert, 248
Brossard, Nicole, 48
Brown, Rita Mae, 48
Bubbles Galore, 253, 259
Bussières, Pascale, 246, 249–50
Butler, Judith, 250
Butterfield, Sarah, 121
By Their Own Strength, 4

caesarean section, 227–8
Camilla, 306
Canada Council, 11, 14, 46, 309
Canadian Broadcasting Corporation
    (CBC), 5, 90, 92, 95, 97–8, 171
Canadian Film Centre, 309
Canadian Film Development Corpora-
    tion, 11, 167
capitalism, 11, 71, 139
Carles, Gilles, 201
Carrière, Louise, 201
Central Character, The, 141–2, 148–52
Challenge for Change program, 5, 44,
    52, 226
Chambers, Jack, 137
Channel Four, 306
Chat dans le sac, Le, 198–200, 206
Cherry, Evelyn Spice, 4
Chinese-Canadian identity, 299–303
Chinese Revolution, 302
Christmas at Moose Factory, 76, 91

cinéma direct, 78, 198, 221, 224, 230
cinéma vérité, 8, 96, 101, 144, 221
class, 55, 69–75, 214, 248, 251, 255,
    293–6, 301
Clement, Catherine, 33
clitoridectomy, 232–3
Clouds, 145
Coconuts/Cane and Cutlass, 126
Cold Journey, 90
Cole, Janis, 6
Collin, Frédérique, 198, 204
colonialism, 78, 80–3, 85, 88, 195, 161,
    165–81, 257–60, 269, 307
Company of Strangers, The, 6, 212–21
consciousness raising, 3, 44–8
Copjec, Joan, 213
Crash, 259
Crawley, Judith, 5
Cronenberg, David, 259
Cuisine rouge, La, 8, 198, 201–3
cultural diaspora, 12
cultural policy, 11. *See also* multicultur-
    alism
Curnoe, Greg, 137
Curwood, James, 20–1

Dale, Holly, 6
Danis, Aimée, 5
Dansereau, Mireille, 5, 8, 198, 200,
    202, 204, 210
Davis, Angela, 308
Day in the Life of Canada, 94
Daymond, Kathy, 145
Deep Sleep, 161
Defiant Ones, The, 307
Demoiselle sauvage, La, 206
Department of Indian Affairs, 77
Dernier Secours, 85
Deschamps, Laurette, 50
Desire, 143

Deux actrices, 244, 249–51
Dialogue on Vision, 145
distribution, 13, 21–2
Doane, Mary Ann, 154, 213–14, 217
docudrama, 109–10, 121, 172, 212–21
documentary, 4, 76–90, 94–107, 109,
    120–32, 148–60, 202, 205, 212–13,
    215, 218–19, 223, 225–33, 282–3,
    286–7, 310; experimental, 141–7;
    pornography, 62–75, *see also* Studio
    D; social realism, 48, 49
domestic violence, 231
domesticity, 261
Double Happiness, 4, 10, 291–3,
    299–305, 308–10
Douglass, Frederick, 304
Doyle, Judith, 122–3
*Dream of a Free Country: A Message from
    Nicaraguan Women*, 50
Driving Miss Daisy, 294
Dulac, Germaine, 19, 24
Dziga-Vertov, 127

Egoyan, Atom, 196, 242, 259
Ellison, Ralph, 304
En tant que femmes, 226
Epp, Ellie, 14
eroticism, 67–8
ethnicity, 7, 10, 291–304
ethnography, 80–1
exhibition, 13, 22
experimental film, 137–46
expressionism, 232–3, 300
Extenderis, 209

Fairfield, Paula, 143
Falardeau, Pierre, 201
Fanon, Frantz, 298
fantasy, 68, 227, 246–7, 277–8, 280–1
Far Shore, The, 10, 33, 139–42, 165–78

Federal Women's Film Program, 51
Feldman, Seth, 141, 279
femininity, 24–31, 35, 139–41, 146, 152,
    228–9, 254, 263, 280
feminism, 122, 129, 148–53, 156–60,
    185, 201–9, 215, 221, 227, 230–44,
    253–62, 269, 275–7, 282, 286–9; femi-
    nist film theory, 9, 18, 24, 48, 64, 66,
    253, 264, 274, 310; French feminism,
    8, 143; liberal feminism, 12–42;
    morality and, 61–2, 73; politics and,
    68–75
feminist cabaret, 51
Femme du l'hôtel, La, 4, 8, 206
Fernie, Lynne, 6, 53–4, 275
fetishism, 81, 192, 220, 260–1, 303, 308
Fille c'est pas pareil, Les, 5
Filles du Roi, Les, 5, 8, 126, 200, 230
Fire, 306
First International Festival of Women's
    Films, 44
First Nations, 7, 42, 56–7, 76–90,
    109–19, 122, 169, 171, 173–4
Fish, Stanley, 281
Flaherty, Robert, 101
Fleming, Ann Marie, 124, 143
Flitterman-Lewis, Sandy, 18, 24
*Forbidden Love: The Unashamed Stories of
    Lesbian Lives*, 6–7, 53–4, 56, 275, 282–8
Forcier, André, 206
Forgotten Warriors, 109
formalism, 300, 309
Fothergill, Robert, 255, 269
Foucault, Michel, 149
Fox, Beryl, 4
Fragments, 143
Fraticelli, Rina, 6, 49–51, 60, 61
French, Marilyn, 230, 240
Frenkel, Vera, 122, 124, 133
Friedan, Betty, 48

Gabriel Goes to the City, 91
Gallop, Jane, 18
gaze, 9, 64, 66, 229–30, 236, 245, 253,
    256, 259–60, 263–9, 285–6
gender, 42, 165–81, 197, 226–9, 237,
    244, 248–51, 255–6, 264–8, 276–7,
    280, 298, 301, 303, 306. *See also* femi-
    ninity; masculinity
genre, 25, 142, 283–4, 300
George, Chief Dan, 111
Gibbard, Susan, 5
Giguère, Nicole, 123
Gina, 236
Girl from God's Country, The, 23
Gish, Dorothy, 19
globalization, 11–12
Glooscap Country, 5
Godard, Jean Luc, 231
Godbout, Jacques, 201
Goddess Remembered, 50
God's Country and the Woman, 20, 26
Goin' Down the Road, 255
Gowdy, Barbara, 262, 264, 267
Grand Manan, 5
Grant, George, 166
Great Grand Mother, 47
Grierson, John, 4, 13, 41, 99–101,
    141
Griffin, Susan, 64, 72
Griffiths, Linda, 184
Gronau, Anna, 143
Groulx, Gilles, 198–201
Group of Seven, 168–71
Grub Stake, The, 21, 28
Gruben, Patricia, 9, 14, 60, 141, 125–7,
    148–62
Guilbeault, Luce, 48
Gunning, Tom, 17, 23, 33
Guynn, William, 99
Gwendolyn, 144

Hall, Stuart, 106, 292–3, 310
Hamilton, Sylvia, 7, 51–2, 53
Hand-Tinting, 9, 139, 140
Hands of History, 110, 114–15
Haraway, Donna, 250
Hartt, Laurinda, 226
Haustien, Lydia, 122
Haynes, Scott, 145
Healing Our Spirit, 109, 113
heterosexuality, 25, 229
Histoire Infame, 123
historiography, 17–19, 24, 139, 144–5
history, 23–4, 146
Hodge de Silva, Jennifer, 7, 94–107
Hollywood, 6, 19, 22–3, 99, 179–80,
    188–96, 212, 214–17, 229, 235, 243,
    268, 301
Home Feeling: Struggle for a Community,
    7, 94, 96, 101–6
Homme à tout faire, L', 245
homosexuality, 197, 202, 257, 263, 275,
    306
Honey Moccasin, 110, 115
hooks, bell, 97, 304
Hoolboom, Michael, 124
Houle, Robert, 86
Hutcheon, Linda, 10, 287
hybridity, 7–8, 12, 102, 141, 148–50
hysteria, 32–4, 139–40

I Love a Man in Uniform, 259
Iconography of Venus, The, 143
identity, 79, 81, 85, 89, 91, 120–32,
    148–61, 183, 195, 197–200, 207,
    211, 238, 240, 244, 247, 250–1, 255,
    258, 260, 264–8, 275, 282, 288, 292,
    300–4
ideology, 231
If You Love This Planet, 6, 41, 50
I'll Find a Way, 50

imagined community, 12, 43, 56–7
impressionism, 232, 239
improvisation, 244
In Support of the Human Spirit, 94, 99, 102–3
In the Heat of the Night, 307
Incident at Restigouche, 83–4, 91
Inside Out, 143
Inside Upstairs, 143
Iribe, Marie-Louise, 19
It Starts with a Whisper, 110–4, 118–19
I've Heard the Mermaids Singing, 4, 8, 9, 14, 183–8

Jacob, Lea, 23
James, C.L.R., 297
Janie's Janie, 43
JanMohamed, Abdul, 293
J'me marie, j'me marie pas, 5, 200
Joe David: Spirit of the Mask, 102–3
Jour après jour, 240
June in Povungnituk, 91

Kanehsatake: 270 Years of Resistance, 7, 76, 79–80, 88–91
Kaplan, E. Ann, 59
Kazan, Elia, 26
Keepers of the Fire, 110, 116–7
Kenora, 91
King, Rodney, 92
Kirby, Kathleen M., 159–60
Kissed, 4, 9, 253–4, 259–60, 262, 268–9, 272
Kiyooka, Fumiko, 145
Klein, Bonnie, 47, 50, 58, 62, 63, 65, 66, 67, 70
Koenig, Wolf, 76

Lac La Croix, 122–3
Lai, Larissa, 125–6

Lanctôt, Micheline, 8, 231, 244–52
landscape, 4, 29, 83–4, 86, 88, 148, 165–81, 188, 218–9, 256, 292, 305. *See also* wilderness
LaRoque, Emma, 78
Lauretis, Teresa de, 48, 59, 145, 165, 175, 219–20, 274–88
Learning Path, The, 110, 115, 119
Leduc, Jacques, 196
Lee, Helen, 145
Lehman, Peter, 254, 256, 262, 270
Lesage, Julie, 44, 58, 101–2
lesbian culture, 275, 282–87
lesbian sexuality, 53–4, 74, 216, 275–6, 279–80, 282, 284
Ley Lines, 148–9, 153, 154, 156, 157–60
Linaae, Karethe, 10, 254, 259–61
Listen to the Prairies, 5
Lloyd, David, 293
Longfellow, Brenda, 60, 128–9, 145, 277
Loon's Necklace, The, 5
Loved, Honoured, and Bruised, 128
Low Visibility, 148, 153–6
Lowe, Lisa, 301
Loyalties, 10, 165, 171–6
Lyell, Lotte, 19
Lyotard, J.F. 281, 286

Macartney-Filgate, Terence, 96–7
MacDonald, Sandra, 57
Maitland-Carter, Kathleen, 143
Man, 124
Man with the Movie Camera, The, 127
Mangaard, Annette, 143, 145
Manning, Frank E., 183–4
Marsh, Jane, 4
Martin, Lee-Ann, 85
Martineau, Barbara Halpern, 45
Mary, Mary, 143

masculinity, 34, 255–6, 268–9, 280, 298
masquerade, 34, 244,, 251
Massey, Doreen, 12
matriarchy, 82
Mayne, Judith, 216, 219–20
McCarthy, Sheila, 185, 191–2
McMahon, Marion, 145
McMaster, Gerald, 85
Me, Mom and Mona, 309
Mehta, Deepa, 4, 10, 291, 304, 309
melodrama, 25, 165, 172, 212, 234,
    236, 282–7
memory, 30, 61
mère en fille, De, 8, 200, 226–30, 241
Miegs, Mary, 216–17
Mildred Pierce, 190
Millett, Kate, 48, 64, 67, 72
Mills of the Gods: Vietnam, 4, 5
minoritarian, 292–3, 305
Mission Colombe, La, 85
Mitchell, William J., 131
modernism, 18, 35, 138, 226, 286–7
Mohabeer, Michelle, 126
Montreal Native Friendship Centre, 85
Montréal vu par ..., 192–4
Morazine, Jeanne, 5
Morgan, Robin, 62, 71, 72
Morris, Meaghan, 35
Morris, Peter, 22, 179
Morrison, Toni, 292, 304
Mother of Many Children, 76, 81–2, 85,
    91
Mourir à tue-tête, 8, 120–2, 127, 130,
    203–4, 226, 230–4, 239–42, 253
Mouvements du désir, 10, 165, 176–81,
    206
Mulroney, Brian, 305
multiculturalism, 42, 55–7, 96–7, 100,
    269, 292–305, 307
Multiculturalism Act (1988), 292

Multiculturalism Canada, 309
Mulvey, Laura, 192, 230, 233, 236
My American Cousin, 300
My Name is Kahentiiosta, 84, 89, 91
Myself, Yourself, 94, 96, 99, 101–2, 106

Nash, Terri, 50, 60
nation, 99, 165–81, 183
National Film Board, of Canada
    (NFB), 4, 11, 41–61, 66, 76–7, 89–90,
    96–100, 102–5, 121, 129, 200, 212,
    220, 225, 230, 243, 282–3, 309
National Film Theatre, 241
national identity, 197–209, 256–8, 269,
    293
national unity, 4, 10, 258
nationalism, 10, 41, 268
Native filmmakers (see, First Nations)
Nazimova, Alla, 19
Neighbourhoods – Kensington Market, 94
Neighbourhoods – Outremont, 94
New Initiatives in Film, (NIF), 51–2
new narrative, 141
New Visions, 309
Newsreel, 42–4
Nice Girls Don't Do It, 145
Nichols, Bill, 82, 91, 218, 287
Niro, Shelley, 7, 109–14
No Address, 85–6, 91
No Longer Silent, 50
No More Secrets, 109, 113
Nochlin, Linda, 238
Noriega, Chon, 78
Normand, Mabel, 19
Not a Love Story, 6, 41, 48, 49–50, 62–75,
    253
Nottary, Elvira, 19
*Nuclear Addiction: Dr. Rosalie Burtell on
    the Cost of Deterrence*, 50
Nursing History, 145

Obomsawin, Alanis, 7, 76–90
Oedipus complex, 260, 263, 295, 300–1
off Key, 254, 259–63, 268
Office national du film (ONF), 5, 8, 225
Oh, Sandra, 299, 300, 303
Oka, 79–80, 88–9, 93, 117–8
Older Stronger Wiser, 7, 53
Onodera, Midi, 14, 60
Ontario Arts Council, 11, 14
Ontario Film Development Corporation (OFDC), 14, 306
oral history, 7, 78, 81, 88, 111
Otherness, 88, 106, 174, 179, 199, 208, 215–9, 258, 296, 304, 308
Our Dear Sisters, 90
Our Marilyn, 129, 145

Passion: A Letter in 16mm, 183–5
patriarchy, 25, 33, 142, 225–6, 231–4, 237, 254–7, 266, 270, 275, 280–1, 289, 302
Patricia's Moving Picture, 47–8, 50
Patriotism, Part One, 253–4, 257–8, 268
performativity, 244, 249–52, 255
Perry, Margaret, 4, 5
Pettigrew, Margaret, 43, 58
Pines, Jim, 105
Poirier, Anne Claire, 8, 120–3, 126–7, 130, 200, 203, 225–43
Pollack, Griselda, 18
Pool, Léa, 4, 8, 10, 176–81, 196, 198, 200, 202, 205
pop art, 140
popular culture, 138, 142
pornography, 62–75, 144–5; gay male porn, 69; violence, 68–9
postcolonialism, 12
postmodernism, 137, 275–6, 281–2, 286, 288

poststructuralism, 226, 268
Poundmaker's Lodge: A Place of Healing, 85–6, 91
Praxis, 309
pregnancy, 81, 227–30
Preobrajenskaya, Olga, 19
Prieto, Claire, 7, 54, 99, 105
private sphere, 139–42, 227, 277–9
propaganda, 230
Prowling by Night, 144
psychoanalysis, 145, 246, 263
public sphere, 146, 227, 277–9

Quebec cinema, 5, 8, 176–7, 197–202, 205–8, 211, 225–43
Quebec identity, 176–7, 228, 230, 281
queer identity, 7
Quiet Revolution, 198, 225, 230

Rabinovitz, Lauren, 140
race/racism, 7, 31–2, 69–75, 76, 84, 86–7, 94–107, 183, 255, 275, 291–304
Radio-Canada, 241–2
Ramsay, Christine, 255–6, 268
rape, 231–42
Rasmussen, Lorna, 47
Rat Life and Diet in North America, 4, 9, 139, 166
Read, Donna, 50
realism, 32, 48, 94–107, 145, 218–19, 231, 278, 284, 300, 302, 306–7, 310. *See also* documentary
Reason Over Passion, 9, 139, 141, 166
Récit d'A, Le, 208, 211
Reel Feelings, 46
Reel Life, 46
Reineger, Lotte, 19
Rescued by Rover, 27
Rich, Adrienne, 143
Rich, Ruby B., 19, 42, 58–9

Richard Cardinal: Cry from a Diary of a Métis Child, 86–7, 91
Riefenstahl, Leni, 19
Rimmer, David, 137
Rioux, Geneviève, 193
Roberts, Cynthia, 253, 259
Rock, Joyce, 6
rock video 123, 129
Rogoff, Irit, 18, 25, 35
Ross, Christine, 248
Rozema, Patricia, 4, 9–10, 14, 183–96
Rubin, Gayle, 263–4
Rubin Suleiman, Susan, 281

Sam and Me, 4, 10, 291–300, 303–7, 309–10
Schwartzwald, Robert, 197
scopophilia, 278
Scott, Cynthia, 6, 212, 217, 220
Sedgwick, Eve, 288
Shaffer, Beverly, 50, 60, 121
Shannon, Kathleen, 5, 6, 43, 48–50, 58, 61
Sheets-Johnstone, Maxine, 254
Shipman, Ernest, 20–1
Shipman, Nell, 3, 4, 17–38; filmography 35–6
Shub, Esther, 19
Shum, Mina, 4, 10, 291, 300–1, 304, 308–9
Sifted Evidence, 125, 148, 151, 154, 253
Silverman, Kaja, 152, 153, 246, 248, 254, 261, 266
Singe Bleu, Le, 207–9
Singer, Gail, 50, 128
Sisters in the Struggle, 7, 53, 56
Smiling Madame Beudet, The, 203
Smith, John, 221
Snow, Michael, 137, 146
social hygiene, 72

Société générale du cinéma (SOGIC), 11
Société Nouvelle, 225–6
Solax, 22
Solser, Adriane, 19
Some American Feminists, 48
Something New, 21
Sommer, Doris, 91
Sonatine, 245–8, 251, 300
Souris, tu m'inquiètes, 5
Speak Body, 141, 142, 253
Speaking Our Peace, 50
spectatorship, 17, 19, 192, 215–19, 221, 223, 231, 234–9, 275, 278–9, 286, 288
spirituality, 215–17
Spivak, Gayatri, 274, 287
Spudwrench, 91
Sternberg, Barbara, 14
Stikeman, Ginny, 50, 53
Stopkewich, Lynne, 10, 253–4, 259, 262–4, 267
story-telling. *See* oral history
Studio B, 212, 220–1
Studio D, 6–8, 41–61, 121, 226, 243
subjectivity, 79, 88, 226–7, 239, 258, 266, 276, 281
Summer in Mississippi, 4, 5
Svilova, Elizabeth, 19

Take Back the Night, 70
Telefilm Canada, 11, 309
Temps de l'avant, Le, 5, 200
Tetsuo, Kogawa, 130–1
Thérien, Gilles, 197
They Called Us 'Les Filles du Roi', 123
Thomson, Tom, 168–71
To a Safer Place, 50, 60
To Desire Differently, 18
Todd, Loretta, 7, 88–9, 109–13, 115–9
Todd Henaut, Dorothy, 62, 69

tokenism 54–7, 213, 216, 222
Trail of the North Wind, 27, 30
Transitions, 143
Trudeau, Pierre, 9, 97, 166
Tuer, Dot, 124
Turim, Maureen, 214

Valiquette, Esther, 198, 207–9, 211
Van Tuyle, Bert, 21, 23
vaudeville, 19, 20
Verall, Bob, 76
video, 80, 138, 146
Vie revée, La, 8, 198, 201–3, 253, 275–82, 286–8
voyeurism, 220, 230, 235, 259–62, 267, 278, 286
Vraie nature de Bernadette, La, 250

Walker, 91
Walker, Giles, 221
Water Sark, 8, 139–41, 143, 253
Waugh, Thomas, 77, 101, 105
Weber, Lois, 19
Weedon, Chris, 226
Weissman, Aerlyn, 6, 53–4, 61, 275
Wellington, Peter, 259
Welsh, Christine, 7, 109–16
Wendayte, Georges E. Sioui, 83
Wescott, Margaret, 48, 50
westerns, 27
Wheeler, Anne, 10, 47, 171–4, 180
When Night Is Falling, 195
White Room, 183, 188–92, 194

Wiegman, Robyn, 276, 286
Wieland, Joyce, 4, 8, 10, 33, 139–41, 146, 166–71, 180, 253–9
Wife's Tale, A, 6
Wild Rice Harvest, The, 91
wilderness, 20–1, 25–6, 34. *See also* landscape
Wilson, Margery, 19
Winston, Brian, 77
Wittig, Monique, 74
Woman's Event, 44
Woman's Film, The, 44
Women Against Pornography, 6, 8, 69
Women Against Violence Against Women (WAVAW), 71
Women and Film 1896–1973 International Film Festival, 3, 45
Women and Film Touring Media Bus, 45
Women Are Warriors, 4
Women at the Well series, 53
Women in Focus, 45
Women's liberation movement, 41, 138, 225, 274–5
Wong, Paul, 126
Wood, Robin, 175
Working Mothers series, 5, 44, 47, 50, 51, 58
Working Nights, 121
Would I Ever Like to Work, 5

Yoshida, Yuki, 43, 58
You Take Care Now, 143, 145